Exit Wounds
Murder, Diaspora and the Irish Troubles

Exit Wounds

Murder, Diaspora and the Irish Troubles

An Irish-Australian Story

Simon Adams

Crossing Press
Sydney

Published in Australia by Crossing Press
P.O. Box 1137
DARLINGHURST NSW 1300
Website: www.crossingpress.com.au
E-mail: sales@crossingpress.com.au
Telephone: (02) 4782 4984 Int+ 61 2 4782 4984

ISBN 0 9586713 9 7

First Published in October 2000

National Library of Australia
Cataloguing-in-publication entry:

Adams, Simon, 1968- .
Exit wounds : murder, diaspora and the Irish troubles.

ISBN 0 9586713 8 9.

1. Irish question.
2. Paramilitary forces - Northern Ireland.
3. Northern Ireland - Politics and government - 1969-1994.
4. Northern Ireland - Politics and government - 1995- .
5. Northern Ireland - Social conditions - 1969- .
I. Title.

941.60824

Designed by Luca Balboni, Sydney and printed by Star Printery, Erskineville

Contents

Acknowledgments

My deepest thanks to those who, in their own unique way, made the writing of this book possible:

IN AUSTRALIA The Adams Family – Peter, Vivienne and my wee brother Máirtin; Bruce Scates and Rae Frances; to all my Irish history students at UNSW who I had the pleasure of learning from between 1994 and 1999; all my friends in Australian Aid for Ireland (NSW), especially Doug Cooper; Patrick O'Farrell, who gave me my first university job teaching Irish history; Danielle Bourke, temporary Belfast research assistant and Diet Coke addict; all my friends at *Conradh na Gaeilge* in Sydney; all readers of my pieces in the *Irish Echo* who very kindly wrote to me; Val Noone at *Táin*; Greg Craven and all my colleagues in the College of Law at The University of Notre Dame; Danielle at 'Canberra Fire' for her unflagging tolerance; Brian, Úna and Kevin from Australian Aid for Ireland (WA); Joe O'Sullivan from the Australian Irish Heritage Association; Graham Bass; Colin Ryan of SBS; Susie Q for her encouragement; Caroline 'Wing Commander' Nicholls; Nick 'Buzz' Perkins and his travelling circus of neurosurgical thespians; Robin Bass for her continual interest and support; Peter Moore, a pillar of support and word surgeon extraordinaire.

Above all others, I would like to thank my comrade in arms, Amanda.

IN NEW ZEALAND Manuel, Raewyn, Regan and Allanah Fairley; Dimmy. And Gordon Coleman, my favourite storyteller: gone but never forgotten.

IN IRELAND Kevin and John Sr from the New Lodge; all my family on Jamaica Street; Yvonne at the Linen Hall Library; Peggy in Andersonstown; all my family in Twinbrook; Ann O'Sullivan and Ella at *Coiste na n-Iarchimí* in Dublin; 'Uncle Gerry' and all the other members of the 1999 Sinn Féin delegation to Australia; everyone at *An Phoblacht* in Belfast; Breandán Mac Cionnaith, Donna Griffin and the Garvaghy Road Residents Coalition; Jim Neeson the Black Taxi man; The McKeown's of the Garvaghy Road; The Devlin family in Andersonstown; all those who allowed me to interview them.

A special thanks to 'Gran', Mrs Mannix Campbell. And to the Andersonstown McVickers, who made it all possible—Sharon, John, Conor, wee Dan and baby Liam.

In loving memory of G. L. Coleman and Jean Veronica Smyth.

Abbreviations

CIRA	Continuity IRA or Continuity Army Council (hardline breakaway from IRA; not on ceasefire)
CLMC	Combined Loyalist Military Command (now defunct loyalist umbrella organisation representing UDA, UFF, UVF, RHC).
DUP	Democratic Unionist Party (Reverend Ian Paisley's party)
GAA	Gaelic Athletic Association
INLA	Irish National Liberation Army
IPLO	Irish Peoples Liberation Organisation (INLA breakaway—now defunct)
IRA	Irish Republican Army (Provisionals)
IRSP	Irish Republican Socialist Party (political wing of the INLA).
LOL	Loyal Orange Lodge
LVF	Loyalist Volunteer Force (splinter from UVF, led by Billy Wright)
NIO	Northern Ireland Office
MRF	Mobile Reaction Force; also sometimes called Mobile Reconnaissance Force or Military Reaction Force; secret 1970s British Army intelligence unit
OIRA	Official Irish Republican Army (on ceasefire since 1972, not to be confused with the Republic of Ireland's armed forces)
PIRA	See IRA
PUP	Progressive Unionist Party (political wing of UVF)
RHC	Red Hand Commando
RHD	Red Hand Defenders (loyalist paramilitary splinter group)
RIR	Royal Irish Regiment (British Army regiment recruited from local Ulster population)
RIRA	'Real' IRA (hardline IRA splinter group)
RUC	Royal Ulster Constabulary (Northern Ireland police force)
RSF	Republican Sinn Féin (political breakaway from SF, linked to CIRA)
SDLP	Social Democratic and Labour Party (moderate nationalists)
SF	Sinn Féin
UDA	Ulster Defence Association
UDP	Ulster Democratic Party (political representatives of UFF/UDA)
UDR	Ulster Defence Regiment (British Army regiment recruited from local Ulster population; now RIR)
UFF	Ulster Freedom Fighters
UKUP	United Kingdom Unionist Party
UUP	Ulster Unionist Party
UVF	Ulster Volunteer Force
32CSC	Thirty-Two County Sovereignty Committee (political breakaway from SF)

Belfast Glossary

Brits	All-encompassing term used by Ulster Catholics/nationalists to describe British soldiers and/or the British government
Bru	The dole. Possibly originally shortened from 'unemployment bureau'
Craic	Ubiquitous Irish word used variously to describe good fun or good conversation
Entry	A small laneway
Fenian	Protestant derogatory slang for a Catholic. Derives from nineteenth century Irish republican movement.
Gurning	Whingeing or whining
Hurley	A stick used in the traditional Irish sport of Hurling
Irps	INLA or IRSP members and supporters
Joyriders	Young people who steal cars for fun
Orangies	Nationalist slang for loyalists
Oul Wan	An old person
Peelers	The police, RUC
Provos	(also 'Provies') Slang for IRA
Screws	Prison guards
Shinner	A member of Sinn Féin
Stickies	Members and supporters of the Official IRA
Taig	Derogatory slang for a Catholic
The Crum	Crumlin Road prison
The Kesh	Long Kesh/Maze prison where the majority of republican and loyalist prisoners were held in Northern Ireland until the release scheme initiated following the Good Friday Agreement
The Morra	Tomorrow
The 'Ra	The IRA
Tiochfaidhs	Pronounced *Chock-eez*. Slang for IRA members (derivative from the Irish, 'tiocfaidh ár lá'—a republican slogan)
Tout	An informer
Wains	Young children

Timeline:
Northern Ireland's Bloodletting, December 1997–January 1998

1997

Sat 27 Dec: LVF leader Billy 'King Rat' Wright (36) shot dead by INLA inside Long Kesh prison at approx 10am. Rioting breaks out in Portadown. That night Séamus Dillon (45) is shot dead in Dungannon. Three others are wounded. Responsibility for the attack is claimed by the LVF.

Tues 30 Dec: Billy Wright buried in Portadown. Séamus Dillon buried a few miles away in Coalisland.

Wed 31 Dec: Eddie Treanor (31) shot dead by loyalists in North Belfast. Five others wounded. LVF claim responsibility.

1998

Sun 11 Jan: Cross-community worker and part-time doorman Terry Enright (28) shot dead by loyalists outside a nightclub in Belfast city centre. LVF claim responsibility.

Sun 18 Jan: Fergal McCusker (28) dragged off the street and shot in the head by the LVF in Maghera.

Mon 19 Jan: Leading South Belfast UDA man Jim Guiney (38) shot dead by the INLA inside his carpet shop in Dunmurry at 11am. That evening Catholic taxi driver Larry Brennan (52) is shot dead by loyalists while sitting in his cab in Belfast. UFF suspected of involvement in his murder.

Tues 20 Jan: UDP leader Gary McMichael insists UDA/UFF ceasefire is still intact.

Wed 21 Jan: Catholic Ben Hughes (55) shot dead in his car after leaving work in a Protestant area of Belfast. LVF claim responsibility. Later that night a Catholic taxi driver, John McFarland (37), is also shot in the head and wounded in North Belfast.

Thurs 22 Jan: Catholic Chris McMahon (29) shot and wounded outside the bakery where he works in North Belfast. RUC chief constable Ronnie Flanagan claims that the UDA/UFF have been collaborating with the LVF.

Fri 23 Jan: The UFF issue a press statement officially reinstating their ceasefire. A few hours later Catholic Liam Conway (39) is shot dead as he works laying gas pipes in North Belfast. No group claims responsibility.

Sat 24 Jan: Catholic taxi driver John McColgan (33) killed by loyalists after picking up a hoax fare from Andersonstown. His body is dumped near the Hannahstown Hill just off the upper Glen Road. No group claims responsibility.

Sun 25 Jan: Catholic truck driver shot and wounded in Lurgan. LVF are believed to be behind the attack.

Mon 26 Jan: Australia Day. UDP temporarily expelled from the Northern Ireland multi-party peace talks in London.

Author's Note

The bulk of this book was written in January of 1998 and is based on the journal I kept while I was in Belfast investigating Jean's death. Historians, political pundits and tabloid journalists will all tell you that 1998 was perhaps the most important year in the history of Northern Ireland since partition in 1921. Only a few months later in April 1998 the 'Good Friday Agreement', a tentative attempt to find a peaceful solution to three decades of 'the Troubles' in Ireland, would be signed at Stormont Castle. British Prime Minister Tony Blair, arriving in Belfast for the final stages of the negotiations, would declare that he felt 'the hand of history' upon his shoulder. In January however, staying in the Irish nationalist (or Catholic if you'd rather) enclave of Andersonstown in West Belfast, the hand of history was not upon anyone's shoulders. Starting with the assassination of Loyalist Volunteer Force (LVF) leader Billy 'King Rat' Wright on 27 December and ending with the murder of Catholic taxi driver John McColgan on 24 January, a total of ten people lost their lives over a four week period. A dozen more were shot and seriously wounded. The hand of history was at people's throats.

Indeed, many would later comment that it was the horror of January 1998, in particular the terrible bloodletting and random revenge murders carried out by loyalists in memory of King Rat, that would re-focus the minds of Northern Ireland's politicians on the fragile peace process and the negotiations that led to the Good Friday Agreement. In January however, none of this was apparent. I was in Belfast for one reason only, to conduct several weeks' research with the aim of trying to solve a twenty-six year old mystery—who killed a relative of mine, Jean Smyth, in 1972 and why? When I arrived in London from Australia on 27 December I called a friend in Belfast and was told that King Rat had just been killed. At that point I had no idea how the story put down in words here would play itself out. How the death of Billy Wright and all the others in January 1998 and the death of Aunt Jean in 1972 were intertwined and interwoven in the same unbroken fabric of suffering. How history works and what the Troubles have really meant for the people who have endured them for the last three decades. It was a lesson that would be well learnt.

Both my immediate and extended families played an enormous role in making this book possible. While the faults are all my own, the strengths come from their telling of the tale. There are undoubtedly sins of omission on my behalf, but I have tried to be as direct and accurate as possible in the retelling of all events and conversations. And yet, given the dark corners of history in which the Troubles often take place, this was not always possible. Facts are never neutral. In Northern Ireland everything is in dispute. While I have checked and double checked all allegations, stories and general facts, small inaccuracies undoubtedly remain. My apologies.

I am also particularly indebted to those people who allowed me to interview them for this book. This was the first time some of the interviewees had been subjected to tape-recorded questioning (although a few of them had had previous experience in an RUC barracks in this regard) and I was continually and pleasantly surprised by the results. I would especially like to acknowledge the risk taken by some ex-members of the IRA who spoke to me about sensitive issues and events. I would also like to thank those whose names can't be recorded here but who provided information that contributed to the overall mosaic. Other names have been changed or masked as requested, or in order to protect some individuals from any further intrusion or threat to their lives.

It's hard to be objective about people who are trying to kill you. I realise that. I know how hard it was for me, writing in the attic in Andersonstown, to suppress my feelings towards the loyalist paramilitaries and how hard it was to try and understand things from their historical perspective. The simple truth of the matter was that while the LVF weren't trying to kill me in particular, they would have happily murdered me in general. Their attacks were directed at Sharon and Big John, at my family, at the local community, at all our people—Irish Catholics. It *was* a threat to me (even as a diminished and hyphenated Irish-Australian) and the killings they perpetrated touched the outskirts of my life. I spoke to one of those murdered in an incidental conversation a few days before he was killed. Another was a youth worker from near where I was staying. Yet another was shot dead inside a pub in North Belfast close to where my father was raised. The last man killed was a taxi driver who picked up his killers after they called a cab from inside the pub where I spent New Year's Eve. Any one of the dead could have been someone from my family or known to me personally.

Through all of this I gained a better understanding, ironically enough, of how the everyday English or Ulster Protestant 'punter' must have felt during the worst years of the Troubles with bombs going off in London or downtown Belfast. Although IRA bombs weren't directed at them personally, they reduced the local bank or High Street to rubble and could have killed that bloke from school—the one in the Army or Police. British people, in particular, found it desperately hard to understand the men and women who shot dead British soldiers, or the distant deadly conflict which suddenly, incomprehensibly, resulted in IRA bombers in their towns. The fact that the British government and media played a determined role in obscuring and distorting the popular interpretation of the conflict does not change the fact that many ordinary British and Ulster Protestant people felt intensely and personally threatened by the IRA.

Let me state unequivocally that I abhor bombs and killing as much as any other decent person. Yet, unlike most Australian media commentators over the last thirty years, who have selectively denounced 'terrorism' from the safe distance of several continents (and have generally ignored or condoned state violence), the Northern Ireland conflict has actually touched my own family intimately. It killed my Aunt Jean. She was innocent in the way that all civilian casualties of war are innocent and she left behind her own share of heartbroken relatives. My relatives. The man who killed her had, I am sure, his own reasons to squeeze the trigger. The men and women, on all sides, who have done these things for the last thirty years always do. I am sure that, like everyone else, he was both a historical product and a victim of the conflict that also claimed Jean's life.

There are those who will undoubtedly read this book and dismiss me as yet another misty-eyed long-distance Celtic romantic. They will probably accuse me of being a Provo-apologist, and of a lack of academic objectivity. On the contrary, I have never been a St Paddy's day rebel and have worked tirelessly throughout my adult life for peace, with justice, in Ireland. That I view the Northern Ireland conflict from a particular perspective, that of Irish republicanism, does not detract from my grim determination to see the gun and bomb taken out of Irish politics once and for all. Moreover, career-wise the easiest thing for me to have done, as an Irish-Australian and as an academic historian, would have been to take the line of least resistance. To denounce 'terrorism' from the safety of 10,000 miles. To relax into smug superiority, looking down on 'two tribes' at war in Ulster. To fake objectivity and to say that the Troubles were just too hard and horrible to understand.

This, I always felt, was not an option available to me. My family's past and the very nature of the conflict in the North of Ireland, in all its intertwined complexity, has always been very personal to me. It was never enough, it seemed to me, just to say that bombs and kneecappings and the mundane terror of urban war were horrible and nasty and wrong. I always felt the pull of family, of bad blood, and of the place my father called 'home'. Despite being born of emigration and living a world apart, I was never entirely free of Belfast. I know the songs, the faces and the voices— I am a conscious part of Ireland's echo in the antipodes. And I always felt, above all else and despite the horrors of the last thirty years, that ordinary Irish people, both Protestant and Catholic, and regardless of political affiliation, possess a remarkable capacity for political clarity, laughter and forgiveness. It has been remarked that Irish history teaches us not to hope. And that the Irish people teach us otherwise.

This book, then, is my first faltering attempt to understand the mangled and bitter history of Ireland. It is about Jean. It is a book that wants to hope.

Simon Adams
Fremantle
Western Australia
October 2000

FOR SHARON

1

Diaspora Child

A generation of one.
Raised on dog eared letters
and weeping from exit wounds.
Blind memories.
No past.
I forget where I am
and who
I am not.

'And a 24-year-old woman was killed by machine-gun fire that tore through the car she was sitting in at a Catholic area of Belfast.'
New York Times, 9 June 1972

I never met my Aunt Jean. She was only twenty-four when she was torn from this world—shot dead by a gunman on a dark, quiet Belfast night. It was 1972 and I was just four years old, living thousands of miles away in New Zealand. What do I know of her? Very little other than fragmented memories scattered over my life by relatives. That she was taken prematurely from this world is indisputable. Jean was killed by a single bullet to the head while driving with her boyfriend on the Glen Road in Andersonstown, West Belfast. There is also universal agreement that she was young, beautiful and had just escaped a bad marriage. Had she lived, she would have been a fine mother to her daughter Sharon. But the reason for her death, and its perpetrator or perpetrators, are open to conjecture and have been the reason for dark secret whispers in my family ever since.

No one was ever charged with her murder and here in Australia or New Zealand oceans of time and distance distorted every rumour concerning Jean's death. Part of the problem was that no one really bothered to ask those back home in Ireland for substantive details. It just wasn't something that was spoken about in that sort of way. There's an Irish saying that has arisen from the last three decades of conflict in Northern Ireland—'whatever you say, say nothing'. As a result, whenever I heard Jean's name as a child it was a whispered secret thing shrouded in mystery, morbid speculation and tragedy. The aunt who was shot in the head and killed.

It always bothered me that no one 'down here' really knew what happened. I always wanted to know who killed her and I always wanted to understand the dark world of 'the Troubles' in a place my father called 'back home'. How could the violent death of a young mother become so entangled in conspiracy and conjecture? As I grew older I started to read books about the cruel little war in Northern Ireland and it seemed to me that it was impossible to confront the reality and reasons behind Jean's murder without confronting the larger tragedy of the conflict in Ireland. Without exhuming the fierce and tragic history of Ulster, Jean's death on the streets of Belfast in June 1972 is meaningless.

■ ■ ■ ■

It was 'the Troubles', and family secrets, that forced my father's side of the family out of Ireland. My father, Thomas Joseph Paul Fairley, like thousands of Irish before him, had left for Australia in 1966, before the most recent bout of the Troubles officially began. He was nineteen. I'm not close to my father, but I can't conceive of how frightening it must have been for him to have walked his bony arse on to that boat in Belfast's cold deep harbour armed only with his youth, a one-way ticket to Australia and a set of rosary beads. It was the first time he had ever really been apart from his parents and the brothers and sisters with whom he had been raised on a poverty-stricken housing estate. What did he think as he sailed out of Belfast (the harbour that launched the *Titanic* no less) and away from the coast of Ireland?

The long sea journey must have been an experience in and of itself. Aboard the ship Tom met other young £10 migrants like himself from England and Ireland—working class lads lured by the promise of Australia. After passing through the Suez Canal he apparently visited his first sex show with some of these 'lads'. Given the oppressive Catholic environment he was raised in, it must have appeared like a modern Sodom to him. So different from the closeted bleakness of Ardoyne where priests still ruled supreme and masturbation was considered a sacrilegious defilement of one's body. As they reached the Pacific Ocean Tom also experienced the disputable joys of sunburn and peeling skin. He arrived in Sydney in April of 1966. Although I am a migrant to Australia myself, I still can't fathom how strange, wondrous and terrifying it must have been for him to walk down that gangplank in Sydney Harbour with the sun glittering off the sea and the seagulls screeching like banshees in their endless search for lost chips. Nothing would ever be the same again.

In Sydney he met my mother, Vivienne, who had Irish grandparents, and they fell in love. In 1967 Tom and Vivienne moved to New Zealand and got married. I was born the following year. For Tom the Troubles arrived in stamped envelopes from home. My mother remembers Tom's growing alarm as letters from his sister Mary in Belfast arrived with news of barricades and riots in the Ardoyne district. Between tid-bits of information about his siblings and parents, there would be mention of someone beaten and taken away by the soldiers, or of the IRA shooting a policeman down the road. Sitting in the small living-room of our council house in Auckland it must have been very worrying. Tom was particularly concerned about his younger brother, Manuel, who was becoming 'involved'. According to my mother:

> Tom was always on about getting your Uncle Manuel and the others out of the Troubles. Your Aunt Mary was writing these letters and it was always barricades this and bullets that and oh, by the way, 'your Ma is in good health'. It was terrible really. I remember him getting the letter where they mentioned that Paddy McAdorey fella, I think that was his name, got killed. Tom had gone to school with him and knew him quite well. By 1971 he was getting really worried. Something happened on Jamaica Street and your Irish granny nearly got hit by a bullet that went through the door. There was always just some frightening story in the letters you see. It was really hard to know what was going on. We were hearing stuff on the news and then reading these letters and I remember one time Tom actually called on the phone. The Fairleys didn't have a phone in their house on Jamaica Street so he had to call the local shop and ask them to go fetch his mother and tell her he would call back at so and so time. And then in 1971 he just decided he really needed to get them out, so I had a bit of an inheritance that had been left to me. I cashed it in and paid for them all to immigrate to New Zealand. No one ever thanked me for it, but I'm not bitter.

Irish history was always an important part of my life. In a way my experience was typical of children born of immigration as I felt caught between two worlds. My father never hid the fact that he left Belfast by boat at age nineteen to escape forever the sectarianism, bleak weather and most of all, the grinding poverty that had mapped out his life until then. As the Northern Ireland civil rights movement of 1968 gave way to the riots of 1969, and as the civil conflict slid inexorably towards civil war, my mother and father had helped Tom's parents, four brothers, two sisters and a niece to immigrate to New Zealand in late 1971. For a while all twelve of us (two children, ten adults—three generations) lived in a small three bedroom government house in Mangere, south Auckland. Despite the obvious over-crowding, my earliest childhood memories are of this period and they are all happy ones. Dispersed to the southernmost tip of the South Pacific by conflict and poverty, my first conscious memories are of an Irish immigrant culture where even the potatoes on your dinner plate had a wider historical significance.

I guess you could call my Irish grandparents and my Irish aunts and uncles soft nationalists. They had just escaped a conflict that was becoming increasingly bloody. Although I never remember anyone advocating the wilful murder of any soldier of the British Crown, I do recall being taught the song:

> I'm off to Dublin in the green, in the green,
> where the helmets glisten in the sun,
> where the bayonets flash,
> and the rifles crash,
> to the echo of the Thompson gun.
> Well I've lived a life of slavery,
> since the day that I was born,
> but now I'm off to join the IRA,
> and I'm off tomorrow morn'.

Indeed, this song forms as strong a part of my childhood memory as any nursery rhymes. An Irish historical tradition was absorbed through song and later on through stories of 'back home' or by listening in when adults discussed the Troubles and the role of our family in them. The bullet through the back door that nearly hit my grandmother. The IRA man who was shot dead in front of Uncle Manuel. The riots. The British army. Prods and Taigs. Loyalists and republicans. Poor dead Jean. I was transfixed by all of it.

Still, there was an obvious sense of detachment as well. Belfast was never home to me. Yet, without ever having been there, I grew up knowing that Ardoyne was 'ours' and the Shankill was 'theirs'. Having never stepped foot in Belfast or Ireland myself I knew about the old egg factory behind Jamaica Street in Ardoyne where my aunts and uncles would play; that the housing in Andersonstown was better than Ardoyne; that if you wanted an ice cream cone in West Belfast you asked for 'a poke' and so on. I developed a queer sense quite early on in life that I was some sort of interloper in the South Pacific. This displaced sense of identity was often bewildering as a child. In a rare moment of infantile lucidity I remember asking my grandfather when I was about six how it was that I was Irish— as he insisted I was—when I had not been born there and we lived in New Zealand. His words, borrowed and bastardised from a famous Anglo-Irish nobleman, have always stayed with me: 'The Lord Jesus was born in a stable, but that never made him a horse.'

If these confusions were difficult to muddle through as a child living in a house where almost everyone I came into daily contact with was from the north of Ireland, they were even more perplexing after my parents divorced. Both my mother and father eventually remarried and due to a fight between my father and his parents when I was about eight, I never ever saw either of my Irish grandparents again. The tragedy of my family was that they came from Ireland to the other side of the world only to be separated by bad blood. I always felt an enormous emptiness because of what was lost and for some strange reason those months in 1971 and 1972 when we all lived in a small off-blue council house in Auckland have continued to hold a particular clarity and fondness for me. They were somehow indelible.

Part of the problem was my name. I was born and given a typically Catholic and apostolic name of Simon Paul Fairley. The surname only became a problem after my parents divorced and eventually remarried. After my mother fell pregnant to her new husband, Peter Adams, I became painfully aware, at the tender age of seven, that my baby brother would have a different surname to me. Eventually my mother got Tom's permission to change my name to Adams by deed-poll and for Peter to adopt me. That was it, I was never Fairley again. And yet, I have heard that when my father told my Irish grandfather, Old Q'ey, that Peter adopting me meant that he, Tom, would no longer have to pay ten dollars in child support each week, Old Q'ey reached into his pants and pulled out a ten dollar bill. He gave it to Tom in disgust: 'There you go, you sold your son and our family name for ten dollars.'

There was also the vexed issue of nationality. For most people this is an incidental matter, predetermined by geography and representing an absorbed cultural commonality. Given that my formative years between the ages of five and eighteen were spent in four different countries, the Irish connection has been one of the few constant things in my life. After all, it's all about blood and ethnicity, not geography (or so I was always told). And yet, my understanding of what it meant to be Irish, or even if it meant anything at all, was distorted by emigration, divorce, bad blood, ignorance and 10,000 miles of sea. It still is.

The connections were there, only weakened by time and distance. For instance, in December 1997 I found an old neglected box that I have carried with me across two continents and a dozen changes of residence. Inside was the obituary notice an aunt sent me when my Irish grandmother died in 1982. Underneath it were other diaspora fragments. A mass card from the funeral of a relative in Belfast, a hand-crafted republican plaque from a relative in Long Kesh prison, and a prayer book sent from Ireland for me when I was a baby.

Somewhat bewildered I contemplated what a strange and disjointed childhood I had had. I was constantly moving schools, cities and countries and always adapting to a new culture. In doing so I had become a professional at fitting in. Blending. Learning new national anthems. Making sure I pronounced things like everyone else. And yet these fragments of an older cultural tradition, of another place and of relatives that I felt had abandoned me—I still carried them around with me in an old box and absorbed them. The evidence was all around me. Above me on the wall of my study in Sydney were my father's rosary beads, given to him when he left Belfast on a boat bound for Australia. I have always kept them hanging near me in every house I have lived in. They represented a link with a place I never really understood but which I was not prepared to completely let go. Perhaps without all the moving, immigrating, emigrating, and fitting in I would never have felt the need to explore my 'Irishness'.

Jean was part of the family my father left behind. She was his first cousin and as children my father and Jean were extraordinarily close. He was deeply wounded by her death. When I was growing up she was always 'your poor Aunt Jean', and I was encouraged to think of her reverently. I'm not sure if it's an Irish thing, or a Belfast thing, or simply an idiosyncratic foible of my family, but we don't go out of our way to draw a distinction between first and second cousins, aunts and great aunts etc. The bottom line is you're either related or you're not—you're part of the *clann* or you ain't. As I was to find out later in my life, there were good reasons for my family to stick to this policy. It was a way of holding onto dark secrets.

What follows is my attempt to understand the terrible history, the hopes and the hardship that drove my family, like countless others before them, apart and from Ireland. In telling Jean's story I hope to recapture her for all our family. I want to take her back from the gunman who made her a statistic. In investigating her death I want to explore the crevices of the dirty little conflict in Northern Ireland and understand why she was killed. My return to Belfast for three weeks' research over New Year 1997–98, in the midst of a faltering peace process, was to discover Jean and in the process learn more about the beautiful, tragic land from which my family originates. I wanted to give Jean back something of the life that was stolen from her and in doing so, recapture something of Ireland and my family for myself.

2

Loinnir

'It was Wellington who first exhibited the splendid fighting qualities of the Irish private solider in the service of the Empire... For more than a century the slum-dwellers of Dublin, the hard-bitten men of Ulster, and the peasants of Munster and Connemara have fought in the van of England's battles... Irishmen of the lower classes do not make leaders. Under British discipline, and led by gentlemen of their own country, they have made history on a hundred battlefields in both hemispheres.'

Ireland of To-Day, 1913[1]

'In all sincerity we offer to the loved ones of all the innocent victims over the past twenty-five years abject and true remorse. No words of ours will compensate for the intolerable suffering they have undergone during the conflict.'

CLMC ceasefire statement, 13 October 1994

Derry journalist Eamonn McCann once wrote that 'Irish history is hair-raising' and that just because 'it is encrusted with myth alters nothing essential'. It has become fashionable within academia in recent years to almost write British blame out of Irish history, just as during the nineteenth and early twentieth century is was fashionable amongst many Irish people to hold the English responsible for every act of perfidy or misfortune visited upon poor Ireland, up to and including its terrible weather. Still, a few uncomfortable truths remain—Ireland was England's colony, its lands were annexed at the point of a bayonet, its people were subjected to countless indignities and suffered intolerable hardships. Over several centuries Irish people were born into a land of tremendous poverty, many reached the conclusion that English domination was the reason for their suffering, but still died without knowing the elemental national, religious and social freedoms now taken for granted. The IRA's 'War of Independence' and the resulting formation of the Irish Free State in the southern twenty-six counties during the 1920s therefore represented a decisive break with Ireland's previous history of miserable colonisation. However, the Irish 'Troubles', as they were already called, did not end there.

After Northern Ireland was partitioned from the rest of Ireland following the War of Independence, the province's first Prime Minister, Sir James Craig, famously declared: 'All I boast is that we are a Protestant parliament and a Protestant state.' And indeed it was. Virtual religious apartheid ensured that Catholics were discriminated against in housing, employment, social services—without objection by successive British governments—for almost fifty years. So unashamed was the discrimination that in 1934 a senior member of the Northern Ireland government, Sir Basil Brooke, publicly recommended that 'those people who are Loyalists not employ Roman Catholics, 99 per cent of whom are disloyal'. He was taken at his word. Although Catholics were roughly one quarter of the population of Belfast by the late 1920s, jobs within the local public service, the Belfast Corporation, continued to go almost exclusively to Protestants. For instance, the *Irish News* in 1927 revealed that of the 181 public servants in the Gas department only three were, to use Brooke's phraseology, 'Papists'. No less than seven of the 'twenty important departments connected with the Belfast Corporation' (including the all-important Police Department) had no Catholic employees whatsoever. And so it continued. By 1969 only 23 of 319 people employed at the higher administrative grades within the Northern Ireland civil service were Catholic.[2]

There was virtually no parliamentary alternative to this state of affairs. Gerrymandering along religious/ethnic lines ensured that the Ulster Unionist Party and their allies within the Orange Order ran Northern Ireland as a virtual one party state. Indeed, the small number of Irish nationalist members of the Stormont parliament only succeeded in passing one opposition bill during the entire fifty year existence of Stormont—the Wild Bird Protection Act of 1930. No wonder that latter day republicans still hark back to these events, denouncing the moderate leadership of the then Nationalist Party for being more successful at protecting birds than defending and improving the lives of their own people.[3]

Something had to change. It all started quite innocently with a few scattered civil rights marches in 1968 and ended four years later in blood-splattered agony on 'Bloody Sunday', 30 January 1972. It was at that point, according to one of those idealistic young social revolutionaries who participated in the early civil rights campaign, that 'I became aware that there was going to be a war in Northern Ireland and that people were going to have to choose sides.' The intervening years 1968–72 had seen a continual escalation of social unrest, political protest and vigilante backlash until the 'middle road' of Northern Ireland politics had disappeared completely. Forty years of religious apartheid left no room for the sorts of social reforms that civil rights activists were demanding and the 'we shall overcome' of the mainly Catholic protesters had been met head on by RUC baton charges and loyalist cudgels.

Civil rights protesters were attacked by sectarian mobs, sometimes in open collusion with the police. One of the very first people to be killed in the modern Troubles was Sammy Devenney, a harmless middle-aged father of nine beaten by the RUC inside his own home in Derry during April 1969. He died later of his injuries.[4] The RUC were then forced out of Catholic neighbourhoods by riots as people viewed them as hopelessly sectarian and unreservedly repressive. Increasingly, Catholics were burnt out of their homes in 'mixed' or predominantly Protestant areas in retaliation. According to official reports, over three terrible nights in August 1969 seven people were killed, 750 injured, 275 buildings were burnt down or otherwise damaged, and nearly two thousand families were forced from their homes—1,505 of these were Catholic families, while 315 were Protestant.[5] This season of violence, epitomised in riots and house burnings, resulted in the deployment of British troops on 14-15 August 1969. Initially perceived as peacekeepers, in the eyes of most northern Catholics they quickly became a foreign force of military occupation. And on it went until that fateful Sunday in 1972 when fourteen unarmed Catholics protesting about the reintroduction of internment (imprisonment without trial) in Northern Ireland were shot dead by British paratroopers in Derry. Although they were not the first civilians to be killed in the Troubles, their deaths on 'Bloody Sunday' certainly marked a bloody degeneration of the conflict in Northern Ireland.

A deadly triangle had asserted itself. On one side of that triangle were many of those idealistic young reformers of 1968 who had come to the concrete conclusion that the minority Catholic community's political aspirations were being silenced by force of arms. As a result they reasoned that they only had two practical options in front of them—submit or fight. In this context the traditional organisation of physical resistance politics, the Irish Republican Army, which had been virtually moribund in Ireland, north and south, since the late 1950s, was able to rise from the ashes of the civil rights campaign.

It is now part of the anecdotal popular history of the Troubles that in 1969 when the British Army was first deployed in Belfast, the entire IRA Belfast Brigade consisted of a few dozen middle-aged men and a couple of shotguns. The sort of people whose stories of past conspiracies were tolerated in West Belfast but were not taken especially seriously. Gerry Adams claims, in his book *Free Ireland*, that in 1961–62 the entire IRA in Belfast consisted of twenty-four people and two short arms. By contrast, after Bloody Sunday in 1972 neither wing of the recently-split IRA could absorb the vast numbers of new recruits they were getting from the Catholic ghettoes of the north. The IRA re-emerged with the furious and unbridled anger of 1960s youth. [6]

The statistics speak for themselves. Northern Ireland is a small place with a population of about 1.5 million people. Between 1969 and 1999 roughly 3,600 people were killed because of the Troubles. In terms of population size this would roughly equal about 100,000 deaths in Britain or half a million in the USA over the same thirty year period. In Australian terms it would mean 43,200 deaths. According to *Lost Lives*, a recent and exhaustive index of fatal causalities arising from the Troubles, between 1969–99 the Provisional Irish Republican Army (IRA or PIRA) killed 1,771 people, including over a thousand members of the security forces. Among the IRA's victims were also 59 alleged informers, 28 loyalist paramilitaries, and approximately 376 unintentional civilian deaths. Most of the killings occurred within Northern Ireland itself, although some occurred in England, the Republic of Ireland and even in Holland and Germany. As such, the IRA have inflicted 48.7% of all the deaths suffered over the last thirty years. In return, about 293 IRA members have been killed since 1969.[7]

The second side of the Troubles triangle comprised the loyalist paramilitaries. Thriving on the historical prejudices of the Orange Order, these organisations saw in the civil rights campaign a threat to the very existence of partition and their Northern Ireland statelet. 'Ulster says no' has been the traditional refrain of every loyalist political movement to emerge in Northern Ireland over the last century. In 1968 working class loyalist mobs joined their political leaders in saying 'no' to the demands of civil rights marchers and in some instances actually assisted police in beating them off the streets. In 1969, in the case of Belfast's Bombay Street and elsewhere, they literally burnt their Catholic neighbours out of their homes. And in the early 1970s they said 'no' to the armed resistance of the IRA and formed their own civilian militias to resist the threat posed by Catholic/nationalist political unrest.

The Ulster Defence Association (UDA) was formed in the days after the introduction of internment in August 1971. A leaflet calling for the formation of what would become the UDA was circulated widely throughout the Protestant areas of Belfast and read, in part:

> Being convinced that the enemies of the Faith and Freedom are determined to destroy the State of Northern Ireland and thereby enslave the people of God, we call on all members of our loyalist institutions, and other responsible citizens, to organise themselves *immediately* into platoons of twenty... Our enemies are the forces of Romanism and Communism which must be destroyed... We must prepare now! This is total war![8]

At swearing-in ceremonies for the UDA, prospective members had to utter an oath of allegiance to the Queen and promise to defend Ulster 'by all and every means possible'. The actual politics of the organisation were well illustrated in a now infamous letter from an anonymous woman that was published in the *UDA Bulletin* of February 1972:

> I have reached the point where I no longer have any compassion for any nationalist, man, woman, or child. After years of destruction, murder, intimidation, I have been driven against my better feelings to the decision—it's them or us. What I want to know is this, where the hell are the MEN in our community?... Why have they not started to hit back in the only way these

nationalist bastards understand? That is ruthless, indiscriminate killing... If I had a flame-thrower, I would roast the slimy excreta that pass for human beings. Also I'm sick and tired of you yellow-backed Prods who are not even prepared to fight for your own street, yet alone your own loyalist people. When civil war breaks out and, God forgive me, but I hope it's soon I, at least, will shoot you along with the Fenian scum.[9]

Unlike armed republican groups, the UDA was not banned by the British government until 1992.

Loyalist politics is a veritable minefield of acronyms and the various paramilitary offshoots include the UVF, LVF, UDA, UFF, RHC, OV and RHD to name only the most recent and/or best known. Between 1966 and 1999 they killed a total of 1,050 people, 28.9% of all the deaths caused by the Troubles. The overwhelming majority of these killings were indiscriminate, consciously aimed at the Irish Catholic community as a collective whole rather than at individuals specifically involved with the IRA. In many ways this was a logical consequence of an ideology that saw all Catholics as 'Fenians'—inherently treacherous, anti-British, seditious and alien. An estimated 144 loyalist paramilitaries have also lost their lives during the Troubles.

The final side of the deadly triangle was made up of the official security forces—principally the British Army, the locally recruited Ulster Defence Regiment (UDR—now the Royal Irish Regiment or RIR) and the Royal Ulster Constabulary (RUC). Since 1969 there have been as many as 30,000 heavily armed British security personnel in Northern Ireland at any one time. The security forces have widespread powers to detain, search, interrogate or use force against those whom they suspect of conspiring to overthrow or undermine the state in Northern Ireland. They also have the logistical support of military helicopters, armoured cars, numerous fortified barracks and some of the most sophisticated surveillance equipment ever deployed against any armed insurgency. While the Army is made up predominantly of working class youths from England and Scotland, the RUC and UDR/RIR are constituted from the residents of Northern Ireland itself. Since 1969, the security forces have caused approximately 360 deaths (about 10% of the total), including 158 civilians and 104 IRA members killed by the British Army. During the same period, 303 members of the RUC, 503 British soldiers, and 206 members of the UDR/RIR have been killed.

In short, the Troubles have produced enough death to keep a legion of statisticians busy. And between each dull number is a personal story of enormous human suffering.

■ ■ ■ ■

I woke up 35,000 feet above Iran. Dawn was breaking outside. If you've never seen it yourself, daybreak at that height over the Middle East is a majestic thing. Pure and brilliant. *Loinnir* as they say in Irish. We then flew over the former Yugoslavia, stopped off in Rome and landed in London. I had been travelling for over twenty-four hours and was feeling decidedly ill-humoured and of ill-odour. In order to cheer myself up I found a British Telecom phone that worked and called Big John in Belfast.

Big John is my cousin Sharon's husband and Amanda and I had stayed with Gran, John, Sharon, and their two boys last time I was in Belfast in 1995, during the first IRA ceasefire. Gran, who appears to be called such by any person in West Belfast under seventy, is my grandmother's sister and the mother of Jean. Sharon is Jean's daughter and after Jean was killed in 1972 she was raised by Gran in the house her mother was herself raised in, in Andersonstown, West Belfast. However, practically the first thing Big John said to me after the mandatory Belfast 'What 'bout ye?', was 'Did you hear the Rat is just after getting whacked in the Kesh by the Irps?'

It was just before lunchtime and this was big news all over Northern Ireland. Indeed, some would later argue that along with the IRA's second ceasefire, this was one of the most important political developments of 1997. Billy 'King Rat' Wright was the notorious leader of the hardline Loyalist Volunteer Force (LVF), an organisation that emerged as the most important loyalist splinter group to reject the 1994 ceasefire of the Combined Loyalist Military Command (CLMC). As a child Wright had apparently played Gaelic football with his Catholic neighbours in South Armagh and had been interested in Irish history. Decades later he would tell a journalist that as a result of this education he 'could well understand the fierce resentment the Irish had against England'.

Nevertheless, as a teenager Billy Wright joined the mid-Ulster youth wing of the Ulster Volunteer Force (UVF), a decision that was solidified when his uncle, father-in-law and brother-in-law were apparently each killed by the IRA in separate incidents. Arrested in 1977 while still a teenager and imprisoned for three years on an arms charge, Wright continued in the UVF upon release from jail. A Protestant fundamentalist lay-preacher, over the years it is believed that Wright may have been involved in planning and killing up to thirty Catholics. By the early 1990s he was the most feared loyalist paramilitary in Northern Ireland. When a journalist asked him what he thought of the murder of half a dozen innocent Catholics in the 'Greysteel Halloween Massacre' of 30 October 1993, Wright simply replied, 'That's just war'.

Republicans failed several times to assassinate Wright and the fearful legend around him grew. When asked about the attempts on his life he insisted, 'I'm immune to fear'. More interestingly, when author Martin Dillon asked Billy Wright about his relationship with God, he was happy to explain the Ulster conflict and his role within it in religious terms. By his own account, Billy Wright turned away from his Lord Jesus Christ principally because of his hatred for the IRA, 'The bitterness that was going on inside me told me I could not walk with God.'[10] Among the killings personally credited to Wright or to his 'Rat Pack' (as his Mid-Ulster UVF squad were called) were those of two teenage girls, Eileen Duffy and Katrina Rennie, a pregnant woman, Kathleen O'Hagan, and pensioners Charlie and Teresa Fox. In July 1996, prior to his break with the UVF and the formation of his own loyalist paramilitary group, the *Irish Times* published the following profile of King Rat.

> He is of average build, about six feet, with close-cropped hair and piercing eyes. 'Not the sort of fellow you would out-stare', according to one acquaintance. He is intelligent and shrewd, doesn't drink or smoke... He has never been convicted of UVF membership or, since reaching adulthood, of paramilitary activity.[11]

Indeed, part of the mystique surrounding King Rat was his uncanny ability to escape prosecution for murder. Perhaps part of the reason for this was, at least according to journalist Sean McPhilemy in *The Committee*, that a number of killings carried out by King Rat were actually abetted by security forces personnel sympathetic to his extreme brand of Protestant loyalism—including the murder of nineteen year old Denis Carville. Carville had been targeted simply because he was a Catholic and was shot dead as he sat beside his girlfriend in a parking spot popular with courting couples near the small town of Lurgan in October 1990. A week or so earlier the IRA had killed an off-duty UDR soldier in the exact same parking area. It is alleged that after being directed to the parking lot by on-duty RUC officers, King Rat walked up to the car Denis and his girlfriend were in and asked for Denis' identification. Satisfied that he was indeed a Catholic, King Rat asked Denis Carville to face forward and look out the windscreen—and then he shot him in the head. A loyalist co-conspirator alleges that King Rat later made an appearance at Denis Carville's funeral. He had dressed for the occasion in a dark suit and tie. As the hearse passed nearby carrying Denis to an early grave, King Rat turned to the fellow loyalist and allegedly whispered, 'I just came to make sure he was dead.'[12]

On the other hand, despite allegations of covert collaboration between the security forces and the Rat Pack, Wright would later assert that he had spent an estimated twelve months of his thirty-six years in Police interrogation centres, claiming he was the most arrested and 'interviewed' loyalist in Northern Ireland. Moreover, his acrimonious break with the UVF's Belfast leadership over their 1994 ceasefire, allegations of drug dealing, and the July 1996 killing of Catholic taxi-driver Michael McGoldrick (which was carried out by Wright's squad in a deliberate breach of the UVF ceasefire), led to the UVF, via the Combined Loyalist Military Command, issuing an order for Wright to leave Northern Ireland within 72 hours or face the consequences. His very public defiance of the CLMC's death threat established Billy Wright as the hardest of the 'hard men' of extreme loyalism. The formation of the Loyalist Volunteer Force, which was based mainly in mid-Ulster around Portadown, consolidated

Wright's paramilitary position. Ironically, given his proclivity for sectarian crimes, when Wright was imprisoned in March 1997 it was for threatening to kill a Protestant woman.

Initially Wright was held in Maghaberry jail, but in late April 1997 he was moved to the Maze/Long Kesh complex where he hoped to consolidate a LVF wing in the prison. The thirty LVF prisoners were eventually given C and D wings of H-Block 6, while just over twenty republican INLA inmates continued to be held in A and B wings. As such, the two groups were separated only by a central administration area which linked A–B with C–D wings and gave the blocks their infamous H shape when viewed from the sky.

King Rat's April 1997 arrival in H6 was not welcomed by the small militant republican group, the INLA. The Irish Republican Socialist Party (IRSP—the political wing of the INLA) denounced his transfer as 'a serious error of judgement' on the part of the prison authorities. An IRSP spokesperson went on to say that if Wright was not moved out of H6 immediately then the authorities 'must be prepared to accept whatever chain of events, inside and outside Long Kesh, that they have set in motion'. The threat was ignored and eight months later the INLA killed King Rat.[13]

According to reports published at the time and evidence later given in court, on the morning of Saturday 27 December 1997 a white prison van arrived at the gates of H6 to take two loyalist prisoners, Billy Wright and Norman Green, from the LVF wings to the prison visitor's centre. The van arrived at about 8:40am. Wright and Green were led out of their wing at about 9:50am, climbing into the van by a sliding door and taking their seats. At the same time, three INLA inmates from the adjoining wing clambered out on to the roof of H6 via a hole in a fence which they had cut earlier and covered-up using a shoestring and a stack of chairs. As the van moved off the three INLA inmates leapt off the roof into the H6 exercise compound and stopped the vehicle by brandishing a handgun at the driver.

Christopher 'Crip' McWilliams (aged 35), armed with a 9mm Makarov pistol, opened the sliding door and ordered the prison guard not to move. Identifying King Rat, he took aim and Wright kicked out in a vain attempt to save his own life. Loyalist prisoners who witnessed the events from nearby windows claimed that McWilliams simply stepped back and opened fire. Wright was hit by 'at least three but possibly seven bullets', including one to the forearm, the left buttock, and a fatal shot to the chest which pierced his lungs, heart and main arteries. The crown prosecutor later argued in court that the assassination was 'a daring plan dependent on split second timing' and that it involved seizing a one minute 'window of opportunity' to kill Billy Wright in the middle of what was supposedly the most secure anti-terrorist prison in Europe. According to Britain's *The Mirror*, King Rat's last mortal words on this earth as his INLA killer repeatedly fired at him were, 'God, let it stop.'

King Rat lay dying on the floor of the prison van (he was officially pronounced dead at 10:50am) as McWilliams and his accomplices escaped back on to the roof of H6 and into the INLA cells in A-wing of H6. After a four hour stand-off and what was described at their trial as 'a tense period of negotiations', the three INLA men surrendered themselves and a box containing two guns and a pair of bolt-cutters to prison authorities. McWilliams allegedly told the prison guards that an INLA operation had just taken place and that 'Youse put him in a block with us. There could have been twenty of us burned because of him.' (This was a reference to the fact that in August 1997 the LVF had set fire to their wing during a protest). At the trial of McWilliams and the other two INLA men in October 1998, it was revealed that when they surrendered the defendants had firearm residue and two had blood matching that of Billy Wright on their clothing. During interrogation McWilliams had allegedly told police that 'Billy Wright was executed for one reason and one reason only, and that was for directing his campaign of terror against the nationalist people from his prison cell.'[14]

Crip McWilliams, like Billy Wright, was no stranger to death. His older brother Paul McWilliams was shot dead while (allegedly) throwing petrol bombs at a British Army observation post in Ballymurphy, West Belfast on 9 August 1977. Paul was sixteen years old and had been a member of the *Fianna*, the youth wing of the IRA. Crip, thirteen at the time, placed a death notice in the *Irish Times* which said of his older brother that, 'He was shot in the back by a coward and died a hero.' Crip would himself join the INLA, becoming a political associate of Jimmy Brown, Gerard 'Dr Death' Stevenson and Gino Gallagher, all of whom would die during bloody internecine republican feuds. As the INLA divided into rival factions— one of which resulted in the creation of the tiny Irish Peoples' Liberation Organisation (IPLO)—the bodies began to pile up. Between December 1986 and March 1987 twelve people were killed as a result of a feud between those who left to join the IPLO and their former comrades in the INLA. In August and September of 1992 a further three people were killed during a faction fight inside the Belfast Brigade of the IPLO.

McWilliams apparently joined the IPLO, of which Jimmy Brown was the principal leader, and was convicted for the 15 December 1991 killing of Colm Mahon, a thirty-nine year old Catholic father of three who was shot dead at the Belfast bar he managed. The IPLO claimed the slaying of Mahon was a mistake and that they were actually after a leading loyalist whom they had earlier sighted in the bar. The reality was far less heroic than even that. Several IPLO members had apparently been drinking at the bar and after getting into a drunken argument with Mahon and being thrown out, Crip allegedly returned and killed him, shooting him dead in front of the bar's patrons. Crip McWilliams was later convicted of Mahon's murder and given a life sentence.

Killings like that of Colm Mahon dredged the depths of drunken maliciousness and besmirched the already tarnished image of Irish republicanism, prompting the IRA to move against the IPLO. The IPLO's penchant for deadly and reckless faction fights did little to mitigate in their favour and increasingly the feeling in West Belfast was that 'something needed to be done' about them. On Halloween night, 31 October 1992, an estimated 100 Provos hunted down IPLO members. Numerous punishment beatings were carried out, a number of IPLO supporters were ordered to leave Northern Ireland immediately and several were 'kneecapped'. The IPLO commander in Belfast, Sammy Ward, was shot dead. After that, the IRA ordered the small group to disband and the IPLO effectively ceased to exist. Crip McWilliams survived this blood-letting and made it alive back into the ranks of the INLA at Long Kesh. In October 1998 he was sentenced to a second life term for the killing of King Rat. The *Belfast Telegraph* offered the following analysis:

> Christopher 'Crip' McWilliams had nothing to lose when he clambered over a prison wall and pumped bullets in to the most feared loyalist in Northern Ireland... He was a loner, unpopular even with the hardline republican terror group he served...
> McWilliams is the most unpredictable and fanatical of terrorists imaginable. He once shot dead a bar manager apparently because he threw him out of a Belfast pub on his birthday. [15]

The *Belfast Telegraph*, not for the last time, had it wrong. Crip McWilliams, like Billy Wright, wasn't a fanatical monster, but a man. For instance, following his October 1998 trial, various newspapers published reports claiming that McWilliams had laughed after shooting Wright. In response, Crip called the *Irish News* from a phone in Long Kesh prison to give his version of events.

> As one of three INLA volunteers ordered to assassinate [Billy Wright], I most certainly didn't derive any sense of malicious satisfaction for being party to the demise of a fellow human being, irregardless of his involvement in any such campaign of slaughter. I am confident that my fellow comrades involved in the operation would offer a similar sentiment in this regard.

McWilliams also strenuously objected to reports which claimed he had smiled in court when he was convicted for murdering Wright. Crip, who had lost his own brother to the Troubles, said he was aware of the presence of the Wright family in the court room:

> At no time did we seek to behave in a manner adding in any way to the sense of loss or grievance. Billy Wright was justifiably deemed an enemy but that most certainly didn't extend to members of his family. [16]

However, the details of all of this were still ahead of us as I stood talking to Big John on the phone from an airport departure lounge in London on the morning of 27 December. Indeed, Northern Ireland radio had only just announced that King Rat was dead.

'What happened?', I asked.

'The Rat was about to go on a visit and some Irps climbed over a roof inside the Kesh and stiffed him in the prison van. Five in the back.'

'Where'd they get the guns?'

'Smuggled them in t' the Kesh up their arses I suppose.'

'Bugger me.'

'Aye. Exactly.'

After a while of this chatter my money started to run out and Big John said he would pick me up from the airport in Belfast in an hour or so and bring me back to their place, which was where I would be staying for the next month. I hung up and sat on a gawdy lime-green British Airways chair near the boarding gate. King Rat shot dead just two days after Christmas. My mother's hopes that all would be peaceful while I was back in Belfast looked like being dashed. So much for a quiet research trip and a low-key family visit. As I sat sipping on a drink looking out the windows at the plane that would carry me to Ulster I began to feel the blood curdling within me. The loyalists will go mad over this one, I thought to myself. Someone will die tonight for sure.

3

Burying the Rat

'In ancient times Belfast was the site of a fort... John de Courcy, soon after his invasion of Ulster in 1177, destroyed the ancient fort and erected a castle on a site near-by. This castle was destroyed in 1316 by Edward Bruce, and again several times in the next 300 years, during which its possession alternated between the O'Neills and the English. In 1574 Brian O'Neill... was, with his wife and brother and others of his followers, treacherously seized by the Earl of Essex during a banquet in the castle and put to death. Thirty years later the castle and lands of Belfast came into the possession of Sir Arthur Chichester, Governor of Carrickfergus, who ruthlessly exterminated the Irish inhabitants of the surrounding territory and planted the lands with settlers imported from Devon and Scotland.'
Illustrated Guide to the Counties of Ireland, 1953

'The axe forgets, but not the tree.' Irish saying

Over the disputed territory of Northern Ireland, descending into Belfast, I looked down at the patch-work of green fields and thought about all the pain and suffering that had been invested there over the last 400 years. Soil soaked in blood and history. As the harbour came into focus my mind shifted to the *Titanic*. Built right there below me in Belfast: impenetrable, luxurious and unsinkable. Strangely, I then began thinking about the pilots who bombed Belfast on 15 April 1941. The Nazis used 180 planes to bomb the city that night. Many concentrated on Belfast's famous docks, devastating entire streets in the surrounding districts and killing 745 people, reputedly the largest loss of life in a single Nazi air-raid on any city in the British Isles on a single night. In West Belfast the dead were taken to the Falls Road public baths and laid out around the pool until space ran out, and then some were actually placed in the empty pool itself. What a macabre scene it must have made. About 120 bodies, some of them unidentified, were later buried in a mass grave.

In all, Belfast was bombed four times by the Luftwaffe in April and May of 1941, killing nearly 1,000 people and damaging 56,000 houses. Tens of thousands of incendiary bombs were dropped on the night of 4-5

May alone. Whole parts of the city centre, docks area and North Belfast were reduced to smoking rubble. About 100,000 people were made homeless. The *Northern Whig* of 17 April reported that 'working-class districts took the heaviest battering'. Apparently, for weeks afterwards tens of thousands of people, both Protestant and Catholic (the bombs didn't discriminate) would sleep out at night in public halls, in schools, under trees in parks and even in the meadows of Black Mountain. So inadequate were the government's preparations and so severe was the shortage of safe housing that they were forced to build prefabricated huts to accommodate all the 'refugees'. Bitterness was at a premium. Unionist politicians admitted their dismay that in the fields of Hannahstown, on the outskirts of Belfast, thousands of bombed-out Protestants and Catholics were sleeping alongside each other in the fields and were all coming to the same conclusion—that the government was no good.[1]

It took Adolf Hitler to unite the people of Belfast.

Air travel also reminded me of Reginald Maudling who on boarding his July 1970 return fight to London after his first trip to Northern Ireland as British Home Secretary, is said to have remarked: 'For God's sake bring me a large Scotch. What a bloody awful country.' Over a quarter century later and with no Scotch being on hand, I simply swallowed my own saliva to brace for landing. We touched down with a jolt on the wet runway at Belfast International as British Army helicopters were taking off on the next runway. It was only then that it really hit me that I was indeed back in Ireland for the first time in almost two years.

I was met by Big John and his boys, Conor (seven) and wee Dan (four). Along for the ride was John's younger brother Kevin who is a plumber and who lives with John's Ma and Da over in the New Lodge in North Belfast where Big John grew up. I then quickly discovered that British Airways had checked my luggage on to the wrong flight and after discovering it was unaccompanied by me they suspected it might be a bomb and it was taken off the plane. My backpack was still in London while I was now in Belfast. No problem, they'd send it over on the next flight. With that sorted out we drove on out to Andersonstown in Wild West Belfast and down into Tardree Park where Gran had an Ulster fry on the table waiting for us. The boys were all over me asking if I had brought them boomerangs again and asking why Amanda wasn't with me this time. In short everything was in brilliant focus. I was back in Belfast.

That night was spent catching up with Big John, Sharon, Gran, as well as reading the boys the Australian books (*Edwina the Emu* and *Blinky Bill*) Amanda bought for them and watching the telly. The news was full of Billy Wright getting killed. There had been rioting in parts of Portadown, King Rat's political bastion. In the equally staunchly loyalist town of Ballymena, a bus had been set on fire. The police fired a single plastic bullet at the rioters, but no one was injured. Still, melodramatic newsreaders put on their deadly serious faces and lamented about extremists dragging the province back to the brink of civil war.

At about ten o'clock Colm[2] from across the road, whose wife happens to be a cousin of Sharon's from the other side of her family, came over for a drink to celebrate the untimely passing of King Rat. He asked us if we had watched the news of how the INLA had managed to shoot Billy Wright dead inside the most secure anti-terrorist prison in western Europe. 'Fucking magic'. Eventually Colm left and after catching up some more with Big John and Sharon I crawled up in to the half-renovated attic where I would be staying for the next few weeks and slipped over into a deep, deep sleep. So subterranean was my slumber that if the Reverend Ian Paisley himself had been preaching hellfire and masturbation from the end of my bed it would not have awoken me. The last thing I remember is lying on my back looking out the skylight at the black ink night of Belfast. Bruised clouds were flying by at a furious pace and swirling over me. As I closed my eyes in exhaustion I prayed that no one would get shot that night in retaliation for the Rat.

I awoke next morning at a ridiculously inhumane 6:46am with what passes for the grey dawn of Belfast starting to filter in through the skylight above me, robbing the darkness of its hold on the day. The sky was already sulking. The first thing I saw when I opened my gluey eyes was a British army helicopter hovering at low altitude over the district. I lay in bed for a while, not wanting to awaken the others below me in the house, watching the chopper and listening to my walkman. Above me Belfast was turning blue-grey, grey-blue as clouds attacked, obscured and then retreated away from both the morning light and the beating blades of the flying war machine.

I also lay in bed thinking about Jean and how to broach the subject of my research with Gran and Sharon. I had touched on it last night with Gran when no one else was in the room, mentioning that one of the things I wanted to do while I was back in Belfast was research the circumstances surrounding Jean's death. She didn't have much to say at all except 'The one that done it, whoever he was, is probably long dead.' That was it. She then looked down and played with the hem on her skirt and I felt like a monster until Sharon and Big John came back in to the room sporting late Christmas presents for me. I felt very unsure sticky-beaking around and hadn't even talked about my idea of looking into Jean's death yet with Sharon. On the other hand I mentioned what I wanted to do to John and he said he was sure Sharon would agree. I was thinking about all of this and enjoying the blue-grey/grey-blue pageant through the skylight when at about 9:15am Big John shouted up from the bottom of the ladder that leads up into the attic.

'Simon, you awake up there?'

'I am, aye.' (I always say that when I'm in Ireland.)

'Three men are after getting shot last night down in Dungannon in retaliation for King Rat.' Good morning West Belfast. Hell of a way to start a Sunday, I thought to myself.

■ ■ ■ ■

A man was dead. His name was Séamus Dillon. He was forty-five years old, worked as a bricklayer's labourer during the day and as a part-time doorman at a hotel at night. He had served a life sentence for a killing carried out in 1980 and had only been out of prison three years. The LVF claimed responsibility for killing Séamus Dillon and wounding three other people when they opened fire on the pub in Dungannon where he worked. The Glengannon Hotel was full of young Catholics out for a Saturday night's fun and dance. Following the death of Billy Wright on Saturday morning, the LVF had issued a statement to the press claiming that 'Billy Wright will not have died in vain' and threatening to widen their 'theatre of operations'. Early that evening the LVF had put on a paramilitary display for the cameras at a wake for Billy Wright in Portadown. Four armed men in combat fatigues and with balaclavas on were photographed saluting their fallen commander. One of them read a statement to the press saying that King Rat was 'one of Ulster's finest' and that 'The torch lit by Billy in a struggle against pan-nationalism and the all-Ireland peace process will be carried on by us all.'

Shortly before 11pm, as I was asleep in the attic in Andersonstown, a red Vauxhall Nova carrying a LVF squad drove into the parking lot of the Glengannon Hotel. It pulled up near the front door, presumably to open fire on the dancing teenagers inside. However, noticing the suspicious vehicle several doormen (including Séamus Dillon) approached the Vauxhall and the two masked gunmen opened fire. It was later reported that approximately thirty-five bullets were fired at the Hotel entrance. In the melee they succeeded in shooting Dillon in the head, killing him and wounding three others, including a fourteen year old boy who was working inside the hotel as a glass collector. The bullet that hit him travelled through two sets of doors and his arm before lodging itself in a music speaker. The 'spray job' completed, the LVF squad then fled the area. The car used in the shooting was later found burned out a few miles from the spot where Séamus Dillon lay dead.

Witnesses and friends of Séamus Dillon later claimed in the press that he was 'a gentle giant', that there 'was nothing sinister in him', and that he died trying to save the lives of others. He was the first person to be shot dead in retaliation for the assassination of King Rat. He was the fifteenth person to die violently in Northern Ireland in 1997. Unfortunately, he would not be the last.

■ ■ ■ ■

Later that day Colm came over again to ask if we had heard the news about the lad down in Dungannon and, by the way, would John mind driving his great-aunt who had been staying with him since Christmas back down to Portaferry on the Ards Peninsula this afternoon. No problem says John and after spending some quality time with Sharon, Gran, Conor and wee Dan I hitched along for the ride, never having been down to Portaferry myself. The drive was pleasant enough, with brilliant landscape and little villages with their red, white and blue curb stones announcing their loyalties. Portaferry itself is the southernmost town of the Ards, a bruised tongue of land about five miles wide and twenty miles long that stretches away from Belfast along the eastern-most coast of Ulster. To the right is the Irish Sea and to the left is Strangford Lough. It was the Vikings who had originally named the lough, calling it *Strangfjord* on account of the deliciously unusual sounds made by the tide when it pushes in from the open sea.

Outside the car the day was a touch foggy but it was still an enjoyable drive down the Ards. Colm was in good humour. On the trip back to Belfast he joked that his family was so poor when he was young that 'if you didn't have a hardie in your pants when you woke up on Christmas morning you didn't have anything to play with.' He suggested we all go out for a drink to The Front Page in the town centre that night and John agreed.

The night itself was less than perfect. The band was hungover and atrocious. Patrons were also a little fearful that loyalists might attack the bar, it being a 'Catholic pub' afterall, and booths at the back were at a premium. Each time someone walked through the door everyone would glance around nervously to check that it wasn't a gunman before returning to the comfort of a pint of the black stuff. Stories about King Rat had also been flowing thick and fast. Danny the Printer (logically enough, he works at a printing business) was drinking with us and mentioned that at the time of the Siege of Drumcree in 1996 a car load of loyalists had pulled up beside him at traffic lights and shouted 'King Rat will get you!' at him. They then screeched away.

'What'd you do?' asked Sharon.

'Shat me daks and drove on, what do ye think?'

We all caught a cab home just before midnight.

■ ■ ■ ■

The next day I had another chat with Gran about Jean. I got her consent to look into Jean's death although Gran assured me that she herself didn't know anything about it.

'No one ever told me nothing. Billy [her deceased husband, my great-uncle] might have known something, but he never talked about it t' me.'

This I could not understand. Here was her daughter, who was living under the same roof when she was shot dead, and no one, not the Police, the Army, her husband or anyone else ever bothered to tell her who had killed Jean, why or how. I couldn't comprehend how Gran could have been kept so much in the dark until I discovered that Gran had taken Jean's death so badly that she was medicated and confined to bed. She didn't even attend Jean's funeral.

Over breakfast, I examined the Monday papers. The news was all bleak.

It was the third-last day of the year, 29 December 1997, and death and despair were everywhere. The southern paper, the *Irish Times*, was fairly representative. Its Northern Editor lamented that 'As darkness closed in on Northern Ireland last night, there was fear in many hearts. After the Billy Wright assassination and the speedy retaliation at the Dungannon Hotel, yet again people asked: 'What next'.' If the *Times*' Northern Editor knew then he wasn't shy in telling you: 'the one gloomy certainty as Northern Ireland faces a new year is that there will be more deaths and further violence.' I wondered how much Northern Editors got paid to write this stuff and if they ever got depressed. He did make a good point regarding the situation at Long Kesh though:

> The past year has been a chapter of disasters from the point of view of the authorities, with republicans trying to tunnel their way out, a republican prisoner escaping in woman's clothes and now the assassination of the jail's best known inmate. [3]

Later on I checked the *Belfast Telegraph* to see if the forecast was any different there, but it wasn't. I also couldn't help but notice the 45 obituary notices published for Billy Wright. Although a number were from grieving relatives and friends, quite a few more were from 'colleagues' and loyalist inmates at Long Kesh/Maze Prison. Members of the LVF wing, for instance, ended theirs with the simple words 'Lead the way'. Numerous others described Wright as a 'patriot', 'a true son of Ulster', a 'true loyalist' and a 'brave and loyal Ulster man who stayed faithful right to the end'. There was even a personal notice from Michael Stone of Milltown Massacre fame, who wrote that: 'You sleep now but the high company of heroes will forever be your Valhalla.'[4]

After the morning newspapers and breakfast I went with Sharon and the boys into town in a black taxi. Black taxis are a cross between a community mini-bus and a proper taxi service. They drive along prescribed routes, the fare is set (usually 70p a trip) and you can get in or out anywhere on the way. You hail the cab by waving it down on the street and if it has room (five in the back, one in the front with the driver) you squeeze in. You get out by tapping on the glass between the driver and the back with a coin and he pulls to the side.

With Sharon and Conor beside me and wee Dan on my knee we travelled down the Falls Road towards Castle Street in the city. On the way I was amazed to discover that although Billy Wright was only two days dead and hadn't even been buried, the graffiti on the Falls was already up: 'King Billy Wright—Rot ye Rat!', 'King Rat—watch your back! Ha Ha!' Nasty gallows graffiti.

It was rainy and cold in town and after exchanging a playstation game the boys got for Christmas, we promptly headed back up Castle Street and took a black taxi back to Andersonstown. On the way we passed a funeral on the Lower Falls. The cortege carried the coffin straight out onto the Falls Road and the mourners fell in behind, in the rain, for the one mile walk up to Milltown cemetery. Everyone in the taxi crossed themselves.

On the way Sharon started talking about Elva.[5] Apparently when Colm was away working in Berlin Elva and her five kids were living up in North Belfast in the 'mixed area' (Protestant and Catholics live there) of Deerpark. One day Elva had a row with a woman across the road who happened to be Protestant. Some words were said and the Protestant woman muttered that 'Fenians' shouldn't be in the area anyway. A few nights later the front door was smashed down and in walked men in balaclavas, one with a shotgun. Upstairs, one of Elva's sons threw her on the ground and lay over her shielding her body from the shotgun blasts. Fortunately, neither of them was killed. The message was unmistakable; the family was no longer welcome in the district. The RUC turned up an hour later to take the family away to a refuge. When Elva returned the next day to collect her furniture, the house had been broken into and the family's belongings were all smashed. That's when Elva and her family moved to Andersonstown for a new beginning.

The walk home with Sharon from where we left the black taxi gave me the opportunity to clear the Jean stuff up with her. I told her of my plans to look into her mother's killing, but only if she gave her permission. She immediately said to go ahead and I was free to sticky-beak around. While on the subject I told Sharon that according to Gran, when I spoken to her that morning, Jean was very republican-minded, always giving the soldiers stick and chasing after the Army Saracens taking men away. She had a wardrobe in the alley behind the house and Gran was convinced she was 'hiding stuff for the boys out there'. She would joke Jean about it and Jean would just shake her head and laugh, 'Catch yerself on Mammy'. I then mentioned that the really odd thing Gran had said was that 'after Jean got shot, sometimes I used t' tell myself that perhaps it was a blessing that she died quickly rather than getting caught up in something and spending her life in jail'. This was interesting because the image of Jean I had always been given was one of someone uninvolved in politics. Sharon said it was all news to her; no one ever spoke to her about Jean at all.

We were still talking as we walked down the hill with Conor and Dan in the Belfast chill. I asked Sharon if she ever remembered the Army coming to the house when she was little. She said she remembered one time when she was about six and the house was being raided in a search for guns, explosives and/or IRA men on the run. A black British solider picked Sharon up out of her bed and carried her downstairs. She remembers being in his arms and was amazed by the size of him and his skin. He was the first black man she had ever seen up close. As she looked over his shoulder other soldiers were on their hands and knees searching under her bed. Sharon was still telling me this story as we reached the front door at Tardree Park where Gran was waiting for us. As we walked inside Sharon asked Gran if she remembered the house being raided in the 1970s.

'Aye, they'd search the entire house trampling over everything and we would all sit huddled downstairs like the Jews.'

Interesting historical analogy, that one. Gran put a cup of tea on and we all agreed that, yes indeed, the seventies had been the worst decade of the Troubles.

■ ■ ■ ■

The noise of children gurning dragged me from my slumber, so I got up and walked up to The Pop—a small old-style convenience store located at the top of the housing estate near the Glen Road. It was cold out and a black miserable Belfast winter sky was hanging bruised and disenchanted above me. I walked out of Tardree Park with my collar turned up to the cold, past the wasteground with 'P.I.R.A' spraypainted on the brick wall and up the path towards The Pop. Inside The Pop, behind windows heavy with condensation, I bought a pan loaf (as they call it in Belfast), a newspaper, and some sweeties for the boys. The lovely woman behind the counter heard my accent and asked if I was from that large sunburnt ex-British colony in the south seas.

'I'm Australian, yeah.'

'My best pal is just back from Australia and she was out in the outback in the west—Perth, I think you call it—and 'tis a bit of a rough town from what I hear.' (This from a woman who lives in the middle of a war zone.)

'And whereabouts in Australia are you from yourself?'

'Sydney.'

'That's where *Home and Away* is filmed, is it not?'

'Tis, aye.' (I always say that in Ireland.)

'It must be lovely.'

She packed up my little bag of goodies and after a few 'cheerios' and 'see ye soons' I was on my way back down the hill under an angry Belfast sky that was starting to spit.

Back in the house, I settled down to see if Tuesday's feature writers could succeed in depressing me any worse than Monday's. Once again the southern *Irish Times*, and its Northern Editor rose to the occasion.

> Gloom and doom are the most plentiful commodities in Northern Ireland this week. The festive season turned to ashes in the mouth after the killings last Saturday.

And on it went, detailing the horror disco massacre that was narrowly avoided by Séamus Dillon's sacrifice of his life at the Glengannon Hotel. Quoting 'Loyalist sources', the Northern Editor also claimed the LVF had 'about 100 nominal members but a much smaller number of effective killers'. Still, the reaction of the LVF to King Rat's death 'could quite conceivably include a pub massacre which only requires a handful of operatives and a single gun'. Accordingly, 'pubs and places of entertainment or worship' in country areas would be the greatest places of risk. After chewing over the Northern Editor's insights, I moved on to the *Irish News*.

The outlook of the *Irish News* was also bleak. In addition to the recent killings, a considerable amount of space was given over to the 'surreal holiday camp' at Long Kesh/HMP Maze. Pointing out that approximately 180 of the estimated 500 inmates—'some of Europe's worst criminals'—were presently on Christmas release, the paper argued that life in the prison 'has been likened to a social club'. Not one I would particularly like to join thank you very much, I thought to myself.[6]

As I sat there reading newspapers, Sharon came in and put the kettle on. With the sky outside continuing its three day sulk, we settled down for a nice cup of tea and a chat. Sharon talked about people remembering her mother as one of those women who would bang the bin lids on the road whenever the soldiers raided the estate at night, warning IRA men 'on the run' to flee.

She also remembered another relative of ours who was always hijacking trucks whenever the rioting would start in the early 1970s. Before burning the trucks at the barricades, the contents would usually be 'liberated' and Sharon remembers one time, around Easter, when this relative came back from a riot to Tardree Park carrying armloads of Easter Eggs taken from a lorry before it was torched in the name of the Irish republic.

'There were Easter Eggs all over the district. You couldn't move for friggin Easter eggs. Easter was brilliant that year, so it was.'

Another time it was lightbulbs, not nearly as good. Two decades later, and now a mother herself, Sharon cried when she heard the first IRA ceasefire had been declared in August 1994.

'I thought it was over. That's what you were thinking at the time. It was like a weight was lifted and for a few weeks it was like living in a new place.'

We talked some more about family gossip and then Sharon had to do some housework, it being her day off work. I decided to make a few phone calls in order to get the research moving. My first, to the Linen Hall library in Belfast city, was an easy one. I had prearranged to gain access, for research purposes, to their world famous political collection. Yvonne and Kieran, the librarians, told me to come in the following day and everything would be fixed up. The second call was a little more difficult as it was to the Royal Ulster Constabulary. I had decided earlier, and I discussed this with Sharon, that I would try to use my academic credentials to gain access to the RUC file on Jean's death. This I knew would be difficult. The RUC are not known for their willingness to cooperate with academics sticking their noses into the security situation in Northern Ireland. We decided that the best course would be for me to play down the fact that I was a member of Jean's family.

After psyching myself up I dialled the media officer at RUC headquarters. He was pleasant enough, I guess that is his job after all, and after explaining my situation to him he suggested I make a formal written request for access to Jean's file. He emphasised that my letter should stress my academic credentials and the fact that I had the consent of the surviving relatives of 'the deceased'. Well, I thought, at least the ball is rolling. After hanging up I reported back to Sharon, who was now cleaning the kitchen floor. She nodded her head and continued mopping.

■ ■ ■ ■

Later, Big John came home from work and put the kettle on. The great thing about Belfast is that there is always someone who will put the kettle on. After chatting about the current state of the peace process we started talking about his childhood growing up in New Lodge in North Belfast. I got out my tape recorder and asked him if he remembered when the British Army came to take his father away.

'Yep, I was five or six. They searched our house. They actually left the house but left it under guard. And then they came back, searched the house again and found a gun in the wall. It was hidden—actually built in t' the wall.'

John had come home to find his dad sitting on the couch under armed guard. He remembers that the British soldiers all had their rifles piled up against one wall as they searched the place. Then they left. But when they came back later, obviously operating on inside information, they found an armalite rifle folded up in the wall. As the Army was photographing the captured rifle and its hiding place, a commotion started in the street.

'There was actually a riot going on outside the house. I remember going out of the house, and you're a kid and you're looking at the neighbours screaming and shouting at the Army and you were shocked— everything was just happening too quick for you. Your eyes are wide open and yer stunned, 'what the hell is happening here?' After that, when me Da went inside [to prison] and we'd go up t' see him, it was weird. It used t' be like a day out, only instead of going t' the beach or something you were away t' see your Da in prison.'

In most places having a father in prison would be an awful social stigma for a child to endure. Not so in the republican New Lodge. Gunner Robert Curtis, age twenty, the first British soldier to be killed by the IRA in the modern phase of the Troubles, was shot dead on the New Lodge Road on 6 February 1971. Three months later the New Lodge Provo who was widely believed to have killed Curtis, Billy Reid, was himself shot dead during another gun battle with the British Army. Coincidentally, he was killed near Curtis Street in the centre of Belfast. Ever since then a frightening and disproportionate number of civilians, soldiers and IRA Volunteers have been killed in the New Lodge area. And over the years the New Lodge has contributed dozens upon dozens to the republican wings of Long Kesh.

'There was so many kids with dads in jail it made no difference. We all just knew the *craic*. There was just so much happening out in the street— shootings, bombings. You were fearing t' put the kettle on in case there might be another shooting. When we went t' school we all did wee drawings of armoured cars and barbed wire and such. Strange. You just put your head down and lived through it. Even when a bomb went off, it was like a bit of a thrill when you were young. You just didn't understand about getting killed or that people were maimed and such. You knew death, but you didn't understand it.'

In 1976, while John's father was still in prison, Sheridan's Bar, across the street from John's childhood home, was bombed by loyalists. The explosion killed two Catholic civilians, wounded a dozen more and caused extensive damage to John's place.

'We were all in the house. Ahhh Jaysus, there was no front left on the house after. No windows in the house either. It was all blown t' fuck. My Ma took all the blankets out and was putting them 'round the shoulders of the injured and such. That was the first real experience I had of killing.'

I then asked Big John about his teenage involvement in *Fianna Éireann* (the youth wing of the IRA). His father was just out from the IRA compound at Long Kesh. Why had Big John never made the common leap from the *Fianna* to *Óglaigh na hÉireann*—the IRA. He replied that he had actually been asked to join 'the movement proper' when he was about sixteen but had declined. Sharon, whom he was already going with at the time, was one reason. The other?

'There was too many numbskulls and touts already by that stage, even by the early 'eighties. I was already in the *Fianna*, learning how t' dig an arms dump, all that shite, but I was looking at the fellas in front of me, those already totally up t' their eyes active in the movement, and I felt I couldn't trust 'em with my life. The top of the movement was brilliant, real smart fellas, but it was the ones down on the ground at the bottom who'd get ye stiffed or banged up in the Kesh. So, basically I turned away.'

After marrying Sharon, John moved out of the New Lodge and into Andersonstown where he and Sharon shared the house at Tardree Park with Gran. John later joked that he had never seen grass or birds until he moved to Andersonstown, 'I thought that was just stuff you only saw on holiday in Donegal.' He eventually got work as a night watchman at nearby Musgrave Park Hospital. The British Army built an annex there thinking its proximity to the civilian hospital would protect it from IRA attacks. They were wrong.

'The reason I know exactly what time the bomb went off was that I was listening t' the radio in the car and Nick Farr-Jones converted for Australia for t' beat the English in the rugby, and then the whole place went up. I had been out playing football actually, and I was driving back in t' the hospital grounds listening t' the radio and the whole road just lifted up in the air. I stopped the car. Smoke started coming out of the buildings at the military base, so I started t' reverse away. Then I was shitting myself in case they were thinking that I might be the bomber, ye know, 'cause I was reversing away from the thing 'n all. None of the Army came out of the base within Musgrave so I was able to back up t' the gate, park my car, get out—still in my football kit—before the RUC arrived.'

The damage to the military base behind the civilian hospital was extensive and as John was both a worker at the hospital and was on the spot, he was asked to help with the injured. And so Big John, Irish republican and former member of *Fianna Éireann,* helped injured, bleeding, stunned British soldiers as they emerged from the rubble. 'It was just human nature to help, it didn't matter what they were.' The military annex was virtually demolished.

'Half the building was bombed out and the roof was blew off it and it had a lot of smoke coming out of it. I was there as they took two bodies out and one of them was a young guy, and he had a short four inch hole in his back, other than that he wasn't touched. He only had a wee hole in him but Jesus Christ some blood come out of him. The second soldier, he was like a lump of meat, completely charred and unrecognisable. His hands were all curled up. Ahh Jaysus, I'll never forget it.'

The bombing took place on 2 November 1991. The two dead bodies were both British soldiers: Craig Pantry (age 20) and Philip Cross (age 33). Eighteen more people were injured when the twenty pounds of semtex exploded. Most had been watching Australia versus England in the Rugby World Cup final on a TV in the military annex. The bombing, the first on a military annex beside a civilian hospital during the Troubles, was later claimed by the IRA. About two days later one of John's friends and a fellow worker at Musgrave, Ciarán, was arrested by the RUC in connection with the bombing. And then the RUC came for John. Coming from strong republican lineage he was a suspect and he was interviewed and reinterviewed by the RUC, but eventually released. Ciarán however, was later convicted of murdering Craig Pantry and Philip Cross and for planting the bomb at Musgrave Park. He received two life sentences.

I asked John how he had felt that first night when he came back from the hospital immediately after the bombing. Sharon told me he threw out all the clothes he had been wearing.

'It actually took me a wee bit longer t' get on after that one. Usually when you see something like that it takes away yer head for a week or two. And it doesn't leave you, it grips you. I remember the smell of burnt bodies clinging t' me. And after that someone says t' me t' take counselling—balls! The things I've seen it would take counselling all week, every week. I've had friends shot dead and lost my cousin. It's frightening. Counselling would be useless.'

That cousin, eighteen year old Gerard O'Hara, was shot dead by the UFF at his home in the New Lodge on 27 September 1992, ten months after the Musgrave bombing. They were after his older brother, who they suspected of being in the IRA, but any male member of the Catholic O'Hara family would do. Gerard was shot dead in front of his mother in the living room of his own home. When the masked paramilitaries burst into the family home Gerard's mother Bridie, Big John's aunt, begged the gunmen to shoot her instead and spare her son's life. They ignored her, opening fire on young Gerard, leaving him dead on the lounge room carpet with his mother screaming on the couch beside him.

Sharon called John at Musgrave Park to let him know that his cousin had been shot dead and a short while later John arrived at his aunt's house in the New Lodge. His aunt Bridie 'went to pieces' over the killing and had a complete nervous breakdown. I asked John if he felt any ill will towards Protestants as a result.

'No. I'm angry at the bastards that shot him, not angry against Protestants. I was out playing football soon afterwards and there were a few Protestants within the team and I didn't want them t' think I'd stoop to the sectarianism of the people that killed my cousin. Some of them apologised for what happened and there was one particular one within Musgrave who sent a mass card. But then there were others I worked with at Musgrave who seen me on the front of the newspaper carrying Gerard's coffin and shunned me for it.'

■ ■ ■ ■

As Big John and I were having our chat, down in Portadown they were burying King Rat. An estimated 6,000 people turned out to bid farewell to the most famous loyalist 'paramilitary' of his time. Shopkeepers were pressured to close down all business in Portadown for the day. LVF supporters handed out a leaflet entitled 'Mark of Respect':

> As a mark of respect to the late Billy Wright, it is requested that
> you accordingly close your premises today, Tuesday, 30th
> December, 1997, between the hours of 12 noon and 6pm. Your co-
> operation is noted and appreciated.

The *Irish Times* the following day conveyed the mood as Billy Wright's coffin made its way along Portadown's cold wintry streets.

> Portadown was dead, shut down, kaput. Every shop from Dunnes
> Stores to the meanest huckster shop closed its doors. Virtually
> nobody was on the streets apart from the ubiquitous men in black.
> There was fear and foreboding in the air. This was a big occasion: a
> caudillo of loyalism had gone down and there would be hell to pay.
> The funeral went at a snail's pace. Groups of mourners took it in
> turns to carry the coffin… No big-name politicians walked behind
> the coffin and nobody with money either… A lone piper played
> 'Abide With Me' before a banner bearing the letters 'LVF'. The sky
> was grey, the wind bitter and biting.[7]

Pastor Kenny McClinton, a former loyalist prisoner turned lay-preacher and a personal friend of Billy Wright's, gave the graveside oration. He praised Wright as being a 'complicated, articulate and sophisticated man of high integrity'. Meanwhile a few miles away in Coalisland, Séamus Dillon, the victim of the LVF retaliation shooting at the Glengannon Hotel, was also being put in the ground. His widow helped carry his coffin through the streets and Sinn Féin's Martin McGuinness attended the funeral. A young girl who had been at the Glengannon Hotel when Dillon was killed told a reporter from the *The*

Mirror that: 'We heard the shots that killed Séamus and we were sure the gunmen were coming after us. He barred their way as he was dying. We will never forget him.'

Big John and I watched these events as the pictures were beamed to television screens across Northern Ireland. John, Sharon, Gran, myself and even the stony-faced newsreaders on TV were all predicting that the LVF would strike again soon. As I crawled up into the attic that night I didn't need the Northern Editor of the *Irish Times* to tell me that 'tension was high' in Belfast. Snuggling up against the cold in bed, I tried to imagine the motivations of armed men who drove around in stolen cars looking for a Catholic to shoot dead in the name of God and Ulster. 'Yabba-dabba-do, any Fenian will do!' as the LVF had painted on the wall of their wing in Long Kesh. I lay on my fold-out sofa bed in the attic looking up through the dark skylight before drifting off to sleep. As I closed my eyes I could hear British Army helicopters off in the distance relentlessly beating their cold steel arms against the black night sky. Don't they ever get sick of looking at us?, I thought to myself as sleep fell upon me. 'Us?'

4

Provo Spice

'Two households, both alike in dignity,
In fair Verona, where we lay our scene,
From ancient grudge break to new mutiny,
Where civil blood makes civil hands unclean.'

Romeo and Juliet, W. Shakespeare

'All the Irish songs are sad and their war nasty.'
American J. Bowyer-Bell in his history of the Troubles

I awoke early, pleased to discover no one had been shot during the night, and caught a black taxi from the Andersonstown Road down the Falls. The winter sun was poking its head out trying to decide whether to make a day of it. I kept my collar down and enjoyed the morning crispness.

Down the Falls I knocked on the window of the black taxi and paid the driver his 70p. I walked a few paces and was immediately in front of the purpose of my visit, the Sinn Féin Advice Centre and Green Cross Bookshop on the Lower Falls. The Green Cross Bookshop is run in support of republican prisoners in Long Kesh and many of the people who work there are related to present or former inmates. I stood outside in the cold and rang the doorbell. Bzzzzzzzz. A middle-aged woman walked gingerly towards the front of the shop, poked her head round the security grill and looked at me. I gave her my best smile and waited patiently. Obviously deciding that she had nothing to fear from this grinning eedjit on the footpath she unlocked the security door by remote control and I was let inside.

Such security precautions may seem excessive as the only things worth guarding inside the Green Cross are books, republican propaganda and a few coffee mugs with Gerry Adams' mugg printed on them. However, the building in which the bookshop is housed has previously had a rocket fired at it by loyalists and in February 1992 an off-duty RUC man ran amok inside the Centre shooting dead three people before turning the gun on himself. Discretionary precautions, such as checking out smiling strangers before allowing them access, are therefore a necessary part of commerce.

Anyway, after spending a small fortune updating my library I waited outside for a black taxi, leaning on one of the huge white rocks placed there to inhibit car bombers. It occurred to me that this might not be such a great place to stand. After all, King Rat had only been put in the ground the day before and the LVF were certain to make someone a widow soon in remembrance of their fallen leader. All alone outside the Sinn Féin Centre I was a perfect target. I felt the fear. It put years on me. All the sins of my life gathered around me (their size and din was considerable). I subtly moved down the road from the Centre and eventually a black taxi came to carry me away.

Back at Tardree Park the Fairleys over in Ardoyne called to tell me they couldn't come over for a visit today, so Big John and I took a run into town to 'collect some messages', as they say in Belfast. In due course we purchased a toilet plunger, some sausages, and some Irish linen for my mother. While in the city centre a British Army patrol came by in an armoured jeep and I had a young boy—barely shaving age—point his rifle at me. We called on Sharon at work and met her work friend, Makela, who is a Protestant. She was very friendly, with lots of questions about Australia and Sharon just happened to mention that I had just spent £150 at the Green Cross bookshop.

'Well, that's more guns for the Provos I guess,' says Makela.

In Belfast some things are best left unspoken.

■ ■ ■ ▫

That evening I went with Big John, Colm, Danny the Printer, and Sean from Glasgow down the road to have a New Year's Eve drink at the Whitefort. It was while we were enjoying the Whitefort's smoky confines that someone phoned to say that loyalists had just shot up the Clifton Tavern over in North Belfast. One dead and several wounded. The publican immediately shut the curtains and the bullet-proof shutters were pulled down over the pub's windows. At the front door, where you already had to get buzzed in by a security guard, precautions were intensified. People were frisked coming in and the security guards kept a constant watch on the street for suspicious looking cars that could disgorge armed loyalists. Inside the Whitefort people weren't exactly taking cover, but they weren't loitering near the windows or doors either. And as we put the last of our warm beers down our gullets, even fearless Big John mentioned that we should get on home before Sharon, Gran and Elva heard news of the shooting and began to worry about us. The night was still young and there was plenty of time for loyalist paramilitaries to hit another pub. We gathered up our takeaway liquor and downed the last of our drinks. I gave mine to Colm to finish off as he looked like he might resort to licking drops of spilt beer out of the ashtray if I didn't. He looked like he had a serious thirst on for the night.

The walk along the Andersonstown Road and back into the estate was frosty and we ran into a British Army mobile patrol on the way. Boy soldiers in camouflage gear pointed rifles at us as they thundered by in their heavily armoured jeep. Behind me Danny the Printer muttered 'Just ignore them lads, let's get on home and have a few drinks instead.' No one said a word as Britain's finest passed us sneering silently in the night. All the way home I kept thinking of the poor dead bastard over at the Clifton Tavern. I didn't know his name—I'd have to wait for the morning papers for that—but the thought of his spilt blood slowly congealing only a few short miles away sickened me.

Back at Tardree Park, the others went over to Colm's place as Big John and I slipped back into the house. The news was already all over the television and Gran was covering her mouth and shaking her head in disbelief. 'What did they go and do that for?' Sharon was beside herself, 'Thank God you never went up the Ardoyne to see them Fairleys today Simon or I would have been sick with worry by now.' I slipped upstairs to the attic to spend a few minutes absorbing things before I went back down to the festivities.

On my fold-out bed was a plaque that John had found when he was renovating the attic and which he had given to me that morning. The plaque was made of lacquered plywood. On the front of it was a hand-painted picture of the Irish tricolour, the starry plough and the rising sun flag of the Provisional IRA. A text underneath said 'Long Kesh 1971–1972'. On the back were the signatures of eighteen republican prisoners in Hut 26 who had signed their names and where they came from. Some were from Armagh, Coalisland, Dungiven, Derry, but the majority were from Belfast. The plaque was Jean's and had been sent out to her by a republican friend. It was placed in the attic after she was killed. Now it was given to me.

I sat on the bed looking at the plaque while British Army rotor blades sliced away feverishly in the distance. The red eye was back up in the sky. A lot of good that would do, I thought to myself, for the person lying dead in the Clifton Tavern right now. Eventually I put down the plaque, climbed back down the ladder and after a few quiet ones, we all went over to Colm's place for a couple of festive and cleansing ales.

■ ■ ■ ■

Over at Colm's house the drink was flowing freely. A good hooley, according to Brendan Behan, who was something of an authority on such matters, involved a bit of a sing-song, plenty of liquid refreshment and a bite to eat. Minus the bite to eat we were giving a good account of ourselves despite the depressing antics of loyalist gunmen earlier in the night. News of the Clifton Tavern shooting trickled in on the teletext and Irish rebel music was blaring on the stereo in the kitchen. In West Belfast Irish rebel music is sometimes referred to as *tiocfaidh* (roughly pronounced 'chockie') music because of its association with the republican movement and their slogan of '*tiocfaidh ár lá*' ('our day shall come'). In keeping with this tradition IRA members are sometimes referred to in local slang not only as 'Ra men', 'Provos' or 'Provies', but also as 'Chocks' or 'Chockies'. Mary Costello, in her fabulous book about Andersonstown entitled *Titanic Town*, also refers to traditional rebel music as 'Comeallyez' songs on account of the oft-repeated call for people to come join the hooley and/or struggle.

Anyway, the *tiocfaidh* music blared—I recall it was a young Glasgow Irish band by the name of *Eire Óg*—and upstairs some of the older children were yelling out 'up the 'Ra!' and such. Elva was not too happy with this and she carefully (she'd 'drink taken', as they say) tip-toed upstairs and advised the children not to chant IRA slogans. I went up after her. As I did her ten year old son, who had been in the house the night loyalist paramilitaries broke in with their shotguns, declared that when he grew up he was going to join the Provos and protect his family from the people who tried to kill his mammy in Deerpark. 'But that's against the ten commandments,' says his sister. To this Elva patted her brave boy on the head and agreed with the sister, 'Tis aye. God bless you son, but it's a sin.'

Back downstairs things were getting noisy as on the stereo *Eire Óg* were singing:

> Go on home British soldiers, go on home
> Have you got no fucking homes of your own?
> For eight hundred years, we've fought you without fear
> And we will fight you for eight hundred more.
>
> If you stay British soldiers, if you stay
> You'll never ever beat the IRA
> The fourteen men in Derry are the last that you will bury
> So take a tip and leave us while you may.

Then Danny the Printer, who I had already taken a liking to, came over to ask me a rather sobering question.

'Does it not seem strange to you, as an Australian, to be in the middle of a war zone on New Year's Eve with people getting shot and Brits cruising the streets in armoured cars pointing rifles at you?'

'Well, now that you mention it.'

'See I never grew up in West Belfast, I grew up out of all this shite and my parents tried t' pretend that there never was any such thing as the Troubles, like if you ignored it it might go 'way.'

This interested me. 'Did it work?'

'No, but it was a nice theory anyway.'

We both nodded and took a sip of our respective beverages. Wiping spilt lager from his lips, Danny had another question for me.

'Are you frightened you might get shot or something while you're here?'

'Not especially, should I be?'

'No. I mean I'm not planning anything, I was just wondering, like. You know ye have t' be careful at the minute.'

We both chuckled and someone put a Bob Marley disc on the stereo. I could see Big John taking a massive gulp of a can of *Harp* lager in the corner. The hooley continued.

■ ■ ■ ■

I fell asleep well after midnight to the by-now familiar and almost soothing dull thud of rotor blades cutting through the heavy Belfast darkness. I awoke eight hours later on New Year's Day 1998 to rain dripping on the skylight and I lay in bed wondering to myself if in a year's time things would be any better for the people of Belfast. Would some widow be waking up on 1 January 1999 grieving for a man shot dead the night before? Jean's Long Kesh plaque was still lying beside the bed where I had left it the night before and I took it with me as I climbed down the ladder to greet everyone on the first morning of the second-to-last year of the millennium. I thought Gran might remember a thing or two about the plaque if I actually let her look at it and hold it.

'No, I told ye, I can't mind a thing about whose it was or where it come from.'

'Gran, do you think it was Jean's?'

'It might have been, aye. There was lots of fellas from 'round here in the Kesh in the seventies and Jean would've known plenty of 'em.'

Gran and I got to talking about the visits she had made out to the prison with Peggy from across the street who had two sons on the IRA wings from the mid-1970s to the mid-1980s. Peggy and Gran had been living in Andersonstown since it was built. Together they had seen their children grow up as the world around them exploded into civil unrest. Gran's daughter Jean was killed and two of her sons-in-law were interned at the Kesh. Gran knew first hand the suffering that the Troubles had brought to ordinary people, including ones like herself who were basically apolitical.

At the same time two of Peggy's boys became heavily involved in the local republican movement and were eventually imprisoned. Indeed, one of Peggy's boys, an IRA Volunteer captured in 1976 after a shoot-out with a British Army patrol in Andersonstown, spent a decade behind bars. He appears under his nickname 'Hector' in the two most famous books dealing with the 1981 republican hunger strike at Long Kesh—David Beresford's *Ten Men Dead* and the collection of interviews with republican prisoners, *Nor Meekly Serve My Time*. These days Peggy and Gran are two old women who sit in each other's homes for much of the day watching television and chatting. Two nicer old ladies you could never hope to meet. Having survived three decades of conflict and immeasurable personal suffering, neither of them has much hope left that the Troubles will ever end.

Gran hasn't visited the Kesh since she used to go with Peggy to visit Hector in the late 1970s. At the time IRA prisoners in Long Kesh were both 'on the blanket' and on the 'dirty protest'—refusing to wear prison uniform (and thus wrapping blankets around themselves) while also refusing to wash and smearing their cells with faeces (and thus dirty). The struggle was about recognition of IRA inmates as political prisoners and resulted, ultimately, in the 1981 hunger strike. Notwithstanding the immense suffering of the prisoners, the blanket and dirty protests were also hard on the mothers who visited their sons in Long Kesh, only to find them emaciated, bruised from beatings, and with long hair and beards like Jesus Christ. Hector was on both protests and Gran went to the Kesh to give Peggy support. Since Hector was released in 1986 Gran has not been back.

'None of our own family were in there by then, Peggy's boys was out and besides, it's a terrible place out there, I'm too old and ye wouldn't go if ye didn't have to.'

Gran did however ask after Ciarán, who she knew I was planning to visit while I was in Belfast. Ciarán had been in the house at Tardree Park several times before he was arrested in 1991 and Gran had fond memories of him.

'Ach, he's a lovely wee fella so he is. If ye go see him, tell him I said 'God Bless' and that I was asking after him.'

It occurred to me that this was the real weakness in the British government's 1970s–1980s criminalisation campaign. Their enormous resources meant that they were largely able to win the propaganda war in the international media. Notwithstanding occasional journalistic criticism of the security situation in Northern Ireland, favourable portrayals of the IRA in the mainstream press in America, Canada, Australia and elsewhere are very rare. And yet these men and women that the British establishment denounced as 'terrorists' were the sons and daughters of ordinary people from a community that still feels that it is under siege from both history and a foreign power. If the British government and its spin doctors couldn't convince the little old grannies along the Falls Road that their sons and granddaughters were murdering swine, then they never really got close to winning the hearts and minds of the local population. Gran is a deeply religious woman who believes fervently in the Ten Commandments and rubs little stones from a holy grotto in Italy on her wrinkled skin when 'the pains' come to her legs. But the community ties that bound her to Hector, Ciarán and the others proved far stronger than all the fortified prisons the British government built in Northern Ireland over the last thirty years.

■ ■ ■ ■

At about this point Big John, who seems impervious to hangovers in particular and the negative affects of excessive consumption of alcohol in general, came in with the morning's papers. Another day of page after page of pure gloom.

The man killed the previous night at the Clifton Tavern was thirty-one year old Eddie Treanor. He had been shot in the head as he enjoyed a New Year's Eve drink with his girlfriend, Roisín, and a few mates. The shooting at the Clifton Tavern was witnessed by a fifteen year old boy called Andrew Rosbotham who had been standing out front of the pub when the car carrying the loyalist killers turned up. Two men wearing balaclavas walked straight past Andrew into the pub's foyer and opened fire on the seventy or so locals, killing Treanor and wounding five others. At the inquest almost a year later, Andrew Rosbotham told the tale of what happened.

> I jumped behind the front door and hid there. There were about ten
> loud bangs and my ears got very sore. When the shooting stopped I
> ran next door to the Chinese [resturant].

Eddie Treanor was hit in the head by one of those bullets. He died right where he was sitting; his body slumped in the seat and his head tilted to the side. His friend Damian McMahon, who was sitting nearby, was shot in the right hand and later testified that he and Eddie had only been drinking in the pub for a few minutes before he heard the 'loud bangs' that took his friend's life. Clearly Damian was lucky to be alive. Just how lucky was revealed by an RUC superintendent who gave evidence at the November 1998 inquiry into Eddie Treanor's death. The superintendent argued that the bloodshed at the Clifton Tavern would have been much worse if not for the fact that an Uzi submachine-gun used in the attack jammed after only firing one bullet, leaving only one working handgun for the loyalists to do the job with. If not for faulty machinery many more may have died.

At the Glengannon Hotel, immediately after King Rat was killed, the gunmen had been prevented from entering the premises by the actions of the doormen, including Séamus Dillon who was killed. At the Clifton Tavern the sub-machinegun had jammed after firing one shot. The other gunman had compensated by opening fire with a pistol. What all of this pointed to was the fact that the loyalists didn't just want to kill the odd doorman or two. They were after a pub massacre like the one at Greysteel a few years earlier. They wanted a big 'spray job' where a gunman would be able to machinegun crowded Catholic revellers. Only the horror of a pub massacre would adequately avenge the memory of Billy Wright. That such a thing had not occurred at the Glengannon Hotel or the Clifton Tavern was due only to bad luck on the part of the gunmen.

Eyewitnesses later claimed that after the men who killed Eddie Treanor finished firing and retreated, a woman was seen in the backseat of their getaway car 'whooping and squealing with delight and laughter'. As the blood soaked into the floor of the Clifton Tavern the LVF released a statement to the press claiming responsibility for Eddie Treanor's murder and threatening that 'This is not the end.' However, despite the LVF's claim of responsibility there was widespread speculation that it was actually 'mainstream' loyalist paramilitaries from the UDA/UFF, still officially on ceasefire, who actually carried out the killing. The *Irish News* went so far as to claim that a 'well-known UFF member' was spotted with the squealing woman in the back of the getaway car.

The UFF had left wreaths at Billy Wright's funeral and hardline Belfast loyalists previously associated with the UDA/UFF published sympathy notices in the *Belfast Telegraph*. Another newspaper report pointed out that the car carrying the loyalist killers of Eddie Treanor escaped up Rosapenna Street, turned on to the Oldpark Road and had then driven off towards the Shankill. The *Irish Times* pointed out that the UDA/UFF had used this escape route so regularly over the years that it was known as 'the death run' by their Shankill supporters. The LVF, by contrast, had no real support base in the Shankill and if the gunmen had driven up from mid-Ulster (where the LVF was strongest) for the 'operation' they presumably would not have been as familiar with local geography. Everything pointed to UDA/UFF collusion at some level. This was a worrying development indeed and was the principal source of the aforementioned gloom in the newspapers. The entire peace process seemed to be fraying at the edges.[1]

The fact that the loyalist killers had used Rosapenna Street reminded me of the fact that Pastor Kenny McClinton had given King Rat's graveside oration a few days earlier. McClinton was an ex-UFF man himself and he had been sentenced to life in prison for murdering two people in 1977. According to Martin Dillon in his book, *God and the Gun*, Kenny McClinton told him that in the 1970s he had favoured beheading random Catholics and impaling their heads on the steel railings of Belfast's Woodvale Park. While on remand in Crumlin Road prison in 1978 McClinton had gone on a famous hunger strike. 'Famous' because he lasted over three weeks and gained a stone in weight—other loyalist prisoners were secretly smuggling him food! Although his dedication to political starvation was somewhat lacking, in Long Kesh McClinton underwent a religious conversion, becoming a born-again Christian and dedicating his life to Jesus Christ. He was baptised in a bath-tub in H-block 8 by a former member of the Shankill Butchers who was himself a recent convert to Christian evangelism. After his release from prison in 1993, having served sixteen years for murder, McClinton became a fundamentalist Protestant preacher, while maintaining his connections with extreme loyalists. He was very close to Billy Wright and had even written poetry about him and the siege of Drumcree. Kenny McClinton was living in the Rosapenna Street area when he was arrested for murder in 1977. All things considered, the fact that the Clifton Tavern killers had escaped through McClinton's old stomping ground was certainly a dark twist of historical irony.[2]

When Eddie Treanor was buried a few days later his funeral bore none of the paramilitary glamour of Billy Wright's, in whose name he had been slain. It was a simple funeral for a simple man who had been killed purely because he was Catholic and accessible. Almost a year later, in November

1998, with no one yet charged with his murder, Eddie Treanor's seventy-two year old mother made the following emotional public plea:

> My brother joined the RAF aged nineteen after the Germans
> bombed Belfast. He flew over Germany and France. He was shot
> down after D-Day over France. He and four of his comrades are
> buried there. The resistance helped the other two back to England.
> My cousin was killed in Italy the following day. He survived
> Dunkirk and the African campaign. Their names are in the Book
> of Remembrance in St Anne's Cathedral, Belfast. The killers of
> Edmund betrayed the sacrifice that they made so we could live. If
> they have any conscience they should give themselves up.[3]

No one came forward.

Sitting at the kitchen table on New Year's morning 1998 in Belfast I felt positively grim. What a way to end the year, I thought to myself. Five men wounded and one dead in the Clifton Tavern. Notwithstanding the stalled peace talks, no one seemed to think that that would be the end of it.

■ ■ ■ ■

Despite the depressing and deteriorating political situation there was still some life left in the day. After lunch Big John received a phone call from an old New Lodge friend who was at the end of a lengthy sentence for IRA activities. He was out of Long Kesh jail for a ten day parole period over Christmas and New Year. That day was his last full day on prison leave; he was due back at Long Kesh the next morning. He asked John if he would like to come over to a bar in the New Lodge and have a drink. Never one to refuse the offer of a friendly lager, especially with an old friend enjoying his last few fleeting moments of freedom, John obliged and the two of us drove over.

New Lodge is a tough working class Catholic neighbourhood that has suffered tremendously over the last thirty years of the Troubles. North Belfast is a patch-work of ethnic enclaves and this has given the political violence there a particular and urgent ferocity. It has been calculated that one third of all those killed in the Troubles have lost their lives within a two square mile area around the New Lodge. Around 500 people from the local area have been imprisoned for politically-motivated offences.

In a bar just off the New Lodge Road we met 'Beefy', a friend of Big John's since they were 'just wee eedjits with no fear of anything and fuck all t' do'. Both grew up amidst arguably some of the worst of the Troubles, when John's father was in the IRA compound at Long Kesh. They were living in a staunchly republican district that seemed to be in constant conflict with the loyalist estates that adjoin it. Among other things, the New Lodge was the scene of one of the earliest atrocities (they are now legion) of the Troubles, the December 1971 UVF bomb attack on McGurk's Bar on North Queen Street which killed fifteen innocent civilians. Three were woman and two were children. All were guilty of nothing more seditious than being Catholic and thirsty. Although the press and British Army spokesmen for many years continued to allude to the bombing as an IRA 'own goal'—claiming that the tragedy was the result of a republican bomb in transit that blew up prematurely—it was later claimed by the 'Empire Loyalists', a cover-name for the UVF. Local people developed a keen sense that they were under siege from hostile loyalist paramilitaries who held their entire community responsible for the IRA's military campaign.[4]

The loyalist area of Tigers Bay is literally a stone's throw away from the New Lodge and dozens of gun and bomb attacks have occurred at the interface between the two districts. Young Catholics growing up in the New Lodge faced a constant fear of attack from loyalist paramilitaries; harassment from British soldiers was a rite of passage; and rioting on a Sunday afternoon was almost a form of recreation. There were also the internecine struggles between the various political factions in the district to deal with.

A picture in Tim Pat Coogan's history of the Troubles, taken in July 1983, shows Gerry Fitt standing in the midst of the charred ruin of his New Lodge home. His face is grim and his business suit, polka-dot tie and briefcase look simply out of place in the blackened burnt shell of a room. Fitt, once leader of the SDLP and MP for West Belfast in the Westminster Parliament, had become increasingly alienated from the constituents he represented. He eventually left the SDLP and continued to denounce the IRA in the British Parliament, including the 1981 hunger strikers. While this won him considerable respect from Margaret Thatcher, it did not go down very well in the New Lodge and along the Falls Road. His subsequent electoral defeat by Sinn Féin's Gerry Adams demonstrated that a decisive political shift had taken place amongst Belfast's nationalist community in the aftermath of Bobby Sand's death. On 3 July 1983 a group of local republican youths broke in to his house in the New Lodge, smashed it up and then set it on fire.

Big John and Beefy were among the handful of young New Lodge republicans questioned by the RUC in connection with the July 1983 firebombing of Gerry Fitt's house. Both proclaimed their innocence: John had been holidaying in Donegal at the time. Meanwhile, during interrogation by RUC officers Beefy pointed out that he had a broken leg. 'So I says, "Now if I had a cast half-way up my arse and all t' fuck, how could I be after smokin' Fitt's house?"' Both Beefy and Big John were released without charge. Fitt meanwhile was compensated for his troubles by Margaret Thatcher who offered him a life peerage, which he accepted, politically retiring to the House of Lords for the rest of his able-bodied days.

I was already aware that Big John had been involved in the *Fianna* during his teens, later dropping out of the republican movement. Beefy however, went on to bigger things, so to speak. In 1991 he was sentenced to sixteen years in prison for attempted murder and was given 399 years in concurrent sentences for a number of other IRA activities.

The bar where we met Beefy was a dank smoky pit choking with people, lung cancer and the smell of stale beer. In the corner John and Beefy reminisced over their past while myself and John's younger brother Kevin chatted between ourselves. Kevin mentioned that his New Years' resolution was to give up the drink and I commended his decision by ordering us two large pints of Coca-Cola at the bar. We talked for a while, until Beefy began singing a rendition of *Waltzing Matilda* that attracted my undivided attention. I duly applauded at the end of it and John pointed a mocking finger in Beefy's direction, 'Provo Spice!' Beefy and I then got to talking about Australia and about how his ten days of prison release were going. He mentioned that the previous day he had actually taken his young daughter to see the *Spice Girls* movie.

'What did you think?'

'Pure shite, it was almost depressing enough t' make ye want t' go back to jail.'

Meanwhile John had emptied the last of his pint of Harp and was back at the bar ordering another. As Beefy and I talked a constant stream of people passed us on the way to the toilets, almost all of whom slapped Beefy on the back and gave him the customary, 'what 'bout ye?' Men were falling over themselves to buy him a pint. It then occurred to me that Beefy was about as far away from the standard Hollywood and British tabloid representation of an IRA man as is humanely possible. He was funny and articulate, a clean-cut man in his early-thirties who had dedicated his life, as he saw it, to the defence of his community. I had one question I was dying to ask him.

'How'd you feel about getting sentenced to 399 years in jail?'

'Pleased.'

I looked at him incredulously. 'Why?'

He smiled. 'I thought I was going to get 400 years.'

Thankfully for Beefy, the sentences were concurrent and with remission allowances he was due to be released in February 1998, after serving eight years in Long Kesh. He then mentioned, after sipping a little more of yet another free pint bought for him by one of the patrons of the bar, that when he got out he had no plans to get reinvolved in the republican movement. Despite his convictions, both intellectual and judicial, he felt he had done his bit for a united Ireland. Instead he wanted to rebuild a life for himself with his de-facto wife and his little daughter who was conceived while he was a free-man and born while he was in Long Kesh.

'Besides, there's too many touts and dough-heads around in the lower ranks of the movement these days.'

John, who was listening to all of this, nodded his head in solemn agreement.

'Aye, steal a box of matches with some of them'uns and they'd get ye captured or killed.'

After some more banter Beefy intimated that the day was drawing to a close and that he wanted to spend the last night of his ten day release with his partner, 'rather than with you fucking desperate cases'. We bade each other farewell. Before he left Beefy said I should come out to Long Kesh and visit him again.

'Just don't come this weekend, I want a nice sleep in after I return t' jail tomorrow morning. The missus asked me if I wanted her t' come up and visit me on Sunday but I told her t' give it a miss because all the prisoners had t' hold fresh discussions on the peace process and we'd be busy. Truth is these last ten days have wrecked me, what with all the drinking and taking the wee daughter t' see the fucking Spice Girls and all that there. I'm looking forward t' a lay-in for fuck's sake.'

John, Kevin and I stayed in the pub for another round and then John and I drove back over to Andersonstown. On the way home the radio was full of speculation that 'mainstream loyalists', rather than the LVF, did in fact carry out the attack on the Cliftonville Road the previous night. Loyalist politicians were warning that King Rat's death may mean that the peace process was over. Republican spokespeople were urging 'everyone in the nationalist community to be vigilant'. As we passed the darkness of Milltown cemetery from the motorway I looked out wishing that no one else would be buried while I was in Belfast. I had been there not yet a week and already three people had been put in the cold ground by political violence. Deep inside I knew that the evil season was far from over.

5

The Severed Red Hand

The sky here
is sad and brittle
and seems clouded with tears.
This morning I walked under
the severed red hand of Ulster
that is carved in stone
above the entrance
to the Linen Hall.
I trembled beneath
its monumental amputation.
Only in Ulster
would they make
a mortal wound
a provincial emblem.

On the second day of 1998 I decided it was time to get to work. It was Friday and five days had passed since I had arrived in Ireland. After breakfast with Gran and a quick wrestle with Conor and wee Dan, who were still on school holidays, I departed for the Linen Hall Library in the fine city of *Béal Feirste*, or Belfast if you prefer.

Now, the Linen Hall at 17 Donegal Square North is a historian's dream—immaculate archives, a massive collection of material on the Troubles, clean toilets (very important in a library) and a coffee shop to boot. In addition, the Political Collection on the Irish Troubles is staffed by Yvonne, one of the most personable and knowledgeable librarians you are ever likely to meet. The library itself is resplendent with atmosphere and tradition. Established in 1788 (the year Britain began colonising Australia) as 'the Belfast Society for Promoting Knowledge' (although originally in a different building) the library has not only collected Irish history, it has survived it. Among other things, it was accidentally bombed by the IRA once and the first librarian was Thomas Russell, a prominent member of the Society of United Irishmen who was hanged in 1803 by the British for treasonous behaviour. In remembrance of the current library's connection with the linen mills that were central to Belfast's development during the industrial revolution, the current library building is draped in stone cloth and sports a rather terrifying severed red hand above its doorway.

The red hand is the historic symbol of the province of Ulster and is still prominent in contemporary political iconography. Several versions of the story of the red hand survive in the popular mythology of Belfast's inhabitants: worth telling for that reason alone. The tale, as I was told many times as a child, goes something like this.

During a Viking raid on the coast of Ulster in the middle ages some of the inhabitants raced to the shore to do battle with the invaders. Casualties were sometimes heavy in such melees and one of the chiefs mentioned to his fellow Ulstermen that this time 'round he had a better idea. The Vikings were almost ashore by this stage and not being particularly anxious to be cleft in two by the battle axes of the Norsemen the Ulstermen decided to hear their Chieftain out. He bade them bide their time and walked down to the water. After dipping his big toe in the cold Irish Sea, he announced to the arriving Viking longships teeming with warriors considerably predisposed to pillage and plunder, that with all due respect and in all fairness, was there not a better way of working this thing out? What did you have in mind, says the Viking's chief from one of the long boats. Well, how about this—first one to lay a hand on this land can take full possession of it, and the rest shall return to whatever sheep-shagging hellhole they happen to come from. Sounds fair enough, says the burly Norseman, reckoning the hairy-arsed Ulsterman to be a bit soft headed. With the terms of settlement agreed upon, the Ulster chieftain then pulled out his sword, cut off his own hand, dropped the sword and threw the severed bloody hand on the ground, thus claiming the land in the name of his people. The Vikings were considerably impressed by this and reckoned the Ulster chieftain to be a bit damaged in the noodle department. And if the knock-kneed men behind this one-handed, bloody-stumped mad Ulsterman were prepared to follow such a fellow into battle they must be no better themselves. Deciding that such people are best not engaged in matters martial, the Vikings announced to all and sundry; fair play to you and this bog is your own from this day to the end of time. They then turned their boats around and headed further down the coast. So impressed were all the other Ulstermen, and all those belonging to them, by these events that a bloodied red hand was eventually adopted by the O'Neill *clann* as their symbol. As the story was passed on from one generation to the next, the severed red hand became the symbol of all of Ulster and survives, in amputated majesty, in the architecture above the Linen Hall Library today.

I was contemplating all of this as I walked in under the red hand and decided that with such popular myths it is little wonder that Ulster has had such a blood splattered history. I met Yvonne, who showed me where I would be allowed to study for the next few weeks in a private loft above the main floor of the library, and I told her about my intention to investigate Jean's death. She cautioned me not to get my hopes up. She told me about a woman who waited over twenty years to get the courage to come in and inquire about her son who had been shot dead by mistake by Crown forces. She was shaking with nervous anticipation and was sure that the librarians in the Political Collection would have an entire file on her son and the circumstances of his death. They had nothing; he was just another statistic in the Troubles. Yvonne mentioned that there was definitely a down side to her job as chief librarian of the Political Collection on the Troubles. I told her I had no false illusions about my research into Jean's death and we moved on to the back corner where I was instructed how to use the photocopiers.

I spent the rest of the day looking at old newspapers. I requested all the papers for the day Jean died, and these were bought out to me in thick full-size leather-bound editions. Despite being winter, the sunlight was strong and warm through the windows behind me as I pored over the brittle pages.

There she was on the front cover of the *Belfast Telegraph* for 9 June 1972. Beautiful, youthful and dead. The newspaper itself was now older than she had been when she died and it was starting to yellow and curl up at the edges. I read all the reports and was struck by the fact that, as always in such circumstances, they so resolutely failed to convey the human tragedy that was tearing a family to pieces. You can never really see the broken lives that lie between the column inches of newsprint. Outside, rain began to fall and the day washed itself down the Belfast gutters as I fortified myself in the warm reading room. I could hear the rain beating the roof and at about 5:30pm I was told by a librarian that the library would be closing shortly and could I please pack up my things and come back tomorrow. The hours had simply disappeared as I had spent the entire day taking notes and writing unanswered questions alongside photocopied newspaper articles concerning Jean's death.

Down on the street it was now dark and from a public phone box opposite Belfast City Hall I called Gran. Sharon was still at work and Big John was over in Glasgow for the day to see the 'Old Firm' grudge match of Celtic versus Rangers. I was worried that Gran may be expecting me for supper and that I had better tell her I was going to be late. However, after a brief chat she revealed that she was thinking that maybe I might like to drop by the chipper down on the Andersonstown Road on my way home and maybe while I was there I could pick up a hamburger and some chips for her and the boys. Within a few minutes I was down to Castle Street and in a black taxi back out to West Belfast.

Sitting in the back of the crowded black taxi, the windows heavy with condensation and the rain riveting across the roof, I thought of my first visit to Belfast. John and Sharon had picked Amanda and I up from the train station. As we drove up the Falls Road into West Belfast it was all so strangely familiar to me. John was giving a running commentary. 'There's Divis flats, planet of the Irps, on the left,' and so on. I already knew it all from a hundred books and half-forgotten stories from my Irish immigrant relatives. It was all such a bizarre thrill to be in the town that my family originated from. Years later, the thrill had not entirely dissipated, though dampened a little by the rain. The black taxi had the musty smell of wet clothing in the back and as we turned right at the Andersonstown RUC barracks and up the Glen Road I thought of Aunt Jean—the face on the front page of the yellowed copy of the *Belfast Telegraph* from twenty-six years ago. This was the very road she was killed on.

The Glen Road must have been nearly barren in those days, certainly up the end where she was shot dead. There would have been very few buildings other than the *Bass* brewery and the road must have been quiet and secluded that night. It was June when she was killed, summer, and I wondered if it had been a nice night out. The press reports said the car was 'riddled' with bullets. What a horrible way for it to end for her. I wondered who had given them the photo published in the newspapers? Someone in the family I supposed, but who? Sitting in the black taxi it was difficult to comprehend that Jean was younger when she died than both Sharon and I are now.

I looked up and noticed that the black taxi was reaching the Andersonstown shops, so I tapped on the window to get out. It was raining outside and as I walked down the Andersonstown Road I could not get my mind off Jean and the newspaper reports I had read. There were just so many questions and the most frustrating thing was that I realised that if I was lucky I would get answers to only one or two. As I finally arrived at the chipper a queue was forming in the light rain outside and an Army helicopter began tracking its red eye across the night sky. Dribbles of rain ran down my neck.

It was still raining when I left the chipper and I had to place our takeaways into my jacket for the short walk home in the Belfast drizzle. As Brendan Behan was known to say on such occasions, 'what can't be cured must be endured', and I set off at a cracking pace for Tardree Park. Gran met me at the door and Dan announced that he was nearly starved to death and that he was thinking of leaving home with his Action Man if he didn't get a bite to eat soon. In the back of my mind I was still fixated on Jean and wondered what it must have been like for Gran on that night in 1972 when the RUC or the Army or whoever it was came to the door to tell her that her daughter was dead.

Gran, the boys and I ate our hamburgers and chips at the table and then Conor and wee Dan raced back into the other room to watch more cartoons, leaving Gran and I to ourselves. Gran put on a cup of tea and suggested I tell her about my day. I mentioned that I had been up at the library reading the news reports from the day Jean died. Gran immediately went awfully quiet and started to stare down and play with her hem. If there are words for such occasions I know nothing about them. I made a decision then and there never to mention my research into Jean's death in front of her again. Gran eventually broke the silence between us by mentioning that before she had children she used to work in one of the old linen mills that were originally situated behind the Linen Hall Library. I had read about the linen industry in Belfast and knew that it was by all accounts brutal, underpaid and extraordinarily hard work. I never knew Gran had been one of the 'linen girls' and this fact now gave the industry an added interest to me.

'What did you do there, Gran?'

'Same as everyone else, murdering m'self for a few shillings a week.'

'Was it hard work?'

I knew it was, but I wanted her to talk about it. Anything to get off the Jean business.

'Hard? Aye. A girl was killed beside me once.'

Gran had said the last sentence with her usual matter-of-fact stoicism, and after some prompting she consented to elaborate a little. It seems a girl who was working beside her got her hair caught in one of the flailing machines and in a split second had her entire scalp ripped right off her head. Laying in a state of shock, she bled to death on the floor of the linen mill before she could receive any medical attention.

Suddenly the phone rang and I was surprised to hear my friend Danielle from Australia. She was currently holidaying in Scotland and was coming to Belfast with the specific intention of visiting me, in a few short days. This was welcome news and I agreed to meet her as soon as she arrived. As I got off the phone from Danielle, Sharon arrived home from work and we sat down to watch the evening news. According to the hairdos reading the tele-prompter extra British soldiers were being put back on the streets of Belfast that night to protect us all from the LVF. The news also showed the 160 prisoners who got ten day releases from the Kesh over Christmas and New Year returning to jail. I kept an eye out for Beefy, but did not see him.

■ ■ ■ ■

Dawn never really breaks in Belfast during winter. 'Break' implies too much of a contrast betwixt day and night. Rather, a Belfast winter day slowly washes away the night, leaving a dirty stain across the morning. By late morning a smudge of grey lingers in the canopy and by lunch the sun has almost finished its frail limp across the horizon. The light is then filtered away. Darkness descends before supper, wrapping the cold pavement and green hedges in its Belfast crispness. Night falls upon you in the entries and icy pathways. Black mountain disappears back into the mist. And finally, morning arrives once again and the cycle continues.

This morning however was black and blue. Lying on my back looking up through the skylight it was like the sky above West Belfast was horribly bruised. No one was awake in the house below and lying in my warm bed in the attic I could hear the gentle rattle of the oil heater in the corner and feel the cold air stab through the tiny holes in the roof tiles above me. In

Belfast the cold speaks to you and I could hear the humming of the bitter draft waiting for me to slip out of bed on to the cold floor. Waiting to bite at my exposed ankles. Waiting for me to bare myself to it. I decided it was safer to stay in bed and drift off back to sleep until I could smell the aroma of potato bread, bacon and toast coming up from the kitchen. Then I would get up, climb down the ladder and go downstairs to sit with the family. It was Saturday and Big John would surely throw together one of his highly-recommended, heart attack inducing, Ulster fry-ups before we left to visit Ciarán in the Kesh. After all, it's always best to visit a prison on a full stomach.

An hour later my desire to urinate finally got the better of me and after doing the business I slipped downstairs and into the kitchen with the hope that John would soon be down to cook. However, my hopes of peace and quiet were extinguished as soon as I walked into the kitchen and was set upon by the boys. A few minutes later Sharon burst into the room and gestured immediately to the kids.

'You and you, out and leave me and Simon in peace.'

'But I'm Hercules and Dan is Action Man.'

'Well Action Man and Hercules better get their wee bums out of this kitchen or Action Mum is going to take them over her knee.'

We sat down for a while and Sharon told me about how a few years previously she noticed that a particular British Army patrol would cut through her backyard at Tardree Park every Sunday morning. The first time it happened John was out 'collecting the messages' and Sharon ignored it. The next Sunday at the same time, they appeared again. John was home this time, spotted them and went out to give them a mouthful. The following Sunday they were back at the same time, cutting across the backyard on their way back to the barracks from patrol. This time Sharon phoned the local Army base.

'So I told the commanding officer that I had no love for the British Army, but I didn't want t' see them killed either and that they were coming in t' my backyard and putting the lives of me and my family at risk. I says t' him, if I can figure out that youse come into our wee patch each Sunday morning between ten and twelve then someone else can too, ye know what I mean? Besides, my husband's forever fighting with yer men and if they get blown up in our backyard I don't want ye pointing the finger at him. I've got a wee boy and my gran in the house and I don't want us being blown up because of yer men either. So he apologised and said it won't happen again Mrs McVicker and it never did.'

We also discussed more recent developments in the Troubles. That morning's *Irish News* had reported that the British Army had resumed daytime patrols in Belfast in the aftermath of the last three killings. It was the first time that such numbers of troops had been on Belfast's streets during daylight since the IRA ceasefire had begun. An opinion piece carried the title 'Another year starts with familiar sadness', while the main editorial argued that 'The last thing anyone wanted to see this year was an increase in security levels. It runs counter to the whole thrust of the peace process which should see our society moving to a situation of demilitarisation.'[1] Sharon was similarly unimpressed.

'All them soldiers supposedly protecting us and they still can't stop a man getting shot as he has a wee drink in a pub. It won't stop a thing. It's just terrible, so it is.'

Big John eventually stumbled in and an Ulster fry was cooked for one and all. Arteries were sufficiently hardened.

■ ■ ■ ■

The drive out to Lisburn after breakfast was pleasant enough except that it was blowing a gale outside. Historically, the area around Lisburn was transformed by the development of the linen industry in the seventeenth century. During the United Irishmen's rebellion a local draper named Henry Monroe led the rebels into battle at Ballynahinch, one of the most important military engagements of the 1798 uprising in Ulster. The rebels were decisively defeated by the King's soldiers and the town was reduced to 'a smoking ruin'. According to Thomas Pakenham in *The Year of Liberty*, after the battle the bodies of some 400 rebels were littered across the battlefield, and those not carried away under cover of darkness and buried by their grieving relatives, were left rotting and became food for the local pigs. Such was the message the British wanted to send regarding the wages of sedition in Ireland. What Pakenham describes as two other 'sad relics' were also discovered on the battlefield.

> They also found the bodies of two beautiful women fantastically dressed in green silk, who had carried the rebel standards. They had been known as the Goddess of Liberty and the Goddess of Reason, and were apparently the town prostitutes.[2]

As for the draper, Henry Monroe, he was captured and went to the hangman's noose less than a week later wearing 'a dark coat, nankeen breeches and white stockings'. After falling in the street he proclaimed to the assembled Lisburn townspeople that 'I'm not cowed, gentlemen', and proclaimed 'I die for my country', before swinging to his death from a makeshift gibbet in front of his own house. The British, after removing the noose from around the dead man's neck, apparently beheaded his corpse for good measure. Spare a thought for poor brave Henry Monroe and his nankeen breeches next time you drive through Lisburn.

These days, you know you are finally approaching Long Kesh prison outside Lisburn because of the security cameras posted on top of lamposts in the surrounding streets. As we turned left into the parking lot of the prison flowers for Billy Wright were tied around telephone poles with red white and blue ribbons. As we slowed past, I noticed that the colours were already starting to fade and bleed down the pole in the relentless drizzle. We pulled into a parking space on the grey dismal gravel and braced ourselves for the cold.

Long Kesh—or 'Her Majesty's Prison Maze (Cellular)' if you prefer—is an enormous construction. Surrounded with walls over fifteen feet high that run some two miles in length, it is nothing if not formidable. Within the core of the prison eight 'H' shaped blocks have housed some of Ireland's most famous and feared loyalist and republican inmates. Each H-block is divided into four wings. Each of the wings (every one being a single upright of the 'H') holds twenty five cells plus communal areas. A wing would normally be allocated to a particular armed group and would then be administered by their own military structures, under the overall 'supervision' of the wardens. The perpendicular bar in the middle of the 'H' is controlled by the warders and is used to administer all four wings. While the British government liked to present HMP Maze as the bright shining jewel in the crown of its criminalisation strategy when the complex opened in the mid-1970s, it has remained a cold heartless hole for the men who have been kept there. Several men have gone to their deaths inside its walls, including the ten 1981 hunger strikers and, most recently, Billy Wright.

The newspapers had recently been pushing the idea that Long Kesh prison was some sort of holiday camp.

> It is a situation that is as farcical as it is frightening... Visiting times last all day and drink and drug binges far into the night. Sex during visiting is routine. Prisoners without wives or girlfriends have hookers supplied by their pals outside... Computers are fitted in cells beside multi-channel tellies... Inmates' leisurely existence is only interrupted for parades—in camouflage military uniforms and with banners flying—or lectures on terror techniques.[3]

Well, standing before Long Kesh, it still appeared a fearful and cold building to behold. It was all barbed wire, corrugated iron and spy towers to me. Not my idea of a holiday camp by any stretch of the imagination. Not least because those inside its cold walls weren't allowed to leave. I also knew that beyond the exaggerations of tabloid editorialists, to the extent that the prisoners of Long Kesh now enjoyed a 'relaxed internal regime' at all it was because in 1981 ten men starved to death to make it so. It got me thinking.

■ ■ ■ ■

In 1981 I was thirteen. My family was living in America at the time and I remember watching the news of the hunger strikes on TV. The young INLA prisoner, Mickey Devine, had just died after sixty-six days without food and there were scenes of fierce rioting in Derry. The footage was shot at night and there were pictures of flaming cars, barricades and silhouettes of teenage petrol-bombers raging against the heavy darkness. Mickey Devine was the last of the ten Irish republican hunger strikers to die in 1981. Some scoffed at his sacrifice and denounced him as a failure because his wife had left him for an ice cream salesman. Tory politicians slandered

Mickey Devine. Stephen Ross MP, speaking at the British Liberal Party's annual conference in Wales in 1981, called the hunger strikers 'cowardly bastards'. Sixty-six days. Mickey Devine's body slowly rotted around him. First he lost weight, then he lost his sight, his hearing, suffered terrible pains and died of starvation unreconciled with his wife, the only woman he ever loved.

Sixty-six days.

When he finally died everything Mickey Devine owned was given to his sister Margaret. A man of twenty-seven, all that Mickey Devine had was 'a plastic bag, a pair of shoes and socks, his glasses and a bunch of letters, and a crucifix'. Had the hunger strike never happened and his lost remission been restored, Mickey Devine would have been out of jail in 1982.[4]

Years later I would make a friend of a man close to my own age who as a teenager had witnessed the furious rioting in Derry after Mickey Devine's death. Sean had actually lived alongside a British army outpost in Derry and remembers being awoken by the ferocious roar of petrol bombs exploding against the side of the British base when the news circulated that Devine had died on hunger strike. For Sean it was like some incomprehensible carnival night with adults running through the streets hurling abuse, stones and Molotov cocktails over the fences surrounding the British soldiers. Northern Irish communities are extremely tight-knit. Mickey Devine was a Derry man and undoubtedly some of my friend's neighbours had known Devine personally, or had at least come across him. He was the third INLA man to die on hunger strike. My friend was both terrified and excited by the fury of the streets that night. It was, he told me, the first time that he became aware that he was living in the middle of a war zone and a divided city.

That same night in 1981, as a thirteen year old sitting watching television thousands of miles away in the warmth of our small south-east Los Angeles apartment, I can only remember thinking: that could be my uncle dead in that prison. That could be my cousins throwing stones at the soldiers. That could be my family. There, but for the grace of God and an immigration boat, go I. I became increasingly aware that it was only my father's leaving Belfast that had saved me from exposure to the nasty little conflict in Ireland. As is often the wont of teenagers, I allowed myself to become deeply moved by this rather obvious proposition. I seem to recall I actually succeeded in getting a knot in my throat about it and alone in my room I may have even shed a tear that night for the hunger striker whose name, at the time, I could not remember.

Compare this experience though, with that of Ciarán.[5] When I was in Belfast in 1995 Big John suggested I write to Ciarán, who was serving life in Long Kesh. He suggested the correspondence because Ciarán, like myself, apparently had 'a head for the books'. The first time Ciarán wrote to me, on a letter stamped with the seal of some British security authority just to remind you that the letter had been read by the powers that be, he tried to explain how he got involved in Irish republican politics.

I was born into a working class family off the Falls road where I lived, right up until I got married. After I married I moved to Andersonstown where I lived with my wife and two sons up to my arrest in November 1991. I was detained in Castlereagh interrogation centre for a number of days after my arrest and subsequently charged with involvement in a bomb attack. After being on remand for a period of two and a half years, I was sentenced in a no-jury Diplock court to two life sentences which I have chosen to serve with my other comrades in the H-blocks. Prior to being incarcerated, I left school at 16 with no qualifications, (thought I'd better things to do than exams!) and went through a variety of jobs.

Like yourself, I was thirteen at the time of the Hunger-strikes and although I was aware before that age of a conflict in the North, it wasn't until the Hunger-strikes that I began to question why this was so. Gradually through reading books of my father's and experiencing first hand, both the oppression of the community where I lived and their resistance to that oppression, I slowly began to become politicised. It was a slow process, impeded in part by adolescence, enjoying life and more immediately bread and butter issues such as finding a job and providing for my family. Ironically, it wasn't until I became imprisoned that I developed a better understanding of not only my country's history but of the factors that necessitated the need for armed struggle and how without it, Republicans/nationalists would not be the positive, vibrant force they are today.

Ciarán was now imprisoned in the same jail Mickey Devine embarked on a hunger strike and faced death in.

■ ■ ■ ■

Big John and I were quickly out of the car, across the parking lot and in through the first of many security gates with the Ulster chill biting in around our necks. Inside the first gate we were welcomed at reception by two largish guards who asked the name and prison number of who we were visiting, followed by our names. John gave his name easily enough but when they got to me the accent got the better of them.

'Simon Lemons is it?'

'No, Adams.'

'Pardon?'

'Add-amm-zz.' I was about to say, you know, like Gerry Adams, but thought better of it. It didn't matter anyway, the guard had it all down on paper now and gave me the nod.

'Right, away ye go.'

From there we went in to another room with cartoon characters

(Roger Rabbit, Porky Pig etc.) painted on the dirty blue walls. This seemed a little strange; Bugs Bunny and correctional facilities not being things I normally associated with one another. More worrying was the grubby decor and crumbling furniture. I expected something a little more upmarket.

'This place could do with a clean couldn't it?', says I.

'Aye, it's desperate', says John.

We took a seat beneath Roger Rabbit and waited.

After about ten minutes sitting in silence waiting to be searched and passed by at least four guards who said nothing, we were informed by a woman visitor that we were actually sitting in the section for women visitors, not men. The men's seats were over there on the other side of the room. Cursing the screws, we moved across, joined the queue for male visitors, and waited some more. And more. Ten minutes passed.

Prisons have a way of making sixty seconds seem like a lifetime.

Finally a door swung open and we heard 'next two gents please' from one of the screws who then led John and I into separate secure cubicles to be searched. Now I don't know if you've ever been searched before by guards in Northern Ireland's most infamous prison, but if you haven't I can assure you that it is not an especially pleasant experience. That is, unless you like having your testicles squeezed by a bearded bruiser with dandruff on the shoulders of his uniform. He also insisted on running one of those ridiculous beeper things over the nether regions of my body.

Beep beep.

'Is that your belt, Sir?'

'Yes it is, aye.'

I then had to give the two guards in the tiny cubicle all my money which they put into a little envelope and promised to give back to me at the other end. I signed a piece of paper with Her Majesty's seal on it and got a frosty 'Thank you', and a receipt from a bureaucrat with rubber gloves in his front desk drawer, which I know from others are not there to keep his hands warm.

Finally I was led in to yet another waiting room where I met up with Big John. I had to ask.

'Did they squeeze your balls, John?'

'When?'

'Just then.'

'No, not me', says John.

'I must have looked suspicious', I said, trying to reassure myself.

'Either that or perhaps he just fancied you', said John smiling.

We chuckled over that and then sat still in that hollow room that stank of damp loneliness. Another ten minutes passed until we were called forth again, this time by a skinny guard with red ears like slices of beetroot.

'Visitors for MacCárthaigh 9889 please.'[6]

A whole lot of other people were called too. We were all put in a van with seats in the back and all the windows obscured with special distorted glass so you couldn't tell where you were. The van was mostly full of young men, but there were also a few families with young children visiting friends and relatives. It was strange looking around and trying to figure out if they were there to see loyalist or republican prisoners. Our knees were almost touching and all twelve of us were crammed in not knowing if the person next to you might be visiting someone who had killed someone you knew. Opposing sides, side by side.

We sat like that for what seemed like an eternity, but it must have only been about five minutes before we slowly began to drive off across the prison and through two enormous fortified gates. During all of this the woman opposite me was smiling and watching her two young girls of about eight and ten messing about playing clap-games of the 'I-see-see-see-you-staring-at-the-sea-sea-sea' variety. I surmised that they were in to see their daddy. The van stopped suddenly and a guard opened the back door to count us all. The younger of the curly haired girls looked around the van quickly at the dozen or so people behind her and said 'seven' to the prison guard. 'Not at my school it isn't,' said her sister and the whole van cracked up laughing.

At the centre of the prison, through yet another enormous gate, we were let into yet another waiting room with stained seats and a smell of stale cigarette butts that would have had the Marlboro Man gasping for fresh air. It was another five more minutes before we were all called again and led off to our respective visiting wings—loyalists to the left, republicans to the right. It was only then that I realised that every other person in the van except us, and including the two wee curly-haired girls, were there to visit loyalist paramilitaries.

Finally, we were there. It had taken forty minutes to navigate our way from the front gate through the tightest security establishment in western Europe and in to the visiting room. A mean-faced guard turned the big metal key and locked the door behind us. We took a seat at the booth on the end and sat down on the hard cold wooden bench. When Ciarán arrived it was handshakes all round. Ciarán had a bag of chocolates and a bottle of softdrink that he had bought from the IRA inmates' personal store on the block. (The store is so prisoners have something to give their kids and friends during a visit.) The room itself was pleasant enough I guess, if you could put the fact that it was in a maximum security prison out of your mind for a moment. There were about fourteen visiting booths, each partitioned off from one another with a table in the centre, and bench space for about six or seven people. The booths themselves could have been from any fish-n-chip joint on the Australian suburban seaboard except that the underneath was blocked off to restrict leg movement and the passing of contraband. In addition, screws were monitoring us from the end of the room.

Ciarán himself was in fine form, looking fit, well dressed (prisoners at Long Kesh wear civilian clothes) and clean shaven. Indeed, his general appearance was a considerable improvement on the likes of John and myself who both looked positively dishevelled by comparison. Or as John put it, 'You look a sight fucking better than the pair of us ye prick.'

And so he did. I was unshaven and John had something of a hangover from the stunning 2–0 victory of Celtic over Rangers. The corresponding boat trip (and drinking binge) to and fro old Glasgow town hadn't helped. Anyway, we sat down for about two hours and the *craic*, as they say, was brilliant. Conversation ranged over everything from the IRA's mistaken bombing of the Linen Hall Library in 1993 (I mentioned I was doing some work up there), the fact that the Rangers' goalkeeper had worn a black armband in honour of Billy Wright,[7] the latest family news and gossip, the attempted republican escape from H7 in 1997, and the state of Irish literature. Ciarán had some particular insights on the subject of the attempted escape because he was one those in H7 who were eighty feet from freedom in an episode republicans now refer to as 'Operation Tollan'. When the guards discovered the tunnel in March 1997 it was seven feet underground, forty feet long, was fitted with electric lighting and had breached H-block 7's perimeter wall. There was only eighty feet left to the outside wall.[8]

Mostly however our conversation revolved around the issue of the utmost importance in every prisoner's mind—the world outside.

'And what's this I hear about girls outside now, the young ones, going about nightclubs and raves 'n' all with no top on over their bras?'

'Aye, it's true', says John, who had worked as a bouncer at a club and was in some position to comment.

'Fuck's sake, I gotta get out more,' said the man serving two life sentences.

After about two hours a guard came over and without a word put a piece of paper at the end of the table that informed us that our visit was officially over. We waited another five minutes, said our goodbyes and then John and I left. As we took the long journey back through the various gates of the prison I had one thing on my mind—Ciarán was twenty-four in 1991 when he was arrested. He was serving two life sentences. I threw my mind back to those ten minutes John and I had been sitting in the smoky dank waiting room after the screw had squeezed my testicles earlier that morning. The time spent in that confined, loveless, heartless little room seemed like an eternity. Even the air seemed heavy and captive, like it didn't really want to be there. What must an entire day in that room feel like? What about a week? Or thirty weeks? Or seven years? It was beyond the realm of my comprehension.

■ ■ ■ ■

On the way out of the prison through the various heavy steel doors and walls, we were crammed into yet another van that drove us all to the front gate. It was the same deal as the last time with the benches facing one another and the windows blacked out so you couldn't get your bearings.

Sitting directly opposite John and I were four young lads who had Red Hand Commando (RHC) banners that loyalist prisoners had made and given to them. That severed red hand again. One of the banners, I noticed, celebrated the 'Irish Street' unit of the RHC. The Irish Street area is in the loyalist Waterside district of Derry. In a survey published in 1998, researchers discovered that in Irish Street 'more than half the households in the district reported unemployment' and residents claimed 'they felt alien from the rest of the city'.[9] These particular young blokes had seen John and I come from the republican visitor's wing and were whispering to one another as they glared at us. Our knees were nearly touching as their eyes betrayed their disdain for our presence among them.

I knew a little about the Red Hand Commando. They had been founded in 1972 by John McKeague who, not prepared to bow to the discipline of other loyalist organisations, wanted a paramilitary organisation all of his own. It was for this reason that he helped form the small Red Hand Commando instead of remaining loyal to the larger and better-established UVF or UDA. McKeague had established a name for himself by playing a leading role in 1969 when Catholics had been burnt out of streets adjoining the loyalist Shankill district. Far from shunning the notoriety associated with this violence, McKeague revelled in it. In July 1969 for instance, it was McKeague who played an important role in not only driving the few isolated Catholic families from the Shankill, but also put pressure on Protestants living in Ardoyne to come back amongst 'their own'. Several elderly Protestant women (including a Mrs Gilmore) who were happy living in Ardoyne refused to leave, and were personally visited by McKeague. A few days later Mrs Gilmore's house was firebombed and she fled Ardoyne. At the time, this action was blamed on Ardoyne Catholics whom it was assumed were striking back for the Catholic expulsions from the Shankill which McKeague had helped organise. However, it was later claimed by a Labour MP at a British government inquiry into these events that evidence suggested it was probably McKeague's men who had firebombed the house of the elderly Protestant woman in Ardoyne. 'Mixing' and 'mixed areas' have always posed an intolerable threat to the loyalist notion of separatism.

When 'the Troubles' truly ignited on 14 August 1969 following Derry's 'Battle of the Bogside', McKeague was in the front lines in Belfast. McKeague's men set fire to Catholic homes at the Crumlin Road/Shankill end of Ardoyne and McKeague later boasted that he and his men had given Ardoyne's Catholics 'a lesson which I do not think they will ever forget'. He was right of course, but not in the way he imagined. In all, at least 113 Catholic homes were set alight that night. Completely defenceless against McKeague's mob—whom a later government inquiry claimed had burnt houses as the RUC looked on—the people learnt a very bitter lesson indeed. From the ashes of these simple homes rose the Ardoyne IRA.

Nevertheless, McKeague was such a loose cannon that as early as 1971 he was targeted for elimination by erstwhile loyalist colleagues who seemed more offended by his secret homosexual lifestyle than by his penchant for sectarian violence. The macho world of loyalist paramilitarism does not look favourably upon what was described at Oscar Wilde's trial as the love that dare not speak its name. In an attempt to eliminate him, loyalists (assumed to be from the UDA) petrol bombed McKeague's house on 9 May 1971, burning to death his aging mother Isabella instead. McKeague founded the Red Hand Commando soon after and soldiered on. Although his personality, politics and lifestyle saw him become increasingly alienated from the mainstream of extreme loyalism, he survived until January 1982 when he was shot dead in his own shop by the INLA.[10]

Despite the death of its founder the small Red Hand Commando continued and had killed thirteen people by 1994. While initially an independent organisation, in later years the RHC came to be a paramilitary sub-set of the UVF, basically operating under the larger organisation's protection. As such, the Red Hand Commando was a participant (with the UVF and UFF/UDA) in the Combined Loyalist Military Command (CLMC) and was party to the CLMC's declaration of a ceasefire on 13 October 1994 (in response to the IRA ceasefire declared in August). However, the organisation's commitment to non-violence was belated.

On 6 April 1994, a few months before the IRA and CLMC ceasefires, a young Protestant woman called Margaret Wright had been attending a rave party at a loyalist band hall in the Village district of South Belfast. Mistaken for a Catholic, she was reported to paramilitaries at the hall who promptly detained her and took her to a private room where she was stripped naked, beaten with pool cues, tortured and then shot in the head. Her badly beaten corpse was then dumped into a wheelie bin and abandoned. Following the discovery of Ms Wright's body, it was revealed that the main participants in the murder had been members of the Red Hand Commando and that several of them had been under the influence of alcohol and/or drugs at the time. There was palpable outrage in loyalist districts across Belfast and the RHC, along with their more important guardians in the UVF, were forced to move quickly to stem the tide.

Five days after Margaret Wright's death the UVF extracted a confession from a twenty-one year old participant in the killing, Ian Hamilton (a Shankill UVF member), and promptly executed him. The RHC was no less forgiving. In the recriminations that followed the Red Hand Commando assassinated Billy Elliot, the organisation's own second-in-command, on 28 September 1995. At the time the RHC was officially on ceasefire. Elliot was killed because of his connection to the RHC members who had murdered Wright, as well as his involvement in illicit drug-dealing (the fact that several of Wright's killers had been high at the time caused nearly as much consternation in the loyalist community as her actual murder). Luring him into a false sense of security, Elliot's assassins had allegedly shared cups of tea with him shortly before shooting him. When the

Margaret Wright murder case eventually came to trial, the RHC ordered all the accused (including Elliot's wife) to plead guilty or face its wrath. A senior RHC commander sat in the public gallery of the court to make sure his former foot-soldiers obeyed. All but one pleaded guilty.[11]

■ ■ ■ ■

The prison van came to a halt, we were counted once again and released. We strolled over to a little counter to pick up our money and the keys they had taken off us earlier in the testicle-squeezing room, and then we walked out through a steel turnstile past a British paratrooper and his loaded rifle. We were back on the outside. The air instantly tasted better and the sky seemed to form an infinite canopy over the dismal corrugated fortress of Long Kesh.

In the parking lot we all moved towards our respective vehicles and there were final dark glances from the loyalist youths with their Red Hand Commando banners. A lad of about fifteen who had been visiting a loyalist prisoner had been so close to me in the prison van that our legs had actually been touching and I had felt the heat of his body through my jeans. As he got in a car across the parking lot to return to Tigers Bay or Sandy Row or the Waterside or whatever loyalist estate he came from, I wondered if he would one day grow up and join the Red Hand Commando, UFF or LVF. What would he recall of that lonely morning when he sat in a crowded prison van with his leg touching that of a balding young Fenian from Australia? Would it make him blink for just a moment in the darkness of night when he was alone with his thoughts? Would he remember the heat from my leg, that he also must have felt through his jeans? And would it make him contemplate the coldness that death brings?

I pondered all of this in the car on the way back to Belfast, getting lost in the winter's afternoon headlights of oncoming cars, and I tried to imagine what that young Protestant boy and the four loyalist youths with their freshly painted Red Hand Commando banners thought of the ceasefire, their friends or relatives inside, the murder of King Rat, and the future of their disputed province. Suddenly John slapped me on the leg, dragging me away from my thoughts.

'What're stewing about over there, Einstein?'

'Celtic two-nil over Rangers at home. What a match, eh?'

'Aye, 'twas.'

We drove on to the glimmer of Belfast as the sleet began to fall.

6

The Dead of Night

I sometimes wonder how
the man who squeezed the trigger feels.
Does he ever lay awake at night
seeing her in his mind's eye
that dead girl in the green car
on that dark road
that he put in the cold ground
long before her time.

'Conceivably it might be necessary to kill the fish by polluting the water...'

Brigadier Frank Kitson, 1971

Back home, up in the attic, I began to sort through the press clippings that I had photocopied from the Linen Hall library and tried to make some sense of the notes I had taken. I also looked over my notes of background conversations I had already had with relatives concerning the night Jean died. As always, I had more questions than answers, but something of a picture of events was forming.

Jean Campbell married Declan Smyth[1] and became Jean Smyth while still in her teens. Declan, a heavy drinker even by Belfast standards, was a far from perfect husband. Jean stuck by him though, falling pregnant with Sharon and enduring until Declan left Belfast to find work in England. With no money or hope left, Jean eventually moved herself and Sharon back into the family home at Tardree Park around 1970. Despite the breakdown of her marriage, it appears that this was a happy time for Jean. She got a job working at Bass brewery up on the Glen Road and started to rebuild her life. She had some money of her own for once and was able to provide for her daughter and to buy little treats for her mother, Gran. Altogether it must have been an immensely liberating experience for Jean, especially given the poverty and hardship that she had previously known. It was also at about this time, and via her work at the brewery, that she met Sean McCann and fell in love for the second time in her life. Like all courting couples, they socialised together in the local pubs and clubs.

Jean had no plans to go out on the night of 8 June 1972. It was Sean McCann who talked her in to it. It was a Thursday, Jean said that she was too tired and that she had to get up early in the morning for work at the brewery. Sean insisted and she eventually relented. With wee Sharon crying at the door, the two of them left for the Glenowen Inn in his car. Once there, they had a few drinks and a bit of a laugh until a friend of theirs asked to be dropped at home. Sean and Jean were only too happy to oblige and the three of them left the Glenowen together. It was a short drive, no more than five minutes, perhaps a mile or so, up the Glen Road. On the way, they passed The Pop and the turn off to Tardree Park. They also passed Bass Brewery and continued up past the Oliver Plunkett school and the bus terminus to the top of the Glen Road. There were no streetlights on the Glen Road at the time. Somewhere along the way they probably passed the men who would shortly shoot Jean dead. After dropping off their friend, Sean McCann turned the car around and came back down the Glen Road towards the turn off to Tardree Park. They never got that far.

Still at the top of the Glen Road, near the brewery where they both worked, Sean heard a bang and pulled the car into the bus terminus beside the Oliver Plunkett school. There was a burst of machine-gun fire from the darkness. Jean was shot once in the head. She apparently died quickly and without an awareness of her terrible injuries.

According to the *Index of Deaths from the Conflict in Ireland*, our Jean was the 366th person to die in Ulster's sordid Troubles. The 197th non-combatant. The mysterious circumstances of her death meant she got a paragraph or two in the following day's newspapers, but Jean was just another Irish nobody killed in strange circumstances. There were plenty of them in 1972. In June alone thirty-eight people died along with Jean—more than one a day. There were sixteen British soldiers, one Irish Garda, two UDR men and three civilians killed by the IRA. One *Fianna* member, two civilians and one loyalist were killed by the British Army. The loyalists, who were only really getting started in 1972, killed at least six civilians and one of their own members in an internal feud during the month. There seemed to be no end to the funerals.[2]

There was no royal tribute and no angered outburst from politicians on television decrying the senselessness of Jean's death. She died on a forgettable June night on a dark silent strip of road in West Belfast. To all but her family and friends, she was forgotten within a month. If the police investigated her murder, they certainly never approached the family about it and no one really expected that they would find anything anyway. No one was ever charged with her murder. The coroner's inquiry established little more than the fact that she was shot in the head in a case of presumed mistaken identity. She became a statistic.

■ ■ ■ ■

If you are so inclined, you can peruse our Jean's death in newspapers now yellowed, creased and dog-eared with age. Even in far off Australia Jean's relatives could read about her death in a very small article tucked away in the world news section of the *Sydney Morning Herald*. Positioned next to a job advertisement the article, 'Woman shot dead in Ulster', details how a 'Mrs Jean Smith' (they always misspelled her name) had been 'killed by a burst of machine-gun fire'. No reason for her death was offered. Jean even made it in to the *New York Times*, where her death was worth about thirty words, an appendix to a much larger article on the resignation of Mr Robin Bailie from the Ulster Unionist Party. Almost as an afterthought we are informed:

> And a 24-year-old woman was killed by machine-gun fire that tore
> through the car she was sitting in at a Catholic area of Belfast.[3]

Again, no attempted explanation or speculation regarding who killed her or why.

The most in-depth coverage was obviously in the Irish newspapers. On the bottom of the front page of the *Belfast Telegraph* for Friday 9 June 1972 you can see a small picture of Jean. Surrounded by stories of murder, bombings and mayhem, Jean's small simple photo stands out. She looks young and happy and when I saw the photo I immediately wondered where it was taken and where the *Telegraph* got it. Underneath her photo are two very simple, typed sentences: 'Mrs Jean Smith, of Tardree Park, Andersonstown, was shot dead last night. Report—Page 3.' They also spelt her name wrongly, a common enough mistake that all the papers would make over the next few days. Beside her picture was an advertisement for new colour TVs which could be rented in Belfast for only £1.12 a week.

Turning to page three, you can see that Jean's death was the major 'human-interest' story of the day. The headline reads, 'Young Woman dies in Mystery Shooting'. We are then given a round-up of the overnight deaths, and bombings in Northern Ireland:

> A 24-YEAR-OLD woman was shot dead in the Glen Road area and a
> Craigavon youth was seriously injured during shooting between
> troops and gunmen in the Lower Falls last night.
> A Gardai inspector died in hospital from injuries received when a
> bomb blew up in his face on a cross-border road near
> Newtownbutler and a UDR private was seriously wounded when
> gunmen ambushed a mobile patrol on the outskirts of Armagh.
> Mystery surrounds the reason for the shooting of 24-year-old Mrs.
> Jean Smith, of Tardree Park, Andersonstown, whose body was
> taken to Andersonstown RUC station by a taxi-driver after a
> shooting incident on the Glen Road just before midnight.

The *Telegraph* went on to claim that, 'As far as can be gathered', Mrs Smith and her 'friend' had been 'turning their car at the Glen Road bus terminus' when 'the man she was with heard what he thought was a tyre bursting'. He got out to investigate 'and then a machine-gunner opened up' on the car.

Mrs Smith was shot in the head and died almost instantly.
Apparently the man was very anxious to tell Mrs Smith's father
what had happened. He stopped a taxi and asked the driver to take
the woman's body to hospital or an Army post.
The taxi driver took it to the nearby police station and his wife,
who was travelling in the cab with him, had to be treated for shock.

That was it. The *Belfast Telegraph* followed up the story three days later
on 12 June when it reported, on page two, that 'Another 3 victims of
shootings are buried'. Jean's funeral was reported and mention was made
of 'a large turnout of mourners'. Then the story, like Jean's short life, just
ended. There were simply too many tragedies in 1972 to be giving over any
more column inches to some young beautiful mum who died in a 'mystery
shooting'. The *Telegraph* moved on.

The coverage in the *Belfast Newsletter*, Belfast's oldest newspaper, was
generally more informative regarding this 'mystery shooting'. There we
find Jean, once again, on the front cover on the morning of Friday 9 June
1972. It is the second largest story on the page, under the headline: 'Taxi
brings mystery body to police'. I scanned the story for every minute detail
and insinuation.

A mystery woman was shot in Belfast late last night and her body
delivered to Andersonstown police station in a taxi. Police said that
the woman had been shot in the head and that her face was badly
mutilated by the shooting.
A taxi driver was stopped at Shaws Road by a number of men, who
then proceeded to dump the body inside.
The driver immediately drove to the police station and detectives
started their investigation into the mysterious death.
Early today police were working on the theory that the woman was
the latest victim of IRA violence although they stressed that this
was still only speculation.
An Army spokesman said shortly after 11:30pm, that a taxi was
stopped outside the Oliver Plunkett school on the Glen Road by
men in another car.
The taxi already had a passenger on board. The men took the body
of the woman from the other vehicle and carried it to the taxi, put
it into the back and asked the driver to take it to Andersonstown
police station.
He arrived at 11:47pm. Five minutes before the taxi had been
stopped two high velocity shots were directed at Hannahstown
sub-station.
The Army returned fire but it is not known if this incident is
connected with the woman's death.
One unofficial report said that the woman was in a car which was
riddled with bullets fired from another vehicle. A man was also
said to have been wounded in the legs.
The RUC had no knowledge of this incident.

This story provided some early clues into how Jean died. The most important sections, in terms of piecing together the events that led to Jean's tragic death, were in paragraphs two and nine. Sean McCann's car was allegedly shot at by people in 'another vehicle'. These people—whom the *Newsletter* was assuming were the IRA—must have immediately realised what a horrific mistake they had made. Jean's bloody body was then driven a short distance back down the Glen Road to the intersection with the Shaws Road. There, a taxi was waved down and the body was transferred to the back seat by a group of men, possibly including some of those who had killed her. Jean was then driven to a local Army/RUC barracks where she arrived at 11:47 pm. She was officially pronounced dead just after midnight. Meanwhile, about a mile away and unbeknownst to the reporters of the *Newsletter*, Sean McCann, the man the 'unofficial report' correctly contended had been wounded in the legs, was knocking on the door at Tardree Park so as to let Jean's father know that his daughter had been killed.

The next day, Saturday 10 June 1972, the *Belfast Newsletter* ran a follow up story. At the bottom of the front page a headline, 'Five die in 24 hours of terror', detailed the multiple deaths around Northern Ireland over the previous day. The paragraph concerning Jean, although brief, was revealing:

> And Mrs Jean Smith, of Tardree Park, Andersonstown, was shot dead while sitting in a car in Andersonstown late on Thursday night. It was thought yesterday that she was the victim of an IRA mistake when gunmen opened up on what they thought was an Army vehicle.

Altogether the two stories in the *Belfast Newsletter* were extremely useful. Sitting in the loft that night reading and re-reading the photocopies I had made I started to build a picture of how things might have happened. I had several pressing questions though. The questions were fairly basic but I genuinely felt that if I could get the answers to them I might be on the way to unravelling some of the confusion in my own mind about how Jean died. First, assuming it really was the IRA who shot Jean, how would I be able to confirm or disprove this? Secondly, why did they open fire on Sean McCann's car? What would make them think Sean and Jean were in an 'Army vehicle'? I picked up some books and started reading.

■ ■ ■ ■

May and June of 1972 stand out as particularly bad months in the history of the Troubles. The death toll for 1972—472 people killed—is the worst for any single year of the conflict.[4] The IRA were intensifying their armed struggle to unprecedented proportions and the Provos genuinely believed that they were on the march, Armalite in hand, to victory. In April *An Phoblacht*, which at the time was little more than a mouthpiece for the

IRA, declared 'Blitzkreig! I.R.A comeback as Peace Proposals ignored'. In May the British Army logged some 1,223 shooting incidents and 94 explosions. By the end of the year there were 10,628 reported shootings, 1,853 bombs had been planted, 1,264 weapons found, 27.4 tons of explosives recovered and 531 people had been charged with 'terrorist offences'. In all 108 British soldiers, 26 UDR members, 17 RUC policemen, 74 republicans and 11 loyalists were killed in 1972. Tragically, the other 258 victims of the Troubles that year were civilians. Despite reassurances from London that it was all just a local civil disorder matter, 'the war' was for those on all sides who were prosecuting it, very very real.

By 1972 most republicans firmly believed that theirs would be the generation to finally break the British by force of arms. The day before Jean was shot a British soldier had been killed by an IRA sniper while on patrol in Tullymore Gardens in Andersonstown. Less than a week after Jean died, on Sunday June 11, Maire Drumm urged a large republican crowd assembled at Wolfe Tone's grave at Bodenstown to make 1972 the year of destiny. Certainly, all indications were that the British were on the back foot. And in republican enclaves like Andersonstown and Ardoyne, they even appeared to be in retreat.

What this meant for the daily lives of ordinary IRA Volunteers in West and North Belfast was to become central to Jean's death. The IRA's bombing campaign was only just getting under way in 1972 and rather than the sophisticated military operations that the Provos would specialise in by the late 1980s, in 1972 IRA Volunteers on the ground were engaging the enemy on almost a daily basis in basic ambushes and sniper attacks. Or as one IRA member explained regarding the operation of the Ardoyne IRA in August 1971:

> The daily routine for company members was to turn up at a call house, pick up a weapon and ammunition from the tiny armoury of two Armalites and a sub-machine-gun allotted to each company, then set off in pairs, usually by car, to cruise the narrow streets in search of a target... Little planning went into the operations. They were simply under orders to engage any troops who entered the district...[5]

The practice of picking up weapons and driving around the district in a car looking for British soldiers to shoot at was called running a 'float' by a former commander of the IRA's Belfast Brigade, Brendan Hughes. Or as Hughes told Peter Taylor in the television series *Provos*:

> That's two men in a car with one man driving and one man in the back with a particular weapon. They'd be 'floating' around the area just waiting until targets came along.[6]

It was an effective strategy for urban guerilla warfare costing the lives of many British soldiers and contributing to a sense in IRA ranks that the republican slogan of 'Victory 1972' was not hollow words. For instance, the British Army lost four soldiers in four separate incidents in the Ardoyne district alone in the weeks following the introduction of internment in August 1971. Every time British soldiers breached makeshift barricades in Ardoyne, Andersonstown, the Bogside and elsewhere, they faced the very real threat of death. However, IRA operations were not just costly for the security forces. Almost as often an IRA Volunteer may be wounded or killed in the exchange of fire and there was always the risk of hitting civilians in the crossfire. It is therefore not surprising that when the temporary June 1972 IRA/British Army ceasefire was called, a great many in the Catholic ghettoes breathed a sigh of relief. The war was literally being fought in their backyards and in the laneways and entries of their narrow streets.

The willingness of the British government to call a temporary truce with these jeans-wearing long haired Provo 'terrorists' must have given hope to many ordinary people in Northern Ireland that a sort of 'peace at a reasonable price' could be arranged. Years later Brendan Hughes revealed that it was also a relief to the average IRA member:

> Most [IRA Volunteers] never lived beyond the next month, never mind the next year. There was no strategy, no long-term strategy to fight the war. And when the British troops were taken off the streets in 1972 because of the IRA ceasefire, obviously people thought, 'this is it'... So there were expectations that the war was over... Most people involved had been on the run and being on the run means living from hand to mouth and depending on people to feed you. It means not seeing your kids, it means not seeing your wife, and it can be a very, very difficult situation to be in. People wanted it to end then. They wanted back to their wives and they wanted back to their kids.[7]

Yet, despite the secret negotiations and the June 1972 ceasefire, the British maintained an undercover war against the IRA. Indeed, the British Army had become experts in counter-insurgency following their various efforts in other colonial contexts. In Africa and Asia in the post-1945 period they had run undercover squads and engaged in 'dirty tricks'. British troops had arrived in Northern Ireland on 14 August 1969 and shot dead their first rioter (a loyalist) soon after. The first British soldier to be killed by the IRA during this most recent phase of the conflict, Gunner Robert Curtis, was shot dead in February 1971. Despite all of this, it was not until 1972 that British Army Intelligence got down to the job of launching a clandestine 'dirty war' against the IRA. They didn't always excel in their early endeavours. For instance, according to the American historian J. Bowyer-Bell:

> On June 22 four men were machine-gunned with a Thompson in the Glen Road, Andersonstown, a Catholic area, by men in a car. The RUC investigation led to Captain James McGregor of the Parachute Regiment and Sergeant Clive Wilson, both operating as members of the Military Reconnaissance Force, an undercover organisation attached to Thirty-ninth Infantry Brigade... But in the din of the IRA campaign, with car bombs taking down the centre

of Northern cities and sniping a constant, such activities were a minor matter.

During the truce these British special operations continued, indicating that whatever the intentions and inclinations of the politicians, the security forces had settled in for the long haul.[8]

The attack by two Military Reconnaissance Force (MRF) members on innocent Catholic civilians on 22 June 1972 occurred fourteen days after Jean was killed, on the very same street, the Glen Road. In fact, the shooting occurred very near to the spot where Jean lost her life. The Glen Road shooting on 22 June also occurred on the very same day that the IRA announced a ceasefire to come into effect in four days' time. What can be made of all of this?

The MRF was pretty much the brain child of Brigadier Frank Kitson. Kitson was a veteran of military subterfuge, having participated in previous British colonial campaigns in Kenya, Malaya and Cyprus. In Kenya, Kitson had been connected to secret British-controlled units of ex-Mau-Mau who ruthlessly hunted down, discredited and/or killed their former comrades. Considered to be something of an expert in the field of 'counter-insurgency', in 1971 Kitson published a book called *Low Intensity Operations* which set out his views on how to defeat 'Insurgency' and 'Subversion'.

In a foreword written by the well-lettered 'General Sir Michael Carver, GCB, CBE, DSO, MC, ADC, Chief of the General Staff', Frank Kitson is described as 'both an idealist and an enthusiast'. Kitson is better remembered by Irish republicans for his suggestion in *Low Intensity Operations* that in some cases 'the law should be used as just another weapon in the government's arsenal, and in this case it becomes little more than a propaganda cover for the disposal of unwanted members of the public'. The introduction of internment in 1971 and the criminalisation campaign of the late-1970s are viewed by republicans as emanating from such a philosophy. More importantly, a significant portion of *Low Intensity Operations* is dedicated to the development of 'specialised units' for gathering intelligence and countering 'subversion'.[9]

Yet, aside from its occasionally frightening insight into the minds of men who plot state-sanctioned murder, *Low Intensity Operations* is a pretty boring read. I was however interested in Kitson's manipulation of Mao Tse Tung's famous analogy of a guerilla's relationship to the local population where s/he is operating being like that of a fish to a pond of water. Just as the fish needs the water to swim in and survive, so too the guerilla requires the support of locals in order to operate successfully. Kitson's take on the fish/water analogy was revealing.

> If a fish has got to be destroyed it can be attacked directly by rod or net, providing it is in the sort of position which gives these methods a chance of success. But if rod and net cannot succeed by themselves it may be necessary to do something to the water which will force the fish into a position where it can be caught. Conceivably it might

be necessary to kill the fish by polluting the water, but this is unlikely to be a desirable course of action.[10]

■ ■ ■ ■

Brigadier Frank Kitson arrived in Belfast in 1970 to take control of military operations in the Belfast area and remained in Northern Ireland until around April 1972. While in command of Belfast, Brigadier Kitson attempted to replicate his Kenyan counter-insurgency experience, actively recruiting disgruntled former IRA members (called 'Freds') to a special unit. This operation, which was under the command of British officers, also recruited British soldiers of Ulster extraction who could hopefully pass themselves off as locals. Together the 'Freds' and local soldiers constituted separate units of the MRF under Kitson's overall command.[11] The purpose of the MRF was to carry out intelligence work and, where possible, secret operations aimed at discrediting and undermining the IRA. Or as Mark Urban writes in his study of the British military's secret war in Northern Ireland:

> MRF soldiers would cruise Belfast's Falls or Whiterock Roads
> accompanied by 'Freds', who would point out characters or places
> of interest... Within months of its establishment, the MRF's
> operations became more unusual... In one operation the Army
> started its own massage parlour; in another women soldiers posed
> as door-to-door sellers of cosmetics. But the MRF's most
> celebrated operation involved setting up the Four Square Laundry.

Four Square Laundry was an operation in which, among other things, undercover MRF members carried out reconnaissance deep in the otherwise impenetrable and unsafe republican heartlands by driving around in fake laundry vans. Apparently the operation was exposed when two MRF 'Freds' were uncovered by an Intelligence Officer from D-Company of the Second Battalion of the Provisional IRA, based in the Lower Falls. The 'Freds' eventually cracked under the IRA's own form of 'deep interrogation' and revealed to the Provisionals various MRF operations and fronts, including the massage and laundry services. After some further surveillance work of their own, the IRA hit back. On the Twinbrook estate a Four Square Laundry van was attacked by the IRA and one of its agents killed on 2 October 1972. An MRF-run massage parlour, the Gemini Health Studio, on the Antrim Road in North Belfast was also attacked by the IRA on the same day. As for the two 'Freds' who were uncovered by the Provos, they were executed by the IRA and secretly buried some time towards the end of 1972.[12]

In the aftermath of the Four Square and Antrim Road shootings, the Provos released a press statement alleging that for 'a number of months' they had been aware of the existence of the MRF which was a 'Special British Army Intelligence Unit' run by a 'Captain McGregor'. The man killed in the Four Square Laundry ambush at Twinbrook was later identified as twenty year old Sapper Edward Stuart, a British soldier and native of Northern Ireland. Publicly exposed, the MRF was disbanded not long after, only to be replaced by various other clandestine units of British soldiers (including the SAS) who would develop their own underground war against republicans. Gerry Adams would later describe the IRA operation against the MRF in Belfast in October 1972 as being 'on a par with Michael Collins's actions against British intelligence in November 1920', a reference to a more famous incident during the 'Tan war' when Collins' IRA had wiped out fourteen British secret agents in Dublin in a single morning.[13]

The episode does not end there. The MRF holds a rather special place in the early history of the Troubles and in Jean's story. For as eminent Irish historian Tim Pat Coogan writes, 'Its stated objective was 'surveillance', but among the 'surveillance' activities which can be attributed to it was a tendency towards shooting at Catholics from passing cars.'[14] Coogan is not, unfortunately, being facetious. Undercover British Army agents were responsible for a fatal shooting in Andersonstown on 12 May 1972, less than a month before Jean was killed. Firing from an unmarked car and dressed in civilian clothes, they shot dead local man Patrick McVeigh and wounded at least four of his companions, who were conducting community policing in the area. The Army initially denied responsibility for the shooting, officially describing it as 'an apparently motiveless crime'. However, at the inquest into McVeigh's death it was admitted that the occupants of the car were British soldiers, members of the MRF, in civilian dress. It was claimed McVeigh's group was fired upon because they fired at the soldiers first, although there was absolutely no evidence that this was the case (not least of all because it was to all appearances a civilian car and because McVeigh and his friends were unarmed). This was prior to the Four Square Laundry incident and the exposure of the MRF, and serves to highlight that by mid-1972 the British Army was involved in various shady clandestine operations, several of which were taking place in the Andersonstown area.

Another strange shooting incident on the Glen Road, near the spot where Jean was killed fourteen days earlier, is even more revealing. On 22 June 1972 a car driving on the Glen Road opened fire, for no apparent reason, on Catholic civilians standing near the bus terminus. Two men were seriously injured at the terminus itself and a third man, who was in a house nearby, was hit by a stray bullet. At the time there was speculation amongst Andersonstown residents that it was a sectarian crime perpetrated by loyalist gunmen. According to journalist Martin Dillon it took a year for some light to fall on this particular dark crevice of the Troubles when a Sergeant Clive Graham Williams ('Wilson' in some books) appeared in court charged with the attempted murder of two of the men on the Glen Road.

According to evidence given in court, the Sergeant had been travelling in a civilian car (a Ford Cortina) and wearing civilian clothes when he opened fire from the back window of the car on the men near the Glen Road bus terminus. While the British Sergeant claimed he fired on the men in self-defence, no forensic or eyewitness evidence collaborated his claim that the men had been bearing arms and had shot at him first. Indeed, all the evidence was to the contrary, indicating that three innocent men had been randomly shot at by a paid soldier of the British Crown for no apparent reason. The important revelations were still to come. In evidence before the court on the second day of the trial, the very same British Army Sergeant apparently revealed that he was in command of a MRF unit which had been operating on the Glen Road on 22 June 1972. He gave an account of the role of the MRF in gathering intelligence behind republican (ie: enemy) lines and then, according to Dillon's account of the trial proceedings published in *The Dirty War*, revealed that:

> In June 1972 there were about forty men in the force, and they were supplied with civilian cars to move about areas and had their own armoury. He had fifteen men in his squad and generally two to four men travelled in a vehicle.[15]

The Sergeant went on to claim that on the day in question he was taking two MRF recruits on a tour of Andersonstown when the bus terminus incident took place. He claimed that on several previous MRF operations he had come under fire from the IRA and he gave indications that he was very familiar with the Glen Road area from previous MRF work. He admitted that he was in possession of a Thompson machinegun on 22 June, but assured the court that this was not normal practice. He admitted he had fired the Thompson at the men at the bus terminus, but reiterated that this was only after having been fired at first. Again, the evidence did not collaborate his account.

Why would Sergeant Williams of the MRF deliberately and maliciously open fire on innocent unarmed men? Was the 22 June Glen Road shooting just the action of a rash British soldier who in the heat of the moment simply decided to take homicidal pot-shots at Catholic passersby? Or was it a deliberate attempt to fan the fires of sectarian hatred, giving the impression of being the work of loyalists, and therefore distracting the IRA from its self-avowed primary goal of defeating British military power in Ulster? Was its purpose perhaps to send a message to the Catholic community that the IRA could not defend them from random attacks by unknown persons, even deep in their West Belfast heartlands? Such a view, if it grew, would certainly have undermined the IRA's profile as the defenders of the Catholic community. Or was the purpose of the shooting simply to sow confusion in republican ranks by exacerbating the tensions between the Official and Provisional wings of the IRA which had, after all, until quite recently been killing each other? The use of a Thompson machine gun (a weapon not regularly issued to the British Army since World War II but popular with the IRA at the time) was, it seems, an attempt to make the shooting appear as if it was the work of republicans. Maybe in the recriminations after the shooting both factions would blame each other and continue to focus their attentions on killing their republican rivals, rather than their British enemies. Or was there some additional aim?

Even at the early stage of my inquiries in Belfast, I had come to the view that the shooting on 22 June may have been a deliberate attempt by British Intelligence to cash in on Jean's death. Jean Smyth, that young mother from down Tardree Park with the wee girl, had been killed only two weeks previously on the Glen Road near the very same bus terminus in mysterious circumstances. The Catholic community in the area where she grew up and died were painfully aware of her death and many would have known the family personally. Andersonstown in 1972 was rife with rumours relating to the Troubles, and in June 1972 rumour already had it that Jean's mysterious death might just possibly have been an 'own goal'— it was even being secretly whispered at Jean's funeral, as her body was being committed to the cold Belfast soil, that the IRA was responsible. This undoubtedly caused tensions, not only between my family and the Provos, but also between the IRA and those in the community who were increasingly of the opinion that maybe the IRA's campaign wasn't such a good idea if innocent Catholics were going to be the ones getting shot. From the point of view of British military intelligence, Jean's death would have been good propaganda precisely because it potentially undermined the IRA's support base.[16]

This is not to suggest that there was a popular backlash against the IRA in Andersonstown in June 1972 following Jean's death. Far from it. Following 'Bloody Sunday' in January 1972 the IRA were ascendant in West Belfast. But given their intelligence profile, the MRF must have been able to see the potential to exploit, even in some small way, Jean's gruesome death on the Glen Road. Most people in Andersonstown would not have known who shot her. Even fewer would have accused the IRA of killing her by mistake. But the potential for tension was there. Mistakes that involve civilian casualties are never popular in any conflict, and in a guerilla war such tragedies can isolate the guerillas from the community they depend upon for protection and political sustenance. Jean's killing had received reasonable coverage in the press. She was young, attractive and she had a child. In short, considerable water poisoning potential.

Given all of these factors, it is open to speculation that someone in the MRF reached a decision that a replica shooting on the Glen Road, again giving the appearance of an IRA operation gone wrong, might just be the straw that would break the camel's back. At the very least, it may have injured the IRA's reputation amongst some ordinary Andersonstown residents.

Of course, in June 1972 the IRA on the Lower Falls was only just starting to unravel the secrets of the MRF and even the Belfast court would have to wait twelve months before a British Army Sergeant would stand up and give his frightful account of his role in shooting at innocent Catholic civilians on the Glen Road with a Thompson machine gun. Remarkably (or some would suggest not), the Sergeant was acquitted of the charges of maliciously wounding the two men standing at the bus terminus on 22 June 1972 and the other man who was hit by a stray bullet within the confines of his own home. The court bought the Army's paper-thin story that it was all an IRA plot and that the wounded men had fired at the MRF agents in the car first.

It should also be noted that Captain James McGregor, a senior MRF commander named in the IRA's press statement after the Four Square Laundry incident, was a passenger in the car that day on the Glen Road. McGregor had arms charges against him dropped in relation to the 22 June incident on the Glen Road and was never forced to stand trial. Still, his presence in the car lends credence to the theory that the decision to open fire on random Catholics on the Glen Road that day may not have been a violent whim, but rather was a conscious decision taken with 'black propaganda' motivations in mind. And it is possible that it may have been connected to Jean's death two weeks beforehand.

As for the Provos, although the IRA only publicly exposed the MRF in October, certainly by early 1972 republicans were aware that the British Army was running undercover operations against them. This knowledge was confirmed by the discovery of specific details about the MRF in mid-1972 and was passed on to all Belfast IRA commanders some time in late 1972. However, even prior to this, awareness was increasing amongst IRA units that British soldiers were carrying out surveillance of republican strongholds in unmarked cars. These cars were, essentially, mobile army observation posts. The Provos were well aware that if they could successfully identify and ambush one of these cars they had a good chance of killing enemy spies. For this reason, as much as for any other, the IRA were driving around the very same districts in their own cars running 'floats'—looking for undercover British soldiers to engage. Sooner or later they were bound to run in to each other. It was a nexus of death just waiting to happen.

7

A knock at the Door

'I regret very much the loss of life in this situation and it doesn't matter whether it's British soldiers or IRA Volunteers or civilians or people in between them all. I think it diminishes all of us.'

Gerry Adams, January 1992

While I had been in Long Kesh with Ciarán that Saturday afternoon, loyalist prisoners in another wing had been making decisions about the peace process in the aftermath of the murders of the last week. Eighty of the 126 UDA/UFF members in H1 and H7 of the prison voted to withhold their support for the peace talks, describing the death of Billy Wright as 'the last straw'.

That afternoon's edition of the *Belfast Telegraph* carried a front page article entitled 'Terror inmates rule Maze'. It also carried an advertisement for the following day's edition of *Sunday Life* (a weekend tabloid) in which a man with a balaclava was photographed holding an AK47. Under the caption, 'Ulster on the Brink', *Sunday Life* revealed that it would be publishing the 'Latest reports from the streets of fear... and as the guns blaze, what hope is there for peace?' Not much evidently. As for the *Telegraph* itself, it was still doubting the actual existence of the 'LVF West Belfast Brigade' which had claimed responsibility for the New Year's Eve attack on the Clifton Tavern that killed Eddie Treanor. An editorialist wrote that the real lesson for 1998 may be that 'We sometimes need to look back into the abyss to realise where our priorities lie.'

Meanwhile in County Fermanagh, at the western end of the 'province', local Catholics were apparently getting dead rats nailed to their front doors in a grim warning of ill will.[1]

As evening fell John and I drove around North and West Belfast on our way to pick Sharon up from work. Armoured jeeps laden with British soldiers passed us on the New Lodge Road and every single Catholic pub we drove by had its shutters down and its doors closed to stop bullets. The city was black as coal and had a nervous tension about it. Billy Wright was seven days dead and ten Catholics had already been shot in retaliation, two of whom had died. Three fresh graves and the end was nowhere in sight. That night I sat in the attic researching Jean's death. Later, as I lay on my back looking out the skylight past the brick chimney and drifting off to sleep, the sky seemed to be closing in.

■ ■ ■ ■

The following day snow fell. At about lunchtime Gran and I were driven by Big John out to the Twinbrook estate to visit my Aunt Pat and Aunt Margaret (two of Jean's sisters) as prearranged. Lunch at Margaret's was unbelievable, with potatoes and meat and vegies piled high. My great-aunt Philomeana, my grandmother's other sister, was there too. After twenty-five years in Australia she'd come back home to Ireland to die. After lunch we all sat around talking about Australia. Various aunts and cousins started drifting in. As usual, everyone passed comment about how I was looking more and more like a Fairley with every year, and that I was the splitting image of my grandfather Old Q'ey, so I was. By the end of the day it was me, Gran, Aunt Margaret, Uncle Bernard, Sarah-Jane, her wee girl Rebecca, as well as cousins Patrice and Lisa and little Aunt Mannix. The boys, Little Frankie and John Paul, were away upstairs. I don't know if it was the potatoes from lunch, but late in the afternoon as snow flaked the estate, I got the courage up to go next door and talk to Aunt Pat about Jean. Uncle Frank, who had done time in the Kesh in the 1970s, was there sitting on the couch, with his brother who had been on the dirty protest in the H-Blocks. Aunty Pat told me to take a seat close to her and 'Pay no mind t' them terrorists over there, now what can I help ye with son?'

'Do you mind if I ask you a few things about our Jean?'

'No Simon, course not, what d'ye want t' know?'

We started talking and I got my micro-recorder out of my jacket. This caused Uncle Frankie to laugh a little and Pat to sit up and protest that she was not going to be speaking into any friggin machine so I could turn that thing off and put it straight back in to my wee pocket right now. However, without even pausing to take in fresh breath she continued with a media savvy that would put Gerry Adams to shame. Uncle Frankie sat back and listened silently as his brother left the room. The lounge room was suitably dark as a light snow continued to fall outside in Twinbrook. Twenty-six years earlier Pat had been sitting on a different couch with Uncle Frankie at Tardree Park on the evening that Jean was killed. Her voice was soft and contemplative as she recalled that terrible night.

■ ■ ■ ■

'It was actually the eighth of June Jean was killed, but the body wasn't brought t' the barracks until after twelve so the Brits said that it was the ninth. We heard the shooting and I says t' him [Uncle Frankie] "don't bother going home." So he went on home anyway and about half an hour later there was a knock at the door and it was Sean, that was the fella that she went out with...'

'Sean McCann,'[2] said Uncle Frank, butting in. Pat nodded her head and carried on.

'And his hands were full of blood. And he just says t' me "where's your daddy?" and he run past me up the stairs. My daddy always went t' bed early, so [Sean] runs up the stairs and next thing you know they come in, the two of them. My mammy was in a terrible state by then, saying "what's happening?", see no one told us what had happened. Nobody told us a thing. And then he says that there had been an accident, a bit of a shooting, but she is ok. He said "she's all right".'

In the darkness outside the front door and a few feet away from where this conversation had been taking place, the car Jean had actually been shot in was sitting against the curb.

'I didn't see the car. He come down in the car she was shot in, but we didn't go outside, we were kept in. We were kept in the hallway. So then my daddy and him went away, but I remember my daddy the next day saying that once he seen the car he knew. It was riddled. But apparently Jean's body had already been taken from his car into the black taxi at the top of the road and it was brought t' the barracks.'

There was a slight pause. I wondered what Jean's father, my great uncle Billy, must have thought sitting in the car that his daughter had just been killed in. There must have been signs of her death all around him. Not least of all, the blood and bullet holes. Did he sit in the back or in the passenger seat where Jean had been sitting only a short time previously, laughing and smiling before the bullets came for her from the darkness of the road? The seat may still have been warm and depressed from the weight of her. What a terrible, terrible thing for any father to endure. In a way I was glad that Billy had died and I never had the opportunity to ask him about that fateful night. Still, I did want to ask Aunty Pat about the taxi that had been mentioned in the press reports.

'Do you know anything about the people who were in the taxi that Jean was carried to?'

'I remember the woman. I have no idea what her name is. I remember her face and I know she came from Lenadoon. She took a nervous breakdown. She came unexpectedly one night t' my mammy's house—in fact it was months and months later—and she sat and she told us everything. My mammy had only just started getting over it a bit when she came, it was terrible. She said that when she arrived at the car and she got in, all she could see was this knot of black hair. She said she lifted Jean's head and put it on her shoulder and she said an act of contrition in her ear and then they took her away.'

Meanwhile back at Tardree Park, Pat had been sent down the road to inform one of her brothers that Jean had been injured.

'While my daddy was away with Sean McCann, we still didn't know Jean was dead. We knew there was a bad accident. I was sent over t' where our Gerry was living in the Turf Lodge at the time and then down t' tell our Síle, and it was then when I come back—it must have been half one in the morning—and when I got back the priest was there and all the neighbours were in the house and I knew.'

The silence returned to the room and Aunt Pat sat looking at the floor, seemingly lost in a moment twenty-six years ago. Uncle Frankie said nothing. Then Pat mentioned that having your sister killed did not give the family any respite from the security forces.

'Even after Jean died our house was always raided—the Army always came t' us. I could tell you, there would have been ten houses in the street and then maybe two or three they should have done, but they always came t' us. No wonder my poor mammy's nerves are wrecked, God help her, timid wee thing she is. She had a wee boy killed at four and then she had that. She'll go straight t' heaven that woman.'

I asked if Pat had read any of the newspapers from when Jean was killed and how she felt about the way they treated her death. How had the press reaction affected the family?

'A while after our Jean died, I opened a copy of the *Telegraph*, it was a paper we never usually bought, but I opened it and there was a big photograph of Jean. I couldn't believe it, nobody could believe it. Really they should have asked permission t' do that. It was about unsolved murders. There were about six cases featured in it and Jean's was the biggest photograph. Looking at you. My daddy went mad and called them up saying they should have asked permission.'

I made a mental note to track down the article in question next time I was at the Linen Hall.

No one was ever charged with causing Jean's death and no organisation ever officially claimed responsibility. So did Pat have a theory on why and how Jean was killed?

'It was an ambush. Jean worked in the brewery, did you know that? What happened was the night before this happened, well, our Síle wanted us t' babysit. So I went over there with Jean that night and Sean McCann. And Sean went out t' get the car and the car was stolen from in front of Síle's door. So we didn't get home 'til about three in the morning and Jean had t' go t' work at five. So when she come home she was really tired. She was doing five t' two shift and she was really really tired. She didn't want t' go out that night [8 June], but he [Sean] was coaxing her t' go. So anyway, they eventually went on up t' the Glenowen Inn and they met up with a couple of friends and they gave one a lift home. That's how come they were up that way. But apparently from what I heard, after the shooting these guys run out and what I heard was that they said they knew her.'

The finer details were missing but it was the single most important part of the story and she repeated it four times so that I did not miss it. The men that killed Jean knew who she was. But what was this about there being blood on Sean McCann's hands when he came to the front door at Tardree Park?

'When the bullets went in they grazed his hands. We didn't see the car. We didn't even see her clothes, her clothes had t' be destroyed. They were sent home and next door destroyed them. We never looked at them.'

I mentioned that Gran had said that Jean was quite republican minded and that this had come as something of a shock to me. That I had always been given the impression she was basically apolitical. At this point Uncle Frankie, who knows a little about republicanism himself, having been interned in the Provo compound at Long Kesh in the early 1970s, chimed in.

'She was. She would have been on the barricades from day one like.'

Pat nodded and offered her opinion on her dead sister's political orientation.

'Well, I always remember the Army would have come up in the Saracens and maybe picked wee boys off the street—young lads, you know, question them and throw them in the back there. And I always remember her running and shouting "give me your name, I'll get in touch with your parents". And I used t' say, you should be careful you're gonna get yerself killed here. She would have hung on t' the back of the Saracen and everything. None of us would have been political. I would say she would have been the only one t' be very republican.'

At this point Uncle Frankie interjected again.

'She'd have gone a long way in the republican movement if she'd been alive. She would have been something in Sinn Féin today.'

Meanwhile Aunt Pat had something else she wanted to share.

'D'ye know what I remember? I remember Sharon slept very late the next morning after Jean was killed and my daddy had t' tell her why everyone was there and what had happened t' her mammy. It was terrible.'

I asked if anyone from what they assumed was the responsible organisation had ever approached the family to offer explanation or apology for Jean's death.

'Not t' my knowledge. I wouldn't know a thing and I tell you, I don't think anyone would know. We weren't told anything. We were told very little. I've heard a lot, but that's it. I don't know. I wish I had been a wee bit older and knew a wee bit more then. I don't know. I think the ones that done it are now dead too—this is only what you hear, mind. They knew her though, they definitely knew her. The ones that done it came from down near where we lived.'

She knew and I knew that there was only one group from 'down near where we lived' who she could have possibly been referring to—the Provisional Irish Republican Army. And what of Sean McCann? According to Pat he had seen these people who had ambushed his car and shot Jean beside him. The car was stationary and then they had come out on to the street only to realise that they had put to death someone they knew. McCann must have seen them. Spoken to them. And yet he lived and walked away. What transpired on the street that night as Jean lay dying in the car? Sean McCann might have even known them himself. I put this question to Pat.

'Now I don't know if this is true or not. Apparently when Jean was buried and afterwards the men all went for a drink, he [Sean] said t' my daddy "I know who done it, but I'm not going t' say"'.

Pat would not be drawn any further on the point and after that Patrice came downstairs, little Frankie and John Paul returned and bedlam resumed. Interview terminated. After finishing my cup of tea I went back across the alley to Aunt Margaret's place where Gran was in the middle of a John Wayne movie. 'Ach, I love his fil-ims so I do.' John Wayne or not, the evening was pressing down and Little Mannix's husband drove Gran and I back to Andersonstown. As I was leaving Uncle Frankie told me to come back again shortly and we could chat some more and have a few beers, just the two of us. On the way out of Twinbrook we passed Bobby Sands' old house and I had time to think about everything Aunt Pat had said. So what had I learnt? It was all still rumour but it was starting to give some depth to the newspaper articles. Jean was probably killed by the Provos. And Sean McCann saw the men who did it. I needed to find Sean McCann.

8

Loneliness without Peace

'Travel is a great inducer of gloom.'

Brendan Behan

Big John and I spent the evening looking through the large plastic sack of Jean's mass cards that he had found in the attic. Literally hundreds of them. Friends and relatives send one of these cards to the family when someone dies. The normal Irish Catholic custom would have been for the cards to be placed in the coffin and buried with the deceased, but as Jean's head wound necessitated a closed casket this was not possible. Instead they had all been gathered up and buried deep in the cobwebbed darkness of the attic, only to be discovered by John a quarter of a century later during renovations. So there we sat, nearly twenty-six years after Jean's death, sorting through the dusty tributes and reading words intended for the dead. Among them were cards from canteen workers at the brewery, several from Sean McCann's family, from Jean's friends and neighbours, and even one from some IRA boys who were in the Crumlin Road jail at the time and came from Andersonstown. We didn't sort through all of the many hundreds, but it was strange to think that somewhere inside there was probably one from my mum and dad also.

After a while we put all the cards back in the sack and lay them back to rest. I was starting to find the whole situation creepy. John had gone in to make a pot of tea and I thought it might be time for me to retire to the attic.

'John, I'm away up to bed now. I'll see you in the morning.'

'Right y're Simon. Can ye do us a wee favour and put them cards back up there on yer way?'

'Sure enough, no problem.'

And so it was that I carried a morbid sack full of my dead aunt's fading mass cards back up the stairs over my shoulder and into the attic. I placed them in a corner as far away from my fold-out bed as I could. I'm not a superstitious person, but there was something about those fragments of death that unnerved me. The cards should have been six feet under cold ground with Jean instead of sitting six feet away from me in a dusty plastic sack. I had a restless sleep and was plagued by what the old Irish sometimes called *uaigneas gan ciuneas*, loneliness without peace. The night chill found my bed and wrapped itself around me.

■ ■ ■ ■

It was still cold when I awoke the following morning and I was not surprised to look out at Black Mountain and discover it was encrusted in snow. After breakfast I was out the door of Tardree Park by 9:30am. A black taxi took me from the Andersonstown Road to Milltown cemetery. The RUC barracks across from the entrance to Milltown cemetery was the reason for my journey and I walked over to it in the crisp winter sun under the shadow of its towering spires and observation turrets. The barracks itself is at the junction of the fork in the Falls Road, where it splits off into the Glen Road on the right and the Andersonstown Road on the left. Simply laying eyes upon the monstrous barracks should do away with any notion that the RUC is some sort of normal police force. Although the population of Northern Ireland is about 40% Catholic, in 1998 only around 8% of RUC members were Catholics. This represented a decline in Catholic participation in the RUC since partition in the 1920s. In 1923 Catholics were only a third of the population of the north and 21% of the RUC. Despite the growth of the Catholic community, by the 1960s only 10% of RUC members were Catholics and with the coming of 'the Troubles' Catholic recruitment declined even further. Even as the overall number of RUC in the north increased enormously, making Northern Ireland one of the most policed societies in the world, Catholics continued to be estranged from the official forces of law and order. Indeed, the physical structure of the Andersonstown police station gave some indication of the nature of relations between the RUC and the local community.[1]

Andersonstown RUC Barracks is surrounded by fifteen foot high concrete walls and reinforced steel gates. Iron cages surround the observation sangers to protect them from rocket attacks. The small glass portholes where RUC officers look out are bullet proof, reinforced roofs protect them from mortar rounds, and seventy foot observation spires stick up into the sky with all kinds of electronic spy cameras and listening devices hanging off them. The Andersonstown RUC barracks is more of a British frontier outpost than a local police station. Still, propriety demanded that fictions be maintained and I was at the barracks to deliver a letter.

When I had originally spoken to the RUC Information Officer on the phone he had mentioned that I should send in a letter officially requesting access to the file on Jean's death. So while at Aunt Pat's house the previous night I had typed out a letter from myself and another one which I got Sharon to sign.

■ ■ ■ ■

Chief Information Officer,
Royal Ulster Constabulary,
Brooklyn,
Knock Road,
Belfast 525 6LE

5 January 1998

Dear Sir,

I am an academic at the University of New South Wales in Sydney Australia and I am currently conducting research in Northern Ireland... Part of my current research involves looking at press coverage of 'the Troubles' in Northern Ireland and especially in regards to innocent civilians killed unintentionally in Ulster since 1969. In particular I am interested in the death of a young woman from Belfast, Jean Veronica Smyth, killed on the night of 8 June 1972. As far as I can tell from my preliminary investigations, Mrs Smyth was killed by mistake by persons unknown in west Belfast. I understand that at least one civilian was with her when she was shot and that several people were interviewed by the RUC at the time regarding the circumstances leading to her death.

If it is at all possible I would greatly appreciate it if the RUC could make available to myself (for copying or examination) the original police file regarding the investigation into the death of Mrs Smyth. My purpose in this regard would be to study all documents relating to the investigation in order to gain greater insight into the circumstances leading to Mrs Smyth's death and as such, hopefully absorb her story into my current academic research as a means of illustrating the enormous cost paid by innocent civilians over the last quarter century of conflict. I would like to stress that I have the consent of Mrs Smyth's closest relatives in this regard and that any examination of these documents by myself would be undertaken with the highest professional respect for the deceased, and with an acute awareness of the greater sensitivity of the issues involved. I would be extremely grateful if the Chief Information Officer could accommodate me in this regard.

I can currently be contacted by telephone in Belfast on ... and would be more than willing to answer any subsequent questions regarding my intentions, professional credentials and so forth. Thank you for your time and I anticipate your reply.

Yours sincerely,
Simon Adams

■ ■ ■ ■

5 January 1998

To whom it may concern,

I Sharon McVicker, the only child of Mrs Jean Veronica Smyth, give my consent to any investigation by Mr Simon Adams of the University of New South Wales in Australia, into the death of my mother on the night of 8 June 1972.

Yours sincerely,

Sharon McVicker

■ ■ ■ ■

And so here I was standing outside a massive British military fortress on the Andersonstown road, only a few hundred metres from where Jean lay in Milltown cemetery, trying to deliver two letters to the RUC on a cold Belfast winter morning. I was told to drop the letters off to the local barracks and they would then send them on to the Brooklyn headquarters.

Getting inside the barracks was a job itself. I had to yell out from an enclosed iron gate about my business to a RUC man in a rocket proof sanger protruding from the concrete wall. He then buzzed me in to an enclosed iron mesh cage and the door opened. After closing that door behind me, I had to be buzzed in through another heavy concrete bullet-proof and rocket-proof door and I was then inside the immediate perimeter of the fifteen-foot concrete walls that surround the barracks. From there I was directed up a pathway to another heavy steel door. The whole way up the pathway I was under cover in a tunnel that was designed to stop mortars raining down on unsuspecting RUC men. At the closed heavy steel door I was let in to a waiting room where a bored-looking young RUC man with a face made for meanness asked me what I wanted. When I explained to him my conversation with the RUC Information Officer, constable mean-face asked to see the envelope in question. And then, without asking and without a shred of embarrassment, he simply opened my envelope, clearly addressed to the Chief Information Officer, and started reading. I was so stunned it took me a few seconds to recover and say something.

'Excuse me.'

He stopped and looked up, a little bothered by the intrusion.

'Yes?'

'That letter is addressed to the Chief Information Officer. I just want you to forward it to headquarters.'

He gave me a filthy look and placed the letter clumsily back into the envelope. He tossed it on the counter.

'Not much I can do with that. You're better off sending it in the post.'

'But they told me to drop it off here and that you would forward it to HQ. They said that would be faster than the post.'

He stared at me for a second.

'You staying 'round here?'

'Yes, but I don't see what that's got to do with anything.'

'Send it yourself.'

And with that he turned away and buried his face back in a copy of *The Sun*.

I left the way I came, with my letter stuffed back in to the warm pocket of my jacket. Back outside the fortified labyrinth of the barracks I angrily strode up the street cursing the RUC, damning them for wasting my time, and quietly hoping that their intimidating fortress would one day crumble. However, noticing that some local wit had spraypainted 'For Sale' on the concrete wall of the barracks facing the Falls Road, my humour lifted and I caught a black taxi into town to do some more research at the Linen Hall Library.

■ ■ ■ ■

I eventually found the article about Jean that Aunt Pat had mentioned had so shocked the family and reopened family wounds after her death. The article in question was published on 22 October 1973 in the *Belfast Telegraph*. It was part of a series entitled 'Seven Baffling Murders', the logo of which was a smoking question mark coming out of the barrel of a pistol. The lengthy article about Jean was called 'Was Jean Smith shot by mistake?' and sure enough her blown-up smiling picture stares up from the centre of the page. More than a year after Jean's death, someone had been doing their research. The journalist, Ted Oliver, set the scene on the Glen Road just before midnight on 8 June 1972 and then replayed the final moments of Jean's life for an inquiring readership. Sean's car turned at the bus terminus near the Oliver Plunkett school at the top of the Glen Road and then:

> A bullet fired from the direction of the Andersonstown estate passed through the rear window on the driver's side and hit Mrs Smith in the head, causing a ghastly wound from which she soon died.
>
> The driver of the car, a young man, thought he had had a blow out, stopped the car, and jumped out to examine his tyres.

That's when, according to some sources, someone opened fire with the Thompson machine-gun, Sean McCann was wounded and the car was 'riddled' with bullets.

The next section however, backed up what Aunt Pat had spoken of in relation to men approaching the car after the shooting stopped.

> A crowd of youths gathered around the car. At least one of them recognised Mrs Smith. She lived in the area at her parent's home. The young man asked them to inform the police of the shooting. They refused, saying they wouldn't go to the police station because they were wanted.
>
> The young man put the woman into a taxi which took her to the

nearby police station. Mrs Smith was either dead when she was put into the cab or she died very soon afterwards.

And that is all that is known about the death of Mrs Jean Smith, a Roman Catholic. Now, 16 months later, no new facts have emerged. There is only speculation.

The speculation itself was intriguing. First of all, the assertion that there were no other cars on the Glen Road when Jean was killed other than Sean McCann's is important as earlier reports and anecdotal evidence pointed to the possibility that the people who shot Jean had fired from a car from which they had possibly seen Jean and Sean travel up and then back down the Glen Road. Mr Oliver of the *Telegraph*, however, seemed to be claiming that whoever it was who shot Jean did so on foot.

Eight days before Jean was killed a British solider had been killed in Andersonstown by the IRA in a 'float' operation. On 31 May Michael Bruce of the Royal Transport Corps was killed while on patrol near the junction of the Andersonstown Road and Kennedy Way. Five shots were fired from a passing car at the Army Land Rover the British soldiers were travelling in. Bruce was hit by at least one of those bullets and died at Musgrave Park Hospital shortly afterwards. Seven days later, on June 7, the day before Jean was killed, the IRA killed another soldier in Andersonstown, twenty-nine year old Charles Coleman, shot in the chest by an IRA sniper near Tullymore Gardens and Rossnareen Avenue. If nothing else, in the lead up to Jean's death there was certainly constant IRA activity in the Andersonstown area.

As for the aforementioned speculation in the *Telegraph* article, it principally concerned who was assumed to be responsible for Jean's death. One of the 'youths' who were around when Jean was shot blamed it on the UVF, but the *Telegraph* quickly dispensed with any suggestion that loyalists might be responsible—providing arguments why the UVF would have been unable to operate freely so deep in republican territory. Ted Oliver of the *Telegraph* had his own ideas.

There is another theory and it concerns the controversial Military Reaction Force (MRF). It appears to hold more water, especially when some of the later events are taken into account.

The *Telegraph* then stated that, for the record, 'neither Mrs Smith, nor the young man, it is believed, were involved in any illegal organisations'.

It was a dark night... The area was edgy, however. At that time of night and in those days there was little peace of mind for the peace-wanting residents and even less for those who did not want peace.

Exactly a fortnight later four men were shot and seriously wounded at a bus terminus, only yards from where Mrs Smith had been shot.

Mr Oliver then gave an account of the 22 June shooting on the Glen Road for which the MRF Sergeant, Clive Graham Williams, later admitted responsibility in a Belfast court. The *Telegraph* article also mentioned the

Four Square Laundry incident out in Twinbrook where Sapper Edward Stuart of the MRF was killed in October, 'again not far from where Mrs Smith died'.

> [MRF] undercover operations were far more widespread than the vast majority of people in Northern Ireland knew.
> Some members of the Provisionals, who claimed the killing of Sapper Stuart certainly knew some if not all of what was going on. There had been claims earlier about the work of Army plainclothes operatives. There had been allegations that they had bombed and killed to place the blame on either extreme Protestants or Republicans.

Oliver went on to argue that Jean 'was 24 and attractive' and that Sean McCann's car may not have been known by IRA men in the Glen Road area.

> Sergeant Williams revealed that the MRF had been in operation in the area around the time that Mrs Smith died.
> And the IRA were undoubtedly at that time starting to build up their dossier on the MRF using their own methods of surveillance and intelligence.
> Were the Provos on the watch that night for the MRF?

It was reassuring to discover that even in 1973 similar questions were running through the minds of some local journalists. Ted Oliver had drawn a conclusion that I had also drawn, based on what Aunt Pat and others had said, but which I was keen to confirm somehow.

> The death of Mrs Smith is still shrouded in mystery. But the most rational explanation from the few facts available is that she was shot by mistake.
> It would appear that a unit of the Provisional IRA fired on the car thinking it was carrying Army personnel.

The *Telegraph* ended by stating that 'there was no organisation prepared to admit killing Mrs Smith'. Ted Oliver could only reach one final, inevitable, conclusion:

> Jean Smith may well have died simply because she, like so many others in Northern Ireland, had been in the wrong place at the wrong time.

And then, at the bottom of the fading, yellowed page, near an advertisement for the new Volkswagon Beetle, a small black box revealed that:

> INQUIRIES CONTINUE
> POLICE still want to gather more information about the death of Jean Smith. Anyone who thinks he or she can help is asked to ring police at Lisburn 77421 or to use the confidential phones at Antrim 3999 or Belfast 652155 or to contact any police station.

I declined to call. It was twenty-six years too late.

■ ■ ■ ■

After spending a few more hours at the Linen Hall Library I went out to meet Danielle, my friend from Australia, who had arrived in Belfast the previous night and was staying in a backpackers near Queen's University. I hadn't seen Danielle since she left Australia three months earlier to travel around western Europe, so it was hugs all round when we met up in, of all places, McDonalds in the city centre. After a Coca-Cola we headed back out west so that Danielle could experience the ambience of Wild West Belfast. We trudged on foot all the way from Divis Street on the Lower Falls to Tardree Park in Andersonstown, stopping at various murals and points of local interest.

Finally arriving at Tardree Park frost bitten and full of history, Gran had the dinner on and Danielle was invited to stay. After dinner John suggested he and I drive Danielle back to her backpackers and on the way he gave her a guided tour of West Belfast far exceeding my earlier efforts on foot, impeded as I was by a lack of direct local expertise and the cold. We drove up as far as Lenadoon and down to Ballymurphy checking out murals and then, for pure scare value, we headed over to the hardcore loyalist Shankill district, driving along the large concrete 'peace line' that divides the two communities of West Belfast. Passing along the length of the wall only ominous silence reminds you of all the house burnings in this area over the years that have necessitated the building of these concrete monuments to human intolerance. In some places derelict ground and dusty bricks remain as a grim reminder that people once lived here who just happened to come from different religious/ethnic backgrounds. Graffiti proclaimed 'Shankill—the loyalist heartland of Ulster': I couldn't help but recall that the name actually derives from Belfast's *Gaelic* past, coming from the Irish *an sean cill*, or 'the old church'.

I was also reminded that when the first 'peace line' was built in September 1969 by the British Army in Belfast it was seen very much as a short-term physical line of demarcation. At the time the British commanding officer in Northern Ireland, Sir Ian Freeland, had commented that 'The peaceline will be a very, very temporary affair. We will not have a Berlin wall or anything like that in this city.' The original peaceline was a small makeshift border of barbed wire separating Ardoyne from the Shankill and intended to stop loyalist incursions into the nationalist area. If it was supposed to make the residents of Ardoyne feel protected, local republicans didn't perceive it that way. Martin Meehan, a famous Ardoyne republican who spent most of the early 1970s either fighting the British Army or in prison, argued that the peaceline 'went up to ghettoise the nationalist community and to keep us hemmed in'.[2]

In a sense Freeland was right all along. The improvised barbed wire barricade of 1969 was a 'very temporary affair'. It was soon to be replaced with enormous walls of concrete and steel. Walls that block out the light and divide communities. Three decades later North Belfast's peace walls, thirteen in all, remain a living memorial to state regulation of human intolerance.

Part of the problem is that since the 1970s the Catholic/nationalist population of North Belfast has continued to grow while the loyalist/Protestant community has dwindled, the result of a declining birth rate and reduced employment opportunities. The contraction of Belfast's heavy engineering and shipbuilding industries, previously dominated by employment policies which favoured Protestants, has sent many Protestants elsewhere for work. Between 1982 and 1991 the number of voters in the Unionist ward of Duncairn dropped by 24%. Throughout loyalist North Belfast Protestant churches have closed and Protestant schools have been forced to amalgamate. Meanwhile the adjoining Catholic/nationalist Ardoyne, Oldpark, and New Lodge districts have continued to expand, with families seeking housing in what used to be solidly loyalist areas. In this context calls for the construction of peace walls were increasingly used by loyalists to mark out territory and contain the expansion of the Catholic community into vacant houses in previously Protestant-dominated areas. Sectarian attacks by the UFF and UVF in the 1980s and early 1990s were designed to reinforce this division and were often directed at those Catholics residing on the fringes of Protestant areas and/or stranded on the wrong side of the peaceline. [3]

From the 'interface', as journalists like to call it, we drove up to the top of the Shankill to where a gate in another 'peace wall' leads to Ardoyne. We drove around Ardoyne and even along Jamaica Street where my father and aunts and uncles all grew up. Around the corner there was a mural of a man in a sash and bowler hat beneath the words 'Orange Free Zone'. And then we drove down the Cliftonville Road, past the Clifton Tavern where Eddie Treanor had lost his life on New Year's Eve. The shutters were still down—out of both respect and fear of further attack—and floral tributes lay on the curbside. From there we drove to the New Lodge, where John is from, and into loyalist Tigers' Bay, past murals of King Billy upon his gallant white charger in 1690. Finally our journey came to a halt in the city centre at the bejewelled, encrusted and illustrious Crown Tavern, where John suggested we partake of a pint of the black stuff before dropping Danielle off. The pint was well enough taken.

Somehow Danielle eventually got dropped off at the backpackers and John and I returned to Tardree Park. It was a quiet night, the air was heavy with coldness, and as we got out of the car kids were sliding down the street on the black ice. For once there were no choppers overhead. Back inside, we warmed ourselves and the late news reported once again that loyalist prisoners had voted against participating in the peace talks when they resumed after the Christmas break. And just in case you weren't depressed enough, there was footage of the funeral of Eddie Treanor as well. I was then on my way up to bed when I whacked my head on the attic ladder and called out six different types of bastardry, much to the amusement of Conor and Dan whom I could hear giggling in their beds. Suddenly John yelled out from below to stop that gurning because Ciarán was on the phone for me. I thought he was joking until I made my way back down the stairs and picked up the phone and there was Ciarán actually speaking to me from inside Long Kesh prison. A quick exchange of pleasantries and a bit of *craic* and he explained the reason for his call. We talked for another minute or two and then he said that other 'POWs' wanted to use the phone. We would talk more when I came to visit him again. We said our cheerios. I went back up to bed, carefully avoiding catching my head on the ladder. Lying on the bed the sky above was murky and silent. Frightfully dark. I lay there thinking about Ciarán, just a few miles down the road in arguably the most fortified prison in western Europe, doing two life sentences. Defender to some, terrorist to others, with access to a pay phone.

■ ■ ■ ■

When I awoke the next morning my head was congested, my ankles ached and I didn't much feel like dragging my miserable self in to the Linen Hall Library as I originally intended. I called the Fairleys over in Ardoyne instead to see if they would like to come pick me up and run me over to Jamaica Street for the pleasure of my flu-plagued company for the afternoon. They agreed. So, all things being fair and equal, I decided to go back to bed until they arrived. After all, I was missing Amanda dreadfully and, overtaken with weakness of the body and spirit, a little lay-in would do me no ill.

While I was wriggling down in the bed, warming it up, Gran shouted up from downstairs that the RUC were on the phone for me. I was out of bed and down the ladder in record time, nearly doing myself a damage on the way as my foot slipped off one of the rungs of the attic ladder. It was the Acting Assistant Chief Information Officer of the RUC or some such thing.

'Mr Adams, I'm just calling you to inform you that we have received your letter and unfortunately we will not be able to meet your request for the file you desire.'

'May I ask why not?'

'All our files are confidential and we do not release them to anyone.'

'But she's been dead twenty-six years and I have the permission of the family of the victim.'

'RUC files are confidential and we don't release them. That's our policy.'

There was no point arguing. The RUC was not renowned for its flexibility in such matters.

'OK thank you.'

Click.

That's it, I thought to myself. *Sin é.* Now what do I do? My little investigation seemed as though it had been terminated before it even really began.

9

Dirty Ardoyne

'Ireland has had martyrs right down
Through the years;
Their families were bereaved,
Their loved ones shed tears;
But to Wolfe Tone and Emmet,
A name we must join;
Add Paddy McAdorey the lad from Ardoyne.'

An Phoblacht, September 1971

'His death put an end to my dreams of a happy future when the shooting is finished.'

Rose McAllister in *Belfast Telegraph*, 12 August 1971

A rdoyne. It was strange sitting in a house on Jamaica Street sipping tea and talking with Aunt Gloria, Uncle Tony, my cousin Caitlín and her husband Mícheál.[1] My father, four of my uncles and two of my aunts had been raised in a house nearby.

It was in Ardoyne that my grandfather, Hugh Francis Fairley (Old Q'ey), met my grandmother, Margaret Mary McGeough (Maggie), and got married. They moved in together on Jamaica Street. My father and six of his brothers and sisters were raised there, in a 'Protestant state for a Protestant people', where poverty, religious apartheid, and second-class citizenship were begrudgingly accepted by many Catholics. Tom left Ardoyne around the time of his nineteenth birthday, in March of 1966, for Australia. From there he moved to New Zealand where he married my mother and I was born in April 1968. Letters from Ardoyne kept arriving with casual news of riots and barricades. In late 1971 my grandparents, four of my uncles and two of my aunts also emigrated to New Zealand. My father's half-brother, Hugh Fairley, took the boat to England. Another aunt joined us in New Zealand after being burnt out by loyalists in the mid-1970s. That left my Uncle Tony, my Aunt Gloria and their two daughters as the only Fairleys in Ardoyne. My immediate *clann* had departed from Ireland's shores.

The story of Ardoyne mirrors the story of Belfast. As Belfast grew under the influence of the booming linen and shipbuilding industries, cheap Catholic labour flowed into the city and needed to be housed. In the year 1600 there were less than 500 people in Belfast and by 1700 the town could still only attract about 2,000 permanent residents. However, following the Act of Union in 1801 and due to the British industrial revolution of the nineteenth century the city forged ahead. The population grew from 20,000 in 1801 to 100,000 in 1851. By 1901 about 350,000 people resided there and it had been fundamentally transformed; no longer a mediocre northern town, it was now the most industrialised and advanced city in all of Ireland. By 1910 Belfast had the largest linen mill in the world and nearby Lisburn had the largest linen thread company, causing some historians to refer to Belfast during this period as a 'Linenopolis'. At the same time, the Harland & Wolff shipyards had the biggest dry dock in the world, and Belfast's ship workers were to build some of the most famous ships of the age—including the *Titanic*.

In this context it is important to stress that Belfast's industrial development was very much a British, rather than Irish, phenomenon. Belfast's industries, principally linen and heavy engineering, depended on British markets and reaped benefits from the expansion of the British Empire across the globe. It was principally the market in British army uniforms during the Napoleonic wars that catapulted Belfast into the industrial age. By 1850 thirty-five major linen mills in the area employed over 30,000 people. In the words of one historian, 'Instead of being the solitary Irish industrial city, Belfast, looked at in this way, becomes an outpost of industrial Britain.' The captains of industry in Ulster integrated themselves into the privileged loyal orders of British colonialism. In particular, the Orange Lodge presided over Ulster society.[2]

Ulster has always been unique in Irish history. Due to the plantation of Protestant settlers after 1610, Ulster has been the only region of Ireland where the descendants of seventeenth century colonisers were able to establish themselves as a lasting majority. The 'native' or Gaelic Irish were often physically driven from their lands during the seventeenth century, and reduced to abject poverty. However, in each of the Protestant British towns and villages of Ulster a Catholic minority remained on the periphery; cowed and resentful. Although a minority in Ireland overall, Protestants constituted a slender majority in the nine counties of Ulster and were absolutely predominant in four of them (Antrim, Armagh, Derry and Down). By 1800 only 6% of Belfast's population was Catholic. However, particularly after the Great Famine of 1845–50, Belfast's industrial expansion provided the lure of factory jobs and impoverished Catholics were drawn to the city.

The arrival (or more accurately, the return) of large numbers of Catholics resulted in several problems, not least of all the sectarian hostility directed against them by organisations like the Orange Order. It was feared that cheap Catholic workers would drive down wages and dilute the culture and dignity of the Protestant workforce. These passions were inflamed by both loyalist employers and fundamentalist preachers who denounced the swelling ranks of 'seditious papists' in their midst. In 1857, 1864, 1872 and 1886 serious sectarian riots erupted in Belfast. In revisiting an unresolved conflict already 250 years old, the familiar delineators of British Protestant settler versus Irish Catholic native were re-animated. Discrimination in employment was open and unashamed, particularly on the shipyards where the workforce was staunchly loyalist.

Shipbuilding was possibly the single most important industry in all of Belfast, yet in 1866 the massive Harland & Wolff shipyards employed only 225 Catholics out of a workforce of over 3,000 men. By 1911 Catholics were 24% of the Belfast population, but still made only 7.6% (518 people) of the 6,809 ship workers recorded in that year's census. The reason for this state of affairs, according to Michael Farrell in *The Orange State*, was obvious: 'Recruitment was in the hands of the Orange foremen and one whole district of the Belfast Orange Lodge was made up of shipyard workers.' Old habits and bitter prejudice die hard. By 1970 there were still only about 400 Catholics employed at Harland & Wolff when the total workforce numbered around 10,000. [3]

The other long-term problem caused by the growth of the Catholic population of Belfast was housing. It seems that there has hardly been a period in Belfast's modern history when there has not been a housing shortage. Places like Ardoyne were built to deal with that shortage, providing cheap accommodation for the mill workers, domestics and 'surplus labour' who constituted Belfast's Catholic working class.

What locals now call 'Old Ardoyne' was originally built as a housing estate for Protestant workers. However, the Catholic overflow was so great that it was largely Catholics like my great-grandmother Sarah McGeough, who ended up moving in. And yet, although Ardoyne established itself as a working class Catholic area, a number of Protestants remained. As a result, even by the late 1960s the densely populated area around Farringdon Gardens, near the Glencairn and Shankill end of the Ardoyne estate, was still solidly Protestant.

Jamaica Street appears in the Belfast street directory for the first time in 1901, the same year that the minimum age for working in the linen mills was raised to twelve. At that time there were only two families on the street—the family of Patrick McCoy, a blacksmith, lived in number one Jamaica Street, and the family of Fred Collins, a joiner, were in number five. The other houses on the odd numbered side of the street, sixteen in all, were empty. The even numbered side of the street had not been constructed; a small creek ran there instead. The 1910 street directory listed only four families on Jamaica Street, but the following year the area appeared to have enjoyed something of a population explosion—almost the entire odd side of the street was now occupied. The listed occupations of the male residents could be considered fairly typical of Ardoyne's proletarians at the time—two 'flaxdressers', a 'tenter', a 'plater', and four labourers. The majority of these people were presumably employed in nearby linen mills.

By 1937 the even side of the street was starting to take form, accommodating a fresh influx of factory workers. The following year number 112, my family's old home, was listed in the street directory for the first time. In 1942 my grandfather made his first official appearance there as 'Hugh Farley'. He had no occupation listed and sitting reading the faded street directory in the dim light of the Linen Hall Library I was amused to see, once again, the name misspelt as 'Farley' rather than 'Fairley'.

My grandfather wasn't the most literate fellow ever born, but he was buried in New Zealand four decades later as a 'Fairley'. There were British 'Fairlies' in Ayr in the 1700s poncing about being bold peers while Irish 'Farleys' eked out an existence in the bogs somewhere. My grandfather is listed in every Belfast street directory from 1937-1975 as Hugh 'Farley' but the name they gave both my father and then me when I was born was 'Fairley'.

By 1942 over 110 families were living on Jamaica Street. Large families. The listed occupations of the male heads of the house included at least forty-four labourers, three dockers, two flaxdressers, two terrazzo workers, two carters, a porter, a saddler, a shoemaker, a boot repairer, a seaman, a hodsman, a weaver and a rougher. Meanwhile, in pre-Troubles innocence, three men living on the street were serving as soldiers in the British Army. Robert McVeigh, a 'carter' who would marry the sister of Hugh Fairley's first wife, was living just up the street from Hugh. In 1947 my father and his twin brother were born. There were already three older Fairley boys, including two from Hugh's first marriage (his first wife had died). After the twins, four more Fairley children were to follow.

Leaping forward in time, by 1968 things had changed. My father was in New Zealand and I was about to be born. The Troubles were also about to erupt. Although Robert McVeigh had died the previous year he was still listed as living in Jamaica Street, occupation 'railway worker'. My great-grandmother, Sarah McGeough, was living in number 18 and Hugh 'Farley', with his wife and six of their children, was still in the tiny house at number 112, occupation 'labourer'. 'Hugh Farley' would continue to appear in the street directory until 1975, four years after most of my family had left Belfast for New Zealand. The Troubles made updating the street directory difficult and deadly.

Many of Ardoyne's older houses were built at the start of the century for linen workers and in its early days there was some local industry in Ardoyne. There was a linen mill on Flax Street and a factory up near Jamaica Street. These days the factory is gone and with the coming of the Troubles the abandoned linen mill became the Flax Street British Army barracks. Even by the late-1960s, Ardoyne was known for its unemployment, poverty and overcrowding.

It was the unemployment and the lack of hope and opportunity which drove my father away. All things considered, I can see why my father opted for a £10 immigration ticket to the sunshine, bleached-blonde hair and boxing kangaroos of a mythical Australia. Even in the boom post-War years of the 1950s, Northern Ireland experienced much higher unemployment than the rest of the 'United Kingdom' it was still officially part of. In January 1972 the average male unemployment figure for Catholics in fourteen districts of Belfast was 16.9%, or twice the overall Belfast average of 8.2%. Add to this the hidden unemployment and under-employment of men and women surviving on minimal income and you get some idea of the poverty passed on from one generation to the next.

When my father, just nineteen years of age, boarded an emigration boat for Australia, like countless millions of our people before him—he was seeking a better life. Indeed, in October 1960 even Gerry Adams Sr, father of the current Sinn Féin president, applied to emigrate to Australia but was knocked back on account of his criminal record (he had been a republican prisoner during the 1940s). Emigration and diaspora is the Irish story. Even in the 1960s, over a hundred years since *An Gorta Mór* (The Great Famine), the constant trickle continued. Not surprisingly, Catholics made up 90,000 of the 159,000 people who emigrated from Northern Ireland between 1937 and 1961. My father, therefore, was not alone in his desire to find a better life in the 'New World'.[4] A few years later the Belfast of his youth would disappear forever as Northern Ireland was plunged into blood.

■ ■ ■ ■

Ardoyne is surrounded by loyalist estates and as the 1968 civil rights movement grew, tensions between its residents and the surrounding loyalist communities intensified. During July 1969 riots and incursions by the 'B-Specials' (an auxiliary force of the RUC) resulted in open violence with nearby loyalists encouraging the B-Specials as they took on 'the Papish rioters in Hooker Street'. One Ardoyne resident remembered the B-Specials charging into Ardoyne:

> As soon as I saw them coming up Flax Street I was terrified, really
> terrified. They had their shields and batons drawn and were
> beating them like Zulus. Ardoyne erupted. The young kids and
> men of the area took to the streets to defend the district, armed
> with bottles and stones… Ardoyne, you see, was originally built for
> Protestants and they always said that they'd get back what was
> theirs. So we knew we were in for it that year. [5]

Soon after, the house burnings began. Catholic houses were torched and residents fled for their lives. Mobs of loyalists and local defenders fought pitched battles in the streets with sticks, stones and petrol bombs. Televised images of the violence forced the British government to act. British troops were first deployed in Belfast on 15 August 1969 in order to restore law and order and protect the Catholic population. The *Irish News* of the following day, under the headline, 'Belfast—A City Convulsed', attempted to convey the terror.

> BRITISH TROOPS went into action in Belfast last night against a background of further killings, heavy casualties, sniping in many areas into Catholic quarters and a total casualty list of 178 injured including 54 shot.
>
> And early this morning 'B' Specials were reported to have gone on a terror rampage in the Ardoyne district where houses in Butler Street and Brookfield Street were ablaze. Wounded were being taken to a first-aid post in Havana Street...
>
> The 'Irish News' received phone messages from Ardoyne early today asking: 'For God's sake get the police or the military or we will be slaughtered.' The callers said the Specials had been sniping from a nearby mill and were firing in all directions. Other 'B' men using an R.U.C. armoured car drove up the Crumlin Road and fired indiscriminately into Hooker Street and Butler Street.[6]

Two Catholic locals were shot dead in Ardoyne by the RUC on 14 August 1969. They were the first in a long list of Ardoyne residents to have suffered violent and unnecessary deaths over the last three decades. Between 1969 and 1993 no less than 58 people, from all sides, died because of the Troubles in Ardoyne.

British soldiers call Ardoyne 'Provo land'. A British Lance Corporal who served in Ardoyne in the 1980s described it as a case of constant overt resistance: 'to the point where they will get out of their cars and fight you when you stop them at night. They'll throw bricks over walls, they'll fight you on a foot patrol. You'll stop somebody and they'll come out swinging; you knock on someone's door and you get nothing but abuse.'[7] Meanwhile, in West Belfast, some people jokingly refer to the area as 'Dirty Ardoyne'. The first impressions of an English feminist author convey something of how the area appears to outsiders.

> It felt like stepping into a Lowry painting of a stifling industrial landscape, except for the fact that there were no factories billowing out their great black puffs of smoke. Army barracks and observation posts had taken their place, and all that remained were the out-dated factory houses with all their attendant ugliness and meanness, as if somehow their reason for existence had ceased.[8]

Welcome to Ardoyne. *The Ardoyne Report*, published in 1982 by a non-governmental organisation, described local residents as 'a forsaken people'.[9] In the words of the report, 'Catholic Ardoyne provides a microcosm of every social deprivation factor conceivable.' Unemployment for 'active males' was estimated to be 54.2%, as compared to the overall, and alarmingly high, Northern Ireland figure of 26.7%. In Ardoyne, the report insisted, 'Unemployment is like a cancer' infecting successive generations with hopelessness and dependence upon social welfare. In terms of the local environment, 'Ardoyne is a disaster' according to the same report. Its terraced housing was monotonous, 'fish and chip papers blow all about the streets, take-away food cartons are thrown into gardens, broken bottles are in abundance as too are contractors' rubble, pot-holes, rats, and dogs' dirt.' Graffiti, 'mostly of a political nature', was also much in evidence. Turning to the political situation, the report opined that 'given the hopelessness of their plight', it was not surprising that people in 'Ardoyne react violently to being treated as second class citizens'. The report concluded that the only response by 'statutory authorities' to the enormous social problems endemic to Ardoyne was to 'cordon the area off with a Berlin-like fence and swamp it with Security Forces'. All this in a small area approximately 8,000 people call home.

While the people of Ardoyne have a deep sense of community, humour and friendliness, outsiders are viewed with suspicion. They have to be. Locals are always alert to the threat of loyalist paramilitaries and nearby pubs have been given gallows-humour nicknames—'The Suicide Inn' or 'The Duck and Cover'. Murals attempt to give people a sense of pride in their Gaelic heritage, promoting the Irish language and images from ancient stories. There is also an overt politicisation to the surroundings. The observation turrets of the fortified RUC base on the hill above Ardoyne cast long shadows.

■ ■ ■ ■

Both Uncle Tony and Uncle Manuel were nearby when Paddy McAdorey was shot. It was the day of internment, 9 August 1971, and it seemed like half of Belfast was already in flames. The British Army had started its raids at 4:30am and by the end of the day hundreds of men had been arrested and imprisoned without trial. It was still morning and McAdorey had just taken up a firing position on Jamaica Street when the fateful bullet struck him in the skull. Or as Uncle Tony put it to me in January 1998 as we sat talking with winter sunlight escaping into the afternoon:

'I seen the Brits blow the head off him. There was brains all over the wall and all I remember thinking was, "I never knew brains were grey".'

The night before the introduction of internment, 8 August 1971, there had been serious rioting in Ardoyne and Paddy McAdorey, an IRA staff captain, was supposed to spend the night in a safe house. Instead he stayed with his wife, Rose, at his mother-in-law's house. Rose had only been out of prison for two weeks, having served a six month sentence for wearing a 'paramilitary uniform'; and she was pregnant. Rose was awoken by the noise of riots breaking out as the British troops began their internment raids in the early morning. Gunfire on the streets outside was already ferocious.

According to Rose:

> There was shooting through the Oldpark Road, shooting from Alliance Avenue, shooting from the other side of the Crumlin Road and even from the grove in the chapel into Ardoyne. And it was sustained... You couldn't even put your head out the door. I

remember seeing the tracer bullets lighting up the sky as they passed overhead.[10]

Pregnant and concerned for Paddy's safety, Rose stood with her arms around him in the kitchen of her mother's home. Paddy left the house for a while and returned at about 9am. He had been out organising the Provo defence of the area and had undoubtedly involved himself in gun battles with the Army. Rose made him a cup of tea and he had just sat down to enjoy it when a knock at the door called him out on IRA business again. Rose watched him cross Etna Drive and crawl along the ground with another man as they sought out the best cover that the narrow streets of Ardoyne could offer. His abandoned cup of tea sat cold on the table.

Paddy McAdorey made it to Jamaica Street via the little entry at the end furthest away from Alliance Avenue, where the loyalists and British soldiers were shooting from. He slipped into the Braniff's home just a few doors down from my grandparent's at 112 Jamaica Street. Assorted republicans were in the house. My Uncle Manuel was there and remembers that 'gear was being handed out and people were getting ready.' With the others still inside the house, McAdorey took up a firing position behind a low wall in the front garden. He prepared to engage his enemies. Or as Rose McAllister tells it:

> What I heard later was that he'd got up and had fired and then got down again. He got up once more to fire and the gun jammed.
>
> That's when they got him. It was the luck of the draw.

He died beside the Braniff's garden wall on Jamaica Street. Uncle Manuel saw the whole thing from inside the Braniff's house. Nearly three decades later he still has vivid memories of what happened next.

'They carried him away but half his head was still lying in the garden. I'll never forget it. He had a wee hole in above his nose and then the whole back of his head was just gone. That was a turning point in my life. After that I just wanted out and away from it all.'

Rose was told of Paddy's death and she was taken around to the school where they had carried his lifeless body. Paddy McAdorey already had a tricolour draped over him and an honour guard of four *Fianna* members were standing to attention nearby. His head was diligently bandaged so as to hide the terrible trauma done to the back of his skull by the bullet that killed him.

If the response of the local community to McAdorey's death was one of mournful respect, others were positively gleeful about his demise. Uncle Manuel remembers that British soldiers came down Jamaica Street the next day singing, 'I woke up this morning and Paddy was gone'. That night, a local pirate loyalist radio station dedicated a song to Rose, his young widow—it was Elvis Presley's 'Are you lonesome tonight?' Meanwhile, the *Belfast Telegraph* for the afternoon of Monday 9 August 1971 ran under the banner headline 'INTERNMENT' and reported that a 'gunman was shot by an Army marksman in Ardoyne'.

The man shot at Ardoyne by troops was later named as twenty-five year old Patrick McAdorey, of Brompton Park. He died almost immediately but as an ambulance was taking his body away it was stopped by an angry crowd. They told the driver to take it to Holy Cross School in Butler St, not far from where he was shot. A spokesman for the security forces said: 'we hope to examine the body later'.

At the official inquest into his death a few months later, no less than three British soldiers apparently tried to take credit for firing the fatal shot that killed IRA staff captain Patrick McAdorey. Ardoyne remembered him differently. The republican newspaper *An Phoblacht* published a glowing tribute in September 1971 and carried a poem praising him as a hero and martyr. In the adjoining article the 'cowardly sniper' who killed the staff captain from 'A Company, 3rd Batt. Belfast Brigade, Irish Republican Army' was chided for thinking that McAdorey's death would somehow weaken people's desire to resist British occupation:

> Paddy McAdorey was a model soldier of the Republic… We his comrades shall miss his leadership but his death shall inspire us to victory. We shall dedicate ourselves to uphold the cause for which he died.

The article offered condolences to the entire McAdorey family on behalf of the republican movement and ended with a quote from the Bible—'No greater love has a man than this: that he should lay down his life for his friends.'

■ ■ ■ ■

McAdorey was the eleventh member of the IRA to be killed in the modern phase of the Troubles, the first following the introduction of internment. His death was not the last. The final body count for Northern Ireland on 9 August 1971 was fifteen: one IRA man (McAdorey), one British soldier, a UDR member, three Protestant and nine Catholic civilians. The *Belfast Telegraph* for the afternoon of Monday 9 August reported that 'a wave of destruction' was engulfing the entire north. Ballymurphy and Andersonstown were barricaded and blazing—children had set up a 'petrol bomb factory' at Beechmont Drive and hijacked vans were being set alight on the Glen Road. By 31 August a total of thirty-two people had been killed since internment began. No one was in any doubt whatsoever that Northern Ireland was at war.

The situation in Ardoyne was desperate. Burnt out buses sealed off Brompton Park, where McAdorey had lived, from the security forces. Besides McAdorey, two other Ardoyne residents were killed on internment day. Fifty year old Sarah Worthington was shot dead by a British soldier inside her own home. Leo McGuigan, who was only sixteen, was shot by the British Army as he walked along Estoril Park, and a twelve year old boy was wounded beside him. A gun battle also broke out between the Ardoyne IRA and loyalists, with the result that the small remaining enclave of Protestant families which had stayed in Ardoyne since the start of the

Troubles suddenly moved out *en masse*. They burnt their homes behind them and two whole streets around the Farringdon Gardens-Valsheda Park area were torched with the loss of 240 houses. It was a tragic end to a most tragic day.[11]

The *Belfast Telegraph* of Tuesday 10 August 1972 had on its front page a large photograph of burnt out remains, captioned:

> All that remains of Farringdon Gardens, Ardoyne. Residents root among the rubble for lost belongings. Behind them, starkly outlined against the sky, the blackened remnants that were their homes.

Another front page item listed the names of the fifteen people who had been killed on internment day. It also reported that about 92 people had been injured in rioting, 39 of whom had suffered gunshot wounds. Twenty-eight soldiers were in hospital. The leading editorial declared, 'God help us all'.

More were to die in Ardoyne over the following weeks, not least because the local IRA were determined to hit back for the loss of McAdorey. On 14 August an IRA sniper fatally wounded a British soldier on Butler Street and on 23 August the IRA killed another soldier standing outside the British Army base on Flax Street. On it went. IRA snipers shot dead a soldier in Brompton Park in September and another on Kerrara Street in October. Two civilians were killed by the British Army in Ardoyne during October. Thankfully, no one died in Ardoyne in November. December, however, brought more heartbreak. Another civilian was fatally wounded by the British Army in controversial circumstances on Butler Street on 10 December and eleven days later, just before Christmas, twenty-three year old IRA Volunteer Gerald McDade was shot dead shortly after being captured by the British Army on Kerrara Street. In all, it was a bloody end to a bloody year. According to my grisly calculations, using Malcolm Sutton's *Index of Deaths* as a guide, a total of sixteen people lost their lives on the narrow streets of Ardoyne during 1971.[12] The Green Howards, the British regiment serving in the area, lost five soldiers in Ardoyne in the two month period after internment alone. It was a time of anger and tears.

On Christmas day 1998 my Uncle Manuel, on the phone from New Zealand, told me that the film *Saving Private Ryan* brought back memories of Ardoyne in 1971 to him.

> *Saving Private Ryan* reminded me of Ardoyne, especially that first bit at the D-Day landing. I came out of the cinema and my feet and hands were sweating. I remember one night back home we'd been pinned down at the back of Jamaica Street. There was four of us. The Brits just saw movement and opened up, thinking we were the 'Ra. We were laying on our bellies on the ground behind some hedges for about 15-20 minutes and they must have fired twenty rounds at us. They couldn't quite hit us 'cause their firing position must have been too high up but the bullets were whizzing by about

ten inches over our heads. It was just pinging like in that movie. We just lay there praying on the ground. One of the fellas actually shit his pants. Finally they stopped shooting and we crawled in to a house where we stayed the night. But for me that's what *Saving Private Ryan* was like—Ardoyne in '71 and like that night, only we didn't have helmets and a gun to shoot back with.

■ ■ ■ ■

There is another terrible side to the Paddy McAdorey story. On 6 February 1971 Gunner Robert Curtis was shot dead by the Provisional IRA in the New Lodge—the first British soldier to be killed by the IRA in the modern 'Troubles'. Soon afterwards, Chichester-Clark, the then prime-minister of Northern Ireland (the parliament was not dissolved until 1972), declared that 'Northern Ireland is at war with the IRA Provisionals.' On the streets of Ardoyne the situation was rapidly going from bad to worse. On 27 February two RUC men were ambushed and killed by the IRA on Etna Drive. The Ardoyne IRA were 'taking the war to the Brits' and developed a reputation for ruthless efficiency.

Then, on the night of Tuesday 9 March 1971, three off-duty Scottish soldiers from the Royal Highland Fusiliers went drinking at public bars in the Belfast city centre. At the time the city centre was generally viewed as 'neutral territory' and the IRA had a policy of not shooting soldiers out of uniform. The young soldiers—brothers Joseph and John McCraig (aged 18 and 17 respectively), and their twenty-three year old friend Dougald McCaughey—assumed that it was safe for them to socialise there.

At Mooney's Bar the three Scottish lads met, unknown to themselves, three Provos from Ardoyne. They started drinking together. After moving on to Kelly's Cellars where additional pints were imbibed, it was suggested that the soldiers might like to join the Ardoyne lads at a party in Ligoniel, on the outskirts of North Belfast. The group set off together in two cars driven by the undercover Provos. On a deserted stretch of road in Ligoniel at about 7:20pm the cars stopped and the three young Scots got out, one still carrying a half-empty beer glass, to pee at the side of the road. While they were doing so, all three were shot in the back of the head by their drinking companions. Following the execution, and in the quietness of the crisp March night, the three IRA men got back into their cars and drove off towards Ardoyne.[13]

When the bodies were discovered in the morning the two McCraig brothers were found lying on top of each other while McCaughey was propped up against the embankment with a half-empty beer glass still in his hand. This was at Whitebrae, a small link road between the old Ligoniel Road and the Crumlin Road. Despite its proximity to the city it was quiet, semi-rural and relatively secluded. The corpses of the Scots soldiers were found by two children. Another man from the area heard the children yelling and ran down the road to the discover the death scene. A fifty-nine year old docker by the name of Sammy Dickson, he later told the *Belfast Telegraph* that 'I thought at first they were gipsies lying drunk, but when I saw the blood all over the face of one of them I stopped... I was afraid to go near them.'

At the inquest into the deaths a few days later, the City Coroner described the killings as 'one of the vilest crimes ever heard in living memory'. He documented that all three soldiers had suffered fatal gunshots to the head. They had been standing in a line and the killers must have used at least two weapons. All had traces of alcohol in their system, and an RUC Detective Inspector testified that when he examined their bodies at the roadside he found that the trousers of all three men were open in the front. The two brothers had been shot virtually simultaneously, which was why they fell dead on top of each other. One was on his side and the other lay over him in a sort of macabre fraternal last embrace.[14]

Politicians and newspaper editorialists reacted with fury to the killing of the three Scots soldiers, two of whom were, after all, teenage brothers. The *Irish News* of Thursday 11 March carried statements from both wings of the IRA denying involvement in the shooting, while others denounced the killers as 'Godless monsters'. A local publican was also quoted as saying that 'Ligoniel has nothing to do with this whatsoever... It is cannibalism.' Meanwhile Thursday's *Belfast Telegraph* reported that extra detectives were being flown in to track down the 'cold-blooded killers' and that a red Mini with men inside with a blanket over their heads had been seen leaving the Ligoniel area at the time of the shooting. The words of the Lord Provost of Glasgow, where one of the soldiers was from, were quoted in the *Telegraph* without riposte:

> My vocabulary is not adequate enough to say how I feel about this—a most dastardly and cowardly act. I feel not only angry but also terribly disappointed at the Irish people for allowing this sort of thing to happen.

Under considerable public pressure as a result of the killings, which had been carried out without authorisation from senior commanders, the Provos continued to deny all involvement. The *Irish News* of Saturday 13 March quoted a second IRA spokesman who, in an innocence long since lost, remarked that, 'We were as horrified as anyone else at the murders. We do not shoot men in the back.'

On 16 March scores of angry loyalist workers marched from various parts of Belfast to attend a commemorative church service for the three soldiers at Belfast City Hall administered by the Reverend Ian Paisley. It was estimated that ten thousand people attended. Even in the republican ghettoes there was enormous unease at the killing of the three young Scots.

> The general response was horror, horror at murder, horror at the murder of three young men, horror at murder under the guise of friendship and horror by many republicans that the cause had

come to this, wee boys on a lark shot in the back. The Officials and the Provos both denied responsibility. Two of the three IRA men were questioned but never charged. McAdorey was later shot dead in a gunfight with troops on August 9 in Jamaica Street in Ardoyne. The British Army announced that all the under-eighteen troops would be withdrawn from the province. Ulster was once again different, too dangerous for boy soldiers.[15]

Established histories of the conflict in Northern Ireland, almost without reservation, name Paddy McAdorey as one of the Provos who lured the Scots soldiers from the bar and shot them while they pissed in a ditch outside Ligoniel. For instance, Patrick Bishop and Eamonn Mallie, in their history of the Provisional IRA, argue that:

Despite the fact that two of the perpetrators were later questioned about the murders, no one was ever charged. The two who were interrogated went on to make reputations as enthusiastic killers. McAdorey survived a few more months before being shot dead on 9 August in a fight with troops in Jamaica Street in Ardoyne.[16]

McAdorey was certainly interrogated by the Army and Police over the episode, but no charges were ever laid. Nevertheless, the jubilation with which the British Army greeted the news that McAdorey had been killed on 9 August 1971 may have been due in part to a perception that he was involved in the deaths of the young Scots. Martin Dillon, in his book *The Dirty War,* claimed that Belfast nationalist parliamentarian Paddy Wilson inadvertently provided 'hard intelligence' to the British Army regarding IRA operations while frequenting a MRF-run massage parlour on the Antrim Road in 1971–72 (the same one that the IRA were later to shoot up). Dillon asserts that Wilson (who was later stabbed thirty-two times by loyalists and murdered, not far from where the Scots soldiers were killed) revealed to a 'masseuse' the identities of the three Provos who shot the three Scots. According to Dillon:

Paddy Wilson was accurate in naming the guilty men, one of whom, Paddy McAdorey, was later shot by the Army during a gun battle in August 1971… What is particularly fascinating about this story is that Paddy Wilson divulged this information in 1971 before McAdorey was killed.17

Dillon seems to imply that a conscious decision was possibly taken to eliminate McAdorey. His position as a high-ranking Provo in the republican stronghold of Ardoyne can't have done him any favours in this regard, and if nothing else the Army would have been hoping that the backlash against internment would cause leading IRA men like McAdorey to militarily engage them in the open.

A number of histories of 'the Troubles' also suggest that the death of the three Scots soldiers may have been the impetus for the 'Tartan gangs' that emerged in some Protestant working class areas in 1971–72. Particularly strong in East Belfast, these gangs wore tartan scarfs and other paraphernalia as a form of collective identification. Fiercely loyalist and sectarian, different tartans identified different gangs. Several historians allege that the Tartan may have initially been adopted by the gangs to identify not only with the Ulster-Scots heritage of many northern Protestants, but also with the three young soldiers who died on that lonely lane outside Ligoniel. By his own account Michael Stone, responsible for 1988's 'Milltown Massacre', cut his paramilitary teeth in the Tartan gangs. By late 1972, many of the gangs had been recruited into the then-legal loyalist paramilitary organisation, the Ulster Defence Association (UDA), or into its secret illegal wing, the Ulster Freedom Fighters (UFF). The UDA/UFF would extract a high price from the people of Ardoyne for their support for men like McAdorey.[18]

■ ■ ■ ■

Patrick McAdorey, former altar-boy and Provisional IRA staff captain, was shot dead on 9 August 1971 on Jamaica Street while sniping at the British Army from behind a garden wall. He was buried in Milltown Cemetery on Wednesday 11 August and the *Belfast Telegraph* of the following day reported that 250 'foot-stamping' mourners had attended his funeral. The *Telegraph* also alleged that McAdorey had been wanted 'for questioning' regarding the two RUC men who had 'died in a long burst of automatic fire' in Ardoyne on 27 February, less than two weeks before the three Scots soldiers were killed in Ligoniel.

More recently, in August 1996 the *Irish Times* ran an article on the twenty-fifth anniversary of internment. The *Irish Times* journalist, who had actually been in Ardoyne on 9 August 1971, claimed to be a witness to the death of Private Malcolm Hatton, shot dead in the early morning as the Green Howards were conducting their post-internment sweep of Ardoyne. Private Hatton was hit by a single bullet fired by an IRA man on the roof of a shop. The Army returned fire but the sniper got away. The journalist claimed that the IRA sniper who killed Private Hatton was Patrick McAdorey.[19]

In January 1998, while we were talking about Paddy McAdorey and his local status as a patriot hero, Uncle Tony mentioned that his stepdad, Robert McVeigh, had actually fought in Dublin during the 1916 Rising. To prove that this wasn't just idle chatter, he dug out a remembrance card for the man and a commemorative medal that was sent to the family by the Irish Government on the occasion of the 50th anniversary of the Rising in 1966. I was reminded that Seán MacDiarmada, a signatory to the 1916 declaration of independence, had lived on Butler Street in Ardoyne for a few years prior to World War One. Indeed, in 1907 MacDiarmada had been made Sinn Féin organiser for Belfast and was given a bicycle so he could get the republican message out to the local population. Maybe it was MacDiarmada who recruited McVeigh to the Irish Volunteers and helped him along the political path that led to Dublin in Easter 1916. For his troubles, MacDiarmada was shot by a British firing squad in Kilmainham jail. Somehow, McVeigh survived Easter Week and later settled on Jamaica Street.

Robert McVeigh died in 1967, a year before the modern phase of the Troubles broke out. I wonder what he would have made of men like Paddy McAdorey who claimed to stand in his tradition. Men who shot unarmed teenage soldiers in the back of the head while they urinated at the roadside. Men who gave their lives beside little garden walls fighting to defend their community from British soldiers and from loyalists who wanted to burn their houses. I wondered. And then I thought about poor Patricia McAdorey, who grew up never knowing the daddy who was killed while she was still in her mother's womb, and I wondered some more.

I remembered that even thousands of miles away across the water, McAdorey is still not forgotten. In January 1996 I had visited my Uncle Manuel in Auckland, New Zealand. Over a few quiet Baileys we had discussed that fateful day on Jamaica Street. Uncle Manuel went in to his bedroom and came back carrying a small memorial card for Paddy McAdorey. He had kept it ever since 1971 and had carried it across the Atlantic and Pacific Oceans to New Zealand. Manuel told me about his memories of Paddy McAdorey from when they were young and what a great bloke he was—'just a really nice, decent fella'.

Paddy McAdorey's death was the reason Manuel left Ireland and my mother and father were the reason he was able to. A number of the boys Uncle Manuel and my father grew up with went on to join the Official or Provisional wings of the IRA. A frightening number of them are now dead. The Braniff family, in whose front yard McAdorey was killed, would later lose two members of their immediate family to the Troubles; one son was shot by the IRA as an informer in 1981, the father was killed by loyalists in 1989. Ardoyne and the Troubles have just carried on.

Still, sitting talking in Jamaica Street during January 1998 we eventually got off the topic of the Troubles and after some family gossip it was time for me to leave Ardoyne and return to Andersonstown. Mícheál ran me back over in the car and on the way we drove through several loyalist districts. Streetlights were starting to come on as we made it safely back to republican Ballymurphy as the dusk started closing in around us. From the top of that estate you could see the old abandoned British Army barracks below us. More spectacularly, further along the road, from the top of the hill above Turf Lodge, the sparkling lights of Belfast were blinking their eyes open for the night.

Even Belfast glimmers sometimes. For all you hear and read about the city, you wouldn't think there was any beauty in Belfast, but there is. It shimmers at night; even in the darkness, the fog and the cold. It brings a warm feeling all over you. And on a frosty January winter's night, sometimes that is all you need.

10

The Man who saw Everything

'It would be a mistake to suppose that the Irish peasant is always saying funny things. Life in Ireland has not flowed for centuries through scenes shadowed by tragedy without receiving a deep tinge of sadness. There is in the Irish nature an underlying melancholy, which at times fills the individual with a strange disquietude as of an impending catastrophe.'

Ireland To-Day, 1913

After Mícheál dropped me back at Tardree Park the full implications of the earlier bad news from the RUC began to sink in. It really was a blow. Now what was I going to do? I took a walk up to The Pop to think about it. I had only two major leads—Sean McCann and the woman from the taxi. I had to find at least one of them. Aunt Pat said the woman from the taxi had dropped by the house once, so maybe Sharon knew how to get in touch with her. I would have to ask. Until then I had been trying to keep Sharon out of things as much as possible as I didn't want to upset her or impose upon her, but now I had no choice. Asking Gran was simply out of the question. Plus, how was I going to tell Sharon the bad news from the RUC. Maybe she'd just ask me to drop the whole thing now? By the time I got back from The Pop with the night's papers under my arm, Sharon was home. She had been in Dublin on work business for the day and I told her about the news from the peelers. She, Big John and I sat in the kitchen and discussed it as Gran sat with the kids in the lounge room watching cartoons. Sharon was angry.

'How dare they? It's my mammy!'

I asked Sharon if she knew the name of the woman who had been in the taxi and who had once come around to visit the family after Jean's death. Did she remember her?

'Of course, Siobhán O'Neill.'[1]

It turns out Siobhán had actually visited the family a few times and had been in and out of institutions ever since Jean's death. Sharon had met her most recently a few years before, and the woman obviously felt that she was somehow inexplicably tied to the family by Jean's death. Ties of blood. So did Sharon have any idea about how I might find her?

'Sure, I might have the poor wee woman's phone number somewhere. I think she gave it t' me last time she called 'round. The poor woman, it wrecked her life seeing my mammy killed.'

Within a few moments Sharon was standing at the phone with a number written in an old address book.

'I've got it.'

She dialled and I sat in the kitchen watching and trying to listen to every word. Desperately pretending not to be on the edge of my seat.

'Ok, thank you. Bye.'

Click.

Siobhán had moved. No one knew where. She had been living in Beechmount on the Lower Falls, but had now moved on. Another dead end. Sharon returned to the table. Then the bombshell fell. It was Sharon again.

'You know, someone mentioned to me a while back that they saw Sean McCann and he was living in a wee flat off the Andersonstown Road. I think I remember the place they mean, I could help you find it if you want.'

Would I?! I wondered why Sharon hadn't offered this information earlier. She said she had even seen Sean McCann down at the Andersonstown shops a few times over the years, but had never spoken to him. 'He walks in a fog, he's never been right since.' I knew this could quite possibly be my last chance of a link to someone who was actually there on the night. God bless Belfast and its can't-scratch-your-arse-without-someone-else-knowing-about-it sense of community that meant that even though she hadn't spoken to him since she was six years old Sharon still had an idea where Sean McCann was living. I went to bed with my mood improved and knowing full well that if Sharon was right about McCann's address, this might be my last hope of unravelling events on the night of Jean's death. For he was the man who saw everything and said nothing.

As I lay in bed that night it was frightening to think of how much one death—a single statistic in the long list of people who have died in three decades of conflict in Northern Ireland—could affect so many people. First there was Sharon, who grew up never knowing her mother. Then Gran, who lost her daughter. All the brothers and sisters. Then poor Siobhán O'Neill who was in the taxi that black night, 'took a nervous breakdown' afterwards, and had been in and out of mental institutions ever since. Or Sean McCann, who loved Jean and was loved by her. Jean was gone and lives were piling on top of lives, one after another, all ruined because of one night, one shooting, one death.

■ ■ ■ ■

The following morning Sharon and I used a walk down to the Andersonstown Road to do some shopping and look for Sean McCann.

The morning was crisp and we avoided the black ice on the pathways as we wound our way across the estate. Just before the Andersonstown Road we passed a drinking club with the gates to its parking lot firmly shut and a sign that said 'gate closed for security reasons'. No pub wanted to suffer the fate of the Clifton Tavern. With the morning traffic breathing dragon's breath out of their frosty exhaust pipes, we walked a while longer until Sharon pointed to an inauspicious small block of flats.

'That's it up there I think, on the second floor. One of them 'uns.'

I asked her if she wanted to come up with me but she shook her head and said she would wait on the street. And with that I walked up a small brick staircase onto a terrace that had a number of doors facing on to it. There were four front doors for four flats. I would have to try each one. Morbid anticipation rose within me as I knocked on the smoked pane glass door of the first flat. No reply.

I waited and knocked again. Nothing.

I moved on to flat number two and rapped on the door. After about fifteen agonisingly long seconds a young woman came to the door with a baby.

'Can I help ye?'

'Does Sean McCann live here?'

'No, next door, but I think he's away t' work.'

'Thanks.'

I felt my stomach go queasy but I slowly moved on to the next door. I knocked on the door and waited, closing my eyes, hoping and counting the seconds in my mind.

Ten seconds. Nothing.

Twenty. I could hear a small dog barking.

Thirty-four seconds and then finally I saw through the smoked-glass the shadow of someone approaching the door. The door creaked open and an unshaven man in fraying pyjamas stood there holding a little lap dog. The man looked like life and the years had not been kind to him.

'Can I help ye?'

'I was wondering if Sean McCann still lives around here?'

'That's me.'

My knees went weak. I had been so determined not to get my hopes up about McCann still living in the same place that I hadn't even bothered to sort out what the hell I would say to him if I met him. And now here I was, face to face.

'Hello Mr McCann. My name is Simon Adams and I'm a historian from Australia and I'm in Belfast researching a book on the Troubles. I understand you were a witness to the shooting of Jean Smyth in June 1972 and I wonder if I could ask you a few questions about it?'

He studied my face carefully before speaking.

'I wouldn't know anything about it, so I wouldn't.'

'Mr McCann, I just want to understand what happened that night.'

'I wouldn't know. That was a long time ago, so it was.'

I noticed that his hands were shaking.

'To tell the truth Mr McCann, Jean was my aunt and Sharon is my cousin. I just want to know what occurred.'

'I couldn't tell you I'm afraid. I don't know anything.'

'Well, could I just ask you a few questions about the type of person Jean was and such?'

'I only knew her from the brewery, that's all.'

'Again Mr McCann, I don't want to bother you, I'd just like to talk to you about Jean and that night.'

'I wouldn't even pass comment. Sorry.'

And with that our conversation was clearly over. He moved the door forward a bit, in anticipation of closing it. The dog looked at me as Sean McCann stood still, his left hand visibly trembling.

'Thank you Mr McCann, I'm sorry for your troubles.'

He nodded and I noticed his eyes appeared to be welling up with tears. I turned away and as I walked back along the terrace I could hear the door gently close behind me. I walked back down the brick staircase knowing that the man who saw everything will take his terrible secrets to the grave.

Sharon was waiting for me on the street. As we walked back to the Andersonstown Road I told her what had transpired. During the time it took, two mobile British Army patrols passed us in their groaning armoured vehicles and I gave one young soldier the evil eye after he pointed his rifle at me. Sharon and I kept talking and walking. She said that no one ever told her anything about Jean and she never asked for fear of upsetting Gran. Gran always blamed Sean McCann for Jean's death. If he hadn't coaxed her into going out that night she would still be alive, Gran would say. When we finally reached the corner where we had arranged to split up on our separate shopping ventures, we stood with our hands thrust deep into our jackets and continued talking while the winter chill gnawed our bones. When the cold finally got the better of us and we split up for the day she hugged me goodbye. It was the sort of embrace that can only come from family and can warm you to the core of your soul. And then we walked off into the Belfast winter morning.

11

A Lock of Henry Joy's Hair

'The rich always betray the poor.'
Henry Joy McCracken's letter to his sister Mary Ann, 1798

After Sharon and I split up I walked to Paul's Barbers on the Andersonstown Road to get my hair cut. Paul's is one of those old style barber's shops with pictures of boxers on the walls and none of the mod cons you would expect in a post-modern *salon*. It's the sort of place John Wayne or Bruce Willis would have felt comfortable getting their locks attended to and I felt my manliness had been considerably enhanced simply by sitting in the establishment. The furniture itself made no concessions to comfort whatsoever. Still, there was a good feel to the place and on the wall across from me was a board with the prices listed on it alongside a notice that said 'No Manchester United fans allowed to talk in my shop—Paul'. While in the barbers I heard the nastiest of the many Billy Wright jokes that had been circulating since his murder a week or so earlier. One of the customers waiting to get his hair cut leaned over and said to me, 'What's the difference between King Rat and a black Taxi?' I don't know, says I. He started grinning before the words were out of his mouth: 'A black taxi can take five in the back.'

After getting my head trimmed I was back out on the Andersonstown Road. I walked a while before catching a black taxi. I finally caught one not far from the block of flats where Sean McCann lives. I wondered if he could see me—that strange Australian who came asking questions about a lover twenty-six years dead. I got in the taxi and as if to prove my barber shop friend's point, there were five of us in the back. However, on the Falls Road our cab was caught in a traffic jam caused by a British Army roadblock as soldiers searched traffic leaving West Belfast. This seemed odd to me. Given that the real and immediate threat at that moment was to the residents of West Belfast from the LVF getting in, why was the Army stopping people trying to get out of the area? Traffic ground to a halt. I tapped on the window, paid my fare and got out of the cab. I'd walk the rest of the way.

As I walked down the Falls Road towards the roadblock I could see RUC officers searching cars and looking through the shopping bags of an old lady in the back of another black taxi. At that point I also noticed that a young British soldier whose torso was sticking up out of the back of his armoured jeep was following my movements through the sight of his rifle. He had one eye closed and his finger on the trigger as I walked down the footpath towards where he and his jeep were blocking the road. He continued to track me as I walked towards him, adjusting the bead of his rifle so the barrel continued to be focussed on the middle of my chest. As I reached the base of the Army jeep the soldier still had his rifle pointed at me, so close now that if I had reached up I would have been able to pull the gun from his hands. He continued to track me as I passed and then he swivelled back to face the footpath and take aim on the next male pedestrian to come sauntering down the road towards him.

As I walked past the jeep I noticed that other British soldiers were in firing positions just over from me at the corners of Rockmore Road and Rockville Street. Another young soldier was standing apart, trying to catch the weak Belfast morning sun, his rifle slung across his chest and at ease. Seeing me coming, he slipped his right hand, which had been in his pocket, back into the trigger guard and smiled. 'G'mornin'', he said in a broad working class English accent, as if this was just another normal morning in a normal town and he was not standing in combat fatigues with a semi-automatic weapon loaded and ready to shoot me dead if I acted suspiciously. I said nothing and kept walking. In England I would have done the polite thing and said good morning back to him. But this was not England.

From Rockville Street I walked all the way down past Conway Mill, just off the Falls Road, passing the famous Lower Falls unemployment office where Gino Gallagher, the INLA's Chief of Staff, had been shot dead on 30 January 1996 while signing on for the dole. It was a particularly nasty moment in the bloody history of the organisation. The INLA was formed in 1975 following a bloody split in the old Official IRA. At least twenty INLA members have been killed in the various ruptures and faction fights that have mapped out its existence ever since. Gallagher had just sat down at a screened cubicle with a female social security employee when she heard a loud bang. She looked up and saw a man pointing a gun at the back of Gallagher's head from close range. According to her testimony at a later trial, 'I heard another couple of shots, one of which pierced the screen, and felt the chips of glass flying around me.' Gallagher was shot three times in the head and died on the floor of the unemployment office. He was thirty-two years old.[1]

I was hoping to visit Danny the Printer but I couldn't find the shop where he works and so I made my way into the city instead.

■ ■ ■ ■

In Belfast city centre there was a large security force presence and I learned that a massive car bomb had been defused in Banbridge earlier in the morning. Dissident republicans were believed to be responsible for the 500lb bomb and that explained, I reasoned, the military show of force on the Falls Road. In town four RUC jeeps were in Fountain Street alone, just around the corner from the Linen Hall, and at least a dozen RUC men were searching cars and pedestrians in front of the Town Hall. I was later to learn from Sharon that it had been the same story up and down the Glen Road all day in Andersonstown. The RUC had been manning roadblocks and searching everything that moved on the Queen's highway.

Anyway, after sifting through the RUC's security cordon I made my way to McDonalds to meet Australian Danielle again. She had agreed to help me with some of my research and we were about to make our way out to the Public Record Office of Northern Ireland (or PRONI) to see what the chances were of getting my hands on the coroner's report on Jean's death. PRONI is located in leafy South Belfast and after arriving we were eventually let in to the main records room where we met a very nice woman with a small cross around her neck who told me that they no longer held coroner's records on site and that I would have to write to the coroner personally. Another damn waste of time, I thought to myself. We were about to walk out when Danielle noticed a piece of paper for public browsers entitled 'Emigration to Australia' and listing the various indices held at PRONI relating to convict transportation and emigration from Ulster to Australia. She passed it to me for a look and I was immediately struck by something—a quote at the top from a carpenter from 'Londonderry' who had emigrated to Australia in the mid-1830s. His comments, most probably from a letter to a relative, spoke of the various fruits and parrots that were assembled in the tree tops near his place of gainful employment in the great southern colony. His name was David Fairley. Fairley!

I remember once as an earnest twelve year old I went to one of those plastic ancestry and heraldry places they have at shopping malls all over the globe and they told me that there was no such name as Fairley in Ireland. Tell that to my father, grandparents, uncles, aunts, cousins and all the rest born and bred in Ireland, I thought to myself. It was a rare name in Ireland though and I remember Caitlín's husband Mícheál once telling me that when he first told some local women that he was going-out with a Fairley they had snidely accused Caitlín of trying to pass for a Protestant by pretending she had a middle-class British name. 'Them'uns is Farleys or Farrells, what's all this "Fairley' shite?" In short, Fairley wasn't a very Irish name and Ardoyne and my family are, well, as working class, Catholic and Irish as you can get. And now here was David Fairley, who emigrated from Derry to Australia in the 1830s. I already knew that my grandfather, Old Hugh Q'ey Fairley's family originally hailed from out Coleraine way in County Derry and came to Belfast for work during the late nineteenth or early twentieth century. It was a common enough story.

All things considered, Danielle and I decided to make the most of our time at PRONI and do some research on the Fairley name. We dragged a number of impressive and weighty looking tomes off the shelves and settled down for some amateur genealogy. We eventually found something in John O'Hart's *Irish Pedigrees: The Origin and Stem*. Apparently a Sir John Fairley came to live in Ireland (presumably from England) around 1572. We also found listings of the Fairley name in some tithe payment books for County Derry 1824-60. An index of birth, marriage and death notices published in the *Belfast Newsletter* between 1738 and 1800 revealed that in 1784 'David Fairly', in 1787 'John Fairly' and in 1788 'Miss Fairlie'—all esteemed members of Londonderry society, had shuffled off this mortal coil. All appeared to be of sound Ulster Protestant stock.

Gaelic surnames generally identified you by your father or earlier paternal ancestors and were altered by gender and marital status. So a man, his wife and their unmarried daughter would all have slightly different surnames. For instance, if the man was Pádraic Ó Conaill (Patrick descendant of Conall), the unmarried daughter's surname would be Ní Chonaill, while the wife/mother's would be Uí Chonaill. Moreover, while Pádraic's wife's name would officially be Uí Chonaill, she would still probably be referred to by her friends and fellow villagers by her maiden name, Ní Cheallaigh, Ní Shé or whatever. One can easily imagine the ire rising amongst seventeenth century British government scribes regarding these Gaelic savages and their impenetrable ways. Therefore, Irish names were often haphazardly or forcibly Anglicised in official documents.

Alternatively, sometimes Irish peasants would voluntarily drop their Gaelic names in order to curry favour with the powers that be. It was, after all, next to impossible to prosper with an especially Irish-sounding name in a colony where Catholics were barred from parliament until 1829 and had been forbidden to own a horse worth more than five pounds. Therefore those Ó Farrells particularly keen to ingratiate themselves to the colonisers sometimes simply dropped the offending Irish 'Ó' and became Farrells, Farrell became Farley, Farrelly or Fairley, and so on. The memory of those who willingly consented to Anglicisation remains in the historical consciousness of some Irish people even today. For instance, Gerry Adams, in his book of Long Kesh prison reminiscences, *Cage Eleven*, relays the story of a good-natured argument between two republican inmates after one accuses the other's family of 'taking the soup'. The accuser has to explain the allegation to Adams and says of his comrades' family, 'They sold their Os for penny rolls and their Macs for bits of Hairy bacon.' 'He's trying to say that we Anglicised our names for a bowl of soup and a crust. It's his idea of a joke,' says the other inmate.[2]

Fairley, Farrell, Ó Farrell, MacÁdhamh, Adams, Farley, MacTómas. The origins of my surname remained something of a mystery to me.

■ ■ ■ ■

On the eighth morning of the year I got up early. I had a long day in front of me. Danielle was keen to travel around some of Ulster and had asked me if I would be her passenger in a one day hire-car jamboree. Northern Ireland is, by Australian standards at least, a remarkably small place. Back in Sydney I had bragged to Danielle that you could drive around the entire six counties in an afternoon. It was an exaggeration, but now that she was actually in Northern Ireland, she had taken to the idea of getting in a car and seeing as much as we could in a day. She picked me up bright and early in the a.m in a shiny little Japanese number with plenty of heating, a new tape player and a full tank of petrol.

We drove out on to the Westlink straight into the Belfast morning fog and didn't stop until we got lost in Randalstown, a nice little loyalist village with red hands of Ulster all over the gable walls and British soldiers patrolling without anti-rocket flaps on their jeeps. Country living! Unbeknownst to my travelling companion Danielle, I had brought along an exquisite tourist guide in order to assist us on our merry way and give some historical depth to our languid surveillance of the countryside. The tome of which I speak was none other than *An Illustrated Guide to the Counties of Ireland*, published in 1953 by *Fógra Fáilte*, 'the national tourist publicity organisation for Ireland'. Now I knew that Danielle was one of those muesli crunching, backpacking types for whom the various *Lonely Planet* guides are veritable bibles. Still, lusciously written and extravagantly illustrated, I really believed you couldn't go past 1953's *Illustrated Guide*. The information may have been forty-five years out of date, but you would certainly never be left wanting for knowledge. Take, for instance, this description of the landscape of Ireland from the foreword:

> The scenery is never marred by screens of smoke from batteries of chimneys such as besiege the skyline in cities and towns of the manufacturing countries. Rivers do not run rancid with the waste of the mills. There are no small mountains of slag like ogres on the horizon. The salmon still come up from the sea through bright waters that are sullied only by the rain. Many a time the Irish have regretted that their country missed the tide of prosperity that flowed in elsewhere with the expansion of mining and engineering. Ireland remained the 'Cinderella' of the chemical age, but it was her sisters in the end who were covered with soot.

Slag mountains and rancid rivers versus Cinderella land. The section on 'Ireland's Attractions' was no less colourful. In true pre-Troubles innocence, we read that:

> **Shooting** is a popular sport all over the country. Where shooting is not entirely free, as it is in several districts, it can be had at a moderate rent from landowners. Certain hotels afford free shooting to their guests.

The 1950s in Ireland were, by many accounts, a rather awful time. In the south the country was tightly in the grip of the Catholic Church and the reactionary conservatism of the Cold War had a particularly nasty chill to it in the Irish Free State. It was a time of poverty, continued emigration, declining population and doubt. However, I was after the *scéal* on Randalstown and I found it on page 524:

> **Randalstown,** on the River Main, 6 miles east of Toome, on the main road to Belfast, is a market town and a bleaching centre. Fishing on the River Main is free, except in *Shane's Castle Demesne*… In the south wall of the tower, about 30 feet from the ground, is a remarkable sculpture of a human head, the origin and purpose of which are unknown… Randalstown was attacked and occupied for part of a day by insurgents after the battle of Antrim in 1798.

There you had, in a few brief lines, all you ever needed to know about Randalstown. I checked the *Lonely Planet* but there was nothing like the same coverage and insight. Apart from mentioning the 'crumbling aqueduct' that leads in to town, all it talked about was the octagonal porch of the local Presbyterian church.

An Illustrated Guide to the Counties of Ireland—1; *Lonely Planet*—nil.

The mention of 1798 was particularly interesting to me. Indeed the Society of United Irishmen—which united Protestant, Catholic and Dissenter in Ireland's first republican movement—had attacked Randalstown on the morning of Thursday 7 June 1798, defeating the local Yeomanry and forcing them to surrender. The rebel commander in Ulster, Henry Joy McCracken, was a close friend and comrade of Thomas Russell, the Linen Hall's first librarian. It was McCracken who had issued the fateful order calling on his 'Army of Ulster' to 'drive the garrison of Randalstown before you'. The order was signed and dated in the style of the French revolution—'First year of liberty, 6th day of June, 1798.' One couldn't help but think of how different Irish history might have been if the pike-wielding rebels had succeeded in holding the town for more than 'part of a day'.

In 1798 Randalstown and County Antrim were hotbeds for a brand of republican radicalism that inspired men like Henry Joy, who came from affluent Presbyterian settler stock, to take up arms alongside impoverished Catholics in defiance of the British crown. Indeed, so noble was Henry Joy's lineage that when he was hanged in the Belfast city centre on 17 July 1798, a month after the attack on Randalstown and with 'an unedifying backdrop of four decaying human heads mounted on spikes', it was on land that his great-great-grandfather had earlier given to the city. Therefore, in deference to the McCracken family's esteemed position in polite society, Henry Joy's British executioners did not cut off his head and place it on a spike outside Belfast's Market House as they had done with the four less respectable insurgents who had gone to the hangman's noose before him. Instead his body was returned to his 'distraught' sister Mary Ann. She complained bitterly that a British officer named Fox had not allowed her to keep a memento which she had procured from her brother immediately before he was taken to the gallows. Said twenty-eight year old Mary Ann McCracken to a scribe from the *Belfast Newsletter*:

...I cut off some of Harry's hair, which curled round his neck, and folded it up in paper and put it in my bosom. Fox at that moment entered the room and desired me to give it to him, as 'too much use' he said 'had already been made of such things.'[3]

When Officer Fox demanded the lock of hair from betwixt Mary McCracken's breasts he played his small part in extinguishing the popular memory of Henry Joy amongst the Presbyterian community in County Antrim. Two hundred years after Henry Joy's boys stormed Randalstown, swathes of County Antrim are now heartlands of conservative Protestant loyalism. The Orange Order, which emerged principally in reaction to 1798 and sought to divide the Irish populace along sectarian lines, is still powerful there. The red hands and fluttering Union Jacks of Randalstown are a constant reminder of the republican dream that was buried with Henry Joy in 1798.

■ ■ ■ ■

From Randalstown we got back on the right road and drove to the loyalist bastion of Ballymena, which is where, incidentally, my maternal great-grandparents were from. We then headed north west to Coleraine, Portrush and then finally to the Giant's Causeway—thousands of oddly hexagonal shaped natural stone pillars reaching out to the sea and to Scotland. I remember as a child, living with my father in Darwin, he had placed a hexagonal Australian fifty cent piece in my hand and told me that there was a place in Ireland where all the rocks on the beach looked like that. Once again, *An Illustrated Guide to the Counties of Ireland* had all the answers.

> One of the world's outstanding geological curiosities, the Causeway was formed by the cooling of lava which burst through the earth's crust in the Cainozoic Period, over an area extending from the Antrim coast to the island of Skye in Scotland. At the Causeway the cooling of the lava resulted in the splitting of the basaltic rock into innumerable prismatic columns, mostly hexagonal, but some pentagonal and others having various irregular numbers of sides.

Personally, I liked the giant story better—the one that has Finn McCool building the causeway so he could visit his Scottish girlfriend across the sea. Nevertheless, as we stood on the slippery shoreline surveying the scene before us, Danielle was suitably impressed by the geographical abnormality of it all. After nearly blowing away in the raging gale that came in to greet us at the foreshore we eventually decided to retreat to the car and its heater. Besides, it was 2pm and we still had a lot of Ulster left to see. We were thinking of continuing our run up the Antrim coast, carrying on northwards towards Ballycastle, but I was reminded of a story I had read in the Linen Hall from the *Irish News* of 5 August 1926:

At Ballycastle Rural Council meeting on Tuesday evening, Mr John Jameson, JP made a strong plea for the securing of better roads along the north Antrim coast. In Ballintoy a few days ago he had been stopped by a party of English tourists, who were motoring round the coast. Putting particular emphasis on Knocksoughey, they said: 'What sort of roads are these? We thought we were coming to Ulster?'

'But', he said, 'you are in Ulster', to which they replied, 'but we thought we were coming to a place fit for heroes to live in, and with roads that civilised people could travel on'.

'Surely', continued Mr Jameson, 'when Churchill takes seven or eight millions out of the road fund, can't we get a share of it? I am a man that has supported Ulster strongly, I was one of the gun-running gang, and I think it too bad to be insulted about the province at my own doorstep'.

The gun-running reference related to the Ulster loyalists who had illegally funnelled thousands of rifles into Ulster in the 1910s and had thus managed to win, by threat of armed rebellion, the exclusion of Ulster from any proposed British government 'Home Rule' legislation for Ireland. For instance, on 24 April 1914 loyalists seized the port town of Larne and landed an estimated 30,000 rifles and two million rounds of ammunition. Protestant Antrim had been a bastion of the anti-Home Rule movement and scores of the 470,000 people who in September 1912 signed Sir Edward Carson's 'Solemn League and Covenant' to resist any move towards Irish independence, had come from the county. Some literally signed the covenant in their own blood. These bold Protestant people were in many cases the Presbyterian descendants of men like Henry Joy McCracken. Their determination to shed blood in public displays of loyalty to the Crown was in stark contrast to the ideals of poor forsaken Henry Joy. A great many of the men—signatories and gun-runners—were also members of the nearly 100,000 strong paramilitary Ulster Volunteer Force (UVF), created in 1913 with the express intention of making good on the covenant. Thousands of these UVF members were later absorbed into the British Army's 36th Ulster Division following the outbreak of World War I.

Ironically, the people the 36th Ulster Division were sent to fight were the very same people who had actually supplied the UVF with their illegal shipment of arms only a few months earlier—the German Army. And the master they served, the British Government, was the same one that only a few months previously these Protestant 'loyalists' (who appeared to be nothing if not obstinately 'disloyal' at this point in history) had been threatening to resist by force of arms should they introduce Irish Home Rule. Those who had symbolically spilled their own blood on the crisp paper of Sir Carson's Solemn Covenant were soon enough called upon to make good on their promise to defend the British Empire at all costs.

At the Somme on the morning of 1 July 1916 a hundred thousand

British soldiers clambered out of their muddy trenches and senselessly advanced (initially walking, later charging) on the German positions. Before the day was done 20,000 of those men lay broken and dead on the killing fields of the Somme—the greatest single loss of life suffered in a single day by any army in World War I. The 36th Ulster Division itself was decimated, suffering an estimated two thousand dead and three thousand wounded in the fighting. Of Captain Crozier's entire West Belfast Battalion, recruited mainly from the Protestant Shankill district, only seventy men survived. Back home in the tightly interwoven communities of Ulster, where loyalist politicians applauded the gallant efforts of 'Ulster's finest sons', the impact of the Battle of the Somme was palpable.

> In the long streets of Belfast mothers looked out in dread for the red bicycles of the telegram boys. In house after house blinds were drawn down, until it seemed that every family in the city had been bereaved.[4]

Nor was that the last sacrifice the 36th Ulster Division would be called upon to make under the fluttering folds of a Union Jack. At Messines in June 1917 the 36th Ulster Division suffered a further 1,129 casualties. Two months later at the Battle of Ypres another 3,441 were to fall dead or were wounded and maimed in the mud. When what remained of the significantly depleted 36th was moved back to the Somme it suffered the full force of the desperate German 'big push' of January 1918—with a further 7,252 men being wounded or killed in the grinding murder of trench warfare. When the war finally ended on 11 November 1918, with a workers' revolution and a military mutiny in Germany putting an end to the madness, what was left of the 36th Ulster Division was permanently disbanded. It had made its sacrifice and its name was committed to the annals of British military history.

No Ulster loyalist myself, I nevertheless sympathised with the frustrations of both Mr Jameson in 1926 and his fellow travellers seventy years later. Whether it be by road or politics, Ulster, despite all the rhetoric of 300 years of English Kings and Queens, British Prime Ministers and Imperial Generals, was never viewed by London as genuinely being 'as British as Finchley'. Despite the demonstrated loyalty of its Protestant subjects Ulster's concerns were always seen as somehow subsidiary to English interests. I couldn't help thinking that perhaps Ulster's loyalist Protestant population would have been better served if they had not volunteered to die for the King's shilling on the fields of France, but had held on to the gospel of righteous dissent elucidated by one of their most brilliant ancestors—young Henry Joy—who had written to his sister before going to the gallows in 1798 that the real lesson of Ulster's troubled history was that 'the rich always betray the poor'.

■ ■ ■ ■

Given the lateness of the day we decided to push south from the Giant's Causeway instead. We drove to Dunluce Castle (built 1300) and then on to Derry as whatever light was left in the day started to desert us. On the way we saw British soldiers disembarking from a large military helicopter that had landed in a field in the middle of nowhere. We also passed through the quaint sleepy village of Greysteel, infamous for the Halloween killings of 30 October 1993 when two masked loyalist gunmen randomly fired forty-five shots into a festive crowd at a Catholic bar. Nineteen people were hit by the bullets, eight of whom died. One of the masked loyalists had entered the bar and shouted 'trick or treat' before raking the crowd with gunfire from his AK47. He walked as he fired, spraying bullets everywhere and after finishing one clip of ammunition, had stopped and reloaded. One of the survivors of the attack, a seventeen year old girl, later told a journalist that she couldn't sleep any more and that whenever she closed her eyes 'all I could see was the dead bodies'.[5]

The UFF claimed the attack at Greysteel was in retaliation for the IRA's hideous bombing on the Protestant Shankill Road a week earlier when a bomb exploded prematurely in a fish shop killing ten people and injuring fifty-seven. In all, twenty-seven people died in Northern Ireland during the month of October 1993. It was Northern Ireland's single bloodiest month since October 1976 when twenty-eight people had been killed. As we passed through Greysteel I thought how sad it was that this innocent little village would now be forever associated with such events.

Finally we arrived in Derry and I don't think I'd be doing the truth a disservice if I said that I gave a good account of myself in the tour guide stakes as I showed Danielle the landmarks of the town with two names. Derry has a troubled and turbulent past. Founded by Christian monks in the year 546, it was originally named *Doire Calgaich* (Calgach's Oakwood) and was later renamed *Doire Cholmcille* in honour of the saint who spent some time at a monastery there. Although Derry (or *Doire*) prospered and grew under the influence of the various monasteries that flourished in the area, between the ninth and eleventh centuries the town was constantly raided by the Vikings. In this context, the English are relative newcomers to the region, only really establishing their power after successfully seizing the town in 1600. In the various recriminations and resistance that followed, the Irish came off second best. The Crown seized over 20,000 acres of land and gave it over to London merchants who established a sizeable colony in Derry town. It was then that Derry's impressive fortified walls were built (completed in 1618) and that the 'London' was added to the 'Derry' in order to give the town a new loyal and distinctively British name.

Londonderry/Derry holds a special place in the heart of both Ulster loyalists and Irish republicans. For Protestants, the 105 day siege of Londonderry in 1689 is a defining moment in their history. It represents the symbolic victory of Ulster loyalists over surrounding disloyal Catholic rebels who they believe are as determined to drive them into the River

Foyle today as they were three and a half centuries ago. For republicans meanwhile, Derry is the city of 'Bloody Sunday', 30 January 1972, when British soldiers fired at least 108 rounds, shooting dead fourteen unarmed civil rights marchers. Just about the only thing Derry's two traditions agree upon is that the eruption of the 'Battle of the Bogside' in August 1969 marked the violent explosion of the modern phase of the Troubles in both Derry and throughout Northern Ireland as a whole.

Danielle was particularly interested in touring the republican Creggan and Bogside areas where we visited some local murals and paid our respects at the Bloody Sunday monument. Continuing on our journey across Derry we passed near Shipquay Gate, which is near the spot where nineteenth century immigrants left Derry by sea, destined for the new world. As we drove by I spared a thought for David Fairley and more tragically, for that vast multitude of others who left Ireland during the Famine of 1845–1850. The earthly remains of 370 unfortunates who perished in Derry, unable to escape to America or Australia, were discovered near the old Waterside Workhouse as recently as April 1996.

We then very courageously—well I was a little nervous anyway—ventured in to the loyalist Waterside district of Londonderry (as its residents would undoubtedly prefer I call it). We found and admired an impressive UDA mural before a mangy old dog started barking at us, chasing our car and driving us from the estate. Coming to the conclusion that loyalist dogs are best left alone at this time of day, we headed out to the Belfast road and were then back on our long journey home to Tardree Park. No sooner were we on the highway than it began to pour with rain, the skies opening up like a gaping wound and pouring down upon us as we crawled along the dark treacherous road. Consulting my trusty guide-book in order to glean additional facts about the city we were leaving behind us in the black rain, I mentioned to Danielle that Derry 'was noted for the manufacture of shirts and collars and has a large bacon-curing industry', but she did not seem to take a particular interest and instead choose to keep her eyes on the wet misty road before her.

When we finally reached Belfast it was early evening and as Danielle turned off the Westlink onto Divis Street she made her only driving mistake of the entire day. Unfortunately she did so right in front of a British Army mobile patrol that was setting up a roadblock in the rain at the front of Divis flats. Driving down the wrong side of the road towards an Army roadblock and then, realising your mistake, slamming on the brakes and swerving recklessly, can be dangerous in Belfast. We very quickly had the undivided attention of the soggy soldiers and at least one was instantaneously in the cautionary process of lifting his rifle towards his shoulder in a firing position. 'For Christ's sake stop Danielle!' I yelled as I had visions of the panicking soldiers shooting us down in the middle of the street. Thankfully Danielle slowed the car to a crawl.

In due course we got back on to the right side of the road and my heart started beating again. We proceeded slowly down Divis Street, passing the wet miserable soldiers without incident. As we were weaving through their little checkpoint I leaned forward and tried to give one of them my best Oh-so-very-sorry-old-chum grin, intimating with my eyes that I was driving with a madwoman who had no inkling of the violent and unintentional danger she may possibly have placed us all in. He nodded back.

We drove on and my nerves steadied as I looked back at the four soggy soldiers standing out in the miserable freezing rain in front of a block of flats wearing camouflage gear. If they really wanted to be camouflaged in West Belfast they should have been wearing track-suit pants, Nike trainers and a Glasgow Celtic jersey. Still, the Queen would no doubt be proud of them as they stood shivering in her name on a miserable Thursday night in the heart of Gerry Adams' electorate. The defence of the realm appeared safe in their damp numb hands.

And with that we finally made it back to Tardree Park. It was Danielle's last night in Belfast and we parted with a warm embrace. Danielle thanked me for the whirlwind tour of the north and for my family's hospitality. I thanked her for the company, for her help at PRONI and for not bringing her Alanis Morissette tape with her in the car. We agreed to meet up as soon as she and I both got back to Australia. And with that she was gone into the night and I went inside. Big John was at the kitchen counter as I walked in. He glanced my way and smiled.

'Is it a cup of tea you'll be after now?'

12

Mo Chroi-se Dubh

You're not really dead,
she told me,
until no one remembers you.
That is why plastic flowers
are so important for a grave.
They don't fade or wilt,
until long after your memory has.

'Tá brón an domhain orm. Mo chroí-se dubh.'
(The sorrow of the world is upon me. My heart is blackened)

Irish saying

The next day was a Friday and as Sharon had the day off work the two of us went down to the Kennedy Centre in Andersonstown to do some food shopping. I needed some new deodorant so I sought out the personal hygiene department. Not being familiar with any of the namebrands on display I settled on 'The Scent of Africa' which I thought might be a pleasant enough fragrance to have emanating from my armpits. Although what business a supermarket in Andersonstown had selling the bottled scent of Africa to the unsuspecting residents of West Belfast is one of life's little commercial mysteries. Nevertheless, groceries and deodorant were purchased and Sharon and I were on our way back up to Tardree Park.

When we got home we had a cup of tea and I read the morning paper. The press had been allowed into Long Kesh prison the previous day and the *Irish News* carried a picture of UDA/UFF leader Johnny 'Mad Dog' Adair on its front page. Adair was photographed standing under a banner with a skull emblazoned upon it which read 'Kill 'em all, let God sort 'em out!' The "em' in this case being, presumably, the Catholics Mad Dog had been responsible for sending to their maker. Adair was the former UFF 'brigadier' who it was assumed had authorised the murder of Big John's teenage cousin, Gerard O'Hara, among more than a dozen others. In September 1995 Adair was sentenced to sixteen years in prison for UFF membership and directing terrorist activities. The latter charge had been proven when Adair openly bragged to RUC officers about being responsible for planning the murders of up to twenty Catholics. These conversations were secretly recorded by the RUC.

There was also a picture in the *Irish News* of Michael 'Milltown Massacre' Stone talking to journalists. As I was reading the newspaper the British Secretary of State for Northern Ireland, Mo Mowlam, was paying an extraordinarily controversial visit to Long Kesh to try and win the loyalist prisoners back to supporting the peace process. Despite the death of King Rat, she somehow succeeded in easing some of their fears and after she left the prison approximately 120 UDA/UFF prisoners voted to recommend that their political wing, the Ulster Democratic Party (UDP), return to the peace talks at Stormont after the Christmas break.[1]

As Gran was over the road with Peggy, I thought it was as good a time as any to go get my micro-recorder out and ask Sharon a few questions. She was nervous at first, but as we began to talk she became less self-conscious and seemed to forget about the recorder altogether. The day marched on as we talked about 'her' and what it would have been like if 'she' had lived. Although Sharon hardly ever mentioned her mother by name, she was always the missing third person.

■ ■ ■ ■

'I don't remember very much really. Only thing I remember is her going to work in the mornings. She worked in the brewery as you know. I don't remember anything before that. So I must have been about five or six and I remember her coming home and bringing me wee sweets and drinks and those kinds of things. The next morning after she died, Gerry came in t' tell me and he was crying and I says "where's my mammy?" and he says "she's not coming home" and I says "why?" He said something and I can't remember what it was but I knew it meant that she'd died. I can't remember what happened after that or the funeral or anything. Absolutely nothing at all. The only thing I can think of is that I didn't want t' remember and no matter how hard I try it just doesn't come back to me, ever.'

Sharon does however remember that she didn't want her mother to go out that fateful night in 1972 and that she had asked her to stay at home.

'I remember standing at the door crying and the car was parked just two doors down. I always used to cry after her, but Gran probably told you that already. I remember Gran saying "come on" and then sitting on the sofa beside Gran and then that's it.'

'What about Sean McCann?'

'I remember him coming in and out of the house but I don't remember spending time with him, although I did. The three of us even went away on holidays together once but I don't remember any of it.'

She only had one memory of Jean's wake. The coffin was in the living room at Tardree Park and she was brought in to the room by her Grandfather to pay her respects.

'I remember seeing the coffin with the lid on it. I remember I asked my Granda' why it wasn't open, I wanted to see her, and all he said was "you can't". And then years later I was told you couldn't because she was shot in the head. That was it. I don't even know if I was at the funeral or not.'

It was when Sharon was about twelve or thirteen that she finally got the courage to go to a relative and 'ask the question' regarding her mother's death because 'no one ever told me voluntarily, like'.

'They said she had been travelling up the Glen Road or down the Glen Road, I don't remember which, but it was near where it meets the Shaws Road, and that there was some kind of crossfire or something and she just happened t' be travelling the road at the time. The story that they got was that it was the 'Ra but they weren't sure. I didn't really have much feeling about it then because I thought to myself, well, nobody's actually sure what happened or who done it. I knew they [the IRA] were involved but I didn't know who else was involved. I thought, "well they wouldn't have been shooting at just nothing, they must have been shooting at something else".'

Sharon had obviously not heard the MRF ambush theory.

'I thought to myself some day I will find out or some day someone will explain it all to me but then nobody ever did and so I thought, "well, nobody wants to talk about it" so I never really asked. Also, because it was so unsure about what happened I was probably afraid of finding something I shouldn't find or something like that. That's why I felt OK about you looking into it, because it was always the questions I couldn't ask. It wasn't that I didn't want to ask, I just couldn't ask, I couldn't bring myself to do it. So if you get the information and build the picture then that's fine, I'd like to see it. It would probably put a lot of things straight for me. Even when I was younger in school kids would say to me "Is your mammy dead? What happened?" And then I'd say, "Umm, she got shot in a crossfire or something" and you'd see people's faces and them thinking "hmm, something not right about that". Because she was innocent and they'd be thinking she was involved, she was in the IRA or was in this, that, or the other, she must have done something, or she was a tout or something. Now I'm older and when people ask they think I just don't want t' talk about it, but I couldn't tell people what happened because I just don't know.'

She had however, heard about Jean's political tendencies.

'From what I've heard, she was a bit of a rebel', she said, laughing.

Sharon was told stories of Jean rioting and being involved in numerous protests and demonstrations. I asked Sharon if she had inherited her mother's republican outlook.

'I don't have any sort of political views at all. It's probably one of the things out of my mammy's death I didn't get involved in. I never had any opinions on it, I never hardly watched the news, or read a newspaper because of that. If things went wrong or they [the IRA] done something I didn't agree with I'd probably have been the one t' say they shouldn't take anybody's life and things like that. I'm not republican minded whatsoever.'

After she grew up, Sharon's work put her in close contact with Protestants—unusual for someone from republican West Belfast.

'There's a lot of people up here that probably wouldn't have a lot of Protestant friends and I've loads. I would say probably 90% of my friends are Protestant. It's only because I've always worked in that environment. And the way that I was brought up; Granny was never republican and neither was my Granda'. I lived a life sheltered from it all. I never got involved in anything at all. And then when I met John it was a friggin shock—he was republican mad and when he used t' come in here I used t' say "don't be talkin' about them things in front of my Granny" and he never really did, like.'

I commented on how different her own background was from Big John's. His father was an IRA prisoner and John had spent his youth rioting against the British Army. I wondered what Sharon had made of him when she first met him when they were teenagers. John had mentioned that one of the reasons why he didn't get involved in 'the movement' was Sharon and I was interested about this.

'All I knew was John was like a hard man kind of thing, nobody would tackle him, but I didn't know much about his background. When I started going out with him, after a couple of months I was at his place and he started telling me about his daddy being in jail and I thought, "oh God, why am I getting mixed up in all of this?" Some of his relatives were republican mad, but what I had said t' John then was that "as long as you don't get involved then I don't care 'cause I don't want to be burying you". So I told him if he joined the IRA then that would be it. At the end of the day, the way I looked at it was I wasn't going to live my life with John being in prison and me on the outside. I just couldn't do it. I couldn't.'

Yet, while Sharon felt that, unlike John, she had been sheltered from the Troubles and had never really experienced the conflict first hand at all, it simply was not true. One of her childhood memories is of the 1974 Ulster Workers' strike when loyalists shut down the entire province for nearly two weeks in their campaign to overthrow the moderate power-sharing Sunningdale executive. Towards the end of the strike loyalist electricity workers succeeded in cutting power supplies to parts of Belfast.

'I remember us cooking potatoes on the fire because there was no electric. There was loads of times when the lights were turned out and there was candles on, but when you were a child it was all a bit of a novelty. You didn't really know what was going on.'

Another time as a child, a passing RUC man in a jeep had fired a plastic bullet at Sharon while she was inside The Pop. She could have easily been killed. Yet unlike John, Sharon had not gone through the West Belfast childhood ritual of rioting against the security forces.

'Up here it was pretty quiet, the only places where that went on was the top of the road and down on the Falls Road itself. Gran and Granda' never let me out if there was any rioting anyway. Once mammy was killed,

Granny was really over-protective of me. I wasn't allowed a bike, I wasn't allowed out after nine o'clock at night, I had t' be in the house. All my friends would go to the youth club and I'd have t' come home.'

Hardly surprising that a woman who had a daughter gunned down in the street would become a little over-protective of the grandchild in her care. Still, the Troubles always found a way of creeping in to your life.

'There was one guy that we went t' school with and he was like really high up in it. He must have been about seventeen, he was a wee bit older than me, and I was at secondary school then. He used to come in t' the youth club because there was always a couple of joyriders and glue-sniffers in there. "Anti-social behaviour" the IRA called it. You knew it was him because he was really tiny and he'd come in to the youth club t' do beatings. He'd have a balaclava on and one night they came in and picked out these joyriders, there was about eight of them, and they lined them all up, turned the lights on and they beat them with hurleys there and then. We were all like "oh my God!" It was terrible. Awful.'

Even when Sharon got a job at a shop in the city where the majority of workers were Protestant, the Troubles followed her. After the signing of the Anglo-Irish Agreement in 1985, loyalists attempted to stage a repeat of their 1974 resistance to the British imposition of moderate reforms.

'I worked beside the City Hall and we knew the loyalists were putting on a big protest so we were expecting trouble and they boarded the whole store up. The store was t' be closed for the hour or so when the protest was on and then reopen later in the day. What happened was we closed the store and I was downstairs doing the banking and the march came by and they all had their banners and Union Jacks and everything. They started shouting in through the windows at the staff because obviously we weren't out joining in and they assumed we were Catholics. So I was downstairs and I heard all this commotion and next thing the windows got put in and all I saw was men with masks pouring in over this hoarding. I'll never forget it, it was terrifying. They had big sticks and I think that if they had've got their hands on any of us we would have got the beating of our lives. There was about ten of us in there that day and we had to run for our lives and escape through the fire exit. We locked the door behind us and climbed out. We could hear them at the door screaming and trying to kick it in. It was terrifying.'

She laughed when I remarked that most people outside of Northern Ireland would hardly consider this as having been 'sheltered' from the Troubles.

'It's sad to say but people think it's normal. Anything could happen here. You could be out one night and go out to the wrong place at the wrong time and never get home. You know what I mean? You stumble in to the wrong area or meet the wrong person and that's it.'

Indeed, it was precisely what had happened to Jean. So how did Sharon feel when the first IRA ceasefire was called in August 1994 and it seemed like there might finally be a small opportunity for peace?

'I cried. It was just like, I don't know, like someone had said to you that it's ended, that's it, there'll be no more shooting and you can go where you want and do what you want. I thought I don't have t' worry about my boys growing up and getting involved in all this any more. And then a year or so later when the ceasefire ended it was awful, it was like going back t' square one again. I thought it would be worse than ever.'

'So do you think there'll be real peace in Ireland in your lifetime?'

'No.'

'A united Ireland in your lifetime?'

'No.'

'So what's going to happen?'

'I think it will just continue on the way it is.'

The slaying of Billy Wright and the recent killings had extinguished the last of Sharon's hopes for a peaceful future. I was rapidly running out of tape and it was almost time to pick the boys up from school so I shifted the conversation back to the topic of Jean. I had a few final questions I wanted to ask. The first was about Siobhán O'Neill, the woman from the taxi. I wanted to know how much Sharon remembered about her coming to the house after Jean was killed.

'She used t' come all the time after mammy died. I remember her coming for like birthdays, Christmas, and each year she would come up and she used t' give me a wee card and she would stay maybe an hour or something. She was in and out of the hospital because she had that nervous breakdown and she was never mentally stable after that. She was in and out of the psychiatric hospital and I remember she used to have this short short hair because she was getting shock treatment and all that. She used to frighten me when I was young. She used t' come up and see me and all she done was bring me presents, or come up and see Granny and say hello, but I remember every time she was here she used to cry. She used to cry all the time.'

Eventually the family lost contact with Siobhán, until years later Sharon received a phone call from her out of the blue, asking if it was all right for her to drop by for a little visit.

'So she come up and I was a bit nervous about seeing her again because I didn't know what way she would react. In the end she just sat and had tea and it was fine. I told her I'd phone her some time before Christmas but I didn't and of course I phoned her for you the other day and her number's not the same. But that was the ruination of her life what happened. That was the end of it for her.'

I then asked the most obvious question of all, what sort of a terrible void had Jean's death left in her own life?

'Even though Granny was here you know, it's just not the same. I mean when I was having Conor and Daniel there was nobody there. Granny had so many children that all the weddings and births and such just kind of went by. It would have been different if she would have been here. Just the wee things go through your head. My Granny goes "oh, you're like your mother" and you never know whether you are like her or if you do the same things she used to do. You just don't know. I always felt I couldn't really go to my Granny because I always thought she had enough worries and enough heartbreak and I never wanted to burden her with any more. It was hard enough for her looking after me so that's why I never gave her any trouble as a child.'

'So how do you think your mother is remembered by the family?'

'I think we've all got very fond memories of her and very sweet memories, because she was a very good person. I think every year when her anniversary comes around it just breaks everybody's heart. She's dead for twenty-six years now and there is never a year they forget about her. I don't think they can ever express how they felt when she died. Ever. I really don't. And although I didn't know her that much, I just miss her. There is a part of you that is just missing. I used to go to her grave whenever I was down or lonely and I would sit down there. I wouldn't have said anything, I just would have sat there and thought things to myself. There's just a part of you that's missing.'

13

The Reluctant Hunger Striker

'Armoured cars and tanks and guns
Came to take away our sons
But every man will stand behind
The men behind the wire.'

Song by P. McGuigan, Long Kesh, 1970s

That afternoon, the 9th of January, I walked up to the Glen Road to collect the boys from school. The school in question, St Teresa's, was in fact the very same one that both Sharon and Jean had attended as children and was just off the street Jean had been shot dead on. In fact, on the night she was killed, Jean and Sean McCann would have driven past St Teresa's as they left the Glenowen Inn. St Teresa's was also the school that had been used as a refugee centre during the violence of 1969 when burnt-out Catholic families slept there before they were rehoused in Andersonstown and elsewhere. Anyway, Sharon and I met wee Dan and Conor as they made their way out of class and we held hands as the lollipop man (as they call him in Belfast) stopped the traffic so children and adults alike could cross the road. As we walked back down past The Pop and onto the estate the Brits were everywhere. In fact, two armoured jeeps full of soldiers were parked in front of Tardree Park itself, pointing rifles at local residents. I gave them the best evil eye I had in my head as Sharon and I walked the boys back into the house.

After a cup of tea and a few games with the boys, I phoned my Aunt Pat's house out in Twinbrook to see if my Uncle Frankie would be there that evening. He would be indeed, she said, and I asked if it would be alright if I dropped around so as to have a little chat with him.

'Yer not bringing that wee recording machine with ye again are ye Simon?' asked Aunt Pat.

'I am indeed', says I.

'Ahhh Jaysus, it's turning into the friggin Oprah Winfrey show out here, so it is.'

When I arrived Uncle Frankie was in his work overalls and he threatened to break a beer bottle over my skull if I didn't get out of this awful polite habit of calling him Uncle all the time.

'Call me Frankie for fuck's sake, you're making me feel even older than I am.'

We sat in the living room, drinking beer and talking as Aunt Pat was sewing a new boot-scooting outfit for a young girl on the estate. We were only interrupted by the constant need to travel to the fridge and bring back more beer. As the evening wore on I was glad the tape was rolling because I knew I had skin full of drink and I was worried that there would be very little I would remember by the time I got home. Like the fact that Uncle Frank had been a steward at Bobby Sands' funeral. Like the stories about Uncle Frank visiting his younger brother in Long Kesh when he was on the dirty protest. And like all the little details that he seemed to remember about Jean and her death.

■ ■ ■ ■

'I was just going on sixteen when it all blew up in 1969. I was going along on the bus one day and a fella says t' me "what about all the trouble and all this crap what's going on". Here's me, "yeah, I'd love t' get back at 'em for it". About three or four days after that there was a fella at the door, "do ye wanna come with me?" "OK, no problem", and away we went. So then I was in the *Fianna*, ye know, and then when you got a wee bit older, say twenty, you were supposed t' progress to the IRA.'

Uncle Frankie's family lived in the West Belfast area of Turf Lodge and he was trained by older men in the IRA.

'They taught ye how t' use weapons and you carried information and stuff from one person t' the next. They'd give you arms training and it was all part of the republican movement at the time. That's the way it started anyway and I just got into it a bit.'

Frankie's father was very republican minded himself and as soon as Frankie entered the *Fianna* he went and told his Da' that he had joined up.

'As long as I wasn't in the Sticks, the Official IRA, he was chuffed. See the *Fianna* wasn't split, unlike the army, between Provisionals and Officials. It was just the one at the time. The *Fianna* was neutral, it was just the breeding ground. But me, I didn't think what the Officials were doing was hard enough, I preferred t' go the more militant way at the time.'

It was while Frank was in the *Fianna* that he met Aunt Pat, Jean's sister.

'I never met our Pat until I was eighteen and that's when I met Jean too and she made it known that she was very republican minded as well. She knew some of them'uns that I knew 'n' all.'

Frank would often talk to Jean when he visited Pat at Tardree Park and he got quite close to her. However, in August 1971 the British government introduced internment without trial in an attempt to smash the republican movement. West Belfast lost many young men to the internment camp out at Long Kesh.

'It was about the 2nd of December 1971 when the soldiers came and raided the house at about two o'clock in the morning. So they came and they didn't know which one of us t' take, me or me Da' because we are both called Frank, so they took the both of us just t' be sure. They dragged me out by my hair and fucked me down the stairs t' the jeep. So I says, "Ma I'll see you later" and yer man says, "I wouldn't be so sure of that", and then we were away.'

At the time Frank thought he was just being taken in for questioning.

'They just lifted you, came in, broke the door down, straight up the stairs and took ye out. That was it. As I said it was December and it was freezing and the ice was on the ground. All I had on me that night was a pair of jeans, pair of slippers for my feet and a T-shirt. So they brought us over t' the interrogation centre. They separated us and interrogated me for about six hours. Then they took us over to Girdwood barracks.'

The interrogation techniques used against internees in 1971 at Girdwood, Hollywood and Palace barracks were so brutal that the British government was later compelled to hold an official inquiry into whether it actually constituted legalised torture. While the initial Compton Report exonerated the security forces, further public outrage necessitated a second official inquiry. The resulting report by Lord Parker found that the methods used were illegal under British law. Finally, in 1978 both the European Court of Human Rights and Amnesty International condemned the techniques which had been used against internees in 1971, with the European Court arguing that it 'constituted a practice of inhuman and degrading treatment'. At the time these torture techniques had been euphemistically referred to as 'deep interrogation' by the security forces.[1]

'At Girdwood they interrogated me again and then they took you out and put ye in these cubicles. Tiny wee things. Did ye ever see them tiles with the holes in them, all holes, well that was all around you and ye couldn't look anywhere but straight ahead. If ye looked anywhere else you got a dig in the back of the head. I had a terrible habit of looking around and I just kept getting a dig in the back of the head, or a dig in the side of the head. Next thing I know, I started seeing these things coming out of the wall.'

The combined practices of sleep and sensory deprivation, extensive interrogation and physical brutality took a toll on internees, often causing them to hallucinate. Add to this the absence of anything to eat and it is understandable why Uncle Frankie started to see things.

'I'd been picked up about 2am Saturday morning and this was now Sunday night. I hadn't slept at all and I didn't eat anything for about two days. I couldn't eat the food because some of the screws had been pissing and spitting on it—it was stinking. So, I started t' hallucinate. I didn't see dragons or anything like that, but what I actually seen was, well, if you can imagine a university with pillars going up and an arch, and it was all outside and there were people walking up and down and I saw my Ma and Da' walking by. I swear t' God it was doing my head in. I kept turning away from it so I couldn't see it anymore and then I'd get some terrible smacks in the head.'

That night Frankie was taken back out of the cubicle and put in to another interrogation room.

'They brought us in t' interrogate us. They put me down and I was only eighteen years old at the time remember. We were going from being eighteen into hardcore fighting and hardcore interrogation and you weren't expecting this. We were told in the *Fianna* what t' do; stare straight ahead when you are being interrogated, pick a spot on the wall and concentrate on it and just deny everything—but it doesn't work out like that. So I never said anything t' them because I couldn't anyway—I was away by that stage, my head was away. I'd been up too long.'

In the interrogation room he was placed in a chair with a blow heater behind him that was turned up so high that within no time it started burning the backs of his legs through his jeans. A number of police assembled in front of him and then a hail of questions started about who was this person and did he know about so and so.

'I denied everything. I even denied knowing my own Da'. They said his name t' me and I go "I don't know him". I denied knowing my own Da'! And then they started saying "your Ma's getting screwed by so and so and he's in the IRA" and all this shite and that just made me angry. Even though I didn't know anything I wouldn't say anything because by then they were starting t' fucking piss me off.'

He eventually asked to go to the toilet and a RUC man led him out to a corridor with three toilets in it.

'He put me into the toilet and he says "there ye go". Coming back out of the toilet there was no sign of the cop. Couldn't see him. I thought, "where is this bastard?" So I'm coming down the stairs and I'm looking all around and I was going t' walk away this different way and there he was standing there with a gun out waiting for me t' take a run so he could shoot me. Just set me up t' see what I would do, like. So I just stood there and I froze.'

He was taken back to the interview room where the heater and the questions raged on without any progress for several more hours. Eventually the interview was terminated.

'I was starving by this time, I hadn't eaten anything in days. So they pulled us out, three of us, and put us into a Saracen and brought us up t' the Crumlin Road and put us into a cell. Me and my Da' in together. And that was the first night I had a bit of a sleep.'

During the night he started to get awful stomach cramps and was ravaged by hunger. His primary focus was now on getting through the cold night in Crumlin Road in order to make it to breakfast the next morning.

'So they took us down the next morning and by this time I was really starving. They brought us down to C-wing, that was where all the internees were. That was actually the death wing, C-wing, and you could go down to the death cell and look in and see where the noose was. But anyway, I went down there and I was starving, I could've ate a horse, and

I arrived as the republican prisoners were having a meeting and they called a hunger strike.'

This caused me to burst out laughing.

'I swear t' God! They called a hunger strike as soon as I got on the wing because the food was crap. Yer man says "so, does everyone vote for a hunger strike?" People were putting their hands up all around. Here's me, "ahhhhh alright" and I put my hand up too. Honest t' fuck, it was another two days we were on hunger strike and at the end of it they agreed t' upgrade the food. So what they done was they couldn't get the kitchens open at that time so they sent out for 150 suppers from some chipper and they brought them in. I swear t' God! And that was my first bite in five days.'

A riot broke out at Crumlin Road while Uncle Frankie was in the place. There were also republican singalongs and plenty of education.

'I just said t' myself, it's like a picture in here. One or two big guys would start singing republican songs and then they'd all come out and all start singing, fuck it was great. And then there was education as well, learning t' set timers, fuses and how t' strip a weapon. They had replicas so they could show you.'

On the 22nd of December, while still at Crumlin Road and three weeks after he had been pulled from his bed in the dead of night, Frankie was served with his internment papers.

'My Da' got my internment papers for me. I just broke down. And then when my Da' got his I just started cheering. I thought thank God, he's coming with me anyway. I spent Christmas in the Crumlin Road. It was a very sad time for me that Christmas. It was the first time I was ever out of the house on Christmas. It fucking broke my heart that, near killed me, swear t' God. Eighteen years of age and I was fucking devastated. About a week after Christmas we got shifted and they took us out by helicopter. It was like something out of the Second World War—all the Brits lined up against the chopper and they dragged you running and threw ye into it. And then the thing took off and landed at Long Kesh and they were all waiting for ye, with guns pointed down at ye, waiting for you t' make a break.'

'So how long were you in the Kesh?'

'Seven months, that was all but it was long enough for me. See the thing was, when you were interned everyone thought it was for life. So when I was eighteen I thought this was it, my life was over. I was never gonna get out. When I was in the courtyard at the Crumlin Road I knew a fella that was inside that had got ten years and he shouted down t' me, "Hey Frankie, I've ten years but at least I know when I'm getting out", and he started laughing.'

At Long Kesh interned IRA members were allowed their own clothes, controlled their own huts, and had free association. Frankie was in Cage Six and then Cage Eight. Ironically, Uncle Frank had actually worked as an apprentice painter on the massive Long Kesh site during the building of the internment camp.

'So I knew, outside of the compounds, how t' get out of the place. I knew every bit outside of the army barracks 'cause I'd worked on it. So for a week I was shoved up on one of the roofs for t' get my bearings. It took me three or four days t' figure out where I was. So I come down and I had t' draw the whole compound and where I thought the way out was. A few weeks later a fella escaped dressed as a priest more or less based on the information I had given.'

Eventually Frank found out he himself was to be legally released from Long Kesh.

'My Da' got out two or three months before me. So I says t' one fella, Tommy, "Hey, I'll never believe anyone that I'm going out unless you come up t' me and hit me a big dig in the ribs and then I'll believe that's me heading out of here". "Alright," he says, "that's a deal." Then one day they come in and says t' me "Frankie, yer wanted at the gate". Here's me, "Ahh sure, fuck off". He says, "I'm telling ye now, go out and see". It was a half an' hour before I even went up t' the gate. So I go up t' the gate and here's me, "what do ye want?" Screw says, "yer getting out, get ready in half an' hour". Here's me, "ahh right, I'm away. Cheerio". I didn't even believe the screw! And then yer man comes up t' me as I'm sitting there getting my fags out and he hit me one big dig in the right side of the ribs. He says, "Frankie yer getting out, it's for definite". I said, "That's fucking great Tommy, thanks very much". Jaysus Christ, he near crippled me but I knew then that I was definitely getting out.'

No one outside knew Uncle Frankie was being released so there was no one there to meet him as he left the Long Kesh internment camp.

'I just walked through the gate and that was it and I went home and someone run out of the house and kissed me. Next thing I knew I ended up at Pat's house at Tardree Park. And she couldn't believe it, because they were always saying t' her, "Hey, Frankie wants you at the door", just t' tease her like. Next thing I really was there. It was that night after we'd all been sitting there and here's me, "Right, I'm going on home now", and when I come out Jean and yer man Sean pulled up. Here's Pat, "There's our Jean" and here's me, "I'm gonna go over". So I seen her looking at me through the car and I walked over—"Hi Jean, how you doing? Alright?" Fuck! She went berserk, screaming all over the place, "You're out, you're out, you're out! Frankie, you're out!" She started hugging me and she brought me back into the house again. Fuck what a night that was. It was great, she went ballistic when I got out. She was over the moon.'

Yet, while Frankie had lost none of his republican enthusiasm, he did not get 'reinvolved' after his release from Long Kesh.

'I don't know Simon, I just thought no, no I'm not going t' do it anymore. I think it all happened to me too young, too soon.'

He had walked out the gates of the Kesh about a month before Jean was killed and I wanted to know a little more about what he thought she was like.

'Jean? One of the nicest people you'd ever meet. She would have given her life for t' help you. She wrote t' me in the Kesh, you know. She came up t' visit me a few times 'n' all too.'

Uncle Frankie was in the house at Tardree Park on the night Jean was killed.

'I remember carrying on with Jean that night before she went out. She didn't want t' go out and she was saying "I'm too tired, I'm too tired" and he [Sean] was saying "Come on Jean, let's go for a drink."'

'So did you know Sean McCann as well?'

'Aye. I liked Sean. I thought Sean was a nice fella. I actually think t' this day that they blamed the wrong guy. The whole family blamed Jean's death on him. But being an outsider, I could see that the guy was fucking devastated and he just doesn't seem t' be the same since. He was always a happy fella. When I first started going with Pat, me and Jean and him always used t' go out. I mean, Jean was twenty-four then, I was only eighteen and Pat was only fifteen or sixteen—she lied and told me she was seventeen the wee bitch—but we were always going out drinking together.'

Uncle Frank was certainly having none of this talk that Sean only knew her from the brewery.

'When I started going with Pat I thought the arrangement was that they hadn't got a house but that Jean was married t' him. They were very serious and he really loved Sharon like.'

Frank and Pat were watching *The Avengers* on television in the house at Tardree Park on the evening of 8 June 1972. Later that night they heard the shooting up on the Glen Road.

'We heard the shooting and I says "looks like the Ra's at it again shooting at the Army". I went over home that night because I had t' go t' work in the morning. I got up that next morning and someone comes over and says t' me, "Jean's dead" and that was it, I never went t' work. I went straight over to the house and it was fucking terrible. Sharon was still in bed, she was only six. She hadn't a clue when she got up and they told her.'

He told me that later that day he went with Jean's brother Gerry and with her father to the British Army barracks in Lisburn to 'identify the body, or something'.

'I stood outside the barracks and they went in. They were very quiet when they come back out. Mr Campbell [Jean's father] never cried. Mr Campbell couldn't cry. Naturally Gerry was crying. We were all very fond of Jean. Jean would have done anything for you, like.'

Apparently there had recently been a pop song that was a big hit on the radio that Sharon had taken to singing all the time—it was called 'Where's your mamma gone?' After Jean's death, Uncle Frank remembers that she never sang the song again. Another song that instantly became taboo in the house at Tardree Park was 'Danny Boy'.

'Jean always tried t' sing "Danny Boy. It was her party piece and she made a bollocks of it every time, she couldn't sing it, she was a terrible singer. I don't know about now, but the Ma [Gran] wouldn't allow it t' be sung in the house after she died either.'

Uncle Frankie attended Jean's funeral and he had much to reveal.

'The funeral was terrible. Shocking. And that's when a couple of fellas come up t' me and told me that it was an accident and sorry it happened. It wasn't the ones that done it. They just said it was a bad accident that happened. It was the car. They thought it was British Army intelligence going up and down the Glen.'

This was the closest thing I had to confirmation that the IRA had killed Jean and of the reason why. Given that it was said to a man who had just been released from the IRA compound at Long Kesh, I wanted to pursue it.

'So were these fellas you mentioned that came up to you at the funeral in the IRA?'

'A few come up t' me and then another fella come up. Let's just say 'Ra men were talking directly to these guys and these guys told me that it was all a bad accident and they apologised. But I don't know if they went up to the Da' or not for to say sorry because the Da' was a very deep man in many ways. Very very deep.'

'So is there anything else you know about the actual shooting?'

'Nothing more than that. It was the car, the 'Ra thought it was undercover Army. There was also a couple of stories that he [Sean McCann] heard a noise, like a bang, and that's why he pulled the car up and he went out t' see 'cause he thought it was a puncture. And when he got out they opened up. That's what I was told, like. I know they opened up with a Thompson and if someone lets go with one of them things and you get it in the head, then there's nothing left of yer head. Jean's was a closed coffin. That's all I know.'

■ ■ ■ ■

And with that we ended. We drank some more beers and I caught a cab back to Tardree Park. On the way we passed an Army foot patrol in the darkness of night, but all I could think about was Jean, the Glen Road and what I had just heard. What those men had said to Uncle Frankie was about as close as you ever got to official confirmation in the shadowy world of the Troubles during 1972. It was probably much more than the RUC ever got.

On the way out the door in Twinbrook there had been much drunken backslapping between Uncle Frankie and I and he had run upstairs and brought me back down an envelope from a letter Pat had sent him while he was in Long Kesh. Sitting in the taxi, I was running the smooth envelope paper, weathered with age and over-reading, between my fingertips as we approached Andersonstown. It had been posted in early 1972, right before Frankie was released from Long Kesh and right before Jean was killed. It was addressed to him at:

Hut 7,
Cage 8,
Concentration Camp,
Long Kesh.

The 'concentration' bit had been crossed out by the British authorities and I had to laugh at the audacity of a teenage Aunt Pat, who claimed she wasn't a republican, writing such a thing on an envelope. I'm sure her rebel sister, Jean, would have been proud of her.

14

Baile Átha Cliath

'It is always winter in Dublin.'

Brendan Behan

The next morning I was back on the road. John and Sharon had planned to spend a weekend in Dublin visiting friends and despite my protests that they should spend a dirty weekend away together, they insisted on me joining them. 'Only dirty weekend I'm likely t' be having is if Sharon pushes me over in a bog', said John. And with that we packed up the car and were away.

We partook of pancakes at McDonalds in Lisburn, only a few miles from where Ciarán and Beefy were waking up in Long Kesh, and then made our way down towards the artificial border that separates the Republic of Ireland from Northern Ireland. I had come prepared, bringing my 1953 *Illustrated Guide to the Counties of Ireland*, but I was afraid John and Sharon might not enjoy its peculiar parlance and penchant for bizarre observation as much as I, so I kept myself to myself in the backseat. As we passed through the hills outside Newry, which naturally separate Ulster from the lands to its south, I couldn't help but note that Newry had for this reason commonly been used as a military fort for centuries. And so it was today, the monstrous British Army base erected on top of the hills outside Newry looking every inch like the intimidating fortress it is intended to be.

From Newry we drove over the border into what Gran still calls the 'Irish Free State' and passed through the quaint town of Drogheda, home of Saint Oliver Plunkett's shrunken decapitated head. As always, the *Illustrated Guide* had all the answers. Some form of settlement seems to have existed at Drogheda since at least about 911 when Vikings established a fort on the site of the current town. Along with Dublin and Wexford, which also blossomed under the influence of the Norsemen, Drogheda was one of the great Viking trading towns of Ireland by the end of the tenth century. I was contemplating all of this when John suddenly spoke from the front seat.

'Wha' ye reading there Einstein?'

'About the Vikings and how they established Drogheda.'

'Ach aye', said John hardly bothering to look at the road as we accelerated over the famous River Boyne, 'fucking tourists, they couldn't hack the rain so they built a town for t' keep the damp off a 'em.'

Notwithstanding John's analysis of the antipathy of the local Viking population towards inclement weather, 1953's *Illustrated Guide* had much to tell me about this settlement.

During the fifteenth and sixteenth centuries Drogheda continued to prosper. The corporation was granted rights to coin its own money and permission to constitute a university with privileges similar to those of Oxford. On occasion meetings of Parliament were held, notably in 1494 when a dominated assembly enacted Poyning's Law, decreeing that no future law passed by the Irish Parliament would be valid unless ratified by the English Privy Council.[1]

However, it is not for its coinage, its Oxford-like privileges in the fifteenth century, or even for its submission to English rule via 'Poyning's Law' that Drogheda is best known. Drogheda is infamously remembered for the massacre of 1649 when Oliver Cromwell seized the town in the name of the English Parliament and promptly slaughtered as many of its inhabitants as he could get his hands on. Cromwell had arrived in Ireland with an army of 20,000 men in August 1649 during the English Civil War. He came to settle accounts with royalists who remained in control of whole swathes of the Irish countryside, but also saw the military venture as a fine opportunity to free Ireland from what he referred to as 'papist barbarism'. In the words of one contemporary, 'he passed like lightning through the land' promising to send any Irishman who opposed him 'to hell or Connacht'. At Drogheda, where the local defences were under the control of a royalist English Catholic by the name of Sir Arthur Aston, Cromwell fought his way into the town with cannons and drove both the royalist soldiers and the local Irish residents before him. In the words of historian Robert Kee:

> Attacking with sword in hand, he and his men drove the defenders back to a high tower known as Millmount. Trapped there, the commander and his officers surrendered, but were immediately put to the sword, though that is a euphemism where Sir Arthur Aston was concerned, for he was beaten to death with his own wooden leg.[2]

Not satiated, Cromwell ordered Drogheda be put to the flame. As many of the town's inhabitants as could be found—including women and children—were cut down. In the words of nineteenth century historian, Mary Frances Cusack, 'Neither youth nor beauty was spared'. With the town in ruins, Cromwell then wrote home about his military adventure:

> It hath pleased God to bless our endeavours at Drogheda. After battery we stormed it. The enemy were about 3,000 strong in the town. They made a stout resistance. I believe we put to the sword the whole number of defendants. I do not think thirty of the whole number escaped with their lives. Those that did are in safe custody for the Barbadoes. This hath been a marvellous great mercy.[3]

Which sort of brings us back to Saint Oliver Plunkett's head. This Olly, unlike the aforementioned Olly, was a man of the Catholic faith living under Protestant English rule. After becoming the Primate of All Ireland in 1670, it is alleged that he confirmed close to 49,000 Catholics in the faith. Now, I don't have to tell you that that's a lot of wafers and wine. This work did not go unnoticed by the government which feared his influence over the local Catholic population. In 1679 Plunkett was arrested for alleged involvement in a 'Popish Plot' and he was hanged for treason on 1 July 1681. His decapitated head was returned to his friends for safekeeping and after travelling to monasteries in Germany and England the relic ended up in Drogheda where it has resided ever since. In 1975 Oliver Plunkett was canonised, joining the pantheon of Irish saints, and his spirit ascended to the holiest corner of heaven. His head stayed in Drogheda.

If you so desire, you can still view blessed St Oliver's wrinkly head in a special case in the north transept of St Peter's in Drogheda. If you are lucky, and so inclined, you can also see his left clavicle, left scapula, ninth and tenth rib, left hemi-pelvic bone and sacrum—all of which are also the property of St Peter's. I had no such desire—not being particularly partial to bones and embalmed heads, whether they be saintly or not—and was therefore pleased enough that we were now out of Drogheda and on our way to Dublin. In the front seat meanwhile, John and Sharon were still discussing the Norsemen.

'Simon, I was just saying t' John that he looks like he might have a touch of the Viking in him himself, ye know, with the blondie hair 'n' all.'

'Ach aye' says I, adopting the vernacular parlance.

Completely free of charge, John then offered Sharon and I the following insight into the ethnic composition of the Irish nation and the remarkable ability of our joint ancestors to 'absorb' the various groups of people who have invaded and settled in Ireland over the last thousand years.

'Ye know, when ye think about it, the Irish are the most mixed-up, mongrelised race of bastards ever t' walk the earth, so we are. Our ancestors bred with Vikings, Normans, Saxons, English, French, who ever. Complete whores, the lot of 'em. What we should have done when they all invaded, instead of fighting the bastards, was walk down t' the shore and yell out, "We're Irish, go on home or we'll ride ye!"'

Sharon and I laughed as we drove along the wet stretch that would carry us all the way to Dublin.

■ ■ ■ ■

We arrived in Dublin and met Sharon and John's friends, Joe and Karen, at a pub near the trendy Temple Bar district where Joe was working. We decided to split up and come back in time for Joe to finish work. Karen and Sharon went on a shopping spree while Big John and I were left to our own devices. In a bold attempt to make a day of it, we walked through the

Temple Bar down to the Liffey where I bought a new Glasgow Celtic top at a sports shop. We then crossed the bridge over to O'Connell Street where we surveyed the remaining bullet holes in the GPO building and I bought a copy of both *Socialist Worker* and *Saoirse* from the agit-prop specialists congregating on the pavement outside. While I was buying a paper off the *Socialist Worker* seller a nun was actually signing their petition in support of a trade union campaign to increase the minimum wage. As we walked back down O'Connell Street, and over the Liffey, I could see that my *compadre* had itchy feet and I had a fair idea why.

'So, Simon what're ye wanting t' do 'til we see the girls later on? Is it sightseeing you're after?'

'No, not particularly John. I've already been to Dublin several times. Why? Did you have something in mind?'

'No, no, not at all. Sharon was wanting me t' show ye 'round but I was just thinking that if it was history you were after I know a wee spot up the road that might interest ye. I remember you speaking highly of Brendan Behan before and his old favourite watering hole is just 'round the corner. We could drop by if you like—just purely for interest's sake like.'

'OK then. Away with us.'

And with that John set a cracking pace for McDaid's, almost trampling over several small children in his enthusiasm to get to the favourite drinking establishment of my favourite Irish author.

McDaid's, off Grafton Street, is one of the million or so pubs in Ireland that can claim to have had the corpulent personality of Brendan Behan within the confines of its four walls. Personally, I had a considerable soft spot for Behan, considering him one of the finest raconteurs ever produced by Ireland. A former house-painter, socialist and IRA prisoner, he was a man of rare distinction. He was also one of the nation's finest and most tragic drunks, drowning and choking his extraordinary talent in Guinness and cigarette smoke—dead before middle age. But if I was within McDaid's to soak up some Behan, John was there purely for the suds, a pint of which quickly lubricated his throat.

'Ahhhhhh, thank fuck for that. I had quite a thirst on there. Not a bad pint either, creamy.'

Given that we were in one of Breandán Ó Beacháin's favourite haunts I was reminded of a little poem by Flann O'Brien which I first read in a book of Behan's. It was Behan who first introduced me to the Irish language and I must say I've enjoyed making its acquaintance although we are not as good a friends as I would like us to be. Anyway, I remember one verse of this particular poem; it is in *Béarla*, 'gibberish', meaning English, so I'll have no trouble repeating it:

> When health is bad and your heart feels strange
> And your face is pale and wan,
> When doctors say that you need a change
> A pint of plain is your only man.[4]

And with that we settled in for the rest of the afternoon.

That evening Sharon, Big John and I had dinner with Karen and Joe and then continued the process of liquidation at a pub called 'The Hairy Lemon' where one of my favourite scenes from the film *The Commitments* was shot—the one where the Da whacks his head while drinking a pint in a snug. However, through the night I kept looking at Sharon and thinking about Sean McCann—about how his life had been wrecked by Jean's death. And what about denying he even knew her: what was the story with that? There was also the matter of the MRF and the IRA. A solid picture was definitely forming. Uncle Frankie mentioned that he and Uncle Gerry (Jean's brother) and Old Billy (Jean's father) had gone out to the barracks at Lisburn to identify the body. I wondered if I could talk to Uncle Gerry about this.

Just then Big John gave me a dig in the arm.

'Right, Einstein, stop contemplating yer friggin belly button and get that pint into ye. We're away t' another pub after this one, so drink up.'

And with that, the night was upon us.

■ ■ ■ ■

I awoke the next morning at about eleven. John and I were supposed to share a bed but I was alone so I assumed John must have eventually passed out on the couch downstairs. Outside the wind was rattling the shutters but I remained shielded from the harshness of the day. I lay on the bed drifting in and out of sleep and waiting until I heard stirrings elsewhere in the house. After a while I decided to do some reading. Having forgotten to bring a book, I was confined to 1953's *Illustrated Guide to the Counties of Ireland* which was fine with me, as I considered the tome to be an exceptional piece of work anyway. All was revealed.

> Dublin is a city steeped in history, tragic and glorious, with haunting memories of great patriots, statesmen, scientists and scholars. Its architecture combines the beauty of more leisured centuries with modern progressiveness. Few other cities provide such a variety of scene and enjoyment.

Dublin only became a significant Irish centre after the year 840, which is when the Vikings arrived; an event that resulted in the invaders and the locals spending the next two centuries fighting over the small fortress town. When the Irish finally defeated the Norsemen at the battle of Clontarf in 1014, Dublin spent at least 150 years free from violent foreign interlopers until the English (actually, the Normans) turned up after 1169. And the rest, as they say, is history. Suffice to say that the English were never completely victorious and the Irish were never entirely broken as an independent people. Which brings us finally to that fateful Easter Monday in 1916 when rebels seized the Dublin GPO and, as they were captured and executed, their deaths caused W.B. Yeats to write that 'a terrible beauty is born'. A guerrilla war, a civil war and a treaty later, the southern twenty-six counties of Ireland got their independence. Dublin became the capital of a free Ireland—except of course, for the north-eastern six counties which were partitioned off and maintained under British rule.

I was still reading about hunting and golfing opportunities in the Dublin environs when John stuck his nose through the door. We whispered conspiratorially.

'Ye awake in there Simon?'

'Aye.'

'I just read on the teletext that another Catholic doorman was shot dead in Belfast last night. I didn't recognise the name. Poor bastard.'

'Has anyone claimed it?'

'No. Though I bet the UFF done it, but the LVF claim it.'

'No claim, no blame.'

'Aye. Arseholes.'

I nodded.

'Simon, I'm gonna cook a fry-up. Shite, shower and come down.'

■ ■ ■ ■

John was right, the LVF claimed the killing but everyone was sure it was the UFF (officially still on ceasefire) which actually did the shooting. The killing took place just after midnight as we had been making our way around the pubs and clubs of Dublin. The Belfast nightclub where the shooting occurred was owned by the sister-in-law of the loyalist Progressive Unionist Party (PUP) leader, David Ervine. Most of the door staff were Catholics and the dead man was married to Gerry Adams' niece. Therefore I'm sure the loyalist squad that carried out the attack thought, all things considered, that they had done a wonderful job. What a bloody horrible mess.

Terry Enright was a twenty-eight year old cross-community worker and a part-time doorman at the Space nightclub in the Belfast city centre. He was from the Whiterock Road area of West Belfast and worked full-time as an 'outdoor pursuits instructor' with the Upper Springfield Development Trust. He was also a member of the Gort na Mona GAA club in West Belfast and coached a girl's camogie team. The young father had two daughters of his own, Aoife and Ciara, aged five and two. Terry Enright had taken on a job as a doorman at the Space nightclub for extra money over the Christmas period so he and his wife could renovate their home.

Just after midnight on the morning of Sunday 11 January a dirty red stolen Ford Sierra pulled up outside the Space nightclub in Talbot Street where Terry was working. Inside the car, according to witnesses and the *Irish News*, were 'two gunmen wearing monkey caps' and with camouflage paint on their faces. One of the men fired from inside the car, while another fired over the roof. Terry Enright tried to run for cover. He was hit in the chest and stomach and died in hospital soon after. As the shock of his death set in, on Sunday afternoon acquaintances of Enright began leaving floral tributes outside the Space nightclub and several of his friends attempted to wash his blood off the cold pavement where he had been slain. Meanwhile the Loyalist Volunteer Force released a statement to an Ulster television station:

> An active service unit of the Belfast brigade of the LVF carried out last night's attack in Belfast in which a leading IRA man was shot dead. This is in direct response for the murder of Billy Wright two weeks ago.

A young husband, and popular because of his cross-community work, Enright's death resulted in a record number of death notices (over 150) being published in the *Irish News*. His widow and two young daughters each published separate notices:

> **Enright** Terry (Murdered)— January 11, 1998. Well Terry this was going to be our best year yet… My heart is broke and the thought of never seeing you again is too painful to deal with… I've tried to tell myself this isn't happening, it's all a bad dream and you're going to be there and put your big arms around me and tell me it's all going to be all right… From your heartbroken wife Deirdre. XXX

Two year old Aoife obviously had to have her notice written for her and it was signed 'your wee Tele Tubbie Aoife'. However, it was the notice of Terry Enright's five year old daughter Ciara that really tore at one's heart.

> **Enright** Terry (Murdered)—January 11, 1998. Daddy, I loved you so much. Why did the bad boys take you away. I will never forget all our wee special times, all the stories you told me about you growing up, now you will never see me growing up, but I will make you proud of me. You'll see. You can watch over me and be my guardian angel. I love you daddy and they will never take away the five years I had with you. Love you forever, your wee Princess Ciara. XXX

The PUP's David Ervine, who had served a sentence in the 1970s for loyalist paramilitary activities, publicly condemned Enright's killers, remarking that 'A fine young man has lost his life, caused by some obscure group of head cases'. Another PUP leader and former UVF prisoner, Billy Hutchinson, who knew Enright from his cross-community work, said he was 'gutted' by the news of the killing. Meanwhile Terry Enright's widow, Deirdre, denounced the men who took the life of her beloved as 'gutless cowards'.

Terry Enright was the fourth person to be killed since I had arrived back in Belfast. First to die had been Billy Wright, and now three random Catholics/nationalists had been shot dead in retaliation—Séamus Dillon, Eddie Treanor and Terry Enright. Everyone was now speculating on how high the body count would have to go before hardline loyalists felt that King Rat's death had been adequately avenged. The peace talks at Stormont were due to resume the following day and it was yet to be seen if Mo Mowlam had really saved the day by visiting loyalist prisoners at Long Kesh prison. The peace process, which had been limping since King Rat's death, now seemed in danger of total collapse.

One of the most contentious issues in this regard was the 'forensic history' of the weapon that had killed Terry Enright. Although the LVF claimed responsibility for the Space nightclub shooting, there was much speculation that the killers were actually members of the UFF. Given that the UDA/UFF were officially on ceasefire and that their political representatives in the UDP were negotiating with all the other parties at Stormont, this was a worrying development. Indeed, one of the main reasons for Mo Mowlam's little visit to Long Kesh a few days earlier was precisely to keep the UDA/UFF prison leadership on board 'the peace train'. However, the getaway car which had been used in the Space nightclub shooting had apparently been stolen from the Lower Shankill, in an area known as an UDA/UFF stronghold.

In previous cases involving the IRA the RUC had sometimes made a point of releasing the forensic history of the weapon to the press. The idea, particularly where the weapon could be linked to a previous killing, was to undermine support for the men or women who had squeezed the trigger. And yet despite public calls by Gerry Adams and others for the RUC to release details concerning the gun that killed Terry Enright, the RUC steadfastly refused to reveal anything about it whatsoever. At best this appeared to most Catholics in West Belfast to be hypocrisy and double-standards on the part of the RUC.

Conspiracy theories abounded. Some people in West Belfast even speculated that RUC members opposed to the peace process were possibly colluding with the LVF and UFF in a campaign of terror against the Catholic community, the idea being to provoke the IRA into breaking their ceasefire. Thus, or so the argument went, the old status quo in Northern Ireland of war and 'the Troubles' would reassert itself and the jobs of the security forces would be secure. Peace had brought uncertainty to the police and 'securocrats' who had spent thirty years fighting a sub-war. Experts sometimes speculated that after 'normalisation' of the situation in Northern Ireland the size of the RUC would probably be reduced from about 13,000 members, to about 3,000 members. Clearly, some RUC men had a political and material interest in maintaining and sustaining the conflict. Why else would the RUC refuse to reveal the forensic history of the weapon when they had done so in many cases involving the IRA?

All was revealed almost a year later at the November 1998 inquest into Terry Enright's death. At the inquest a RUC Detective Inspector testified that the gun that had killed Terry Enright had actually been stolen from the home of a member of the security forces in East Belfast prior to the Space nightclub shooting. Just how or when this had happened the RUC Detective did not reveal, except to say that somehow another legally-held weapon had made its way into the hands of loyalist paramilitaries. Gerry

Adams, the uncle of Terry Enright's young widow, responded to the RUC's remarkable admission by telling journalists that:

> At the time of the killing I called for the publication of the forensic history on the weapons used. The RUC refused. Today we have discovered that one of the weapons was a licensed gun allegedly stolen from someone inside the British forces. This belated disclosure is outrageous and disgraceful.[5]

Certainly it was a source of considerable embarrassment to the RUC and shed some light on their absolute refusal to reveal the forensic history of the weapon in the day's immediately after Terry Enright's death.

■ ■ ■ ■

Back in Dublin, after a late breakfast we all got in the car and drove up in to the hills above Dublin to visit a famous drinking establishment by the name of Johnnie Fox's. According to its calling card Johnnie Fox's was established in the revolutionary year of 1798 and is 'the highest licensed premises in Ireland'. Moreover, 'the first owner of these lands was the famous Daniel O'Connell and it is here in the penal times he gave refuge to the men of 1798'. I'd have to take their word on that one. Still, 1998 was the 200th anniversary of the United Irishmen's rebellion and I genuinely wanted to visit the pub: this gave John and Joe all the excuse they needed. Sharon, however, was unconvinced and had, as they say in Ireland, taken the hump.

'Sharon love, yer wee cousin the scholar is needing t' go for the purposes of research.'

'All you've done is friggin drink since we've been in Dublin. John, we're supposed t' be having a wee holiday, and that means a holiday from the drink too.'

'Sharon love, who am I to stand in the way of university research?'

And so Big John drove us all up into the hills above Dublin to stand outside the pub in the cold waiting for it to open at 4pm. Only in Ireland would people line up in the freezing cold on the side of a hill in the middle of winter in order to get through the door of a pub and have a pint on a wet Sunday afternoon.

The pub opened at 4pm on the dot and people actually started clapping as we went through the doors. Inside we found a table near a turf fire and settled in. All the walls were adorned with pictures and trinkets. The mantelpieces had on them everything from old boots to cross-bows. Pictures varied from original nineteenth century nationalist posters to the front page of a Dublin newspaper on the day JFK was killed. Indeed I couldn't help but notice, over the rim of a warm Bailey's, that we ourselves were sitting under a brilliant portrait of James Connolly, one of my favourite figures in Irish history. On the wall on the other side of the pub was a fragment of Ireland's less glorious past, a poster calling for volunteers to join the Irish Brigade and go fight alongside Franco's fascists in the Spanish Civil War. A few pints, Baileys and other assorted beverages later we were out the warm cosy door, back down to Dublin to pick up the bags, and then the three of us were back on the road to Belfast.

The journey back to Belfast was nothing spectacular, mainly because it was dark and I was sedated, although crossing over the border into the north I did feel for the first time that much talked-about sense of mild foreboding. A lingering regret that 'Derry' or '*Doire*' would once again become 'Londonderry' on the roadsigns. A small tinge of anxiety knowing that the Celtic football top I had on would be enough to get me killed if I walked into the wrong pub or on the wrong street. There was also the fear that since King Rat's death the entire peace process was slowly and inexorably edging towards collapse. Passing under the huge British Army military outpost at Newry did not lessen this anxiety, it heightened it.

I kept returning to the issues surrounding the death of Terry Enright. Assuming it was the UFF rather than the LVF which actually shot him, what did this mean for the peace process? In the murky underground world of the Troubles, symbolism is everything. If the UFF killed Terry Enright, they were sending one hell of a signal to their enemies. Consider this. Terry Enright was a cross-community worker. He was the husband of Gerry Adams' niece. He was working at a club that was connected to loyalist leader, David Ervine. From the point of view of the men in 'monkey hats' who killed Terry Enright, they had simultaneously shot dead someone connected to both the hated Sinn Féin and the UFF's political rivals in the UVF and PUP.[6] They had successfully killed someone who had tried to breach the sectarian divide that was so important to them. And they had shot dead a Taig. All of this added up to one single message that was completely in keeping with imprisoned UFF leader Johnny Adair's 1994 comment that 'You can shove your dove!' They were obviously not going to let the death of Billy Wright pass unanswered. And although the all-party peace talks at Stormont Castle were due to resume the following day, this did not bode well.

We arrived back in Belfast at about 10pm and were greeted by Gran. Everyone was exhausted so we all retired to bed, although in my particular case I lay awake a while longer looking out the skylight and listening to the sharpened arms of the Army helicopters as they cut their way across the night sky. I was back in West Belfast and they were up there in the sky with their blinking red eye; patrolling, observing, protecting, surveying, or doing whatever it was they said they did up there. Down below me everything was silent in the house, everyone was asleep except for wee Dan who had school in the morning and whom I could hear had crawled out of bed and was secretly playing with a toy in the darkness at the foot of his bed as his brother Conor lay sleeping. I knew this because every thirty seconds or so the following message would emanate from the gravelly voice-box of a battery operated Darth Vader doll—'Never underestimate the power of the dark side of the force'—followed by Dan's muffled giggle. With that mad soundtrack below me, there was only one other thing to think about. Before she went to bed, Gran had mentioned that someone had phoned earlier asking for me. She didn't know who it was but his accent was local and he didn't want to leave a message. He said he would phone back later.

Now who could that be?

15

Whatever You Say, Say Nothing

I had been talking to the man for about five minutes about Jean's death. I can't say who introduced me to him or why he agreed to talk to me. I can't tell you anything else except that he was the one who phoned while I was in Dublin. He wouldn't speak on tape. He didn't even want me to record the date on the piece of paper I was transcribing his words on to. Every word was deliberate.

'The 'Ra were on the road that night and they seen the car go past up the Glen Road. They thought it was undercover Army because of the colour. Then they seen the same car start t' come back down the Glen Road again a wee while later. They waited for it and then they opened fire on it.'

He didn't have much more to offer about the actual ambush. After all, he hadn't actually been there. Quickly, we got to the point where I thought I might as well ask the big questions.

'So is it your belief that it was definitely the IRA who killed her?'

'Yes. Definitely.'

'And do you have any idea who the person was that actually shot Jean?'

He was apprehensive.

'Who is this for again? Where is this going?'

We'd run though this already. If he had any doubts he wouldn't have agreed to speak to me in the first place.

'This is just my research, nothing to do with police or anything. As you know, Jean was a relative and I'm working on a book about her death, like I said before. It's for the family.'

There was a pause. And then it came out. No mystery, no build up of tension.

'Well I was told it was the guy that crushed the Maguires. Remember the whole Peace People thing that started after that IRA Volunteer got shot dead and lost control of a car and killed those children?'

'Yes.'

'Him.'

I couldn't believe what I was hearing. It was only one of the most famous tragedies of the entire Troubles. I didn't know the name of the IRA Volunteer in question, but I knew I could find out easily enough. I must have looked gobsmacked because he sort of grimaced a little and leant back.

'I'm only telling you what I heard.'

A thousand and one things were whirling around my brain. I had to ask more.

'Is that 100% certain? Where did you get this information from?'

My committed interest unnerved him.

'No it's not. And I'm not going to tell you where I heard it. It's just what I was told.'

'From someone in the IRA or was it just gossip?'

He shrugged off my questions and started to get defensive.

'It was from a fella who knew a bit about it, let's just say that.'

'Who? Can I talk to him?'

'No.'

'Is this information repeatable?'

'No.'

'Do you believe it?'

There was another awful pause while countless unanswered questions ran through my head. He looked like he was deep in contemplation as he spoke.

'It could just be that blame was laid at his door because he was dead. Maybe he just got the blame for everything after that Maguire business, including that earlier shooting up on the Glen Road [Jean's]. That's probably it. This place is that small that the gossip just flies around. I'm not saying definitely that it was him and I'm not saying it definitely wasn't. I'm just answering yer question and saying what I was told, what I heard. Nothing here is 100%. About 80% is gossip and bullshit and people just pretending they know about things they know fuck all about. But it's the other 20% that's got some truth in it. Maybe. You asked me what I heard and I told ye.'

There was another pause and we sat looking at each other across the table. The skin on his face appeared to tighten as he spoke.

'Look, don't be getting me or yourself in trouble. Don't be printing rumours and don't be disrespecting the dead.'

That was it.

■ ■ ■ ■

Now what the hell was I going to do? One second he seemed to definitely state that he had inside information, the next he was admitting it might be all gossip and innuendo. Why did he want to tell me this in the first place? For the family's sake? Just to play with my mind? To make himself look good? He didn't have the history and didn't seem like the type for that, but who knows? What was his motivation in all of this? What was to be gained and lost? What was I going to do? Whatever you say, say nothing.

I now faced a real moral dilemma. Right or wrong, accurate or inaccurate, I had a name. Should I use the information or was it all just speculation? What about the dead IRA Volunteer? I didn't want to go slandering his name. What if it wasn't him, as was probably the case? The name had come so easily. Was I just lucky, or was it just that, all too easy? Should I tell Sharon and John? He said the information was unprintable, so why go to the bother of telling me?

Eventually I decided to run it past Sharon and Big John. The three of us sat down at the kitchen table as I explained the information I had been given. John thought it was backyard gossip and that I should pay it no heed. Sharon wasn't so sure. She thought I should try and get confirmation or denial from someone else. It was then that John came up with the idea of maybe talking to Peggy's son, Hector. He was originally from Tardree Park, he grew up with Jean and knew her, and he had been in the IRA in Andersonstown in the 1970s. Would he talk to me? Certainly. But would he talk to me about IRA stuff? Probably not. It was worth a try though. I should go to Peggy and see if she would call and ask him if he would drop by and have a chat with me. And I should make sure I knew more about this fella who accidentally killed the Maguire kids before I talked to anyone else about anything.

16

The Dead Volunteer

'Merlyn Rees has said that only one per cent of the Irish people would support the Republican movement, but if you people who are assembled here are only one per cent then God help England if we had two per cent.'

Maire Drumm at a republican rally, 8 August 1976

'We have only one message for these demonstrators, and for all the politicians who are frantically climbing on the peace bandwagon. Our message is this—the war goes on.'

IRA spokesman, *Belfast Newsletter*, 16 August 1976

I was standing in front of the bus depot just across from the Andersonstown RUC barracks at the fork in the Falls Road waiting for a black taxi. On the other side of the street was the Gothic entrance to Milltown Cemetery and a low bright winter's sun was piercing Jesus rays through the gravestones. If nothing else, it certainly took the edge off the morning chill. I looked over at Milltown, squinting in the light, and thought of poor Aunt Jean in that cold frozen ground. I also thought of Sharon, who never really knew her mother and would sometimes sit in that miserable graveyard when she was lonely—and all of a sudden I was sad. Sad for everything that had been lost. Sad for what never was. And sad that I knew I would never really be able to get the answers why.

As I allowed melancholia to roll over me in the cold morning sun I was finally saved by a black taxi which came to carry me in to town. On the way down the Falls we passed no less than three British Army patrols, including one near Rockville Street, the spot where I had been stopped only a few days previously. The young men with guns were, as usual, encased in their metal jeeps pointing rifles at passers-by as RUC men on foot did ID checks. Behind the soldiers was a painted mural of an IRA Volunteer on a gable wall and the words, 'You can kill the revolutionary, but never the revolution'. Perhaps the soldiers were playing some post-modernist prank on the people of West Belfast, using their jeep and rifles in an elaborate piece of live art—deliberately juxtaposing themselves against the mural in order to make some sort of a statement on militarism and culture. Then again, maybe it was just an easy place to park and they didn't give a fish's tit about post-modernism, subverting paradigms, or any Fenian mural. I couldn't decide. My mind was focussed on one thing only. What was the name of the IRA Volunteer who died during the fateful crash that killed the Maguire children? I was going to find out all I could about that man and I was going to the Linen Hall Library to do so.

■ ■ ■ ■

Danny Lennon was typical of the generation who hit their teens as the Troubles exploded all around them in the late 1960s. He was sixteen when the civil rights movement took off in 1968 and his mother Eileen had been a member of *Cumann na mBan*, the women's auxiliary to the old IRA, in the 1940s. After 1969 Danny Lennon was drawn into the riots against the British Army in Andersonstown just like everyone else. He eventually joined 'B' Company, 1st Battalion of the Belfast Brigade of the IRA in 1970. He was eighteen. By the time his brother Sean was interned the following year Danny had already come to the attention of the British Army and was on the run, living from one safe house to the next. He was eventually captured in October 1972, four months after Jean was killed, on his way back from an IRA operation. He was sentenced to six years in prison and served his time in the Cages of Long Kesh. In prison Danny consolidated some of the friendships and personal allegiances that would map out the rest of his short life—he was a close personal friend of Bobby Sands and was well known and liked by Gerry Adams. It was also while in Long Kesh that he was given the nickname of 'Dosser', on account of his diligent avoidance of early mornings. After three and a half years in Long Kesh, Danny Lennon was released from prison in early 1976. He went straight back on active service with the IRA.[1]

In 1976 the British government abolished political status for all newly sentenced IRA prisoners. On 8 August 1976 Marie Drumm, vice-president of Sinn Féin, told a crowd at a rally on the fifth anniversary of internment that if political status was not given back to IRA prisoners in British jails then 'Belfast will be pulled down stone by stone'. Drumm also predicted that if political status was not restored, 'Long Kesh will burn again and we will destroy this town and any other town and that goes for Britain as well'. Addressing the audience as members of 'the risen people', she alluded to the 'fighting girls and boys' who would free Ireland and made a plea for the crowd not to confront the security forces that night—'That is the job of the IRA and they will do it.' That night and over the following days the IRA did indeed engage the security forces.

A front page editorial in the *Belfast Telegraph* of 10 August entitled 'Dogs of War' reported fifty-five attacks on the RUC, twenty-seven on the Army, thirty shooting incidents and twenty bomb attacks across Northern Ireland over the previous day and a half. 'This', the editorialist commented, 'is a catalogue of war.' It was not to end there.[2]

Around 3pm on 10 August 1976 three IRA Volunteers ambushed a British Army patrol from the King's Own Border Regiment near a butcher's shop on Rossnareen Avenue, roughly half-way between Tardree Park and the spot on the Glen Road where Jean was killed—right in the heart of Andersonstown.[3] None of the soldiers was hit by the IRA unit that August afternoon. As the shooting finished one IRA member fled the area on foot while the other two IRA men, Danny Lennon and John Chillingworth,[4] quickly made their way to a stolen blue Ford Cortina. They turned on to Shaw's Road and sped away. While the IRA men were fleeing in the car several British Army jeeps converged on the area in an attempt to intercept, detain and/or kill them. During a high speed chase up Finaghy Road North, still in Andersonstown, a British Army Land Rover opened fire on the car, hitting both IRA Volunteers. Chillingworth was shot through the stomach and legs. Danny Lennon, who was driving, was killed and lost control of the car.

Disastrously, the car careered off the road at high speed, mounted the curb, and struck Mrs Anne Maguire and her young family, who were walking on the footpath. Anne Maguire was crushed against the iron railing of St John the Baptist Primary School. Two of her children—Joanne, aged eight, and Andrew, six weeks—were killed on the footpath. John Maguire, aged two, was seriously injured and died in hospital the following day. (Miraculously, young Mark Maguire who was walking behind the main family group, was not hit and was uninjured.) Another local woman, Betty Williams, arrived at the scene a short time later: one can only imagine the horror she witnessed.

The car had smashed into the iron gates of a schoolyard. Danny Lennon was dead behind the wheel, John Chillingworth was bleeding from gun shot wounds beside him, and the Maguire family lay crushed, bloodied and broken on the pavement beside the wrecked Cortina. Anne Maguire had two broken legs and was in a coma. Three children were dead or dying. The baby's pram was smashed to pieces. Eight-year old Joanna's bike lay mangled beside her.

The tragedy hit the news that night with general dismay at the monstrous loss suffered by the Maguire family and vitriolic denunciations of the IRA. It made it into the major newspapers throughout the world the following day. Yet another unimaginable atrocity from a little corner of the world that had gone quite mad. In Andersonstown some locals constructed a small impromptu shrine in front of the twisted metal gates on Finaghy Road North, leaving religious icons and flowers for the slain innocents. Shortly afterwards an interview with Mairead Corrigan, the understandably heartbroken aunt of the three dead children, was broadcast on television. She had had to identify the shattered bodies of her young nephews and niece, and made a very heart-felt public plea for an end to the violence.

Corrigan's tearful words on television that night so inspired Betty

Williams, who had been at the scene of tragedy, that she decided to start a petition for peace. Within the space of two days she collected six thousand signatures and was seen on television talking about how she was afraid of the IRA, but she felt that someone had to do something to stop the killing. The press immediately realised the potential of the story and widely published Betty Williams' call for a peace rally to be held a day after the Maguire children were buried. Approximately ten thousand people turned up for the rally on 14 August, although the exact figure was hard to gauge. Nevertheless, Corrigan and Williams clearly tapped into some very raw emotion generated by the tragic and senseless deaths of three young children. Virtually overnight a mass movement, the Peace People, was started.

The Northern Ireland Office (NIO) saw in the deaths of the three Maguire children an enormous stick with which they could beat the IRA. Northern Ireland Secretary Merlyn Rees publicly commented that the Peace People had 'shown the way… The terrorists can be beaten only with the support of the entire populace'. Betty Williams and Mairead Corrigan were lauded in the press as modern-day Ghandis who had come to deliver their people from the scourge of violence. An Australian book on the Peace People published in 1977 described Corrigan and Williams as 'Daughters of Destiny':

> Mairead, the virgin martyr, sacrificing her youth and her personal desires on the altar of a higher destiny. Betty, the epitome of motherhood wielding the tools of that trade—patience, humour, wisdom and love—as weapons in an ideological war against violence.[5]

By contrast Danny Lennon was demonised and given sole responsibility for the deaths of the Maguire children. In an article published on 12 August and entitled 'No cause to smile in Provo gangster land', the *Belfast Newsletter* reported that Lennon had just been released from prison after serving five years for robbing a bank for the IRA. He was a second lieutenant in the Provos and a hardened 'terrorist'. And yet Danny Lennon was arguably as much of a victim in all of this as anyone else: the car left the road and hit the Maguire children because Lennon, its driver, had been shot dead. Still, he was an easy target for the tabloids—a terrorist bankrobber madman who had recklessly caused the deaths of three innocent children out walking with their mother.

Meanwhile republicans in West Belfast drew a circle of covered-wagons in tight around themselves. An article entitled 'In Defence of Danny Lennon' was penned inside Long Kesh prison by no lesser inmate than Gerry Adams, already a leading light in the republican movement. In the article Adams offered his 'sincere condolences' to Mr Maguire, who had just lost three children and whose wife was still in hospital:

> 'I know there is nothing I can do to break down the feeling of animosity which the families bereaved in the past few years may hold towards those they feel are responsible for their loss.'

Then, in a long apologia to the Catholic/nationalist people, Adams directly confronted the tragedy on Finaghy Road North.

> I intend speaking here for the young man who was killed. I am deeply sorry that three young children died. I know that he would feel the same and that he would have done everything in his power to prevent injury or death to those innocent of any responsibility for the situation in which Irish people now find themselves. Children are always innocent. The Maguire family were not Danny Lennon's enemies and he was not their enemy. They were victims of circumstances created when he was shot dead... Danny Lennon went out with a weapon against the people he had identified as enemies. He went out against the British Army... He meant no harm to anyone other than the people who eventually killed him... Danny Lennon became involved in the republican movement in August 1971. He came into jail in October 1972 and he was released on 30 April 1976. He did not have to go back to the IRA... Second-timers (those who have been in and out of jail) know what it's about. Danny Lennon cared nothing for myths, for personalities, for glory-hunting. He sidestepped the petty material things which could have been his... His death, which robbed the Maguire children of their lives, was a contradiction of a life spent fighting for young children such as they.[6]

Later in the same article Adams wrote that Lennon 'had human feelings and weaknesses like the rest of us. Like us all he made mistakes but he was a good young man, a socialist by instinct and an IRA operator by choice.' He ended the article by relating to the desire for peace in the aftermath of the tragedy, and with a subtle plea for the Catholic/nationalist people to continue to support the IRA's ongoing war.

> You may believe that violence is never justified. You may have suffered; you may not want any trouble. You may be weary, sick, old or tired... I only ask that you accept that the Danny Lennons within the republican movement would, if given the chance, help build a society in Ireland worthy of the men, women and children of Ireland and that they are engaged in a struggle for this without thought of personal gain or recognition... Jesus have pity. None of us stands guiltless; only our children are innocent. It remains for us to ensure that we build a society in which they will not be robbed of their innocence. Then and only then will we have the peace that ordinary people everywhere deserve and desire.

Then and only then.

On Thursday 12 August 1976 IRA Volunteer Danny Lennon was buried at Milltown cemetery and nearly seventy obituary notices appeared in his name in the *Irish News*. That same night about a thousand women gathered at the site of the tragedy on Finaghy Road North, said prayers and pledged themselves to peace. The following day, Friday 13 August, the three sad little white coffins of the Maguire children were lowered into the ground. Thousands turned up to pay their last respects. Journalists battled for prime position in order to record Belfast's mourning.

■ ■ ■ ■

Liz Curtis later pointed out in her book *Ireland: The Propaganda War*, that in 'the newspaper reports, the role of the British troops in the deaths of the Maguire children was obliterated'.[7] This was by no means accidental. Indeed, the British Army's press people had gone to some lengths to deflect any suggestion that the men who killed Danny Lennon shared any responsibility whatsoever for the deaths of the Maguire children. And in order to do this it was necessary to get across the idea that Lennon and Chillingworth were completely responsible for the tragedy that occurred on Finaghy Road North. Or in other words, it was necessary to lie.

The British Army's version of events was diligently set down in print, for posterity's sake, by Colonel Michael Dewar in his book, *The British Army in Northern Ireland*. It deserves quoting.

> It was on 10 August 1976 in Andersonstown in Belfast that a Land Rover patrol of the King's Own Royal Border Regiment gave chase to a Ford Cortina carrying two gunmen who were escaping from a shooting incident in which they had opened fire on troops of the same regiment minutes earlier. As the Land Rover chased the car, an Armalite was seen to be pointed rearwards from a window of the car. The patrol fired four shots, seconds later the car swerved out of control, mounted the pavement and ran down a mother and her three children… As the patrol drew up at the scene of the accident one of the gunmen attempted to fire. He was shot and wounded. The driver was found to be already dead of gunshot wounds.[8]

The key point here was that one of the 'gunmen' (meaning, presumably, John Chillingworth) had pointed a rifle 'rearwards' at the pursuing British Army patrol. This had been a key point in almost all the press coverage at the time. The *Belfast Newsletter* of 11 August 1976 had, for instance, claimed that:

> As they passed an Army patrol, one of the men in the car took aim at the soldiers. The soldiers fired six rounds at the car, and hit the men in the car… Later, the Army discovered that in the exchange of gunfire one occupant of the car had been killed, and another wounded in the leg and abdomen. An armalite rifle was found in the car.

The implication of all of this was that, but for the IRA 'gunmen' pointing or shooting a rifle at the Army, the Land Rover would have been content to chase the IRA car and apprehend the suspects in a safer set of circumstances. Thus, the deaths of the Maguire children were the result of some IRA madman's desire to escape capture at any cost—recklessly firing at his Army pursuers despite the presence of civilians on the street. The problem, from a technical point of view, was that this was not actually true.

Eyewitness reports and accounts published later stridently claim that no gun was ever pointed at the pursuing British Army Land Rover by the IRA men in the car. There was apparently no gun in the front of the car at all. The Armalite that had been used to snipe at the patrol earlier was discovered partially disassembled and stored away in the back of the wrecked Cortina. If true, Chillingworth obviously did not, and could not, have threatened and/or fired on the Army with it from the front. This then brings us to the issue of the number of bullets fired at the IRA car. The Army historian (Dewar) says four shots were fired, the *Belfast Newsletter* and other sources said six. This is not a quibble over a bullet or two; there is an important point here. The Army claimed, and the press subsequently reported, that only a small number of shots had been fired by the Army, giving the impression of careful deliberate shooting at identifiable targets. However, relatives and historians have claimed that over sixty bullets were actually fired by the Army at Lennon and Chillingworth that day. This number was calculated, in part, by the number of bullet holes discovered in the wrecked car.[9]

Therefore, a detailed examination of the events that led to the deaths of the Maguire family reveals that the recklessness of the British Army contributed to the tragedy. It was the Army, pursuing IRA suspects in a stolen Ford Cortina, which had opened fire, spraying bullets at a car that was travelling at a high speed down a residential street. The fact that the Army was able to manipulate the tragedy to their advantage proves nothing other than that the British Army were more efficient propagandists than the IRA.

Meanwhile, in Northern Ireland there was a movement to promote. The death of the Maguire children and the advent of the Peace People was a big story for the Irish, British and world media. At last, out of the messy confusing little conflict in Northern Ireland came a story that seemed to balance tragedy with hope. Above all else, the lines between good and evil seemed so clearly defined—Maguire family/Peace People, good; Danny Lennon/IRA, evil. It was a story tailor-made for international consumption and journalists enthusiastically promoted the emotive appeals of the Peace People as the solution to Northern Ireland's Troubles.[10]

The tabloids, in particular, were enraptured. The British *Daily Express* put Betty Williams on their front page, Joan of Arc-style, with the crusading headline 'Why I must stop the IRA'. Meanwhile the rallies in Belfast continued: ten thousand, mainly women, near Finaghy Road North on 14 August and twenty thousand people (both figures were disputed) in Ormeau Park at the end of August. A week later an estimated twenty thousand marched up the Shankill Road, spreading the movement to the Protestant areas and thousands marched in Dublin. Soon after there were rallies in Derry, Coleraine, Strabane, Dungannon and all across the north. 'Down South' the movement was also advancing relentlessly, with hundreds of people marching in small towns like Drogheda, Dundalk and elsewhere. In September the Peace People made their international debut, with rallies in Liverpool and Glasgow. Media engagements, requests for interviews and speaking invitations for Betty Williams and Mairead Corrigan began to pile up.

I first remember hearing about the Peace People in 1977. It was around the time that they won their Nobel Peace Prize that October. I was nine years old and I saw them on the TV talking about peace and loving one's neighbour and an end to violence. Even from a distance of thousands of miles, it was all very moving. Especially the stuff about the dead Maguire children. Who could not but admire the courage of these women who in the darkest days of violence and terror stood up for peace? It is no exaggeration to say that the Peace People or, more correctly, Betty Williams and Mairead Corrigan, became media darlings. And it's also no exaggeration to say that the media, in promoting the Peace People, did so for commercial reasons much more than for any genuine desire to end the conflict in Northern Ireland. Above all else, it was good copy.

Corrigan and Williams were feted across Britain and Ireland. Liz Curtis' study of the media and the Troubles tells how the two women travelled to a peace rally in Derry in a large limousine paid for by the BBC whose staff also conducted an 'exclusive interview' during the journey. Indeed, Curtis passes some rather harsh judgements on the role of the press in the Peace People affair. She seems to imply that British journalists latched on to the story not because of any great remorse for the tragedy of the Maguire family *per se*, but more out of antipathy towards the IRA and because it was a 'good story' at a generally slow news period in the UK. The reluctance of Corrigan and Williams to condemn the security forces when they shot dead thirteen year old Brian Stewart in the Turf Lodge in October also proved that they were 'safe' in the eyes of the British media and the NIO. The Peace People could be trusted not to attack the status quo in Northern Ireland, focussing their energies and criticism almost exclusively on the role of the IRA as the primary source of violence, instability and death in Northern Ireland. In October 1976 they even issued a statement contrasting the 'vicious and determined terrorism' of 'paramilitary organisations' to the 'occasional instances when members of the security forces stepped beyond the rule of law'. Such views understandably won them favour with the powers that be.[11]

However, after the initial searing burst of enthusiasm these muddled politics were their downfall. The Peace People focussed on violence and conflict in Northern Ireland as moral issues. The peace they called for was an abstraction devoid of a pragmatic program to solve what was, quite obviously, a complex historical conflict. In the words of historian J. Bowyer Bell, 'Peace was simply, if at all, defined as an absence of the unpleasant and deadly'. Of course, so defined, everyone wanted peace: ordinary people, the churches, the British government, loyalist paramilitaries, the IRA and the local milkman were all committed to the *idea* of peace in Northern Ireland. But what kind of peace? At what price? On whose terms? Whether the Peace People wanted to acknowledge it or not, peace, in any meaningful sense, was going to have to be a political rather than a moral process.

Corrigan's and Williams' audience with the Queen in August 1977 and the announcement in October of the same year that they had jointly won the Nobel Peace Prize may have prolonged international interest in the Peace People as media personalities, but as a movement they were already withering. Indeed, the unwillingness of the Peace People to condemn state violence (such as the killing of Brian Stewart with a plastic bullet) with the same passion that they condemned the IRA, meant that they undermined and then alienated themselves from their support base in the republican ghettoes of Belfast and Derry. There were personal issues too. Mairead Corrigan and Betty Williams, against the wishes of many of their supporters, kept the money from the Nobel prize for themselves. It was at that point that the media, once their most noble supporters, turned nasty, reporting dissension in the peace camp and stories of fur coats and largesse.

Media hypocrisy knows no bounds and suddenly the two modern day Joans of Arc were nothing more than money-grubbing little fuss-pots who were spending half their lives on free peace junkets around the globe. Directionless, the Peace People divided in acrimony. With the political and commercial value of the story declining, the newspapers simply moved on. The three little coffins containing the broken bodies of the innocent Maguire children were all but forgotten, buried under a mountain of media manipulation and heartbreak, their memory only resurrected briefly in 1980 when their grieving mother took her own life.

Anne Maguire suicided in January 1980. It was a tragic end to the most tragic of stories. Since 1976 she had desperately tried to build a new life for herself, even emigrating to New Zealand for a short while. And yet she just couldn't escape Finaghy Road North. Even New Zealand, at the bottom of the earth, wasn't far enough away. Anne and her husband returned to Belfast shortly before she killed herself. According to Eileen Fairweather, Roisín McDonough and Melanie McFadyean in their book on women in Northern Ireland, *Only the Rivers Run Free*, several weeks before her death Mrs Maguire went to visit Danny Lennon's mother. Any conversation between tragic Mrs Maguire (whose family was killed) and bereaved Mrs Lennon (whose son was deemed responsible) would be of considerable interest to historians of the northern conflict. However, if the evidence presented in *Only the Rivers Run Free* is true, the visit was positively revealing. Among other things, Anne Maguire apparently told Mrs Lennon that she did not think Danny Lennon actually killed her children.

> She told Mrs Lennon that she was convinced that two of her three children had been shot by the army, and were not in fact killed by the car as it went out of control. Mrs Maguire said that after the

initial shock had worn off she had a clear picture of the tragic scene, and that in her memory she could see the children already felled before the car hit them. She is said to have written a document detailing this and to have approached various officials in connection with her intention to reopen an investigation.[12]

Her pleas to reopen the case were ignored and the remarkable allegations published in *Only the Rivers Run Free* sank almost without a trace.[13] With the Peace People gone, and press attentions focussed elsewhere, such revelations could serve no purpose. Mrs Maguire, however, was a broken woman and in a final act of dreadful lament she took her own life. As for Mrs Lennon, in 1982 she too passed away. John Chillingworth survived the shooting and crash on Finaghy Road North and served his time in Long Kesh. He was eventually released and still lives in Andersonstown. Betty Williams now lives in Florida in the United States. Mairead Corrigan married her dead sister's husband. The three Maguire children are buried and the journalists and television press men who got so emotional about their passing in 1976 have all but forgotten them. Only the graves remain.

■ ■ ■ ■

Gerry Adams has never forgotten his old friend Danny Lennon. In his important 1986 political treatise *The Politics of Irish Freedom* he remembered his old comrade and the events of that fading summer of 1976, commenting that 'in the nationalist ghettoes popular mobilisations were at an all-time low and the prevailing atmosphere was one of war-weariness'. According to Adams, while 1976 saw the British government intensify their efforts to criminalise IRA men charged with 'war-related offences', the political side of the republican struggle remained weak. Sinn Féin was only experiencing 'the first stirrings of a feeling that it needed to develop itself as a political organisation' and remained little more than a 'support group for the IRA'. In this context the Peace People provided the British government with a wonderful opportunity. The Peace People filled the political vacuum while in the mainstream press the public faces of the republican movement—including Sinn Féin vice-president Maire Drumm—were continually vilified as heartless terrorists responsible for the murder of children. Drumm was even called 'the Godmother of Hate' in some newspapers. In October 1976, as the Peace People campaign reached its peak, fifty-six year old Maire Drumm was shot dead while receiving treatment in Belfast's Mater hospital.[14]

The British press, still relentlessly promoting the Peace People, gloated over Maire Drumm's death at the hands of loyalist UFF assassins. The *Daily Mirror* carried 'Hate Granny Shot Dead' across its front-page while two *Sunday Times* journalists suggested a fitting epitaph could be had by 'removing the final 'm' of her surname and spelling Maire Drumm backwards: MURDER I AM'. Unlike the Maguire children/Danny Lennon case, there was scant condemnation of her killers—the emphasis was on the fact that the middle-aged grandmother had dug her own grave by associating herself with the IRA.[15] To many people along the Falls, such coverage confirmed that the death of an Irish republican meant nothing to Fleet Street journalists.

Twenty years later the emotion remains. In the 1995 edition of *Free Ireland: Towards A Lasting Peace* for instance, Gerry Adams commented that:

> I have very strong feelings about the 'Peace People' campaign of 1976. The IRA man, Danny Lennon, who was shot dead in the incident which gave rise to the campaign, had been a particular friend of mine since we had met in Cage 11 in Long Kesh. It was tragic enough that he and the Maguire children had been killed, but, when the British lie about his death was picked up by the media and gained general acceptance, I found it a great deal more difficult to deal with.[16]

Other republicans were even less forgiving. In volume one of *Belfast Graves*, published by the republican movement in 1985 to commemorate the lives of each fallen Belfast IRA Volunteer, the section on Danny Lennon was positively scathing of the peace movement that his death had generated. The 'British propaganda machine' and 'anti-republican media' were particularly singled out:

> With the help of some self-seeking individuals, and many misguided people, they created the ill-fated and so-called 'Peace People'. But while the treacherous pro-Brit antics of this organisation were soon exposed and discredited, the self-sacrifice and heroism of young IRA Volunteers like Danny Lennon shall be written into the history books and looked upon as a source of strength by the new generations of Irish men and women in a free republic.[17]

The reason people like Gerry Adams continued to revisit Danny Lennon's death was not just personal. Republicans realised only too well the corrosive effect of incidents like the tragedy on Finaghy Road North on support for their entire movement. Take, for instance, Jean's death. Within days of Jean being killed rumours were already circulating in Andersonstown that it was the IRA that had shot her in a case of mistaken identity. Jean had been an essential part of the republican social and political fabric in Andersonstown. Although Jean held no formal position in 'the movement', she argued the republican perspective amongst her friends in pubs and clubs, she collected money for IRA prisoners at her workplace, and local Volunteers would have known, as one put it to me, that she was 'sound' and could thus be relied upon in an emergency to open a door to facilitate an escape, or to warn activists when the security forces arrived on the estate. In 1972 it was the thousands upon thousands of ordinary people like Jean among 'the risen people' who made it possible for the Provos to operate. Without them, the IRA simply could not survive.

In a direct way then Jean's death, like the deaths of the Maguire children, undermined the republican struggle—ordinary people in Andersonstown and elsewhere could hardly be expected to be enthusiastic about the republican struggle if they were going to continually be cut down in the crossfire, blown up by mistake, or crushed by runaway cars. After all, in the early 1970s the IRA's popular support was predicated on the notion that the Provos were the defenders of the Catholic community. It was hard enough dealing with the security forces and the UFF, the 'risen people' didn't want to have to be defended from their defenders.

■ ■ ■ ■

By the late afternoon I felt I had read or photocopied almost everything there was on Danny Lennon and it was time to leave the library. For the trip back to Andersonstown I was in the back of a black taxi with a young mum, a gorgeous wee girl, a howling babe in arms, and (as they say in Belfast) an 'Oul Wan'. On the way up the Glen Road we passed some British soldiers who were lying in people's front yards taking aim at nothing in particular and everything in general. A lone solider with shaving rash was standing all by himself in the cold—shivering and looking frightened. I tapped on the window up by The Pop and the black taxi pulled over into the icy gutters to let me out.

As I walked down into the estate I decided that although Danny Lennon probably didn't shoot Jean, it was still a line of inquiry worth investigating. What I needed to do now was talk to someone who had also been active in the IRA in Andersonstown in the 1970s and knew what the *craic* was. Someone who I knew would not tell me anything unless it was 100%. Former IRA Volunteers are not renowned for their love of prying questions, but maybe I could use Sharon's advice. Hector fitted all the essential criteria and had the added qualification of having grown up just across the road from Jean. I didn't really know Hector, but I knew enough about his reputation to know that he was not the type for stories or elaboration. He had a hard honesty to him that was born of a decade in Long Kesh. I wondered if he would talk to me on tape? Maybe, just maybe, he might allow me to ask him some questions. And if so, and if I thought things were going well, I might just be able to raise the Jean stuff and Danny Lennon's name and see what his reaction was. It was risky business, but what else did I have?

The truth was that Danny Lennon could have killed Jean, but then again so could have virtually any IRA Volunteer in West Belfast in 1972. Jean was only one of 142 civilians unintentionally killed between 1969 and 1993 during IRA attacks on the security forces. She could just as easily have been one of the nearly 200 civilians killed by the security forces during the same period.[18] Her death, like the deaths of the three Maguire children four years later, was a tragedy born of the fact that there was a nasty little war going on in Northern Ireland. It was the Troubles that produced Danny Lennon, King Rat, Crip McWilliams, the IRA, INLA, LVF, UFF and all the rest of them. And it was the Troubles that killed our Jean. It was as simple, and as complicated, as that.

17

Of Skeletons and Closets

You planted our family tree
in poisoned soil.
Unknown to ourselves,
regurgitating untruths,
and folding away our dirty linen
beside the skeletons in your closet.
Indiscretion and deceit.
A cathedral of tears.
Praying on broken knees
that this litter
will never discover
the terrible secrets
of the last.

After a full day at the Linen Hall Library I wasn't really planning on spending the night doing any more work. However, after dinner Gran mentioned that she had been thinking about something I had said the other night about letters from overseas and she remembered that she had an old biscuit tin put away somewhere with letters from Australia and New Zealand and pictures of the family. Would I be interested in looking at them? And that was the rest of the night for me. I sat down in the kitchen pouring over dog-eared photos and well-loved letters as hour after hour went by. At first I was joined by Conor and wee Dan who sat at the table with me reading a Batman book and drawing on scrap paper. And then it was just me. Hours trickled away. The house was dark and silent. Gran, John, Sharon and the kids were in bed as I continued to sift through three decades of family memories and diaspora fragments.

The first item of interest I came across was Jean's marriage album from when she was wed to Declan Smyth. It was terrifying to gaze upon Jean so young and beautiful in her wedding dress knowing that she only had a few years left to live. At the back of the photo album I discovered a pocket with a single photo tucked into it. I immediately pulled it out to discover a large black and white photograph of a little less than A4 size. It had obviously been taken by one of those photographers who walks from one restaurant or club to another taking photos of happy couples and sending them the picture later. I immediately noticed that it was the one the *Belfast Telegraph* had used, enlarging the portion with Jean's head and shoulders, for the front page when she was killed.

The complete photo was of Jean and Sean McCann. No date, although I assumed it was probably taken late in 1971 or early in 1972. Jean and Sean are sitting at a table facing the photographer. They are smiling. Jean's hair is pulled back off her face and she looks happy. The table is covered with drinks—empty pint glasses in front of Sean and Jean has a glass with a white creamy liquid and a straw in it. Jean has her hands crossed on the table in front of her—her right shoulder is touching that of Sean beside her. They look quite the happy couple.

I was stuck by how different Sean McCann appeared then. Younger obviously, but the photo had clearly been taken before the weight of his sorrow had crushed him. He is smiling and bold in a garish 1970s suit with an alarmingly vibrant tie. His smile is that of a man content and with everything to live for. What a different image compared to the unshaven, shaking fellow I had met just down the road a quarter century and a violent death later.

In the background, behind the area illuminated by the flash and the smiles of the happy couple, are the dark shapes of men with their pints. Two of the dark shadows in the background are looking at the happy couple getting their photo taken and smiling. I wondered who the men were. I wondered if they came to Jean's wake or even if, by chance, they were also there on the Glen Road that night when death came to Jean. It was the darkness behind Sean and Jean that bothered me. It appeared to be crowding in around them. In the photograph Sean and Jean's faces and lives are lit up and captured forever. I thought it bitterly appropriate that the newspapers later cut Jean out of this picture just as Jean had been cut from Sean's life.

■ ■ ■ ■

Inside Gran's biscuit tin were literally dozens of photos that had been sent home from Australia and New Zealand by the Fairley side of the family. Pictures of my cousins Monica, Kevin and Thérése sitting on Santa's knee at Mangere town centre in Auckland during Christmas 1976. A picture of two other cousins at a Gaelic dancing competition in Australia. There was also a photo of my father and his brothers and sisters outside the house in Mangere standing under green, white and orange bunting having a party. I remember the occasion because I was there also. Another picture was of my grandparents' grave in Mangere Cemetery in Auckland—one of the only Irish graves in the cemetery, with its shamrocks in the corner to mark out their ethnic space amongst the Samoans, Maoris and Tongans buried all around them.

There were other diaspora fragments as well. Near the bottom I found three sad photos. One is of Jean's grave, no one around it, and a pile of fresh dirt behind it. It was obviously taken the day she was buried. The grave is covered in flowers and you can barely make out the word 'Smyth' on the gravestone behind the massed flora. In the photo the view behind Jean's grave is of Milltown cemetery and the distant motorway. Jean is surrounded by green fields and wild grass, a small dirt path, a wire fence and a few scattered graves. These days it is all filled in and if you were to take the same photo the nearby republican graves of Bobby Sands and others would partially block your field of vision. The green field of 1972 is now awash with the dead, all too many of them put there prematurely by the Troubles.

The second photo is exactly the same as the first—a snapshot of Jean's fresh grave on that bright June 1972 day—except it has Sharon in it. Sharon is standing beside her mother's grave and some of the flowers are even touching her white knee-high socks. Her hands are at her sides and she has a blank expression on her face. No emotion. Just a pretty little girl in an ironed mini-skirt outfit; freshly washed, hair brushed, standing in the sunlight with a wisp of her jet black hair blowing in her eyes. Directly behind her is the pile of leftover dirt from her mother's grave and the wide open expanse of Milltown cemetery. Sharon looks desperately adorable and alone in that photo. Like a wee girl who should be playing games in that field rather than standing, unsure of herself, hands firmly at sides, beside her young mother's final resting place. God love her, as they say in Belfast. It would break a heart of stone.

The third picture is of the exact same spot a few years later. Sharon is once again forced to stand beside her mother's grave for a posed photograph. This time she is older and bolder—eight or nine years of age. She is staring straight into and through the camera. Her hair is off her face and you can see her mother in her already. Except that she is not smiling. She is grim. Sharon says people never really understood how much she was aware of her mother's death as a child. She wasn't too young, she does remember. This picture revealed all. In the background Milltown is filling up—the green field is now covered with graves and the small pile of dirt behind Jean's grave is gone. But the look in Sharon's eyes is unmistakable. She is a little girl who understands only too well what she has lost and who lies cold in the ground beneath her.

■ ■ ■ ■

Also in the biscuit tin were letters from my family in New Zealand.[1] One, from my Aunt Maeve Fairley (my father's sister) written in October 1979 spoke of her ongoing homesickness for Ireland. Another, from my Aunt Margaret written in Mangere in February 1980, reported living in a 'state house, which is like a council house at home'. She too missed Ireland and commented: 'I would rather have snow at Christmas, still it's quite a laugh when someone had said to us let's go to the beach and have Christmas dinner.' Yet another letter to Belfast from my Aunt Maeve rattled a few of the skeletons in our family closet.

In a letter dated 18 October 1979 Aunt Maeve spoke of a terrible falling out between Old Maggie, my grandmother, and Aunt Nimh, a woman whom I and every other relative of mine had always been told was my grandmother's sister. Aunt Nimh, her husband and her children had been burnt out of their home in North Belfast in the early 1970s and had stayed with Gran at Tardree Park before emigrating to New Zealand. Aunt Nimh and her family had then 're-emigrated' from New Zealand to Australia in the late 1970s. Or as my Aunt Maeve explained to Gran (Aunt Mannix):

> I tell you Aunt Mannix, she [Nimh] has caused mum so much heartache, that she broke down one day and cried herself nearly sick and rued the day that she kept her. Nimh has still got the cheek to allow her kids call mum Maggie, not even auntie. I feel so sorry for mum sometimes as I am in the boat that she was in at one time in her life. The difference is Thérése knows and calls me mum and mum is granny.

Interesting boat. The rest of the family only found out about it when my grandparents died in New Zealand in 1982. Aunt Nimh wasn't my grandmother's youngest sister. She was her daughter. It's a sad, and all too common, 1940s Irish story. One of forbidden love and Catholicism and bitterness and lies.

My grandmother had an 'illegitimate' child before she married my grandfather, Old Q'ey, himself a widower with two young boys from his previous wife. Some time in the mid-1940s, in circumstances that lies and deception have subsequently obscured, my grandmother, who was still young Maggie then, fell in love with a married man from down the Falls Road. They courted, began a sexual relationship and she risked banishment from her own community by moving to Coventry in England with him. He was there for work, leaving his wife behind on the Falls Road. Young Maggie followed him soon after by similarly pretending to be 'taking the boat over' in pursuit of employment. They lived, unmarried, as virtual husband and wife in England defying the religious laws and social conventions in which my grandmother was always such a fervent believer. She deceived her family and defied her Church. And then she got pregnant.

Somehow, as always seems to happen, she ran into a woman who knew her from back in Belfast. The woman was sworn to secrecy about Maggie's pregnant state and became the Coventry confidant of young Maggie. However, when the baby, Aunt Nimh, was born, Maggie developed severe medical complications. The aforementioned Belfast woman, fearing Maggie was about to die without the solace of her family around her, contacted my great-grandmother, Granny Sarah McGeough in Ardoyne. Granny McGeough immediately dispatched herself to England to come to the aid of her sick and shamed daughter, my grandmother Maggie. Eventually a deal was put together. Maggie was never to see the Falls Road man again and Nimh would be brought up as Granny Sarah McGeough's youngest daughter. This would save Maggie the shame and stigma of being a soiled and unmarriable maiden. And so it was. Granny McGeough, Maggie and baby Nimh returned on the boat to Belfast and to a life built behind a veneer of lies.

While the entire episode may seem remarkable to us now, it was quite a normal thing in 1940s Belfast. Community customs demanded that 'little mistakes' had to be covered up. The resulting lies and deception poisoned family trees forever. Indeed, it should be remembered, that Old Q'ey, Maggie's future husband, had two sons himself and that after his first wife died of TB these boys were raised in the families of his dead wife's sisters. One sister took Tony and the other took Q'ey junior. They were brought up with different surnames and as cousins. They continued to live on the same street, not knowing that 'Old Q'ey Fairley' was actually their father and that the subsequent Fairley children were their half brothers and sisters. Uncle Tony only discovered the truth when he signed on at the dole office at age fourteen and a desk clerk informed him that his legal surname was 'Fairley' and not the name he had scrawled on his dole card. Such was life in Belfast at the time.

My grandmother, Old Maggie, was a pious religious woman deeply affected by the shame of 'illegitimate' childbirth. A love child to another woman's husband no less. I think I know how she coped. She covered up her 'mistakes' by becoming the most devout and rigid of Catholics. She spent half her life on her knees in Catholic churches and one can only imagine the sins, both real and imagined, she confessed there. The guilt twisted inside her and the lies festered and rotted. No wonder she became such a bitter woman. She compensated for her own transgressions by filling the rooms of her house with religious icons and instilling a terrible fear of God in her children and grandchildren. She frightened me. I do not think she loved me. I only remember her speaking to me with words laced with sanctimonious bitterness.

Old Maggie obviously regarded what had happened to her as her personal cross to bear. Aunt Nimh was raised as my great-grandmother Granny McGeough's youngest daughter. My father and his siblings grew up with her being their 'Aunt Nimh' when actually she was their half-sister. Although all of this was only really revealed to me and others in the immediate family when Old Maggie died in 1982, it was clear from Aunt Maeve's letter of October 1979 that she knew. There was a good reason for this. Aunt Maeve, as she said in her letter, was in 'the same boat'.

In Belfast in 1970 Aunt Maeve had fallen in love with an Afro-Caribbean airman stationed in Northern Ireland. She too fell pregnant out of wedlock and had to go away to a special convent in the border town of Newry run by nuns who looked after young girls 'in trouble'. It was there that she gave birth to my cousin Thérése, only returning to Belfast to join the rest of the family when they all emigrated to New Zealand at the end of 1971. Indeed, the fact that Maeve's baby was black played a major role in the decision to leave Belfast. It was felt that besides the shame that would be inflicted on unmarried Maeve for having a baby, people would not accept the presence of a so-called 'half-caste' amongst them. Belfast, to this day, is still a remarkably white society—until recently practically the only black faces you would see there were those (ironically) of British soldiers. A black baby would have been viewed with at best suspicion, and at worst with racist contempt. It was an additional cross Old Maggie was not prepared for her daughter to bear. Or perhaps it would be more accurate to say it was a cross she was not prepared to bear for her daughter.

However, the Catholic mind can be a strange landscape in which all manner of contradictions can be readily contained. Thérése is unquestionably black. Yet, when I was a child my grandmother sometimes told people that Thérése's father was 'Mexican'. This, presumably, was seen as being less black and therefore somehow more acceptable. Still, in fairness to my grandmother, she did love Thérése dearly. Far more dearly, indeed, than she ever loved me. Yet I always felt sorry for Thérése. Growing up in white New Zealand was always going to be hard for an Afro-Caribbean girl. Add to this the fact that she came from a white Irish immigrant family and you get some idea of the hardship she endured. She was an outsider within the outsiders. She didn't fit in with the Maoris, pakehas, or with the Irish community. Yet Thérése grew up to become as beautiful and proud a woman as any you will ever meet. And she still gets a kick out of the look on people's faces when they ask her where in Africa she's from and she replies 'Newry'.

■ ■ ■ ■

Finally at the bottom of the biscuit tin were some letters that had been written back home to Ireland by Sharon when she came to Australia for a holiday in 1981. She stayed with Aunt Nimh in Sydney as the hunger strikes in Long Kesh reached their final deadly stages. Aunt Nimh was living in Sydney's western suburbs and Sharon was about sixteen years old. In the first letter, dated 15 July 1981, Sharon, born and raised in Belfast during the Troubles, gave her impressions of Australia:

> The shopping centres and the main parts of the town are very big and the clothes and stuff are not as cheap as everyone says… The TV goes on all night and when this letter gets to you it might be a bit late as there is a post strike and they only send letters when they feel like it… I went to a sanctuary and we seen Kangaroos and Koalas. I took a lot of pictures. Hope everything is keeping well over there and there isn't too much trouble… It is great over here you want to see the work and the money they get for it but the clothes and things aren't all that cheap.

A following letter, dated 2 August 1981, contains Sharon's first direct reference to the hunger strike, mentioning that she had heard on the radio that another one of the prisoners had died and that she hoped 'the troubles doesn't turn out too bad'. Just over a week later both Sharon and my cousin Úna wrote letters to Gran. Both had been watching the news and had seen the pictures of Northern Ireland in flames after the successive deaths of Bobby Sands, Francis Hughes, Raymond McCreesh, Patsy O'Hara, Joe McDonnell, Martin Hurson, Kevin Lynch, Kieran Doherty and Tom McElwee on hunger strike. Only Mickey Devine was left to die. Úna mentioned that 'we heard on the news that another hunger striker died, God rest him' and asked 'are the troubles very bad?' Sharon, meanwhile, was hoping 'you are all keeping well as I heard the trouble over there has got worse since I phoned you'. Between the death of Bobby Sands on 5 May and the death of the last hunger striker, Mickey Devine on 20 August about fifty people were killed. These included the ten hunger strikers themselves, at least eight members of the RUC and no less than eight British soldiers. A twelve year old girl walking down the street, Carol Anne Kelly, was shot dead by a plastic bullet fired by the British Army in Twinbrook. Another civilian was shot dead by a British Army sniper in Ardoyne while he stood outside his own home. It was an altogether bloody and desperate time.

As I put down Sharon's letter it was well after midnight and my eyes were swollen and puffy with all the squinting. My hand was sore from transcribing the text into my research notebook. The house was silent except for the distant sounds of British helicopters. I was hoping that tomorrow I would hear from Hector, who had actually been in the H-Blocks during the hunger strike. Still, right now sleep and the attic beckoned. I placed the buckled photographs and smudged letters back into their envelopes and into the biscuit tin. I pushed down on the rusty lid, re-sealed my family's past and went on up to bed.

18

Hector and his Plastic Fork

'It is not those who can inflict the most, but those who can suffer the most who will conquer.'

Republican hunger striker Terence MacSwiney, 1920

'Pay them back woe for woe,
give them back blow for blow,
out and make way for the bold Fenian men!'

19th century Irish rebel song

I spent the whole of the following day in the library researching aspects of Jean's death and the origins of the Fairleys in Ireland. By the end of it I was so tired I didn't give a fish's tit where the hell anyone came from anymore. I left the Linen Hall disgruntled in the teeming rain and caught a black taxi on Castle Street to take me back home to Andersonstown. With the grim light in the back of the cab matching my mood, my spirits were buoyed considerably by an old man with about five teeth in his entire head who, after hearing my accent, insisted on talking to me. His running commentary on the price of travelling to Ireland by boat *vis a vis* air travel, and other insights were a considerable amusement to both myself and my travelling companions.

'I hear that wee accent on ye, is it New York you're from or Boston?'

'Sydney.'

'That's not in America!'

'No, it's in Australia.'

'Well why ye speaking with an American accent then? Impersonating an American are ye?'

'It's an Australian accent.'

'Are ye sure 'bout that?'

'Aye.'

'Now it's Irish yer after using. Are ye sure yer Australian?

'Yes I am.'

'Tell me, do ye surf?'

'Not me personally, no.'

'Why do ye not surf, I thought youse were all mad for it down there? I think I'd like t' maybe surf one day, but I've not got the knees for it anymore. But that's all that's holding me back, like.'

Thanks to the Oul Wan I made it back home to Tardree Park in a better mood and we were sitting having dinner when there was a knock at the door. It was Hector.[1] He said he was just over visiting his Ma and heard I was wanting to have a chat to him about something. He apologised for interrupting our dinner and said I should drop over afterwards to his Ma's house. With that I set about finishing my tatties and sausages and desperately started trying to think of intelligent questions as wee Dan kept making secret faces at me from the other side of the table. After I finished supper I was clearing the table and preparing to do the washing up when Sharon came and snatched the dishes out of my hands.

'G'wan! Away and see Hector, ye might find something out.'

It was a short wintry walk. Black Mountain glowered above me, frosty and unwelcoming. I rapped on the cold glass of Peggy's door and was ushered inside by Hector. As Peggy sat watching game shows in the front room, Hector and I made our way to the kitchen where I was grilled for a good ten minutes on exactly how I was related to Sharon, my academic credentials, my political motivations and my literary intentions.

I had read about Hector long before I ever met him or realised that he was Peggy's son. A former IRA prisoner in Long Kesh during the blanket and dirty protests, as well as the hunger strike, Hector appears in the two most famous books dealing with the republican prison struggle—*Ten Men Dead* and *Nor Meekly Serve My Time*. He is one of those countless ordinary young men who suddenly found themselves in extraordinary circumstances when Northern Ireland exploded around them in the late 1960s. Hector, like many northern Catholic youths of his generation, became a foot soldier in the IRA. And like quite a few others of his generation, he was eventually captured and spent over a decade in a concrete cell. And through it all he maintained the rage that had originally pulled him towards the Provos as they burst on to the political scene at the beginning of the 1970s.

After our little inquisition we settled down around the kitchen table and Hector said that before he could talk to me he wanted to know where this was going and for whose ears was it? I explained once again about my research into Jean's death and he seemed neutral on the matter—neither impressed nor uninterested.

'So why do ye want to talk with me?'

I thought it was best to tell him that I principally wanted to hear about his time in the H-Blocks. I was worried that if I told him about confirming or denying 'the name', he might simply refuse to talk to me. Besides, I was genuinely interested in finding out about his time in prison.

He took a puff on a dying cigarette and informed me that pending approval from someone else whom he would have to check with, he would be willing to talk to me next Thursday at 7pm in his mother's house. I thought we were all wrapped up and I was about to stand up and leave when we broke in to what I guess you would call (in more normal circumstances) small talk.

'So you'll be wanting t' tape this wee chat ye say?'

'Aye.'

He pointed his glowing cigarette butt at my balding head.

'I could tell ye stories about the H-Blocks that would make yer hair grow back.'

Hector's eyes were the palest blue I had ever seen, like the lack of natural light in prison all those years had caused them to fade. He was in his late forties and meticulously clean and tidy. Men like Hector are who the press have in mind when they go on about ex-IRA 'hard men'. And yet Hector was not some fanatical violent lunatic, but a man unbowed after thirteen years in jail and twenty-five years of war. This was a man who had suffered tremendously and whom (I felt it was safe to assume) had probably inflicted suffering.

He was also a man who had a rather irritating and simultaneously worrying habit of poking his finger about three inches from your face to make a point. And yet it was he who seemed uncomfortable as we spoke, my little questions causing him to stand up and walk around the room, distracted as he tried to relight the stub of his smoke on the stove and slowly answering my queries. He was nineteen when he went into jail and thirty-two when he got out. I already knew he had been on the blanket and dirty protests and had survived the heartbreak of the hunger strikes inside the walls of Long Kesh. But what did it all feel like?

'You know, if you are committed 100% to the cause ye can do thirteen years standing on yer head. If you were wearing nothing but a blanket 'round your waist and sitting in a cell, the walls covered in shite, freezing, and I told ye t' hack through a brick wall with nothing but a plastic fork you would do it if ye fucking had to. You have t' because it's either do it or accept defeat. Do it or the Screws beat you. We did it.'

We chatted a while longer and then he reiterated that he wanted to check some things out before he agreed to talk to me on tape. That was something, but what if the answer was no? The suspense and my impatience were killing me. I decided to risk asking the question I most wanted answered.

'Besides the H-Block stuff, I do have one sensitive question I want to ask you.'

I explained that in investigating Jean's death a name of a dead IRA Volunteer from Andersonstown had come up as the 'gunman' that fateful night in 1972. I was immediately assailed with a long diatribe on the importance of avoiding vocabulary relating to any alleged 'gunman'.

'Using those words could get ye in a lot of trouble with some people 'round here if ye know what I mean?'

Indeed, I could imagine only too vividly.

He then recounted that he was actually in prison when Jean was killed and that he had read about it in the paper. Was I sure it was definitely the

IRA who did it? He thought it was an unsolved shooting.

'No, my information and every indication from the press, from our family and from others is that it was the IRA.'

Hector mentioned that that was news to him. But what about this name—the dead Volunteer.

'Don't say his name. Just tell me how the Volunteer died and if he's from 'round here I'll know who it was you think might have shot Jean.'

I emphasised again that I understood the Chinese whispers nature of Troubles rumours and that I didn't want to falsely accuse anyone. But this name had come up in a discussion with someone who claimed to be in possession of reasonably trusty information. I mentioned the circumstances of the dead IRA Volunteer's death. The answer was instantaneous and unflinching.

'Wee Danny Lennon never shot Jean.'

That was it, the name was out there now.

'I spent a lot of time with Danny when I got out of the Kesh in 1975 and we were like that.'

He squeezed his two fingers together so that his fingertips went white with the pressure.

'I knew Jean. I knew Danny. If he was involved in any operation where a mistake was made he would have told me. Especially if it was Jean.'

He then mentioned that whoever gave me Danny Lennon's name shouldn't have. And he had a point to make in this regard.

'If I ever heard anyone, anyone at all, IRA or not, saying who did this operation or shot this 'un or whatever… [edited]. Talk costs lives. [edited] Even if the Volunteer in question is dead it doesn't matter. Talk can put a man behind bars or down a hole. They shouldn't have said anything t' ye.'

I felt my stomach getting butterflies as he then turned back to the matter of Danny Lennon.

'Danny was as sound as a pound. If you told Danny to walk into the heart of a monster he would. He'd do his job and get out. He was a true republican. And I'll tell ye this for nothing. If I knew who killed Jean I would tell ye, for no other reason than for wee Sharon and Mrs Campbell and their piece of mind.'

We left it at that and both agreed to meet again, as arranged, on Thursday night pending consultation with whoever he had to talk to about talking to me. He showed me the door, I shouted goodnight to Peggy and Hector shook my hand. His handshake was firm and I noticed that although he was a fair bit shorter than I he seemed taller. Here was a man who would never give in. Quite literally, you could shoot him (they did), incarcerate him in a concrete cell (they did), leave him without clothes in a cell with shit all over the walls (they did), grind him down for thirteen years (they did) but he would always continue to come back at you. If he had to he would scratch his way through a concrete wall with a plastic fork just to show you that you could not break him. To me, despite the fact that he was no longer a member, he was the IRA personified.

As I walked back home with a light rain falling on my face the clouds were strangling the light of the full moon. I stepped over puddles of black water and wondered to myself if I would ever find out who killed Jean.

19

A Visit to Long Kesh and a Funeral

'Our people and more and more of the Protestant people are coming to recognise that these people you see on television have lived on all of this fear and the threat of death over the years. They have lived off the misery of the people. It will never affect them or their children or anyone belonging to them. It's always working class kids like our Terry.'

Terry Enright's father, January 1998

After a long sleep I got up, shaved and read the morning papers for 14 January. The British government had released their much anticipated 'Heads of Agreement' document which was basically a proposal for a revamped version of the 1973 Sunningdale power-sharing agreement. The papers seemed to be suggesting that the peace process had been saved by this latest brilliant British political intervention. But how was this going to get the LVF to stop shooting Catholics? How was it going to end the root causes of the conflict? Such were the questions going through my head a few hours later as I stood outside the Sinn Féin centre on the Falls Road waiting for the bus service they provide for people who want to visit friends and family in Long Kesh. Standing beneath the flaking mural of Bobby Sands that covers one whole side of the building, the morning was bitterly cold.

As I stood with my hands thrust deep in my pockets waiting for the bus I could feel my toes slowly going numb. Even Bobby Sands, up on the wall above me, appeared considerably worse for wear and his cheeks seemed flushed red with the cold. After about ten minutes of standing in the vicious winter breeze, a woman in her mid-thirties with dyed blonde hair came along.

'Is this where ye wait for the Long Kesh bus?'

'Aye, I think it is.'

She looked at me inquisitively.

'You living in Canada?'

'Australia.'

She nodded her head and rubbed her hands together in cold agreement.

'You've got a wee bit o' Belfast mixed in t' yer accent there. You originally from here?'

'Only for the last two weeks and a couple of previous generations, like.'

A particularly nasty little stab of winter breeze came down against us, causing me to shiver. My suicide-blonde friend seemed none too pleased with the climate either.

'It'd freeze the life out o' ye out here, wouldn't it?'

'It would, aye.'

'Probably warmer in Canada.'

After another few minutes of reckless exposure to the ravages of Belfast winter, a young Sinn Féin apparatchik in a green suit, a tight haircut and with a *Saoirse* pin in his lapel walked past and asked us why we were standing on the street waiting for the Long Kesh bus when we could be sitting inside in the special waiting room beside the electric fire. He indicated to a little reinforced steel door which he said led in to the waiting room. I didn't know whether to kiss him or poke him in the eye. So, inside we went, beside the fire we sat and bored we were. Bored but warm, at least.

The walls of the waiting room were adorned with portraits of Bobby Sands, with shields thanking the drivers who take the relatives out to Long Kesh, *Saoirse* posters and other republican memorabilia including little wooden plaques (like the one of Jean's that was given to me) made by prisoners. Eventually, both the bus and John's younger brother Kevin arrived and we were away to the Kesh. Other than the fact that the woman in front of me was billowing cigarette smoke as she belted her ill-behaved child, the trip out to Long Kesh was pleasant enough and as we turned into the street leading to the prison a shift of guards was leaving in a special van with a RUC armoured escort. Next we turned onto the Bog Road and as we moved slowly into the gravelly prison parking lot we passed that pole with flowers for King Rat tied around it. I noticed the rain and bleak cold of the last weeks had taken its toll—the flowers were now very wilted and pale brown with the red, white and blue ribbon drained and diluted of colour. A memorial card was still pinned to the flowers and I assumed its message was vastly different to the nasty graffiti that continued to surface on the walls of West Belfast after Billy Wright's death—'Early Parole for King Rat', etc.

Regardless, we alighted from the bus and scuffled our way across the gravel and into the prison where we were greeted, as per usual, by reception area guards who had faces built for meanness and deficient in colour. Standing in line waiting to be processed, this time I resolved to pronounce my last name with an Ulster accent and therefore avoid going through the 'Lemons' humiliation of a previous visit. I briefly considered giving my name in Irish, Síomónn Pól MacÁdhamh, but thought better of it.

'Name?'

'Aaad-ems', I said, giving it my best Belfast touch.

'Adams, is it?'

'Aye.'

The guard jotted it down and then took a long hard stare at my face and grumbled something under his breath in the direction of the guard sitting beside him. From there Kevin and I sat with the others in the waiting room and then we were, as per usual, called in to the search rooms one by one. The search was a little lacklustre this time around—no squeeze of the testicles. Coming out the other side I entered the second waiting room and found myself sitting opposite a group of four middle-aged loyalists waiting for a visit. I knew they were loyalists by the Glasgow Rangers pins on their jackets. They were all giving me the stare of death and one, with cruel acne scars trenched up and down his cheeks, looked like he was about to come over and scratch my eyes out. I looked around for someone from the republican bus to sit beside, but there was no one there. If I got up and moved away by myself that would be seen as a sign of weakness. And so I sat, staring straight ahead at them as they stared back at me, trying not to flinch or blink—all of us sitting in silence—as we played out our own little immature version of an ancient conflict.

Finally Kevin made it out from his search and entered the second waiting room. Looking first at the four angry middle-aged loyalists and then at me and my pathetic attempt to stand my ground, he tugged on my jacket sleeve.

'Simon, away over here and sit with me while I have a fag.'

And with that I surrendered my seat opposite the loyalists and moved to the other side of the waiting room with Kevin. As Kevin set about sucking down a smoke, I noticed that on the wall behind us someone had written 'Bangle your sell out ceasefire. INLA'. To 'bangle' something was Long Kesh slang for the most common method used by republican prisoners to get contraband materials in to the prison—by sticking it up a carrier's arse. This method was successfully used to get secret messages, 'coms', out of the jail and (as the INLA had proven only a few weeks previously) everything else, up to and including guns, in. The tiny INLA had always been a poor cousin to the IRA and although it was still not on ceasefire, its stocks had risen considerably in republican areas with the killing of King Rat. Hardened Provos couldn't help but admire their audacity and even moderate nationalists opposed to violence found it hard to shed a tear for Billy Wright.

Anyway, the waiting room slowly filled with people from the republican bus and eventually a guard came in, called our names out and loaded us in to a special van to carry us over to the visitor's wing. As they counted Kevin and I and all the others into the van I couldn't help noticing that this time, unlike my last visit, republican visitors and their children considerably outnumbered loyalists. Indeed, the four loyalists were all alone in the prison van and they sat down the far end, creating as much distance between us and themselves as was humanly possible. I also couldn't help but observe that above us a large 'LVF' had been scorched onto the interior ceiling of the van with a pocket lighter. Striking a blow for the Union I suppose.

After the short, slow and now familiar trip through the various gates and across the prison, we shuffled back out of the bus at the other end and were taken to the final room where visitors waiting to be called on to the visitor's wing were watching a rather interesting British TV talk-show about sex workers and nude modelling. I was actually starting to enjoy the show myself when a screw bellowed out our names—'McVicker and Adams!' and we were let in to B-wing. I took the seat beside the radiator at the booth and Kevin sat opposite me looking a touch worse for wear. He had made it known he had been out the night before.

'You hungover again, Kevin?'

'A little, aye.'

'You're a desperate case aren't you? I thought your New Year's resolution was to get off the grog?'

"Twas, I told ye that, and then I resolved t' get back on it again.'

After a few minutes of banter Beefy arrived and squeezed in beside us. The first thing he mentioned to me was that 'the Shinners' on his wing had read my discussion document on links between the South African and Northern Ireland peace processes and had held a discussion group on it.[1] We then talked about Beefy's family—his girlfriend who he is marrying in some two months when he finishes his eight years in jail; his daughter who was born right after he got put inside—and then we got down to business.

■ ■ ■ ■

Beefy was captured on IRA active service following a bomb explosion that injured two British soldiers in the New Lodge area of North Belfast on 10 January 1990. He had been standing too close to the bomb when it went off. He was looking through the back windows of a vacant house and waiting for a British Army patrol that was due to pass along the front of the house on Stratheden Street. As they passed at about 9pm, the switch was flipped on almost two pounds of semtex. Beefy saw the flash and was blown back across the laneway, through the air, and in to a brick wall. In his own words:

'Saw the flash, felt the air suck out o' me and was lifted away. Speedy Gonzales, that's me. Blew back all t' fuck through the air like a fucking human hovercraft.'

After hitting the brick wall he lost consciousness but woke up a few seconds later. He looked over at where he had been standing and saw that the house was blown to pieces. He could see one of the injured British soldiers lying in the street out where the front of the house had once been and he remembers thinking that 'if he sees me here he's going t' get up and shoot me dead'. Beefy got up, pulled off his gloves (used to avoid fingerprints and DNA evidence) and could feel the blood dripping off his fingers. The side of his face was also warm from the copious quantities of blood flowing generously down it. And yet somehow he got himself together and was away, alluding the security net that was already closing in around him.

He was captured by the British Army a day or two later. He came out the front door of his girlfriend's block of flats and had two rifles pressed up hard against his skull. They dragged him by the neck into the street, asked him his name and told him he was under arrest. He denied he was himself. They showed him a picture taken of him from a RUC spy tower. He continued to claim it was a case of false identity. Finally an RUC officer arrived and quickly tired of the charade. Beefy was put into the jeep and taken away.

In court in April 1991, Beefy pleaded guilty and was sentenced to a total of 399 years for multiple IRA-related activities over a two year period. The sentences were, lucky for him, concurrent, meaning he would only have to serve the longest single one. Or as the *Belfast Telegraph* of 15 April reported:

> A SELF-CONFESSED IRA man was jailed today at Belfast Crown Court for 16 years for a catalogue of terrorist crimes including five murder bids and two murder plots. Among the offences committed by [Beefy] was the takeover of a building site in October 1989 while a massive bomb, to be used in an attempted mass escape of prisoners from Crumlin Road jail, was put into the bucket of a digger.[2]

I'd already heard a thing or two about the mechanical digger and its 750lb bomb. The rescue attempt was foiled because someone sabotaged the operation by letting down the tires of the digger. The *Irish News* of 16 April 1991 also covered Beefy's court case and reported that he had pleaded guilty to forty-four offences including 'five murder-bids on the security forces, two conspiracy to murder, possession of guns and bombs and IRA membership'. According to the *Irish News* Beefy also admitted to 'a series of gun, blast bomb and drogue bomb attacks on army posts and vehicles, including a mortar bomb attack on Girdwood Army base in August 1989, in which a 16-year-old cyclist was injured'.

Beefy had got involved in the IRA for all the usual reasons— harassment at the hands of British soldiers on the streets of the New Lodge as a teenager, the murder of a close friend by the UVF, riots against the British Army, the Orange marching season etc. There was never any shortage of reasons for young working class Catholics or working class Protestants to become protagonists in the conflict. Beefy joined the *Fianna* and was recruited to the IRA around 1988. He was captured in 1990.

Beefy was not optimistic about the peace process. While he was happy that prisoners were regularly briefed by Sinn Féin and mentioned that they were '100% behind the republican position in the negotiations', he was still not confident about the possibility of a peaceful future.

Only a few weeks previously Beefy had played Santa at the republican H-Block Christmas party where wives, relatives and children got to come in to the prison to visit their loved ones and have a little party for the day. One IRA prisoner, Liam Averill, had his picture taken sitting on Beefy's knee as one of Averill's kids sat on the other. Later that week, at another H-Block Christmas party for a different group of republican prisoners, Liam Averill escaped from Long Kesh prison. His was the last escape from the Long Kesh prison complex in its troublesome three decade history.[3] When I sat with Beefy in January 1998 discussing Averill's escape and the peace process, Beefy only had two months left to do on his own sentence. I asked him what he was going to do when he got out. He gave it a long hard think.

'I don't know, but I'm not going back on IRA active service no matter how this peace process thing works out. I've done me bit and done me time.'

Instead he wanted to get married, get a job and spend some of his life with his daughter. I asked him if he was thinking much about his release date now that it was so close.

'I think about the front gate. About walking out that gate for the last time. That's it.'

Republican prisoners give a farewell speech the night before they are released and Beefy was dreading his. He knew he would be leaving a lot of good friends and comrades behind. He said to me that one former IRA prisoner had told him that the walk down the wing on the way out to freedom was one of the worst experiences of his entire life. There was an empty feeling that came from leaving behind friends and comrades— some of whom are lifers. Beefy was given some sound advice by the former Kesh inmate. 'He said that when the day comes t' do the walk, don't look back at the faces behind you, 'cause it'll tear the heart out of ye.'

Beefy, Kevin and I chatted for about another hour and then the visit was over and we stood up to leave. I asked Beefy if there was anything he needed.

'No, Kevin and the boys look after me just fine. I'm not wanting for anything except out.'

We shook hands and my thoughts were on his approaching release date.

'Next time I see you it will be in better circumstances.'

'Aye, it will,' he said and smiled.

■ ■ ■ ■

On the way back to Belfast the sun pin-pricked its way through the windows. Eamonn McCann was on the radio, followed by the news—a RUC man shot and wounded an undercover British agent in a bungled operation and the funeral of Terry Enright, who was killed the previous Saturday night, was due to be held in West Belfast shortly. So, after getting dropped off at the Sinn Féin Centre, I said goodbye to Kevin and decided to make my way up to Terry Enright's funeral.

I caught a black taxi up through Whiterock and got out at the top of the Turf Lodge. It was only a short walk down the hill to Holy Trinity Church and as I arrived a crowd of hundreds of mourners, media and locals was already assembled in the bitter cold outside the church listening to the sad eulogies of weeping children being broadcast over loudspeakers attached to the church walls. Presumably the chapel itself was already packed to capacity. A bitter wind blew off Black Mountain and what sunshine there was, was weak and miserable.

Irish 'Troubles' funerals are desperately sad things. Not one of the more than three thousand people who have been killed over the last thirty years of conflict ever needed to die. Each one was a life cut unnecessarily short. Each death, on all sides, was particularly tragic for the family left behind. Nothing and no one is forgotten. The cold frozen Belfast soil, rich in blood and history, forbids it.

According to the reports I read or watched on television later, about a thousand of us assembled outside Holy Trinity in the freezing cold as the frail winter sun failed to beat away the chill of death from around us. An estimated ten thousand later lined the funeral route or walked behind the cortege, making Terry Enright's funeral one of the largest in West Belfast since the 1981 hunger strikes. Terry's popularity as a cross-community worker was the main reason for this and journalists commented on the large number of young people at the funeral. One remarked that Terry Enright 'was the only person I ever really looked up to'. Another said that 'I was a nobody and he made me feel like somebody'. One of the priests at the funeral commented that Terry had 'reached out in a very special way to the most marginalised in society and given them hope'.[4] When the Bishop of Down and Connor, Dr Patrick Walsh, commented in his speech, which was broadcast on crackly speakers to those of us outside, that the period from 1969–98 was one of 'agony piled upon agony', I realised that my fingers had gone numb. And just when I thought I might freeze completely, the coffin started to make its slow path out of the chapel and I cursed myself for my selfishness.

In front of the funeral cortege was a line of eight teenage girls from the local GAA whom Terry Enright had helped train and who were carrying a large banner made from red flowers that read 'A true Gael'. The bare legs of the girls looked blue and frozen in their camogie outfits as they linked arms and walked with teary eyes past us up the street. Behind them the coffin carrying young Terry Enright was being borne on the shoulders of relatives and behind them were family and friends. A wreath spelling the word 'Daddy' was prominent, presumably put there for Terry Enright's daughters, Aoife and Ciara. Terry Enright's father would later tell journalists about how Terry's five year old daughter had told her three year old cousin that 'bad men had shot her daddy'. He would also comment that press reports that had emphasised that Terry was related by marriage to Gerry Adams had almost legitimised the LVF's argument that he was a political target—guilt by association. Terry was not in the IRA. He was killed for being a Catholic in Ulster. No other reason.

As the procession passed us, onlookers fell in behind, paying their respects and walking a while with the deceased. I fell in too. The pallbearers kept changing over as we moved up the hill and after a while I noticed that both Gerry Adams and Martin McGuinness were walking almost directly in front of me. Each of them took a turn helping carry the coffin. I noticed that Gerry was looking old and I couldn't help but wonder how many of these sad Belfast funerals for young men and women shot down before their time he had been to over the years. Far too many. Looking down at the street I also noticed—and this will never leave me—that at irregular intervals there were small splattered wet drops on the pavement (like the ones you get when rain starts) caused by the cascade of tears slowly dropping from the eyes of those walking behind the coffin. A human downpour of sadness.

I walked with the cortege for about a mile and then I dropped off to the side. I watched the sad parade disappear down the street through the end of the Turf Lodge and on towards the city cemetery. Another statistic for the history books. Another family broken for all time.

I made my way back down from the Turf Lodge to the Glen Road and then strolled on towards Tardree Park. On the way I passed two young boys of about nine or ten sharing a cigarette on the derelict ground at the top of the road. Seeing me coming, one of them stubbed the cigarette out on the brick wall behind them with 'P.I.R.A' painted on it and put the butt in his pocket. As I passed them I wondered if they would survive the Troubles, or if the Troubles would survive them. I remember thinking that there was nothing in the British government's 'Heads of Agreement' paper that wasn't on offer at Sunningdale in 1973. If you could pile up all the mass and remembrance cards that came about as a result of the Troubles, even since 1973, you could build a tower taller than the observation post at the Andersonstown barracks. I thought of all those funeral corteges end-to-end like an enormous trail of tears snaking over the horizon. And of course, I thought of Jean and I wondered when it would all end.

20

Gran, Uncle Gerry and the Titanic

'McDONNELL, Joseph (18th Anniversary)… Our family chain is broken, nothing will ever be the same, but as God calls us one by one the links will join again. Sadly missed by…'

An Phoblacht, 8 July 1999

I watched the coverage of Terry Enright's funeral on the television that night. I didn't see myself, but I did see Gerry Adams and Martin McGuinness and I was right, Gerry was looking worn down by the weight of too many funerals and a failing peace process. After the news finished wee Dan came in to announce to me that he had been made class captain by his teacher at school and to show me his official captain's badge just in case I was in any doubt as to the authenticity of his claim. I saluted him and he marched out of the room. He was replaced by Big John who announced that supper was on the table. Plenty of spuds and plenty of peas—a good solid Belfast dinner. Sharon was still at work, wee Dan was in the lounge room practising being class captain and Conor was throwing a wobbler upstairs about something, so Big John, Gran and I ate without him. Sharon arrived home as Gran and I were doing the dishes. After Sharon and John left the room and while we were wiping up warm plates with soggy dish towels, I asked Gran one final time if she would talk on tape about Jean, about growing up in Belfast and about the *Titanic*. She wouldn't talk on tape but she would talk.

The story about the *Titanic* was that Gran's father, my great-grandfather Frank McGeough, worked on it. Belfast was one of the world's most important shipbuilding ports in those days, the *Titanic* had been built there, and old Frank McGeough worked as a boilerman on the boats that frequently sailed in and out of Belfast harbour. As such, and as a reasonably experienced ship-hand, it is not especially surprising that he got a job as a boilerman on the *Titanic*. What is unique is that he lived to tell the tale. After reporting for duty he sailed on the *Titanic* from Belfast to Southampton—bound for America and the icy depths of the Atlantic Ocean. While in England however, he and some fellow boilermen were doing some touch-up painting work in the boiler room and, to cut a long story short, he drank a cup of paint thinners by mistake (he thought it was water) and nearly died. He was taken to hospital and the *Titanic* left port without him. He was an ill man for the rest of his life but all in all that's got to be better than drowning or dying of hypothermia off the coast of Newfoundland. Makes for a good story too.

Impressed by the *Titanic* tale, I didn't press Gran about the olden days and all the rest of it. All she was willing to say was that she lived in Ardoyne, then she got married and they moved. I pressed her a little more regarding Jean but the best I could get was, 'Simon, son, don't be asking me about Jean for I'll only cry and cry and ye don't want t' be seeing me wailing now do ye?' She looked at me for confirmation. 'Jean went out and never came back, that's it.' And so it was.

■ ■ ■ ■

I still had the *Titanic* and Jean on my mind as I sat losing at Playstation yet again to Conor—a wee boy who was damned lucky that I did not give him a dig in the head for laughing at me when my video snowboarder kept crashing in to the side of the mountain. With the agony of defeat pressing down upon me I decided I might as well follow everyone's advice and give Uncle Gerry a call. Uncle Gerry answered the phone and immediately suggested I call around for a beer and a chat. As the night was young and John was obliging with a lift, I made my way over in the car. On the road we passed a British Army foot patrol and a convoy of three armoured jeeps. John dropped me off at the front of Uncle Gerry's house and I told him I would catch a taxi home later. Aunt Margaret the Third as I called her (on account of 'Aunt Margaret I' being my father's sister, 'Aunt Margaret II' being Jean's sister and she, married to Jean's brother, therefore being 'Aunt Margaret III'—less confusing that way) was at the door. She quickly dragged me in out of the cold.

'For God's sake, get in here before ye catch yer death.'

'Is that our Simon?', Uncle Gerry hollered out from the lounge room.

''Tis, aye,' said myself with regard to myself.

As Aunt Margaret III put on a cup of tea, Uncle Gerry and I watched the end of the Arsenal match and then moved into the kitchen where I got the *scéal*. As we sat talking, the youngest was practicing her Irish dancing in the other room. Aunt Margaret told me how she had won a place in the upcoming Irish national championships but her fear of public performance meant she might drop out. I watched her dance through a smoked glass window of the sliding kitchen door as Gerry sipped his tea and remembered Jean and the events surrounding her death two decades earlier.

■ ■ ■ ■

'Did anybody else tell ye anything, family-wise?'

'Aye. A bit.'

'Sharon? She wouldn't have known a lot about it because she was too young at the time.'

'I've spoken to Sharon a wee bit and to Aunt Pat and Uncle Frankie and some others.'

'Hmmmm'. He took a sip of tea and began.

'Me and Margaret were living up the top of the Turf Lodge at the time. Turf Lodge, it was mad up there in '72, people getting killed and shootings and, fuck, there was everything going on up there. We used t' live in this block of flats and ye used t' come home at night and there was shootings and what-have-you in the flats, it was fucking unbelievable. I remember one Saturday afternoon there was a football match on, England was playing Germany. Anyway, the front of our flat, the kitchen, faced out on t' Kelly's Bar on the Whiterock Road. Germany had just scored a goal and I called Margaret in. And as she come in, the car bomb outside Kelly's Bar blew up. The whole front of the flat come in around us: glass, doors, the whole lot. Margaret had been standing at the sink and if I hadn't called her in she would've been cut t' pieces. The screaming was terrible outside.'

The Kelly's Bar bombing took place on 13 May 1972, less than a month before Jean died, and was attributed to the West Belfast section of the Ulster Volunteer Force. Over sixty Catholic civilians were injured in the blast, one of whom later died. Even in the midst of such tragedy, people attempted to bring a black sense of Belfast humour to things. One local called Hugh McCormick, for instance, was at the back of the pub when the bomb went off and later remarked that it was 'the strongest drink of my life. I had just put the glass to my lips when the world went up around me!'[1]

Immediately after the explosion a three-way gun battle broke out between the IRA, the British Army and UVF snipers who had taken up positions in the nearby Protestant housing estate of Springmartin. The UVF gunmen had earlier positioned themselves in buildings overlooking the republican enclaves of Ballymurphy and Turf Lodge, opening fire as the victims of the Kelly's Bar bombing were being taken away to hospital. The Ballymurphy IRA then returned fire on UVF snipers in Springmartin and at the British soldiers who had set up positions on the ground as UVF members in the flats continued to pour fire into the neighbouring republican areas. At least five people were shot dead in the gun battle that raged into the night and continued the following day. Cusack and McDonald, in their history of the UVF, claim that this engagement was, 'the most intensive gun battle to date in the Troubles'. Some estimated 400 bullet marks were later found on the Springmartin flats, fired by the Ballymurphy IRA at the UVF snipers and British soldiers there.[2]

Gerry and Margaret must have almost been able to watch the ferocious gun battle from the front of their flat. Several of those killed came from streets nearby. Tommy McIlroy, a fifty year old Catholic, was the first to die, shot dead by UVF snipers shortly after the bomb exploded at Kelly's Bar. Thirteen year old Martha Campbell was also shot dead by the UVF as she walked through her local area. On the Protestant side, seventeen year old John Pedlow was killed by a richochet, fired by either the Army or the IRA. A British soldier, twenty-two year old Alan Buckley, was shot dead by the IRA. Finally, ten days after being injured in the Kelly's Bar bomb, John Moran, a nineteen year old Catholic, died of his wounds. Funerals were arranged, bodies were buried and the Troubles raged on. Our Jean had less than three weeks to live. I asked Gerry how well he remembered the night of 8-9 June 1972.

'One of the neighbours came up t' the flat and knocked us out of bed. It must have been half twelve and the guy was standing there. He says t' me "Gerry" and I says, "what's wrong?" He says, "Jean's been shot" and I looked at him and I says, "what do you mean shot? Is she alright?" But I knew right away. He knew she was dead but he didn't want t' say it t' me so I had t' go down t' my mother's and Sean McCann was there at that time. He'd been shot in the leg but it wasn't a big wound it was just a graze on his ankle. He had blood all up his jeans on his legs. And then they told me that Jean was dead.'

At Tardree Park it was all tears and confusion. Despite the fact that Sean McCann was sitting in the house, and knew the truth, initial suspicion for Jean's death fell on loyalist paramilitaries.

'Nobody knew what had happened. We thought that the other crowd had done it. Sean McCann was saying this, that and the other which we weren't listening to. You didn't want t' know because you were too much in shock anyway. But it was way after that, maybe two, three weeks after, when things settled down, that I thought of Sean McCann and I knew there was something wrong with this guy. I thought, he knows more than he's fucking letting on here. And I was told that he knew or he seen the people that done it, that come over t' the car. They come over and said t' him "we're sorry 'bout this" or whatever they said, I don't know what the fuck they said. But he seen 'em and he didn't make an effort t' do anything about it. Which t' me, he should've done. I never liked the guy from that day t' this, for doing nothing.'

'I saw him the other day', I said.

'I haven't seen him in years myself. McCann has t' live with what happened but I was gonna say t' ye that the guys that done it at that particular time in '72 they were all kids, young monkeys...'

At this point we were interrupted by Arsenal scoring a goal. The televised howl of the crowd drew Uncle Gerry out of his seat to watch the replay. A few moments later we shut the kitchen door again and resumed our conversation. Uncle Gerry continued, talking about drinking at pubs down on the Glen Road in the months after Jean was shot and making his feelings clear to people connected to the IRA.

'I knew by then that it was the fucking 'Ra that done it but not one person has officially said t' me that it was them'uns. But I let them'uns know, "I know you fucked up big time here. Somebody say something!" No one said nothing. At that particular time, a lot of fellas that was in the 'Ra, they were all young fellas like I was in '72. The 'Ra never came afterwards to the house t' my knowledge. Even at the funeral, nothing was ever said. See, they fucked up and they didn't want t' make themselves look bad. Jean actually collected money for them'uns when she worked in the brewery. She actually collected money for Provo prisoners in the Kesh.'

I asked if it was him who had told Sharon that her mother was dead the morning after Jean was shot. Sharon still had strong feelings regarding this incident and it was one of her only memories of the time of her mother's death.

'Me? I don't know, I don't recall. Sharon was very very young at the time. It could have been me. Sharon was only a baby and Jean and I were always very close, there was only a few years between us. It could have been me but I don't know, Simon, I don't remember if I did or not.'

'I was also told that you went out to Lisburn with your Dad and Uncle Frankie to identify the body, is that right?'

'No, I never seen her face because the face was blew off her. This was the next day. We actually had t' go t' Lisburn barracks because that's where her belongings were kept. Because, as I was saying t' you earlier on, this was in 1972 and an awful amount of people died. Mostly through sectarian murders. So, to the Brits it wasn't a big thing that somebody else was shot, because there was maybe four or five people getting killed every other day so it was nothing t' them'uns.'

Gerry was right, there had been three other people killed on 8 June 1972 alone. One was a Catholic civilian murdered by loyalists at his workplace in Belfast. Another was an Irish Garda (policeman) killed by an IRA booby-trap bomb on the north-south border, and the third was an Ulster Defence Regiment soldier who died of wounds inflicted by an IRA sniper three days earlier.

Given Jean's terrible wounds, the horrible task of actually identifying her had fallen to a local priest.

'The priest done that because of the way she was. You know the coffin was never open. The coffin was closed because the bullet goes in and makes a wee hole and comes out a big hole. An exit wound. It leaves you in a terrible state. She was gorgeous too, so she was. She was my sister but she was lovely.'

To Gerry, his father and Uncle Frankie (then Pat's young boyfriend) fell the task of driving out to Lisburn Army barracks to retrieve Jean's belongings.

'We had t' go to Lisburn barracks t' get her belongings. That was a terrible day. We went up and they just handed it over the counter; this was her watch and her rings and they were still covered in blood. Nobody cleaned 'em, why they didn't clean 'em I don't know. But I remember looking at her ring and the blood was still on the ring. She must have put it up t' her face when she got shot. So we got her bits and pieces and that was the end of it.'

I asked about the coroner's inquiry some months afterwards. Did he attend?

'No. I never went. My Da went. There was nothing in it. It was just a tragedy.'

I asked if Jean's death changed the way he felt about the IRA.

'At that time yeah, big time. But see now I've watched 'em, as you probably have too, and through history they've got an awful lot better and educated and they know what they are doing now. As I said before, at that time kids were just joining 'em so as t' get a gun. At that time in '72 you joined the 'Ra and you ended up in the Kesh within six months or you were dead. It was that bad, that was the way it ended up.'

Gerry belonged to the generation that had come of age during the civil rights explosion of the late 1960s. I asked him what his first memory of the early Troubles was.

'I went to London to live in 1968, the civil rights had just started, and I got this paper one Sunday and looked at it and yer man Gerry Fitt was on a civil rights march and his face was covered in blood. And I looked at it and thought "what the fuck is going on over there?"'

Gerry came back to Belfast, moved back into the family home at Tardree Park and got involved in the civil rights movement; marching with thousands of other young Catholics against the institutionalised discrimination that had mapped out their lives under the Unionist-dominated Stormont parliament. And like most of the other young working class men of his generation, he was often drawn into the rioting that increasingly eventuated between the RUC and sections of the marchers. Throwing petrol bombs at the police became a generational rite of political passage.

'They used t' barricade all the streets off. Down at Fruithill Park, at the bottom of the Andersonstown estate, they used t' have barricades all around there. And you'd have them up on the Glen Road at the bus terminus as well. It was t' stop anybody getting in but the fucking soldiers used t' get in in the middle of the night anyway.'

If not for the fact that by 1970 increasing numbers of people were getting killed, the riots could be tremendous fun. Not least of all because of the thrill of being involved in something so obviously dangerous and seemingly meaningful. It was living history.

'We used t' have some fucking laughs throwing petrol bombs and all that. You could have heard the Brits coming down the street and we used t' hide behind the barricade and throw the petrol bombs at the soldiers. Jean was into all that business too until she died, but I don't know that much about it.'

I guess hanging out at the barricades with your sister was not the done thing. Still, he did remember one time when he was questioned by the British Army in the street, only to be dragged off into an armoured jeep. It was Jean who came down to the Army barracks to get him out. I also asked Gerry about Hector, who had grown up with them in Tardree Park, and who, unlike Uncle Gerry, joined the IRA.

'Do you know what happened t' Hector? There's a bar called the Black

Swan. Over there it was all Protestants in '70 or '71 before Jean was shot. So he went in t' blow it up with a bomb. He got caught and did some years for that. So, he did his time and gets out of jail and he's out about six months and he's up on one of them avenues off the Glen Road. He had a rifle and he's standing in the middle of the street firing at the Brits and they shot him. He got caught again and he got another bunch of years! Eventually he got out of jail in the 1980s.'

I mentioned that I had spoken to Hector a few nights previously.

'Hector just got caught up in it all like everyone else.'

Growing up in Andersonstown at that time, Uncle Gerry had also known the young Joe McDonnell. Joe was the fifth of nine children born to the McDonnell family on the Lower Falls. At nineteen he started a family of his own with his young wife and they moved to the Andersonstown area. Like Hector, Joe joined the IRA and would die in prison on 8 July 1981 after sixty-one days on hunger strike. Joe had actually been arrested with Bobby Sands following an October 1976 IRA attack on a furniture shop. Like Bobby Sands he got fourteen years imprisonment. Apparently, on the day his wife told their children that their father had gone on hunger strike his daughter had immediately burst into tears, sobbing 'He's going to die, he's going to die, I know he's going to die, they let Bobby die'. Meanwhile his youngest son fantasised about Joe escaping from prison and wrote a story at school about it that ended with the line, 'And now all the daddies are home with their children'. On the day he was buried the same son clung to Joe McDonnell's coffin, weeping and trying to keep his father's cold body in the house he had so seldom ever been in.[3]

At Joe McDonnell's funeral a famous fracas took place when the British Army attempted to capture McDonnell's IRA honour guard. After travelling from Joe McDonnell's widow's house and down the Shaw's Road the funeral party stopped for the traditional final volley of shots over the coffin near some shops in Andersonstown. Patrick Adams, a member of the firing party and younger brother of Gerry, was shot and captured by the British Army as he attempted to flee the area. After a small riot, during which mourners in McDonnell's funeral procession tried to prevent the British Army taking the wounded Adams into captivity, the cortege continued down the Andersonstown Road. Joe McDonnell was buried in the republican plot at Milltown Cemetery with Bobby Sands. Our Jean lay resting in peace less than a hundred metres away.

'Joe was a good guy. We both used t' go to dance halls in town before all the trouble started. I knew him from just knocking about, ye know. He was a bit of a hard man even then. After he got married he used t' live up the way near where Hector got shot. I used t' see him at the dance halls in town before the Troubles started and then after that Joe fell in with the Provies.'

'So did you still see him then?'

'No, no. See when the Troubles all started people changed their attitudes and everything. People drifted that way and drifted this way. I know a lot of guys like Joe McDonnell who ended up getting shot dead or all the rest of it. Then the hunger strikes happened. Bobby Sands died, he was the first, then they all started dying and you'd be waiting on certain ones t' die because you knew them or whatever. For me it was Joe McDonnell, 'cause I knew him from earlier on. And once a hunger striker died there was always trouble, riots and shootings and everything else. Finally, it got to the stage where it was like, this is wrong, we don't want t' see another one die, stop this fucking thing. It was getting nowhere fast. I didn't know all those hunger strikers personally, but they were all just ordinary guys.'

We then started talking about Ardoyne and my immediate family. I asked if he remembered the Fairleys leaving Belfast and if he spent much time with them when they were all young. His memories were of the old pre-Troubles Ardoyne with its indomitable sense of community.

'I used t' go sleep in the house in Jamaica Street where your father Tommy lived. I remember my mother used t' go over there for t' visit and we would sometimes sleep over for the weekend. But Ardoyne has changed so much now, it's not the same anymore. When I was younger I used t' love to go over there with my sister Síle. We used t' go over to do our shopping on the Crumlin Road. We'd catch bus number seventy-nine and go over t' do the groceries and then get back on the bus and come back over to Andersonstown. One time Síle lost the grocery money on the bus and that was a week's groceries gone as well. But I used t' love to go over Ardoyne and see the Fairleys as a kid. Used t' love going down all the back entries and there'd be wee dogs barking and everything. There was something so nice about it all, ye know. There was an atmosphere in Ardoyne then.'

After some more Ardoyne reminiscences, the conversation turned back to 1972 and Jean's death. I wondered if Uncle Gerry had any more information about who did it or what happened that I hadn't heard yet. I asked him if he still blamed Sean McCann for her death.

'I only blamed him in that he should have done something about it. See, apparently her last words were "Oh Sean", that's what he said. All he heard was "Oh Sean". See Simon, t' me this goes back t' what we were saying earlier on that there was that many people getting killed then. You were dead, you were gone and you were forgot about 'cause someone else was getting killed the next day and then someone else was getting killed the day after that. I mean there was even people using the Troubles as an excuse t' kill people and getting away with it. Some of these things weren't even getting investigated.'

I asked if he remembered Jean's funeral.

'I remember very little of it. Oh God, I remember coming out of me Ma's house and there was people everywhere. I was in another world when that happened. I was just gone. I helped carry the coffin for a spell. I think we walked the coffin t' the chapel and then took it out and put it in the hearse but I don't really recall. My Da was in a terrible state. My sister Síle was the same. She would never speak about it. I don't think our Síle will even go down t' the grave. It just affects people in different ways, ye know.'

He remembers Sean McCann being at the funeral. And although he had skirted the question only a few moments earlier, he now reiterated his feelings regarding Jean's former boyfriend. It was interesting to see how he apportioned blame.

'I never forgave him for what he done. He should have died with her, that's what he should have done. I still feel the same way about it. I don't feel the same about the 'Ra now though 'cause they just kept getting better and better at what they were doing. Ye know, there were different people taking over and all that. But they were not the organisation they are now, back then. Twenty-five years ago they were nothing. It was like "here's a gun, away and go shoot a Brit". So there were mistakes.'

Given all of this, I thought Gerry had an unusual perspective on the peace process. The IRA had called a ceasefire in August 1994 and it lasted until February 1996 when the British government's insistence on the IRA decommissioning as a precondition to negotiations had caused the Provos to return to war. Uncle Gerry was not unhappy when the IRA detonated a 500lb truck bomb at London's Canary Wharf, causing £150 million worth of damage.

'I was never for the ceasefire, God forgive me. See, t' me at that time the 'Ra was winning the war. They were winning the war and they called a ceasefire. Then just before the end of the ceasefire I was in a bar and this guy I know, he says t' me, "the Troubles aren't over". A few weeks later the ceasefire is finished—BOOM! I was here, sitting in the house when Canary Wharf went up. See, you've got t' remember, Simon, that the ceasefire had gone on for over a year and nothing had happened, everything was the same as it always was. Sinn Féin had nothing t' show for it. As long as the Troubles were in Ireland the British government didn't give a shite. If that meant one or two Brits getting killed every now and then, they could live with that. But see, when the IRA blew up London they didn't like that, especially Canary Wharf, that cost them some serious dollars.'

It also cost the lives of two innocent civilians. Still, I wondered if the latest ceasefire, which had been called in mid-1997, had changed his mind at all. Sinn Féin were now in peace talks with all the other main parties and despite the loyalist killing spree that we were presently in the midst of, it seemed as though there was still some chance of a peace settlement being brokered.

'I think it has a chance of working out now. The only ones that are going t' go fuck it up now are these other ones, the LVF. I probably won't live t' see a united Ireland but it will happen and they know that. They are losing their little statelet bit by bit and they know it. It's inevitable now.'

With that we were finished. After some more banter Aunt Margaret III and Gerry drove me back over to Andersonstown. On the way I thought about Belfast and the *Titanic*. And I worried about a peace process that was slowly sinking.

21

The One Handed Provo

'When you get into jail, the strength gets into you. You come out fighting more than when you went in.'
Maire Drumm, *Sydney Morning Herald*, 12 August 1976

'The heartbroken mother of UFF murder victim Gerard O'Hara today told how she pleaded with the terrorists to shoot her instead of her schoolboy son.'
Belfast Telegraph, 28 September 1992

Night passed over me and I awoke to yet another crisp Belfast morning. It was already 15 January, I had been in Belfast more than two weeks and I felt no closer to finding the answers to my questions. Indeed, I felt cranial gridlock setting in. A good bowl of cornflakes and a trip to the library can sometimes be a suitable palliative in such situations. This being the case I promptly breakfasted, washed and made my way into the Linen Hall Library, my progress only slightly impeded by yet another combined RUC/British Army roadblock on the Falls Road. As I alighted from a black taxi in the city and strolled towards the library's dripping red hand I was thinking again of Jean and about everything Uncle Gerry had told me. It amazed me how little family members seem to have told each other about what they knew of Jean's death. So much was unspoken. Questions were not asked. The experiences of each of Jean's brothers, sisters and in-laws seemed to have been splintered, fragmented and isolated. I opined that perhaps Uncle Gerry was right, maybe that was just the way it was in 1972—there were just so many getting killed, so many confusing circumstances, so much grief and suffering, that it just didn't bear thinking or talking about.

In the dusty volumes of back issues of the *Irish News*, *Belfast Newsletter* and *Belfast Telegraph* I found more details relating to my research. Later, in the political collection, I asked Yvonne if she could help me with a reference I was having trouble finding. After locating it for me she asked how my investigation of Jean's death was going and for some unknown reason I unburdened myself to her—revealing all my pent up frustrations, my personal doubts and fears, the RUC's lack of co-operation, my confusion, the silence, the quarter century of sadness, and my unease regarding the deep sense of estrangement I felt towards the Fairleys in Australia and how that related to my deep sense of connection with Sharon in Belfast. She listened intently, obviously having heard such self-absorbed waffle from academic interlopers many times before, and offered some sound advice. Then she nodded meaningfully and smiled her lovely warm Portadown smile. I had to ask.

'Why are you smiling?'

'I'm sorry, but you know Simon, I must say, it's strange talking t' you. You have a strong Australian accent but you are so Belfast in every other respect. I was telling another researcher that we had an Australian up here working at the minute and she said "where's he from?" and I said "Ardoyne". You are so Belfast it's frightening. Especially when you are complaining! I'm sorry but I find that amusing.'

This led us on to other things and as we stood whispering between the shelves (trying not to disturb one of the other researchers), she told me about her liberal Protestant upbringing in Portadown. As a child her mother had had her praying at night for both the soul of Reverend Ian Paisley and for that of the old Official IRA leader, Cathal Goulding. Many years later Yvonne remarked to her mother that all those prayers for peace hadn't appeared to have worked. Her mother's reply was typically Ulster:

> Think of how bad the Troubles might have been if you hadn't been praying for Paisley and Goulding, love.

Eventually I got back to the books and dusty newspapers and put in a few more hours at the photocopier. As we reached the stub of the day I packed up and prepared to leave when Yvonne called me over to her desk to meet a friend of hers. It was Sinn Féin Belfast City Council member, Tom Hartley. A rotund republican, he was hospitable enough, and we conversed briefly regarding the peace process. I mentioned my comparative work on Northern Ireland and South Africa and he mentioned he had to go. He'd only dropped by to donate some Sinn Féin election material and was due back at Sinn Féin headquarters very soon. I took the hint, but restrained from mentioning that I too had very important business to attend to. A seven year old called Conor McVicker was expecting me home soon so he could humiliate me once again in Playstation snowboarding. I bid fare thee well to Yvonne and left with some of my dignity intact.

In the black taxi home we were stuck in a traffic jam caused by yet another RUC/Army road block on the Falls Road and I began thinking of the killings of the previous two weeks. All the names were already starting to blur. For a very brief moment I couldn't even remember if it had been Eddie Treanor or Terry Enright's funeral I had been at the day before. I then thought about how it must have been in 1972—the bloodiest year of the Troubles. Three others on the day Jean died alone. There was a numbness then, let alone twenty-five years later. The lives—all exceptional, all important—became trivial and statistical, remembered only by relatives and obsessive historians. In my case, both. I was getting well into this rumination as fog steamed up the black taxi's windows, providing a thin veneer against the brittle frost outside. Above us a brilliant dusk sky was deep blue with big brushes of black across it—as dark and dramatic as the city beneath it.

Suddenly I was jarred from my philosophical musings by the sharp nasal accent of a young woman in the taxi with me. She was clearly, undoubtedly, unquestionably, 100% Australian—with an accent you could sharpen a rusty saw on. The Australian was being asked by the woman next to her about the price of sausages in Sydney and how it compared to Belfast. The older Belfast woman, it soon became apparent, was the young Australian woman's aunt, with whom Rusty-Saw was staying while in Belfast. Rusty-Saw was born and raised in Australia to an Australian father and an Irish mother. Horrified, I sat there in silence as all of this was revealed to the other occupants of the taxi. Each occupant, in turn, bid the young Australian woman a good stay in Belfast and, just down from the Glenowen Inn where Jean spent the last hours of her life, Rusty-Saw and the aunt got out of the taxi and walked home. I sat in the black taxi in mortified silence. Another one. An Irish-Australian with a hyphenated existence. I felt my fleeting and pompous sense of uniqueness fall away as I tapped on the taxi window, got out at St Theresa's and walked down past The Pop to Tardree Park. Two of us within a one mile radius. Diaspora children. As the cold bit in to me I wondered which one of us wanted to belong more. Me, I bet.

After dinner I got out the fairy-liquid (great Belfast phrase that one) and did the dishes. Conor helped me dry up. Meanwhile wee Dan was terrorising the floor—pointing at it and threatening, 'Floor, I'm gonna punch ya in the mick!' I told him to stop saying rude words, even if it was only to the floor, or I'd belt him myself (Belfast extended-family child rearing). He chuckled and told me that if I did, then he'd do his karate on me. Not to be bested by a four year old, I picked him up and tried to force him in to the tumble-dryer, an act which caused his brother considerable amusement. Somewhat subdued by the threat of thirty minutes on hot cycle, things calmed down and Conor and I finished the dishes. Afterwards I made the three of us chocolate milk and Dan succeeded in simultaneously getting it in his belly button, all over his face, down the back of his pants and on the floor. Generous lashings of chocolate sauce adorned the kitchen walls. Fearing that Big John would come in and line the three of us for a good hiding, I cleaned the mess up on my hands and knees as the boys took pot-shots at my arse with the damp dish towel.

I was already putting on a cup of tea when John's Da arrived and the pair of them, John McVicker Senior and Junior, came in to the kitchen. Two things are probably worth mentioning at this stage. In keeping with Belfast tradition Big John is named after his father, and therefore Big John is actually Wee John and his father is John Senior. Secondly, John Sr only has one hand, although this seems to have not hampered his previous proclivity for armed struggle. Indeed I'd once heard one of his sons remark, in a moment of good natured slagging, that John McVicker Sr was the only Belfast republican to have literally taken on the Brits single-handedly. Regardless of all this, we three talked for a while about that day's news and the state of the Troubles. Then Big Wee John sent the children out of the room and suggested I go get my micro-recorder. When I returned, Big Wee John got up from the table and made to leave. 'Away you go,' he says to his dad, nodding in my direction, 'interview with a vampire'.

■ ■ ■ ■

'The way I got involved in the republican movement, I can hardly remember except that at that particular time I was working at Mackies which was predominantly Protestant. It was 1968 or 1969 perhaps, the start of the Troubles. I used t' get the worst of work, but that wasn't the real problem.'

The real problem, in John Sr's eyes, was that Protestant members of the auxiliary police force, the B-Specials, used to come to work and polish their guns in the workshop. Sometimes they would even point the unloaded weapons at him and make threatening sectarian comments. It was a situation which quickly made him come to the conclusion that 'these boys here are for real, and they certainly don't like Catholics'.

As the Troubles increased in ferocity, John Sr felt his young family in the New Lodge were under serious threat of attack from loyalist mobs. This was no melodramatic fantasy. Catholics were being burned out of their homes all across North Belfast. It was as Belfast descended into violence in 1969 that John Sr first contemplated approaching the IRA.

'I approached the 'Ra. I approached them'uns. In the early stages there was hardly any 'Ra t' speak of though. There was hardly any weapons in Belfast at all. When the Troubles started we were actually going around asking if anyone had private weapons: shotguns, .22 rifles, anything at all, because we were trying to defend the Lower Falls. There wasn't a weapon t' defend them Catholics with so we were searching for any legally held weapons. I even know of a case where some of the older IRA from the earlier Troubles came to Belfast t' suss out some of the older members who they knew had been former QMs [Quarter Masters] to see if they knew of any dumps, t' see if there was any weapons in them, and t' see if they could get them. Problem was, there just wasn't really anything much at all.'

John Sr decided he wanted to join the IRA because of its traditional role as defenders of the Catholic population and because everywhere he looked Catholic houses seemed to be going up in flames. However, the big Provo-Stickie split was just making itself felt and John Sr had to choose sides.

'I just approached someone I knew and told him of my desire t' become part of the Irish Republican Army. First of all you were sent on a training course over the border and you did your weapons training and so on. I went with the Provisionals simply because the Catholic people were being burnt out of their homes, being burnt out of their streets, being shot dead, being shot at and the Provisionals were the ones doing something about it. When people are getting burnt out, it's a situation where you begin t' imagine that this is going t' come back t' your own district eventually. Looking at it from New Lodge there was already a lot of incidents—shootings, Catholics getting put out of nearby areas. So I made my decision.'

Following the IRA's successful defence of the Short Strand, the Provos achieved something approaching broad popular support in the Catholic ghettoes of Belfast and Derry. In light of subsequent political and military developments, it was an amazing time to be an IRA Volunteer.

'You could have run up the street with a rifle, no mask or disguises of any sort, taken up a firing position and fired, and go back down the street with no problems whatsoever. People stood about in the streets and actually gave you good cover if you know what I mean, because no one could pick you out. At that time the Brits weren't as established in their observation posts either, so it was easier t' do. You could run about, especially when the "No Go" areas went up. Then there was absolutely no soldiers, nobody came in, they couldn't get in. The New Lodge had every entrance sort of barricaded.'

If early IRA Volunteers had far more freedom of movement in the early 1970s, compared to their comrades in the 1980s and 1990s, they also had a far shorter life expectancy. I was reminded of Uncle Gerry's comment that you were either dead or in prison within six months. John Sr was arrested in 1972. I had heard the story earlier from Big John. He was a young boy when he saw his dad taken away by the Army, and I wanted to hear what John Sr's perspective was on the whole thing.

'I got lifted in '72. I was caught with an AR-180, which was an Armalite with a fold-in butt. A very nice weapon. A great "terrorist" weapon, if you'd like t' call it that. It could be concealed very easily in your trousers; you just put a long coat on over the top and you couldn't see it. I don't know how they found out I had it but all of a sudden they come banging at the door. They were in for a search and there was maybe a dozen soldiers in the house and more outside securing positions. They went to various rooms in the house. I was asked t' go upstairs with the officer while they searched, which at the time I thought was a wee bit peculiar. And when I was upstairs they were messing about taking sashes away from the windows t' see what was behind them. And then one of the other soldiers downstairs called the officer back down and that's when he said he discovered the weapon. The weapon was in a concealed hide-out. It looked very neat. It was over a fish tank where I had a sort of door that blended in with the background. You couldn't see the hinges or anything like that. And it was hidden inside there. The officer who I was with, I didn't think he was all that surprised that it was discovered and I was caught. So, I do believe that someone must have said something along the line.'

John McVicker was one of the first IRA Volunteers ever to be captured with an Armalite rifle. The Armalite was more than a weapon, it was a phenomenon. It is hard to imagine now, but in the early 1970s it had captured the imagination of the IRA. For instance, Brendan 'the Dark' Hughes, in an interview for the TV documentary *Provos*, conveys the enthusiasm the weapon generated in republican ranks in the early 70s.

It could be folded up, dumped in rivers, buried, almost anything. Everyone was talking about it—this 'Super Weapon'. The brochure said if a person was shot in the arm, it would break every bone in his body. It was light and it was powerful. Everyone went wild about it because up until then there were only M1 carbines, .303's and old Second World War weapons... If it [the Armalite] did half the things that it was supposed to have done, the war was going to be over in a couple of years... I remember a car driving up. The boot was opened and there were ten to fifteen Armalites in it. The magic Armalites were there.[1]

In short, the Armalite was the weapon that was going to shift the balance of firepower between the IRA and the British Army. The Armalite would end the partition of Ireland. In the early 1970s the Armalite was sung about in republican ballads and was immortalised by Danny Morrison at Sinn Féin's 1981 *Ard Fheis* when he asked delegates 'will anyone here object if with a ballot paper in one hand and the Armalite in the other, we take power in Ireland.' In journalistic shorthand 'the Armalite and the Ballot Box' was used to describe the republican movement's entire political and military strategy during the 1980s.

The AR-180 was indeed a fine weapon for urban guerilla warfare. Its folding stock meant it could be reduced in length and hidden almost anywhere. It fired a .223 round that was forced out of its barrel at 3,250 feet per second—it could penetrate body armour and kill from a considerable distance. And John Sr was one of the first IRA men ever to be caught with one. It must have scared the life out of the British soldiers who arrested him to get confirmation that the days of the IRA begging around for old shotguns and hunting rifles were over—the Provos were geared up for war.

I also asked John Sr if he remembered Big John, who was still only Wee John then, being in the house when the Armalite was discovered. I was interested about this because the event forms a significant part of John's childhood memory.

'I honestly don't remember. It was a very long time ago.'

Nevertheless, John Sr was interrogated and taken to jail. I asked if the RUC gave him a hard time at the barracks.

'The interrogation, I didn't think it was too severe that time. It was just an interview really, I was caught red handed. What can you do?'

He was charged with possession of the Armalite and got five years jail. At the time IRA prisoners had 'special category' status and were treated virtually as captured soldiers by the prison authorities. John was sent to an

IRA compound at Long Kesh prison.

'I went t' a Cage in Long Kesh which was initially divided between the Stickies and ourselves. I did three years and four months. What you've gotta do when you're sentenced is accept what is happening t' you and make the most of what you've got. I eventually got in to a *Gaeltacht* hut where we concentrated on Gaelic language and Gaelic culture.'

In the Cages of Long Kesh John Sr was incarcerated with several republicans who would later become important leaders within the movement, not least of all Gerry Adams. I asked John Sr what Adams had been like as a young prisoner in 1972.

'I like Gerry Adams and he was just as he is today. We had a great Cage t' be quite honest with you. Unfortunately there's been about six or seven deaths of people who later got out and were blew up or shot dead. I mean Bobby Sands was one.'

'Who else was in that Cage?'

'Adams, Dark Hughes.'

Brendan 'the Dark' Hughes—he of Armalite enthusiasm—was a former Belfast Brigade commander. A very important republican who was central to the formulation of IRA strategy and tactics in the early 1970s.

'Both Adams and Hughes impressed me very much. Both were quiet in their own way of going about things. Very dedicated, very intelligent, good organisers, especially Adams who was unbelievable. Dark couldn't talk like Adams could talk. Adams could talk riddles around anybody and he always had an answer. I'm not just saying it, he really did. Gerry would organise lectures and education. He wasn't a trigger man, he was the brains. I got on alright with Gerry, I got on alright with most of them.'

In his book *Cage Eleven* Gerry Adams writes about his time in Long Kesh. When I re-read the introduction a few months later I was impressed by the list of important republicans—like Hughes, Sands and Brendan 'Bik' McFarlane (from Jamaica Street, Ardoyne and later the IRA's Commanding Officer in Long Kesh during the 1981 hunger strike in which Bobby Sands died), all mentioned by John Sr—who had indeed shared their time of imprisonment in Cage Eleven. And I thought of John Sr as I read Adams' remarks that:

> The rest of the men were equally remarkable; not so well known, but each unique in his own way. We did our time together, and this is my attempt to evoke, minus most of the f-ing and blinding, the atmosphere of that strange yet familiar world we shared.[2]

However, sitting in the kitchen at Tardree Park that night, I mentioned to John Sr that my impression was that the process of interning and incarcerating republicans in 'the Lazy K', as some prisoners called it, seemed to have the reverse affect to the one the British had hoped for. Far from demoralising captured IRA Volunteers, it hardened and politicised them. Many came out more dedicated than ever to the republican cause. John Sr agreed.

'When you're inside it's like an academy. Your whole way of thinking is in a military fashion and actually you are still having your training courses inside anyway: gun lectures, bomb lectures. There's different groups and actually we had a tunnel group going too. Ye knew the tunnel wasn't going t' get too far but it was morale building, ye know. We were always doing something, whether that be training or rolling over the tops of the huts. The *craic* was always good too. I got out in May 1976 and I went back on active service. I only lasted for another nine months and I was back in prison again.'

If the first time he'd been caught red handed, the second time he was falsely accused. I was particularly interested by the moral arguments he offered in terms of different aspects of the IRA's armed struggle.

'I was accused of a bombing. It was a building down off Corporation Street in the Docks area. There was no one killed and it was a commercial target. See in my opinion bombings were a better way of going about operations. When you go out with a gun and a bullet you are actually going out to take away life, that's the whole purpose of it. But when you go out t' bomb a commercial target the idea is to try to make it economically unfeasible for the British government to remain in Northern Ireland and hoping that no one gets caught in the bomb. So it's not a deliberate act of taking away life, it really isn't.'

Nevertheless, John was arrested for the bombing. He was kept in prison on remand for over a year, but was not convicted in court. Two other people he was charged with got fifteen years prison each for the bombing. John Sr's overview of the trial was brief.

'These police got up in court and swore blind that it was me they seen there but I knew I wasn't there. So they tried t' fit me up but I got off.'

I then asked why he eventually moved away from the IRA, ceasing 'active service' and dropping out of the republican movement in general.

'You wouldn't believe this, but the reason why I done it was that I was becoming a one man show. I was a QM, I was the man who had t' go out of the area t' get the gear, whatever it may be. I was the man going out on operations. Everything was coming down t' me and I just got thinking that this is not right here, a one man show can't happen, I was going t' go down again or get blown up and killed. So I thought it was time to get out.'

That was around 1978 and I asked how, now on the outside, he viewed the IRA. His impression was almost the direct opposite to Uncle Gerry's.

'They've changed immensely. I feel that most of the lads from my particular time were a very decent kind of person, but they'd still go out t' kill ye so it's a tough thing t' say isn't it? But they were good people t' be honest. Whereas today it seems they've gone all wrong. I mean there's people being beat up, held t' ransom, it just seems they've gone wrong.'

I asked then, given these comments and his own history, did he still consider the IRA to be the defenders of the Catholic community.

'I would have t' say yes. They certainly are needed. Don't forget that without the 'Ra things wouldn't have progressed the way they have progressed. We'd still be dominated by the Unionist Party which would have kept us down, kept us unemployed, and continued t' give us second class housing.'

I asked if he had any regrets about his involvement in the IRA.

'I do, I sure do. The only regret I have is family, that the family was neglected. I really do. I can recall sometimes having been with John and the others when they were little but there were lots of things I missed. When you get involved in the IRA you just turn yourself off and it's only later on in life that you think "I wish I had of" blah blah blah. That's my only real regret.'

Did it not worry him then when he discovered that John, as a teenager, was starting to move on the active periphery of the republican movement?

'John was a bit of a hot head. He only went as far as the *Fianna*, but I mean the *Fianna* was obviously a training ground for young recruits for the IRA, it was weaning them. John never told me he joined, I probably found out through some of the locals that I knew. I was worried perhaps that he would get caught in a trap and killed. Ending up in jail, that's OK, no problem, but ending up dead, that's something else entirely, isn't it?'

Given John Sr's history as a former IRA Volunteer during the early 1970s, I assumed he had probably been involved, in some way, in inflicting suffering on the security forces of Northern Ireland. I also knew that John's family had itself suffered tremendously, not least of all due to the loyalist murder of innocent eighteen year old Gerard O'Hara, John Sr's nephew. John Sr was working a shift as a taxi driver on the day he got the news.

'That was a Sunday afternoon and another taxi driver radioed the news through t' me. By the time I got there the police were there and Gerard was lying on the ground with his head facing the door. Gerard was hit something like six times in the head, he died instantaneous. The mother, my sister-in-law, saw all of this going on and she pleaded with the gunman to shoot her instead of him.'

Gerard's nickname, 'Soggy', was apparently given to him because he often sold the *Belfast Telegraph* in the city centre in the rain. His regular selling spot was at the entrance to the Cornmarket, not far from where Henry Joy McCracken had been hanged in 1798. Gerard's sister described him as, 'a quiet fella and still young for his age. He just lived for music and discos.' At 5pm on an ordinary Sunday afternoon during September 1992 a UFF squad burst in to the living room of the O'Hara house. His mother watched as one of the men with balaclavas on took aim.

> He was sitting in the chair when they burst in and shot him… I screamed 'Please don't shoot my son, please shoot me instead'.
> Then one of the gunmen went down on his knees and shot him at point blank range in the head. He just went on shooting and shooting… He was my youngest son. He hadn't even left school.
> He was at St Patrick's Bearnageeha and he had a wee part-time job selling the *Belfast Telegraph*. Why did they kill my boy?

The desperate act of a mother begging in vain for the life of her eighteen year old son captured the imagination of journalists and British politicians alike. Who could not help but feel sorry for this innocent boy gunned down by the UFF in his own home simply because he had the misfortune to be born Irish and Catholic in Belfast? A spokesman from the Alliance Party described his killers as 'Godless and savage people'. Even the British Secretary of State, Sir Patrick Mahew, was personally moved to publicly condemn the sectarian killers and their act of 'scarlet wickedness'. He said he would always remember the name of the young newsboy who died as his Mother begged the killers to shoot her instead.

One of Soggy's brothers had actually been upstairs in the shower when he heard the shots that claimed Soggy's life. James later told the *Belfast Telegraph* that:

> I froze, I was too scared to move. I knew what it was and if I went downstairs I'd be shot as well… When I went down he was lying in the corner, blood pouring out of his head. I knew to look at him there was no hope. He was dead.

The UFF later issued a statement claiming that Soggy was a member of the IRA, but no one outside of hardcore loyalist circles believed it. Yet, having said that, when a picture of Big John and John Sr carrying Gerard's coffin at his funeral later appeared in the *Belfast Newsletter*, Big John claims he was shunned by some of his Protestant workmates at Musgrave Park hospital. Meanwhile Gerard's father, James O'Hara, was interviewed by the press and pleaded for no retaliation. 'I would hate to see any ordinary Protestant going through what my wife and I are going through.' The UFF were unmoved. On a wall of a derelict building on the nearby Limestone Road they left a chilling painted message for Gerard's brother Maurice—'Soggy R.I.P. Morris is next'.[3]

My interview with John Sr was by this stage starting to wander a bit and I thought I might be able to re-focus it by talking some more about John's time in Long Kesh. Besides, I was intrigued by the fact that he had been locked up with the likes of Gerry Adams, Dark Hughes, and Bobby Sands. I asked who else was in the Cage and it was then that he inadvertently mentioned the last name in the world I was expecting to hear.

'There was this other wee lad called Danny Lennon…'

I near sprayed spittle over him in surprise.

'You were in the Kesh with Danny Lennon!?'

I knew Adams had been in prison with Lennon and that John Sr had been in prison with Adams, but for some reason (stupidity perhaps?) I hadn't connected Lennon and John Sr. He looked at me and seemed genuinely surprised by my interest.

'Yeah, why?'

'Nothing really, it's just his name keeps popping up lately. What can you tell me about him?'

'Danny was called "the Dosser", 'cause he liked t' sleep. Again, Danny was OK on his own. He was quite close to Sands. I came across Danny many a time on the football pitch, so I did. I did my best t' knock him around a bit. He was alright but I didn't associate with him. T' be quite honest with ye the only thing that really stood out was when he was shot dead. I was surprised about that. I didn't get the impression that he was committed t' the IRA at all. I really didn't.'

'Was there anything else about Danny Lennon you can tell me?'

'Not really, just that he really liked t' sleep.'

Indeed, Danny Lennon appears as 'the Dosser' in Gerry Adams' *Cage Eleven*. In a story called 'Sláinte', about the clandestine in-house production of *poitín* ('potsheen' or 'moonshine') by republican inmates, Dosser is the prime-mover and chief brewer of alcoholic beverages in the Cage. Later in the same book he reappears in a serious and solemn chapter entitled 'In Defence of Danny Lennon', originally written by Adams in the immediate aftermath of the Finaghy Road North tragedy. I wanted to ask more questions about what Danny Lennon was like in the Kesh but by this stage we had been talking for over an hour and I could see John Sr was getting restless. I asked him one final question about the peace process and I wished that maybe he would give me some hope that it might all work out after all. That there might be life after the death of King Rat. His reply was obviously tainted by his years in prison and as a witness to three decades of conflict.

'I say to myself "where are we going t' go?" We don't seem t' be going anywhere and I just don't know. I get confused sometimes.' He looked me in the eye and then finished off the last of his now cold cup of tea. 'Talking is not part of my game by the way, I've never been a talker. I was just an ordinary foot soldier.' He nodded and we were done.

After that Big John came back in to the room and we moved to the lounge room where we all watched a show on UTV about sectarianism in the RUC. And then finally John Sr was away, Big Wee John drove in to town to pick up Sharon from work, and Gran was away to bed. Being the only three residents left in the house, the boys launched a vicious campaign of terror against me—jumping on my back and trying to wrestle me to the ground. Tiny fists rained down upon me. I only pacified them by promising to play car racing games with them on Conor's Playstation the following day after school. I felt like Chamberlain at Munich in 1938; it was a simple case of peace at any price.

22

A Christmas Card for Thomas

'…but the fools, the fools, the fools!
– they have left us our Fenian dead,
and while Ireland holds these graves,
Ireland unfree will never be at peace.'
     Pádraig Pearse's graveside oration for O'Donovan Rossa, 1915

I slept in for once and was only woken by the screeching of Conor and wee Dan as Sarah-Jane (Aunt Pat's and Uncle Frankie's oldest) arrived to drag them off to school. It was Friday 16 January and after a while just lying still and enjoying the warmness of the sheets I came down from the attic to have some breakfast and talk to Sarah-Jane (John and Sharon were already at work which was why Sarah-Jane was taking the boys to school). Rebecca, Sarah-Jane's wee girl, was watching the Teletubbies on the television. Over a cup of tea Sarah-Jane and I discussed what we were going to do that night and I mentioned I might go down to The Felons for a Green Cross fundraiser in support of republican prisoners.

'You should go too, Gran,' says Sarah-Jane.

'Aye', I say, 'you like *tiocfaidh* music don't you Gran?'

Gran spoke with deadpan grimness, never lifting her eyes off the TV.

'Hate it and hate them. If it wasn't for them'uns I'd have a daughter alive today.'

Sarah-Jane and I just looked at each other awkwardly. Later on Gran went upstairs to 'get a wash', as they call taking a bath in Belfast, and I talked to Sarah-Jane about the to-ings and fro-ings out at Poleglass where she lives. I asked if they were still having problems with joyriders.

'No, there's not much trouble with joyriders at the minute. We've got them other hoods, them vigilantes, all over the estate instead.'

'Who?'

'The Provies.'

Sarah-Jane was notoriously anti-Provo which I found was a little odd given that her father, my Uncle Frankie, had been interned in the IRA compounds at Long Kesh during the 1970s.

'Last few nights they've been walking around in groups with walkie-talkies and scarves around their faces, looking for hoods and joyriders. Standing on street corners and all, so they are. Patrolling I guess. They've got a cheek though, don't they? They hijack cars 'n all themselves, so they do.'

I was going to debate community-policing with her but decided to leave her and Rebecca to the Telletubbies and set off for Milltown cemetery instead. I wanted to visit Jean's grave and collect my thoughts a little. As I yelled out cheerio to Gran and Sarah-Jane and walked out of Tardree Park I ran straight in to a mobile British Army patrol. Two Army jeeps were turning into North Link Road and as they drove past me the soldier in the front passenger seat gave me a dirty stare before returning to his fold-out map. I carried on walking up the road to The Pop only to find a RUC jeep with two peelers sitting behind bullet proof glass inside, reading a newspaper. Turning right onto the Glen Road, directly in front of me on the footpath, two peelers in bullet-proof vests were grilling a suspect. He was about eighteen years of age and was shaking as he smoked a cigarette defiantly. He had a tight haircut and an amateur tattoo on his smoking hand. I had to force my way past the three of them on the footpath, bumping into one of the RUC men on the way and he said something curt and unintelligible as I passed.

I couldn't hear what that particular peeler was saying because I was concentrating on the words of his fellow officer of the law. He was questioning the suspect, asking him if he knew anything about a stolen car and where was he last night, etc. The sort of youth/police conversation that could take place anywhere in the western world at any moment on any city street. Mundane stuff. Mundane except that in Northern Ireland in order to conduct this conversation in safety the police had to saturate the area with combat troops. There were four soldiers in camouflage gear in staggered positions up and down the road around the RUC men and the suspect, with another two taking up positions in the hedges of someone's front yard nearby. And on the other side of the street were two more, covering the ones covering the peelers.

As I walked down the Glen Road away from the peelers and their suspected joyrider, I had to squeeze past a British soldier and his machine gun on the narrow footpath. The barrel of his gun was no more than the length of my index finger away from me and pointed downwards, at my waist. Easing past the barrel I immediately found myself walking past yet another soldier; this one was taking cover behind a hedge and said hello to me. He was young, with bum-fluff on his chin and he looked like a nice enough fellow, but I walked on.

I continued on my journey down the Glen Road towards Milltown cemetery and was ruminating over the ridiculousness of all of this when I ran into yet another British Army foot patrol as I crossed Kennedy Way. Coming up towards me on the footpath, at intervals, were now 1-2-3-4 soldiers in single file; one was carrying a heavy calibre machine gun. As we walked past each other in different directions, I ignored them and they ignored me. In this sense it was like we were all pretending this was just another uneventful pedestrian stroll except that they were walking in military formation, wearing combat gear, were heavily armed and would have shot me dead if I made a suspicious move. To these soldiers (who were assuming I was a local) I was just another resident—probably inconsequential but still potentially hazardous to their health. I wondered if they felt that same uneasy fear I felt when I walked past them, like they were waiting for me to throw a nail bomb or otherwise attempt to bring death down upon them?

Finally I made it down to the bus depot just over from the Andersonstown RUC barracks and across from Milltown cemetery. The bus depot, in earlier and only slightly less turbulent times, was the barracks for a regiment of British calvary. Now the buses have replaced the horses. Regardless, I crossed the street and as I walked through the gates of the cemetery the sun actually poked its face out of the clouds for a few seconds. I stood still for a moment with the weak warmth of the January sun on the side of my face.

On the way to Jean's grave I stopped to look at the INLA/IRSP plot nearby. The Irish National Liberation Army's official Belfast plot is a rather unspectacular piece of engraved granite that sits less than fifteen paces from Jean's final resting place, near the back wall of Milltown cemetery. A tri-colour and a starry plough are engraved in each top corner of the gravestone and are connected by a Celtic weave that leads to the middle of the headstone where there is a red star with a fist holding aloft an AK47. Below are carved black words.

ROLL OF HONOUR
In proud and loving memory of those members of the Irish National Liberation Army and the Irish Rep Soc Party who gave their lives in the cause of national liberation and socialism.

Quite a few of the names etched below the inscription are of Belfast INLA and IRSP members killed in bloody internal feuds—including those murdered in the violent dispute between the INLA and the Official IRA as the former split from the latter in 1975. The names of Volunteers killed on 'active service' are also listed. And on the left corner of the gravestone is a special small plaque for 'Staff Officer Gino Gallagher, Assassinated 30 January 1996'. Gino was shot dead in the Falls Road unemployment office in front of Conway Mill. Several remembrance cards lay scattered around the grave, the two year anniversary of Gallagher's death being only a week or so away.

Gino had something of a formidable reputation. Following his death, a reporter claimed that Gallagher had once apologised to him for his awkwardness in talking to the press—'I'm more used to working with a balaclava on'. Only thirty-three, he had been in prison three times, having joined the INLA's youth wing as a teenager during the 1981 hunger strike.

He was first arrested at age seventeen and spent the bulk of his adult life in custody. Apparently his favourite saying was, 'A revolutionary is a dead man on leave'. And if the rumours were to be believed, Gino had allegedly put a few men in the ground himself, including three UVF men shot dead on the Shankill Road in 1994. Earlier, in 1984, he had been sentenced along with another INLA comrade for involvement in a shoot-out with police in which a RUC man and an INLA member were both killed. His co-accused was none other than Crip McWilliams, the man who shot King Rat dead in Long Kesh prison.

It was his own side who eventually killed him—Gino being only the most famous and recent INLA member to be killed in a faction fight. When Gino's family attempted to bury him on 1 February 1996 they were prevented from doing so by the RUC who objected to the INLA honour guard accompanying his coffin on the way out of the family home in Andersonstown. Police waded into the crowd outside the house with batons, bloodying some of the mourners. The coffin and its honour guard then retreated back into the house, a siege ensued, and the funeral was eventually cancelled for the day. After extensive negotiations, the RUC finally allowed the family to give Gino Gallagher the funeral he would have wanted the following day. His weeping mother helped carry his coffin as the funeral cortege walked down the Glen Road and towards Milltown cemetery.[1]

From the INLA/IRSP plot I walked the few paces along to Jean's grave. I only realised when I reached the grave itself that I had come to say something. I knew I would feel stupid doing it but I really wanted to. And so I started saying everything I wanted to say to a woman over twenty-five years dead... Finished, I stood silent for a moment. I bent down and tidied the weeds away from around Jean's grave. I stood in silent contemplation for a moment longer and then I walked away.

■ ■ ■ ■

Back up the wet muddy path near the INLA/IRSP memorial, I turned right and headed down towards the Provos' plot. Less than eighty paces from Jean's grave is the principal IRA burial place in Belfast, holding within it the remains of some of the names most hallowed by the modern republican movement in Ireland. The long rectangular strip of graves surrounded by a low green fence, is like a mini-graveyard within a graveyard. In order to pay your respects you have to step up a few paces on to a narrow wet tiled path that separates the graves. Running perpendicular to the path on both sides are IRA Volunteers buried three deep on top of one another in plain simple graves set out with inauspicious markers. There is little room for pageantry or poetics aside from the plain plastic green, white and orange wreaths that sit atop some of the cold headstones.

Walking along the narrow path I immediately noticed the name of

Thomas Begley etched upon one of the small headstones. His name is well known for all the wrong reasons. It was Begley who was killed on 23 October 1993 along with nine innocent civilians when the IRA bomb he was carrying exploded inside a crowded fish shop on the Shankill Road. The IRA later revealed that the bomb was intended to kill the leadership of the UDA/UFF meeting in an office above. Begley and another IRA Volunteer, Sean Kelly, were meant to place the bomb on the floor of the shop, forcibly evacuate the shoppers from the area, retreat from the premises themselves, and then the bomb would detonate, killing the loyalist commanders upstairs. Such intentions did little to alleviate the sorrow and anger of people from the fiercely loyalist Shankill, some of whom literally clawed at the rubble of the shop with their bare hands as they searched for survivors. British Prime Minister John Major immediately denounced the Shankill bombing as 'sheer bloody-minded evil'.

The Shankill bombing was an IRA operation that went terribly wrong. The office above the chip shop was indeed used by the UDA and it seems several senior loyalists had in fact held a meeting there on the day in question. These intended 'targets' were UFF leaders whom the IRA held responsible for the recent increase in random loyalist attacks on Catholics. By the year's end the UFF and UVF would make 1993 the first year in the history of the Troubles that loyalists killed significantly more people than republicans. A few days before the Shankill tragedy the IRA had responded to this intensified campaign by publicly promising to 'exact a price' from those 'involved with loyalist death squads' and the Shankill bombing was intended to make good on that promise. In particular, the IRA was keen to kill Johnny 'Mad Dog' Adair, the UFF commander. However, unbeknown to the IRA the meeting which they hoped to blow up had already finished. There was no one left upstairs. Instead, on a warm Saturday morning the downstairs fish shop was full of customers and other shoppers were busily making their way up and down the Shankill Road outside.[2]

So even before IRA Volunteers Thomas Begley and Sean Kelly walked through the door of Frizzell's shop dressed as fishmongers, their mission was destined to fail. That the operation ended in complete bloody tragedy was due to the fact that as Begley placed the box containing the semtex bomb on the floor of the shop it exploded prematurely. Bodies were blown to pieces and the building collapsed in a heap of rubble and dust, spewing bricks out into the street. Nine civilians were killed along with Begley, and another fifty-seven people were injured, including Kelly. In the street outside the collapsed building people lay bleeding with debris embedded in their faces, while dozens more were concussed or struck silent by the shock and grim horror of it all. When Begley's remains were later recovered from the wreckage of the building they had to be carried out in two body bags. (Kelly, although badly injured, somehow survived and was later given a life sentence.)

The Shankill bombing set off a season of accelerated bloodletting.

Loyalists threatened massive retaliation, with a UFF press statement indicating that 'John Hume, Gerry Adams and the nationalist electorate will pay a heavy, heavy price for today's atrocity'. Within hours of the bombing the UFF shot and fatally wounded a twenty-two year old Catholic delivery driver in Belfast. On Monday 25 October the UVF shot dead Sean Fox, a seventy-two year old pensioner. On Tuesday 26 October the UFF killed two Catholic council workers and wounded several others in a West Belfast shooting spree. On Thursday 28 October an eleven year old Catholic girl watched as masked UVF men killed her two older brothers in Lurgan. And finally on Saturday 30 October—a week after the Shankill bombing—two UFF gunmen opened fire inside the Rising Sun bar in the sleepy village of Greysteel, killing eight people and wounding thirteen.

The short period between the Shankill bombing and the Greysteel massacre stands out as one of the darkest weeks in the history of the conflict in Northern Ireland. Overall, October 1993 is remembered as the second bloodiest month of the entire Troubles, with a total of 27 people dying in a four week period. Loyalists were determined to match the Shankill bombing body count, corpse for corpse. Not a day seemed to pass without some terrifying killing or heartbreaking funeral.[3]

In the minds of tabloid editorialists, Thomas Begley was established forever as a sort of moronic puppet to IRA Godfathers who pulled the strings in the Northern Ireland conflict and deliberately blew innocent people to pieces. The rest of the media was only slightly more restrained, actively contributing to, rather than attempting to alleviate, the sense of foreboding in the North. On 25 October the lead news story on ITN started with a statement that the Hume-Adams peace initiative had been 'buried in the rubble of the Shankill bomb'. The overall political climate was one of rabid condemnation in which the Sinn Féin leadership were presented as the evil ambassadors of homicidal maniacs.

On Tuesday 26 October Trooper Andrew Clarke, on patrol with the British Army in Ardoyne, opened fire on mourners outside Thomas Begley's house from an Army Land Rover. Trooper Clarke fired twenty rounds at the men and women standing in the front garden of Begley's house and hit Eddie Copeland, a man in his mid-twenties and a leading local republican. Copeland was seriously wounded in the incident and was lucky to come out of it alive:

> I was struck in the back and the bullet entered my bowel and came out through my abdomen. I underwent emergency surgery… I had to wear a colostomy bag for eight months until my bowel was restored, although I have been left with hernia problems and will require more surgery[4]

It is interesting to note that when this matter was later dealt with in court the British soldier who had been standing beside Trooper Clarke in the Land Rover at the time of the shooting incident explained that he and other soldiers had been shown a photo montage of suspected IRA members a day or two previously. When questioned about the feelings of Clarke and other British soldiers after the Shankill bombing, Trooper Lee Potter remarked that: 'He may have gone a bit mad. Maybe he just had enough.' Trooper Potter explained that as their patrol had passed the Begley house Trooper Clarke had just opened fire without warning: 'There was smoke coming out of the barrel and he was pulling the trigger and shouting "you fucking bastards".'[5]

Although Trooper Clarke was later jailed for ten years for attempted murder, Eddie Copeland had to fight for financial compensation for his injuries as the British Ministry of Defence denied any responsibility for Clarke's actions. At the time of a court hearing in January 1999, one of Copeland's lawyers commented on the absurdity of the situation:

> They give young men guns, train them in the use of these weapons and warn them about people they consider to be terrorist suspects but baulk at responsibility when the young man in question actually pulls the trigger.[6]

In the aftermath of the Shankill bombing even John Hume, who was painstakingly attempting to find a way of politically engaging with the republican movement in order to bring them in from the political cold— as a precursor to convincing the IRA that their war could and should stop—was pilloried in the press. For daring to have established a political dialogue with Sinn Féin president Gerry Adams, Hume was accused by a senior Unionist of having 'sold his soul to the devil' and a columnist in the Dublin *Sunday Independent* insisted he was 'intent on sucking us into an immoral relationship with active terrorists'. He was called upon to contemplate retirement. The sycophantic praise heaped upon John Hume by these very same newspapers five years later when he was announced as a joint winner of the 1998 Nobel Peace Prize could not have been more hypocritical.

When Gerry Adams appeared at Thomas Begley's funeral on Wednesday 27 October—four days after the Shankill bombing—and helped carry his coffin through the streets of Ardoyne, the media went apoplectic. *Channel Four* news in Britain, for instance, declared that any dialogue with Adams was now out of the question and that the peace process was 'beyond recovery'. *The Sun* declared 'Gerry Adams' to be 'The two most disgusting words in the English language'. The *Daily Mail* opined that the relationship between the IRA and Sinn Féin was summed up in Adams carrying Begley's coffin—the two groups were 'divided only by the thickness of an undertaker's plank'. Very few in the media actually took the time to notice that in the aftermath of the Shankill bombing Adams had actually gone much further than any leading Sinn Féin member then or since in publicly criticising an IRA operation. Adams didn't condemn the IRA itself, but he did say that the Shankill bombing was inexcusable. Not that this would have provided much solace on the Shankill Road.[7]

■ ■ ■ ■

Thomas Begley was raised in Ardoyne, less than a mile from the Shankill Road. His family home was near the local Sinn Féin Advice Centre, outside which is a memorial to all the people from Ardoyne who have been killed in the Troubles. Paddy McAdorey's name is on that list. Growing up in the cramped working-class ghetto of Ardoyne, 'Bootsy' Begley couldn't help but have been aware that over eighty of his neighbours had fallen as IRA Volunteers, been shot dead by loyalists, or been killed by the security forces. Others had simply been killed by mistake, like Jean, or caught in the crossfire. Everyone was in some way intimately connected to the sorrow and suffering.

Thomas Begley was born into the Troubles. He left school at sixteen and like many young men in the district, he never knew regular employment. He lived at home in a room he shared with his brother. The physical environment around him was marked out by 'peace lines' separating the Ardoyne from the Shankill and beyond which one could not step without fear of death. Although by no means bookish, according to his family Bootsy had read 'over and over' Martin Dillon's terrifying history of the Shankill Butchers—a loyalist gang which had kidnapped and then used butcher's knives to torture to death over a dozen innocent Catholics in the 1970s. When a journalist visited the Begley family after the Shankill bombing, she discovered that a copy of *The Shankill Butchers* was the only book in Thomas' bedroom.

According to my copy of *Belfast Graves Volume 2*, which is published by the republican movement to commemorate fallen IRA Volunteers, Thomas Begley is a hero. Begley, like most of the other IRA members in the book, has one small page commemorating his passing: page 52 carries a picture of a young Bootsy Begley looking impish and smiling. Viewing such a photo it is hard to imagine the horrific explosion that literally tore his body and those of nine others to pieces. A much larger adjoining photo on the same page is of three IRA Volunteers firing an honorary volley of shots at Velsheda Court near Begley's house in Ardoyne as an IRA officer looks on. All are uniformed and wearing balaclavas as the three Provos point their AK47s into the dark Belfast night sky. It is the IRA's traditional and highly symbolic final tribute to one of their fallen comrades.

The text of *Belfast Graves* provides an interesting insight into the attempt of the republican movement to explain the atrocity on the Shankill Road, and deserves quoting at length.

> Born three years into this present phase of the conflict, Thomas Begley was to grow up in a community besieged both by British forces and their loyalist death squad allies.
>
> It was Irish Republicanism, the desire for freedom, justice and peace that motivated Thomas. He was by no means sectarian. He had worked with Protestants and as a Republican his wish was to see an end to all sectarianism.
>
> Thomas 'Bootsy' Begley joined the ranks of Oglaigh na hEireann in January 1993 and was immediately recognised as having great

potential. He was quick in comprehending the methods and techniques used by his comrades. Bootsy's eagerness and dedication… was evident in the many military operations he was involved in against crown forces.

The tragedy in which Thomas Begley and nine civilians died on the Shankill Road, marked another terrible milestone in the present stage of conflict. Part of that tragedy was the misrepresentation in many quarters of the motives of a young man who went out not to commit a sectarian act, but to try to help put an end to the oppression of his community and his country.[8]

The interesting thing about this entry is that I met the man who apparently wrote it and he told me that he had personal reservations. As he saw it, the Shankill bombing was the result of an ill-conceived mission that couldn't help but go wrong. Nevertheless, he felt it was important to defend Begley precisely because an attack on him was really an attack on militant republicanism. He saw it as yet another attempt by the British press and the Northern Ireland Office to demonise the republican cause by demonising IRA Volunteers who sometimes commit horrific blunders in its name. It was all about politics and defending your own. Even the Shankill bomber. Even someone like Bootsy Begley. Especially someone like Bootsy Begley.

That's the point that was missed in all the media vitriol directed at Gerry Adams for carrying Thomas Begley's coffin. Apparently John Major, in confidential talks with the then Irish *Taoiseach* Albert Reynolds, used the fact that pictures of Gerry Adams carrying the Shankill bomber's coffin had appeared on the front cover of every major British newspaper as a reason why he would not, and could not, negotiate with Sinn Féin. On 1 November 1993 in the British parliament Major even went so far as to publicly declare that negotiating with Gerry Adams would 'turn my stomach' and 'I will not talk to people who murder indiscriminately'. Such a viewpoint was completely at odds with the view of the Dublin government and even with that of RUC Chief Constable Hugh Annesley, who understood why it was important for Adams to carry Begley's coffin.[9]

At the time Gerry Adams addressed the issue himself, saying that 'I am not going to abandon Thomas Begley, a lad in his early twenties, or hurt his family any more than they have been hurt'.[10] But more than that, if Adams, the elected political leader of militant republicanism, had chosen not to carry the coffin of Thomas Begley, he would have been seen as betraying not just the Begley family and the IRA, but the entire population of republican Belfast. These people a senior member of the British establishment had once publicly described as 'the terrorist population of West Belfast', saw themselves as a community under siege. The louder the din grew regarding the 'evil terrorist' who had been raised amongst them and had gone out and blown nine innocent civilians to pieces, the greater the need to stand together. Adams had no choice but to carry that coffin. Everything in republican history and in the political culture of republican

Belfast said so. Had he chosen otherwise, his political influence within the republican movement would have been shattered. And that would have made his professed task of winning the IRA over to a 'totally unarmed strategy' almost impossible. Those who condemned Adams for carrying Begley's coffin in October 1993 failed to understand the dynamics of modern republicanism and the political process that would ultimately make the August 1994 IRA ceasefire possible.

To this day the memory of the Shankill bombing still ignites intense passions. In 1998 Michelle Williamson, a young woman whose parents were killed in the bombing, wrote to Sean Kelly in Long Kesh jail. In January 1995 Kelly had been given nine life sentences plus an additional twenty-five years in prison for his role in the Shankill bombing. However, following the Good Friday Agreement of Easter 1998 it was announced he would be released from jail early. This caused Michelle Williamson to take pen to paper:

> You are like a disease in my bones and the only cure is justice. To say I hate you doesn't begin to describe how I feel. I know you will rot in hell.[11]

Meanwhile back in Milltown cemetery there was no Satanic glow of what John Major called 'sheer bloody-minded evil' from the grave of Thomas Begley. Only tri-colour floral wreaths for Bootsy and a sad Christmas card from his family with a white flower printed on the front.

■ ■ ■ ■

Buried on the other side of the IRA plot, opposite Thomas Begley, are Bobby Sands and Joe McDonnell, two of the martyrs of the 1981 hunger strikes. Thousands upon thousands of mourners had gathered around their graves as their coffins were lowered into the ground in 1981. Indeed, the funeral of Bobby Sands was possibly the largest republican funeral to ever take place in Belfast and represented the re-emergence and re-invigoration of Sinn Féin as a political movement in the north of Ireland. Further down are the graves of IRA Volunteers Mairéad Farrell, Dan McCann and Sean Savage, all of whom were shot dead by the British SAS in Gibraltar on 6 March 1988. It was a famous and extraordinarily controversial episode. The 'Gibraltar Three' as they were later called, were on a mission to reconnoitre a target for the IRA to bomb on 'the Rock'. While walking unarmed down a main street the IRA 'scouting party' was ambushed by an SAS team which had been specially flown in for the job. Before they could surrender they were cut down in a hail of gun fire. At least twenty-seven shots were fired at the three IRA members: the dead body of Sean Savage alone bore sixteen gunshot wounds. One witness claimed that after the initial volley of fire one of the SAS men had run over to where Savage's body lay, 'placed his foot on the republican's chest and continued firing into his head at close range'.

Despite the protests of the British security establishment, it was clear to almost everyone who examined the case in any sort of detail (especially the evidence of the Spanish eye-witnesses) that what had taken place was a cold-blooded execution. When *Thames Television* later advanced such an argument in its April 1988 documentary 'Death on the Rock', the British government attempted to have the program banned. Regardless, in September 1995 the European Court of Human Rights found that the Gibraltar Three had been unlawfully killed by the British.[12]

The solemn turnout in Milltown cemetery for the burial of the Gibraltar Three on 16 March 1988 was one of the largest since the hunger strikes. However, as mourners gathered around the republican plot to view the coffins of Farrell, Savage and McCann being lowered to their final resting place a lone loyalist gunman, Michael Stone, threw several grenades into the crowd. Searing shrapnel ripped into the flesh of some of the mourners and people threw themselves to the ground in fear. Stone then retreated slowly from the graveyard, shooting at mourners as he did so. At first the crowd was terrified and then enraged. A group of young men pursued Stone, hiding behind gravestones as he continued to fire and hurl grenades at them. In the process Stone killed three of his pursuers, one of whom was an IRA Volunteer. Nevertheless, Stone was eventually caught by the enraged mob as he reached the motorway where he was beaten until the RUC intervened, undoubtedly saving his life. Stone was later sentenced to life in prison and by January 1998 had risen to become one of the most senior UDA/UFF commanders in Long Kesh jail.

But even that was not the end of it. On 19 March 1988 a funeral procession for one of the three people killed by Michael Stone in Milltown cemetery, IRA Volunteer Caoimhin MacBrádaigh (Kevin Brady), was slowly making its way through Andersonstown. After being spotted by funeral stewards sitting in their unmarked car, two plain-clothes British soldiers, corporals Derek Wood and David Howes, drove at speed into the funeral cortege in a desperate bid to escape the area. Mourners, fearing a repeat of Stone's attack the week before and thinking that Wood and Howes were loyalist paramilitaries, blocked the car's exit route. What happened next was captured by the TV cameras and was seen around the world. Surrounded by furious members of the funeral cortege, one of the corporals attempted to disperse the angry crowd by producing a pistol and firing it in the air. In a frenzy of fear and rage, young men then grabbed his arm and attempted to pull the soldier from the car. As the mob closed in the windows of the car were broken, the two soldiers were dragged from inside and were kicked and beaten on the street. Television cameramen were pushed away as the two dazed and terrified corporals were dragged to a spot in nearby Casement Park, away from the prying eyes of satellite television. At this point the IRA became involved, moving the doomed corporals to nearby wasteground. After a rudimentary interrogation, the two soldiers were stripped down to their underwear and shot dead with one of their own weapons. As a hovering army helicopter watched from the dark skies above, their bruised and bloodied bodies were abandoned on wasteground in Andersonstown. One of the two alleged IRA men later convicted of their murders was Alex Murphy who, in the early 1970s at age fifteen, had been the youngest person ever to be interned without trial in Long Kesh prison.[13]

In all, it was a horrifying two weeks that began with the state-sanctioned murder of three unarmed IRA members in Gibraltar and ended in terrifying scenes of frantic violence on the Andersonstown Road. Standing in Milltown and looking at the final resting place of Mairéad Farrell and the other members of the Gibraltar Three, I tried to figure out where Stone's grenades had landed on the day of the funeral. I had sat transfixed and nauseated as I had watched the original news footage on television in Australia in 1988, but standing at the graveside ten years later, the chaos and terror made it hard to figure out the logistics of the thing. I chided myself for such obsession to peripheral detail and instead focussed on the small memorial plaque dedicated to the three young men 'killed in defence of their people 16 March 1988 at the burial of the three Volunteers murdered by the British in Gibraltar'.

It was after I had stood in front of the graves of Mairéad Farrell and the others that I realised that I hadn't seen a marker for Danny Lennon. I assumed that his name would also be on the main Provo commemorative 'Roll of Honour' monument, which was nearby, and I decided to stroll over and have a look.

The Provo 'Roll of Honour' for County Antrim is a multi-sided granite construction. Names are diligently carved on all its sides, listing those who have fallen for the republican cause in County Antrim and including the names of fourteen people hanged in 1798 for being members of Henry Joy McCracken's republican insurrection. On another side are listed the names of those republicans killed between 1867 and 1953, but the bulk of the monument is given over to the modern phase of the conflict. The untimely death of every Provisional IRA member in County Antrim since the outbreak of the conflict in 1969 is meticulously listed. Danny Lennon's name is there.

Vol. Daniel Lennon. 10-8-1976. I.R.A.

At the foot of the monument I also noticed a small plaque dedicated to the 1981 hunger strikers. A few wreaths, faded with the rain and cold, were scattered around it. Laying wet and withered was also a single red carnation with a small card attached from a still mourning child.

All that death. Generation after generation of it. Name after name of republicans killed in 1867, 1921, 1944, 1986 and so on and so on. There were graves and monuments in Milltown for men hanged by the British for treason in 1798, or blown up by their own bombs in 1971, and even one for 'Lt Gen Joseph McKelvey, I.R.A, executed on 8 December 1922 whilst a prisoner in Mountjoy, by Free State Forces'. The grave of a Belfast republican killed after the split in the IRA that led to a full-scale civil war in Ireland between 1922–23.

I'd had enough. All that death and the winter cold were getting to me.

I walked back up Milltown's muddy laneways between the graves and used the Andersonstown barracks observation post as my compass point out of the cemetery. I braced myself against the January cold and the looming shadows of granite Celtic crosses.

23

Óglach Eachtar

'We are witnessing the greatest prison struggle of all time here in Ireland today, carried out by naked prisoners of war in the face of the most skilful and most totalitarian British propaganda machine ever seen. This current protest for recognition as prisoners of war is without parallel anywhere else in the world today.'

Republican News, 22 April 1978

'I must have died last night, because when I awoke this morning I was in hell.'

Bobby Sands, *Republican News*, 1 July 1978

Big John came home from work and I was sitting having a cup of tea with him when an advertisement for the kid's book series 'Where's Wally?' came on the TV.

'Did ye ever look for that wee fucker?' says John, 'I did once with the boys and it near put me friggin' head away.'

Just after six o'clock Hector phoned again to check that I was able to meet him at his mother's house at 'seven bells'. I said I was. After getting off the phone I went and had a shave and then got together my dictaphone and a spare tape. I thought I'd better take a pen and my notebook as well. I loaded them into my jacket and went down to say goodbye to Gran, John and the boys.

I met Hector at the front door of his mother's house and he let me in from the cold. We sat at the kitchen table again while Peggy watched television in the next room. Although I knew that Hector would never really trust me, I felt we had established some sort of rapport after our last 'wee chat'. I set the tape recorder on the table between us as he fidgeted with an unlit matchhead. We spoke about his fifteen years fighting Ulster's cruel little conflict.

'I don't want a medal, right. I'd just like t' sit down and talk t' somebody when I know that this war is over and nothing will happen t' me and I'll not go back to jail again. I'd like t' tell someone about my bit of a life story, about from where I joined the IRA t' where I ended. I'd like t' some day sit down and talk to somebody about the whole bloody lot. I'm telling ye now, when this war is over and there'll be no repercussions with anybody going t' jail because of what they've done in the past, you come and sit and talk t' me and you'll get some fucking yarns, alright?'

I agreed that we had a deal and he told me what he could about his story.

'I could go back to 1964 to start with. That's when they had that trouble on the Falls Road when Paisley made the RUC come down to take the tricolour off that building and there was rioting. I went down that time, I was only about fourteen. I knew nothing, I was just a nosy parker, I just went down t' see what was going on. And the place was just debris all over. That was it; then came 1969. In your teens you're young, you're into dances and a few drinks and what not—well, that was basically my life before 1969. Then things did start taking a bit of a turn in 1968, with the civil rights marches and all that and then Derry started to explode. I remember up the top of the road at The Pop there, there was these Queens University types one day, civil rights types, and they were talking about Belfast oughta be doing something to alleviate the pressure that Derry was having. We wanted to start something up here to take the pressure off Derry. I think back now and to me then it was really just a bit of *craic* and nothing else.'

In the Autumn of 1969 things went from bad to worse in Northern Ireland. Hector was actually out in Lisburn on 14 August when British troops were deployed to Northern Ireland—ostensibly to restore order in Derry and, later, to protect Catholics who were being burnt out of their houses in Belfast.

'I got back into Belfast that night and the Falls Road was burning. Literally, burning. So I got involved in the rioting and then slowly one thing just led t' another. You were just reacting to what was going on—you got involved in the riots and then the guns came out. I actually got involved in the auxiliaries then, looking after the defence of the area. And then from the auxiliaries I went into the Irish Republican Army.'

Hector joined the IRA in 1970 when he was twenty years old. At the time, the organisation was tearing itself in two in a bitter split between the Official and Provisional wings. It was an internecine struggle that would eventually see former comrades shooting each other dead on the streets of Belfast. I asked Hector how his political allegiances had been determined.

'To be quite honest with you, in terms of political awareness, I hadn't a clue what I was. I didn't know if I was a Stick or a Provo. I remember standing outside St Teresa's chapel one morning when we were selling these papers and a bit of a row started between the Sticks and the Provos and my mate—you mentioned wee Danny Lennon the other night, this was his brother Sean—he was standing next t' me and I says, "What the fuck are we? Are we Sticks or Provies?" 'Cause I hadn't a clue what we were. That's the way the whole situation was, with confusion and not being politically aware we were just reacting to whatever was going on.'

Eventually things solidified. The Provos' mark of distinction was, above all else, their effectiveness in waging war against the British Army.

'Gradually we knew who we were—the Provos. I became a member of the Provisional IRA. Things started happening then with the bombs and shootings and what not and getting involved in operations. I was caught in the Black Swan on the 27th of November 1971. I was aiming t' blow the bar up. The bar was frequented by the security forces, it was a known haunt. The operation was t' go in and take them out. Give civilians so many minutes to get out and then level the bar. If there was any identified members of the peelers or Brits in the bar then they had t' be taken out there and then. As simple as that. I had a sub-machinegun and the bomb. The bomb didn't go off and I was caught, but the rest got away. I got five years out of that.'

We were about to get in to talking about his time in prison, but before we did I wanted to ask if he remembered Jean at all from his time rioting on the streets of Andersonstown at the start of the Troubles. He did.

'I remember one thing in particular that happened down on the North Link. The Brits lifted a few guys outta their houses and Jean went berserk. She went haywire. I remember Jean plain as anything because she was standing there just screaming her head off at the Brits.'

He paused for a moment and was obviously choosing his words carefully. While Hector had grown up across the street from Jean, his involvement in the IRA meant that by 1971 he was hardly around the estate any more. Known IRA activists were continually moving from one safe house to another trying to stay one step ahead of the British Army.

'I was very rarely 'round here during that period. I was always out somewhere. I wasn't staying here because the peelers had raided here a few times, but I knew Jean was republican minded and I seen her down the North Link that one time getting stuck into the Brits. Jean was there alright. Now whether she was a member of the movement or not, I don't know. But she had her republican tendencies, there would have been no problem. She didn't like what was going on, it was as simple as that.'

Nevertheless, following the failed 1971 pub bombing Hector found himself incarcerated in Belfast's crumbling Crumlin Road prison. The Victorian-era building was notorious for its appalling conditions and had once compelled another Belfast republican, Terence 'Cleeky' Clarke (whom Hector would later share a cell with), to comment in a moment of dark humour that 'The Crum's so bad it would put you off going to jail'.[1] In the early 1970s the Crumlin Road was packed to capacity with internees waiting to be sent out to Long Kesh and IRA men on remand. Hector spent two years in Crumlin Road before being sent to Long Kesh in 1973. He was released from prison in 1975 and went back to war. He lasted one more year before he was badly wounded and was captured again.

I asked Hector how he coped with prison.

'The first thing you have t' keep in mind when ye go in prison is that 99% of your keepers in there are from the other side. And there's a lot of them that are connected t' the Orange Order, or the UVF or the UDA or whatever. And they were the ones that were supposed t' be looking after us! I don't want to dehumanise people, but when you are up against somebody like that and their main objective is to destroy you morally and physically, you learn a great deal very quickly.'

After coming out of prison in 1975 one of the Andersonstown IRA Volunteers whom Hector had a lot to do with was Danny Lennon. I asked him what Lennon was like. Given our previous conversation, in which Danny's name had 'come up' in relation to Jean's death, as well as the blame that had been heaped on Lennon after the deaths of the Maguire children in August 1976, I was intrigued by Hector's careful response.

'As a man he was like me or you. No different. Not bad. There was no malice and no badness in him. He had a job t' do when he joined the Irish Republican Army and he did it to the best of his ability. As a man, you wouldn't have got a better person. That's 100%. As a kid he had been what you would call a juvenile delinquent. But we were all growing up and getting into mischief and he done nothing bad. It was more for excitement than for badness or evil. Danny was similar to ourselves and he was a very good Volunteer.'

It was familiar territory but I felt I had to ask again about Jean. I wanted Hector's rejection of the idea that Danny Lennon was involved in Jean's death on tape. I asked Hector if he was sure that if Danny had been involved in Jean's death then he, Hector, would have heard about it.

'I would've known. That's 100%. I would've known one way or another. That's 100%. He could have, or he couldn't have, but as far as I know; nothing. But like I said to ye before, when you're out doing operations, at the end of the day you are not going t' go and tell anybody. Your life's on the line and the time is on the line with you—twenty or thirty years in jail.'

I was confused by these mixed messages. For every 100% guarantee that Danny Lennon did not kill Jean there was a sub-clause of doubt. I also felt there was a slight tension in the air; I was, after all, asking Hector if a fallen comrade and personal friend of his had killed my aunt. My questions were based completely on rumour and innuendo. I moved on. I asked Hector to talk about the second time he was captured. I had heard snippets of the story from my Uncle Gerry and others, but I wanted to hear Hector's version. It occurred on 9 August 1976, the fifth anniversary of internment (and Paddy McAdorey's death) and one day before Hector's comrade Danny Lennon and the Maguire children would die on Finaghy Road North.

'I was involved in an operation in August 1976. We attacked the vehicles the Brits were in. It was up near the brewery, just off the road there. We opened fire on 'em and on the way back t' base I ran into two jeep loads of 'em. I was on foot. They were firing from their vehicles and I was hit. I managed to get in t' a house but they took me out and threw me into a field. I didn't know if they were going t' do me off there and then, I hadn't a clue. They booted the shite clean outta me. I was shot through the leg and they stood on it and booted it stupid. I was taken from there into one of the barracks where I was given another tagging. This big captain he knew me and he says to me, "Hector, where's Danny and Sean?" That was the intelligence they had on us, they knew Danny Lennon was active and they knew I was active, but Sean wasn't an active Volunteer. They had that wrong but they were still looking for him. Straight on from there they took me to hospital where I spent six months, then back into the Crum, into a Diplock no jury court, and then into the H-blocks, all while I was still on crutches.'

He then reached down to show me his leg. As soon as he rolled up the cuff on his jeans I knew I should never have leaned over for a look. I'd seen healed bullet wounds before. In South Africa I had worked for a while doing research in Soweto and one of my closest friends was a former ANC activist called Kaizer Mohau who was one of the 'young lions' of the 1980s township rebellions. Kaizer had been shot by the South African army during a protest and one day he showed me the scar on his leg. On the front just to the right of his shin was a small round mark about the size of a five cent piece where the bullet had gone in and at the back was a larger scar, about the size of a twenty cent piece, where the bullet had exited.

Hector's wound was something different entirely. First of all there was the matter of his leg—I wanted to pretend not to look shocked but where a calf muscle should have been there was nothing but bone wrapped in skin. The whole back of his lower leg had been literally blown away and it looked as if someone had just carved a huge hunk of flesh off his calf. I was later to learn that he had lost a good portion of bone in the exit wound as well—it had been blown out the back of his leg with his calf muscle. So extensive was the mutilation caused by the bullet's exit that the doctors had initially wanted to amputate Hector's leg below the knee, but he had refused. And now he was showing what was left to me.

I was relieved when he pulled down his pant leg again and pulled off a boot on the opposite foot. This foot was normal except for the fact that the big toe had been half blown off by a British soldier's bullet. Hector wiggled his mutilated piggie at me. Then he pulled his sock back on, slipped on his boot and resumed his story.

'See, what had happened was that there was two of us and we had opened fire on them. As I said, we were making our way back t' base and he went his way and I went mine. I still had an armalite and I run into two jeep loads of them and they started firing. See they came 'round the corner and I was running down towards them so I just kept running at them. I got two or three rounds off and my gun jammed. I got shot and whack! [he hit his hand for emphasis] I hit the ground like a ton of bricks. I don't know where my weapon went. It was about ten to fifteen paces from the road up the path into a house. I remember there was pebbledash walls and I crawled up this path and there was a child standing there outside the door. The child was about eight or nine and was outside his door screaming for his Ma. They were still firing at me and the pebbledash was coming down and I got t' the door and I was just holding the child and the child was screaming. The mammy opened the door and the child got in and then the door was shut on me. I was laying there shouting "let me in missus I'm hit, I'm hit!" Fair play to her like, I mean I understand that woman's situation because there was bullets flying everywhere. They were still banging away at me but they couldn't hit me because I was in behind a wee canopy. The bullets were still hitting the pebbledash and it was falling like snow all around me. So, she opened the door anyway and I got in. I managed to crawl in t' the house and I got my gloves off and the hood off. I was actually able t' look out the window 'cause I was laying behind the couch and I could still see the two jeeps and I knew I was caught.'

Hector knew that this was the most deadly moment. He had engaged and fired at British soldiers and he was now seriously wounded and defenceless. The soldiers eventually came bursting in to the house.

'Them'uns finally came in and they later had it in their depositions that I said "please don't kill me", but I can't remember fucking saying that. It was at my trial and I was embarrassed. I rubbed that out myself 'cause I never said that.'

I was slightly amused by his rejection of what most people would consider to be a normal human response to his predicament. I asked Hector if he remembered being afraid he might die from his wounds.

'You don't think. You don't think about dying or nothing. My whole thing there was t' get away and nothing else. I knew they had me 'cause they'd seen me crawl in and I knew I wasn't going t' be able to crawl out the back because my leg was—well, there was nothing there, it was just hanging. I never felt any real pain at this stage t' be honest with ye. That wasn't until much later.'

Indeed, Hector was very seriously wounded and could have bled to death. This seemed not to especially worry his captors.

'They eventually came in after me and they took me out. They beat me and then they drove me through the area for a while with the armalite. They had my weapon and they drove round the area waving it from the jeep. Showing off. They took me down to this big fort of theirs and then battered the shite out o' me some more. This big intelligence officer, a captain, came in and pulled them off me. He said, "It's Hector, leave him alone! Search him!" So when they searched me they got a box of ammo and then they went bananas cause they'd captured a box of ammo. Then that's when they asked me, "where's Danny and Sean?" I never said nothing because by this stage I was in a state of shock. "Right", he says, "get him to hospital." So they put me into a meat wagon and took me to hospital.'

The *Belfast Newsletter* of Tuesday 10 August 1976—the day that Danny Lennon and the Maguire children were later killed on Finaghy Road North—carried a small story on the front page about Hector's capture. He wasn't mentioned by name and the version of events was sanitised:

A man is in the Mater Hospital after a shooting incident involving security forces in the Andersonstown area yesterday afternoon. It is understood that his condition is satisfactory. According to an Army statement, a gunman opened fire on a security forces patrol at Ramoan Gardens. He fired three high velocity shots which missed. The patrol returned fire, and the gunman was seen to fall. Shortly afterwards the patrol picked up a man with a gunshot wound in the leg. In the vicinity was found an Armalite rifle.

Ramoan Gardens is only a five minute drive from Tardree Park and a few minutes' stroll to the Tullymore Gardens/Rossnareen Avenue area where Danny Lennon and his two comrades would engage the British Army in a fateful ambush later that day.

It was a long and painful convalescence for Hector. He eventually arrived in the H-blocks of Long Kesh in 1977 as the campaign for the reinstatement of political prisoner status was beginning to escalate. For rejecting criminalisation and for refusing to wear prison uniform, IRA prisoners were denied clothes, exercise, reading and writing materials, radios, and furniture in their cells. They were kept on permanent lock-up and a 'minimalist' diet. The closest thing they had to entertainment was shouting out stories and songs at night through locked cell doors, or dangling food on a wire and watching the rats attack each other to get at it. Altogether it was the beginning of a struggle inside the prisons that would see 400 IRA prisoners (the majority of whom were between 17 and 25 years old) 'on the blanket', would result in the 'dirty protest', and would end with the 1981 hunger strike. Hector was inside the IRA wings in the H-blocks during this entire period. He knew several of the hunger strikers personally. He suffered the same indignities as them and fought the same battles inside the concrete walls of Long Kesh.

I had read the two most famous books of the H-block struggle and the 1981 hunger strike, *Ten Men Dead* and *Nor Meekly Serve My Time*, and was aware of the inconceivable hardship endured by IRA prisoners at that time. One has to be extraordinarily desperate to turn one's own body into a weapon—wiping your own faeces on the walls or starving yourself to death. Catholic priests, the only people from outside the prison system who had any sort of regular contact with the blanketmen and dirty protesters at this time, reported to the media about:

> …outbreaks of scabies; skin infections; intestinal and stomach disorders; hepatitis; muscle wastage through lack of exercise; cramps; failing eye-sight; perforated eardrums; broken limbs and old wounds reopened, as the result of beatings; malnutrition through poor diet and food made inedible by the urine, disinfectant, glass and spit sometimes added to it by warders and Loyalist orderlies; above all, extreme nervous debility.[2]

Although anecdotes about Hector told by other IRA inmates feature in both *Ten Men Dead* and *Nor Meekly Serve My Time*, this was the first time Hector had ever sat down and spoken on tape about his experiences in Long Kesh himself. I felt he was unburdening himself.

'So I was still on crutches when I arrived at the H-blocks. When you arrive they strip ye naked 'cause I wouldn't wear the uniform—ye know, I wouldn't touch the prison garb they give ye. Then they march ye up into the wing and they put me in a cell. They give ye a wee blanket t' wear and then that was you twenty-four, seven a week in that cell. Four weeks a month, twelve months a year, that was you. You never moved out of that cell. Even if ye wanted to see the doctor ye had t' put on the prison trousers which we refused t' do. The only time we wore the trousers was when we went t' mass on Sundays and a lot didn't even go t' mass. I was in a cell with big Cleeky Clarke at first and then later on with a few other fellas. But there was fellas in cells nearby who ye never ever even seen because you never left the cell.'

I'd heard of Terence 'Cleeky' Clarke. He came from Ardoyne and went to school with my father. My Uncle Manuel remembers him as always being 'a wee hard man and a ringleader. He always had a gang around him as a kid.' After 1969 Cleeky became involved with the Provos in Ardoyne and was captured by the security forces in 1971. He was sent to Crumlin Road jail where Gerry Adams reports he muttered that dark jibe about conditions being so bad it would put you off going to prison. That November, just before Hector arrived at the prison, Cleeky Clarke and eight others escaped by climbing over the Crum's high walls. They were known thereafter as the 'Crumlin Kangaroos'. Clarke took up IRA active service again and was recaptured in October 1972. Between 1971 and 1996 he served about twenty years in prison and was one of the men sentenced for the March 1988 funeral incident on the Andersonstown Road when two undercover Army corporals had been apprehended in their car, beaten and later killed. But in the late 1970s Cleeky was in a small cell with Hector, shivering in a blanket and denied all forms of leisure or comfort other than talking to each other.[3]

I asked Hector what a typical day for a blanket man in 1977 was like.

'The doors were steel doors and them'uns all had batons and they battered your door at six o'clock in the morning and they give you yer breakfast. The breakfast was cold porridge and two bits of dried bread. If you wanted t' go to the toilet—this was before the dirty protest was on—you had t' ring and ring and ring the bell. There'd be no response and that would go on for quite some time. And then when you did get out t' go to the toilet you were harassed: "you Fenian bastards", "you scumbags", "youse are just like yer priests, youse are all sewer rats". And then sometimes you were just battered. It was the exact same on the visits.'

Visits in Long Kesh during this period were notorious. The haggard physical appearance of the blanketmen put immense strain on the families and after each visit prisoners were subjected to violent internal searches to try to stop them smuggling notes or tobacco in to the prison up their arses, in their mouths, or under their foreskins.

'Afterwards they'd strip ye naked and put you over the mirror. You refused t' go over the mirror so they'd force ye down over the mirror.

Batter you down. They'd flashlight search yer back passage, stick it up t' see if you were carrying anything inside ye. Then they got the table. Three or four of them would come get ye from the cell and they'd lift you up and throw ye on t' the table on yer belly. They'd be one on each side of ye holding yer arms and more holding yer legs open. Then another one would spread yer cheeks open and stick his fingers right up inside you. Then they would open yer mouth and use them same fingers for t' check yer mouth as well. They were real bastards. They were raping us. Literally, that's what they were doing, raping us. But they couldn't break us.'

Indeed, if the first hand accounts in *Ten Men Dead* and *Nor Meekly Serve My Time* are anything to go by, Hector was decidedly unbroken and unbowed. One short anecdote from Joe McQuillan serves to illustrate the point.

> One such screw we had named 'Vinegar-face'. In response to this, Teapot and Hector scraped the words 'Vinegar-face has no balls' onto their cell door. That afternoon when Vinegar-face came around with the tea, he noticed the writing and said, 'Whoever wrote that has no balls; they wouldn't sign it'. That night when he came around with the supper the notice had been amended, 'Vinegar-face has no balls, signed Teapot and Hector'. Teapot and Hector stood at the door and said to him, 'Who has no balls?' He just closed the door and walked away.[4]

Still, it was the endless harassment meted out by groups of 'screws' on the way to and from the toilets that led to the escalation of hostilities and eventually to the dirty protest. Hector was in the frontline as usual.

'At the time it felt like there was nothing else we could do. I was on the dirty protest for years. There was a terrible cloud of depression at the time. There was always a dark depression that hung over the H-blocks, but it was just like we weren't going t' take the beating on the way t' the toilets any more so we started doing it in the cells. And we started wiping the excrement all over the cells with our bare hands. It was a way t' keep them'uns off yer back, because you didn't want them'uns touching ye or coming near ye. It got t' the point at one stage that we even discussed washing ourselves in it, just t' keep them'uns away from us.'

I asked what his cell was like.

'Well, you had excrement up on the four walls of the cell and then ye had a wee corner for yerself. You had yer rubbish lying in the corner. If you had a half decent summer the blue-bottles were in and they were laying their eggs and then you'd wake up in the morning and the maggots would be all around yer bed. Maggots fucking everywhere. And then the worms started crawling outta people. Sometimes there were wee things floating about the cell in urine as well. We'd put all our windows in and you only had a wee blanket around ye so in the winter you had the snow coming in. You'd be blue. Then you'd have t' move wing every three days into a clean wing. See, after we'd leave they'd clean the wing with power hoses and these wee mad suits 'n' all. And then you'd be in a clean cell and it would just start all over again. It was just a vicious circle. Every three days you were moved. Every three days you were battered. I lived like that for five years.'

The desperation of the dirty protest led eventually to the IRA prisoners' final stand—the hunger strike of 1981. Hector had had a cell near Bobby Sands right before the strike started. I asked him what Sands was like and Hector got an awful serious look on his face.

'Bobby Sands. Defining Bobby... [long pause]... I guess yer expecting me t' say that Bobby was one of the finest blokes you'll ever meet, but he was. And that's not because he died on hunger strike. He was just an ordinary guy. Bobby would never have fucking died on hunger strike if this war hadn't started.'

There was another long pause.

'He liked singing, he liked playing the guitar, that was him. And the stories, he loved telling fucking stories. I don't know if you've ever read the book called *Jet*, it's an American book about these bikers and I tell you what, you ask any blanketman if Bobby told any stories in the H-block and they'll say "*Jet*, and it was fucking brilliant". You thought ye were actually watching a film because he was that good it captivated you. Now he made that last for about four or five nights, everybody would be like "Bobby wait a minute, I'll just settle down".'

It was nights like that that made the unbearable endurable. Deprived of reading material and locked up for twenty-four hours a day in their own excrement, prisoners had to rely on themselves for entertainment. Songs and stories were shouted out through the bars at night. According to Hector 'some of the talent in there was bloody marvellous'. Among others, Bik McFarlane from Ardoyne, IRA Long Kesh commanding officer during the hunger strike, was a great whistler and would whistle songs for his wing from the cell door. Others would sing, shout out Irish language lessons, recite poetry or give classes in Irish history. Bobby Sands was apparently matchless and Gerry Adams later tried to explain his motivations:

> It takes bone-deep commitment to lie naked and alone in a prison
> cell in your own excreta, systematically beaten and brutalised,
> scrubbed with yard brushes and hosed with industrial disinfectant.
> But it is soul-deep commitment to rise above all of this to stand at
> the cell door telling of films or books you enjoyed, and enthralling
> and uplifting others in the telling.[5]

Bobby Sands died on 5 May 1981 after sixty-six days on hunger strike. In the British Parliament Margaret Thatcher commented that: 'Mr Sands was a convicted criminal. He chose to take his own life. It was a choice that his organisation did not allow to many of its victims.'[6] Undeterred, an estimated 100,000 people joined Bobby Sands' funeral procession from Twinbrook to the republican plot at Milltown cemetery. Rioting broke out across Northern Ireland and even in Dublin it took massive police intervention to prevent a large and angry crowd from torching the British

Embassy. Nothing would be the same in Long Kesh or in Northern Ireland ever again. A lot has been made of the fact that in ancient Gaelic law you fasted against someone who wronged you—starving yourself to death and leaving your ghost to haunt the conscience of your transgressor. Certainly the hungry ghosts of Bobby Sands and his nine dead comrades have continued to haunt the British government. They failed to understand that in Irish history sometimes you can win more by dying than by living.

Hector was finally released from Long Kesh in 1986. He had only been twenty years old when he had joined the IRA in 1970. He had been in jail from 1971 to 1975 and then from 1976 till 1986. He'd spent fourteen years, nearly half of his life, behind bars—surviving on the blanket, enduring the dirty protest and struggling through the hunger strikes. I asked him how he coped being back on the outside.

'The day I got out of prison they were an hour late releasing me and I thought I was going t' be kept in. I thought they had something else on me and I started t' panic. When I finally walked out my brother practically had t' carry me 'cause then I knew it was real. I remember that first night but then for the two weeks after that I haven't a clue. It's a blank in my head. I don't know where those two weeks went and whether I was drinking or what, but I haven't a clue. It's just a blank. Even now sometimes at night I still wake up sweating. Or sometimes I wake up thinking "where the fuck am I? Am I in the house or am I in jail?" You do get that. People say I've got post-traumatic stress disorder. Whatever that is or if I do have it or not, I don't know. I went in to a counsellor one time and before I went in I was sitting reading a magazine and it was about a Brit who fought in the Falklands giving his experiences after the war and how he felt and all. What he was actually describing I was going through; the sweating and the waking up and the whole lot. It's only now, ten years after getting out, that I'm getting it together. I'm doing better than some of these others that have ended up swallowing the river—choking on their vomit. These are ex-republican POWs, blanketmen who literally ended up drinking themselves to death—swallowing the river. I was on that river myself but I got out of it. I think there is just a lot inside you that won't come out until this war is all over.'

I was about to finish the interview right then and turn off the tape when to my surprise Hector returned to the issue of Jean's death. He remarked that he was in Crumlin Road jail in 1972 and that someone had shown him a newspaper with a picture of Jean in it.

'Paper said someone from Tardree Park had been shot and I realised who it was and I couldn't believe it. I just couldn't believe Jean was dead. It didn't hit home, I mean she only lived across the street and I just couldn't believe it. That's how I found out, from the *Irish News*.'

Encouraged by his willingness to return to the subject I asked him how he felt when he found out that it was rumoured that the IRA were responsible. I knew it was a controversial question; it's not like the IRA has ever publicly accepted responsibility for killing Jean. I had no idea how

Hector would respond. There was a long pause, almost ten seconds. Hector spoke softly and quietly.

'Obviously it hurt. To kill one of yer own in an accident when they are after a military target, it's fucking deadly. It's hurtful because it's one of yer own. But not only one of yer own, but someone you know pretty well.'

That was it. I knew he wouldn't tell me any more even if he knew. I thanked him for his time and he bade me farewell, closing the door behind me and going in to talk to his mother.

As I walked home I thought about the recent outrage in the press over the escape of Liam Averill and the killing of King Rat. There had been suggestions that Long Kesh had become a paramilitary holiday camp. I knew that to the extent that the prisoners there had relaxed conditions it was because of ten dead hunger strikers and due to the suffering endured by men like Hector. Men who sat in cold concrete cells twenty-four hours a day for years on end with shit-smeared walls and maggots wriggling in their uncut hair. Hardened men who regarded themselves as prisoners of war whether the British government wanted to recognise them as such or not.

I walked on.

24

Liam Averill's Undies

'I am standing on the threshold of another trembling world.'
Bobby Sands' diary on the first day of his hunger strike.

John and I sat in the car at an intersection on the Andersonstown Road behind two armoured British Army jeeps which were farting hot fog out into the brittle Belfast winter morning air. We were on our way out to the Kesh to visit Ciarán again and had briefly stopped off to pick up some newspapers. As we came out of the parking lot we had run straight in to a mobile Army patrol and got stuck behind it. We sat there at the traffic lights sandwiched in between the anti-rocket armoured flaps of the jeeps with their copious exhaust belching all over Big John's little car. 'This is fucking ridiculous, isn't it?' said John. I had to agree that yes, it was a little unusual.

Other than that, the now familiar drive out to Lisburn and Long Kesh was uneventful. Outside in the fields and farms around Lisburn cows and farmers were going about their frosty damp early morning business. We arrived at the prison without incident and I gave my name to the guard at the front desk again in a Belfast accent, thus avoiding the embarrassment of having to spell my name out at volume.

Today the visitors wing was packed with children, wives and loved ones down for a weekend visit. I had been in B-wing on the previous Wednesday and there had hardly been a soul about. Today there were children and babies everywhere. I went over what I had read about the IRA operation that had led to Ciarán being charged with double murder and sent to jail for life.

■■■■

The bombing took place at Musgrave Park hospital on Saturday 2 November 1991. An IRA unit cut through a reinforced door and planted twenty pounds of semtex in an underground duct that ran into the military annex beside the hospital. When the bomb exploded two British soldiers who had been watching the Rugby World Cup on TV were killed instantly: Private Craig Pantry (age 20) and Warrant Officer Philip Cross (age 33). At least seven other people, including the five year old daughter of a soldier, were wounded. Cross, married with children and from north-east England, had been in the Army seventeen years. Pantry was single and had only been in the Army nineteen months after giving up his job as a postman.

The bombing was the first IRA bomb attack on British soldiers to be carried out on the grounds of a hospital. The media and politicians reached for their thesauruses to find new words of condemnation for the bombers as the papers rolled off the press on Monday morning. The *Belfast Telegraph* of 4 November carried the bitter heartbroken words of the widow of one of the soldiers, Janet Cross, who made the dubious claim that 'even Hitler' would not have carried out such an attack. She added, 'I still cannot believe they blew up the hospital with no warning. That I will never forgive.' David Pantry, an uncle of the other soldier, was similarly outraged by the death of his Army ambulance driver nephew:

> I just can't see what they hope to gain by blowing an ambulance man into eternity. He never so much as picked up a rifle in anger. He was over there doing a humanitarian job and this is what happened. It is hard to understand what anyone can gain by blowing him to pieces.

The *Irish News* of the same day also ran with the story on the front page accompanied by two pictures of the blast wreckage and a photo of each of the dead soldiers. The Anglican bishop of Connor, Dr Samuel Poyntz, was quoted as saying that he was exasperated by 'the depravity of terrorists'. The minister for Northern Ireland, Richard Needham, meanwhile condemned 'the godfathers of the IRA' for putting the lives of sick children at risk and said that the Musgrave Park bombing proved that the IRA were 'fascist beasts who belong in hell'. Such colourfully violent rhetoric clearly found an audience amongst the far right of Northern Ireland politics. DUP councillor Sammy Wilson promptly responded to Needham's remarks by saying that 'Instead of rhetoric, lets have some reprisals which ensure they are dispatched to Hell as quickly as possible'. With slightly more restraint, Ken Maginnis of the Ulster Unionist Party called for the reintroduction of internment without trial. The Lord Mayor of Belfast, Nigel Dodds, commented that 'An organisation which stoops to bombing a hospital deserves to be shown no mercy'.

Nor was the wave of condemnation confined to the Orange-tinged side of Ulster politics. Joe Hedron of the nationalist SDLP denounced the 'Provo's savagery' and the Dublin government's Minister of Foreign Affairs, Gerry Collins, said the attack was 'a most heinous violation of the most basic standards of human decency'. Meanwhile, the hospital's white collar union, the MSF, said the bombing was 'a new low' in the Troubles, and Dr John Alderice of the Alliance Party declared it to be a 'devilish atrocity'. The general consensus seemed to be that something hideous, unforgivable and new had occurred. Desperately fighting a rearguard action in the propaganda war, Sinn Féin president Gerry Adams responded to the public tirades in comments which were printed separately in Monday's edition of the *Irish News* under the headline, 'Killer bomb attack is defended by SF chief'. Adams refused to condemn the bombers:

> Many people will note that British ministers and other politicians are not as outspoken about other deaths arising out of this conflict. Unlike them, Sinn Féin regrets all deaths and injuries. The politics of condemnation are no substitute for a real process towards peace.

Later in the same article the *Irish News* also quoted a separate statement released by the IRA to, in their words, counter the 'intense disinformation' about the bombing of 'an operational British Army base situated adjacent to a hospital'. The IRA spokesman who phoned the *Irish News* emphasised that 'The IRA states categorically that this was not an attack on the hospital' and went on to accuse the British Army of using civilians as 'human shields'. 'It is not the IRA, but the British Army and their political masters who have chosen to build military barracks adjacent to hospitals and schools and on top of nurses' homes and residential blacks of flats.' Such arguments may have slightly eased anxieties down the Falls or in South Armagh, but many others were unmoved.

The following day, Tuesday 5 November, the first public allegations surfaced about the involvement of someone inside the hospital in the bombing. The *Irish News* opened with 'Killer bomb "was result of collusion"' and quoted an Ulster Unionist councillor who alleged that 'Someone certainly working on that block supplied information to the terrorists'. In a separate article it was also reported that Janet Cross, the widow of one of soldiers, had flown to Manchester to inform her sons of their father's death, declaring the IRA to be 'monsters' before departing Northern Ireland. The story then disappeared until Friday, 8 November, when the *Irish News* covered the funeral of Craig Pantry and reported that 'A 24-year-old hospital porter has been remanded in custody in Belfast charged with murdering the two soldiers and the attempted murder of two other soldiers and a five-year-old girl'. That was Ciarán. The RUC believed they had captured the 'monster' who had bombed Musgrave.

Saturday's *Irish News* (9 November) carried an article detailing the previous day's funeral for Philip Cross in Manchester. In front of five hundred mourners Rector Philip Foster stood and declared that Warrant Officer Cross had died in pursuit of a noble cause:

> The Army is in Northern Ireland to pursue the cause of right. Of course, it will make mistakes, errors of judgement. People do. But the cause remains. The cause is to stand facing the armalite to defend the ballot box. The cause is to maintain peace and security for the people of Northern Ireland… The cause is right. But the cost is monstrously high.

One couldn't help wondering how the families of the fourteen unarmed civilians gunned down by British paratroopers on Bloody

Sunday in January 1972 felt about this 'cause of right'. Or what of the first eight people to die in July and August of 1969 during the opening moments of the modern Troubles—seven of whom had been killed by the RUC, two of them beaten to death? Was the price *they* had to pay for the British presence in Ireland not 'monstrously high'? Were their deaths any less tragic? The British officer who commanded the paratroopers in Derry on Bloody Sunday, Lieutenant-Colonel Derek Wilford, was never vilified as a 'monster', a 'devil', or a 'savage' in the British press. He was awarded an OBE by the Queen instead.

I think it was Voltaire who once said that killing fellow human beings is considered murder unless it is carried out to the sound of trumpets. And therein lies the problem.

■ ■ ■ ■

Ciarán came on to the visitor's wing sporting a freshly grown moustache and I immediately told him that his 'mo' made him look like a Mexican bandit. He smiled and apologised for being so late; he had been given quite a lengthy search before being let in. The visit went the same as last time, good *craic* mixed in with gossip and politics and John would tell me later on that he thought Ciarán appeared more relaxed this time. During our visit Ciarán emphasised that while he was serving his prison sentence on an IRA wing, he had never been charged with IRA membership (an offence in both Britain and Ireland). As a 'republican activist' he had simply 'chosen to serve my sentence with republican comrades in the H-blocks'. He also reminded me that he had been sentenced for allegedly bombing Musgrave and killing two soldiers in a Diplock, no jury, court where he had pleaded not guilty.

Identified by an eyewitness as travelling in the car that brought the bomb into Musgrave Park, Ciarán's defence in court had been that the car which he was identified as having been in was hijacked and he had been forced to go with an IRA Active Service Unit to the hospital. He signed a statement for the RUC to that affect and pleaded not guilty to the charge of blowing up the hospital and deliberately causing the deaths of the two soldiers. He got a double life sentence anyway.

Cairán elected to serve his sentence on an IRA wing in Long Kesh. His uncle, now a leading member of Sinn Féin, his father and at least one of his cousins had all done time on IRA wings before him. As a child he had grown up with male relatives interned and incarcerated in the Kesh. In both a figurative and literal sense therefore, Ciarán was following in the footsteps of his family.

At about 12pm a guard laid a piece of paper at the end of the table informing us that our visit was officially over. We said our goodbyes a few minutes later. I knew that this was the last time I would see him before I returned to Australia. The moment must have shown on my face because Cairán immediately said, 'Now I'm not going to be getting all emotional for ye Simon'. We simply shook hands and I promised to write and to visit him next time I was in Belfast. And then we turned and walked away.

■ ■ ■ ■

The trip out of Long Kesh was uneventful except for one moment when a guard opened the packed visitor's van to count us and a child of about five or six immediately chimed in with a loud classroom-like 'present!', much to the amusement of one and all. Outside the prison walls I picked up a book Ciarán had left for me while John picked up a sack containing the dirty laundry that he had agreed to drop off at Cairán's mother's house. With his own money Cairán had bought me a book and it was waiting in a special office at the front of the jail in a thick brown envelope with 'On Her Majesty's Service' printed on the side. I opened the envelope to find a copy of *Nor Meekly Serve My Time*, the famous account of the 1981 hunger strike. There were anecdotes about Hector in the book and it is possibly the most important 'inside history' of the IRA wings at Long Kesh ever written. Moreover, Cairán had got all the prisoners of H8, his wing, to sign the book for me and many had written their prison sentence below their name and place of origin. It was terrifying reading—'Bun McCullough, Ballymurphy, 20 yrs', 'Pat Martin, Belfast, 35 yrs', 'Kevin McShane, Beechmount, 16 yrs', 'Patrick Murray, A'town, 23 yrs', 'Gerry Butler, Ballycastle, Life', 'Paddy O'Dowd, Lurgan, Life', 'Peter Markey, Newry, Life', and so on and so on. Hundreds of years of prison time etched in small signatures. Near the back of the book I noticed that Pádraic Wilson, the IRA's Commanding Officer in Long Kesh at the time, had also signed. It was a gift that required some effort on Cairán's behalf and I wished I could have walked back in to the prison to thank him personally. Instead I had to content myself with walking over to where John was at a different desk waiting for Cairán's dirty laundry.

An elongated middle-aged guard was rummaging around at the back of the office looking at the names on the side of various sacks of dirty laundry while John and I stood at the counter waiting. On the wall in front of us was a large chart with the names of all the prisoners in the jail and their prison numbers. Various marks had been made beside their names which obviously represented when clothes had been taken in and out of the prison. I noticed the name at the top of the list was 'ADAMS', for Gerry's cousin Davy I presumed, as I knew he was doing twenty-five years in the Kesh for 'conspiracy to murder' a senior RUC detective.

John then pointed out that the second name on the list was 'AVERILL' for IRA prisoner Liam Averill. Averill had actually escaped from Long Kesh a few weeks earlier during a Christmas party held on 10 December for the children of inmates. Averill, disguised as a woman, had quietly slipped on to the visitor's van and simply slipped out of the jail. His cross-dressing exit from prison caused a major scandal in Northern Ireland. It was the first IRA escape from Long Kesh since 1983, and Unionist politicians went apoplectic. How, they argued, could a convicted double-murderer dressed as a woman simply climb in to a van with common visitors and walk out the front gate of the most secure anti-terrorist prison in Europe? It was simply inconceivable. The newspapers were also astounded. The *Irish Times* was stunned into stating the bleeding obvious in their 'IRA prisoner escapes from Maze prison' story the following day, remarking of Averill that 'Apparently he was not eligible for Christmas leave'. Loyalist ire was further provoked when Gerry Adams, speaking on radio, was asked what he felt about Averill's unapproved Christmas leave. Adams replied that 'While there are prisoners, there will be prisoners who try to escape. I tried it myself. Liam Averill succeeded where I didn't. Good luck to him.' Averill's photograph later appeared, smiling and free at some undisclosed location, on the front cover of *An Phoblacht*.[1]

John mentioned that maybe the prison authorities were leaving Averill's name up on the board in the hope he might return to pick up his dirty undies. Then they could nab him and put him back in the Kesh. We had a giggle about that until the guard returned with the sack of Ciarán's dirty laundry and we, like Liam Averill, left HM Maze Prison.

■ ■ ■ ■

Cairán's mother met us at the door and ushered us inside her small house in a street off the Lower Falls. 'Come in before ye catch a death out there,' she said, beckoning us in to a room where Cairán's sister and two of her children were sitting on the couch. The children were watching 'Barney' on the TV and I noticed that a copy of *An Phoblacht* was resting on the floor alongside the couch. We exchanged pleasantries, John handed over the sack of dirty laundry and Cairán's mum asked how I was enjoying Belfast.

'It's good to see family again and the *craic*'s fantastic, but you can keep the weather.'

'Aye, ye poor wee thing, you'd not be used t' this sort of cold air down in Australia now would ye?'

We all agreed that my delicate disposition left me unsuited to the Ulster climate. After a while John mentioned that Averill's name was still up on the laundry notice in Long Kesh and Cairán's mum had a funny story to tell us of her own about all of that. She had actually been at the Long Kesh Christmas party in question, having taken one of Ciarán's sons up to have a visit with his father. Liam Averill, unbeknown to her, had been dressed in drag and was sitting in the van with her and her grandson on the way out of the prison. In an interview later published in *An Phoblacht* Averill mentioned that a wee boy had ducked down when a screw had taken a head-count in the van and that this had caused some confusion. The numbers didn't match. Averill, at the time, thought he had been discovered. The wee boy in question was actually Ciarán's son. Eventually he bobbed back up, the head-count was taken again and everything was sorted out. Averill made it out of the prison and made his escape. Cairán's mum was none the wiser until she heard that an IRA man had escaped from Long Kesh that day and read Averill's own account later in *An Phoblacht*.

The centre-spread of the 8 January edition of *An Phoblacht* carried a lengthy interview with Averill and featured a large picture of him holding a copy of the previous edition of the paper in which his escape had been heralded on the front cover with the headline, 'Out for Christmas'. The smile on his face said it all and he was not shy in detailing the humorous side of his departure from Long Kesh. Apparently the night before the big escape he lay awake in his cell and then decided to put the wasted sleep to use by shaving his legs. He spent the following morning helping out at the Christmas party and remarked that there were 'about 108 kids there, absolute bedlam, but great craic'. At about 2:25pm he went and changed, putting on a wig and make-up. According to Averill, 'I spent about 20 minutes with the make-up and felt "transformed" in my new gender'. He then mingled with the crowd and made his way on to the visitor's van at the end of the party. The van was driven through several checkpoints and then a head count was taken. That's when Cairán's mum and son enter the story.

> At the last check the screw counted a few times and I thought the worst but the screw realised that a kid who was messing about by hiding popped his head up as he [the screw] came down the bus. The screw, now happy with the count, let the bus go and before I knew it I was in the car park. I felt so elated, it was brilliant.

Averill, who was already being referred to as 'Comrade Doubtfire' by some Long Kesh prisoners, ended his interview arguing that 'it is impossible to imprison an ideal' and remarking that, yes, he had heard that people had been phoning radio stations and requesting the song 'Sometimes it's hard to be a woman' in his name.[2]

A few weeks later Cairán's mum was back in the Kesh again visiting Cairán when King Rat was killed. No one had any idea at the time what was going on. She remembers sitting in the waiting room after being searched as the first visitors were sent back from the visitor's wing. After some confusion and delay she still got to visit her son and it was then that she discovered the news of the death of Billy Wright. At this point Cairán's sister, who had been quietly sitting on the couch, chimed in, 'Only God can judge, but that'un was the devil's own'.

I told Cairán's mum to contact me if he was ever wanting for anything and then we left.

■ ■ ■ ■

Gran had an Ulster fry waiting for us when we got home. After a morning in the Kesh I felt happy to be warm and protected and amongst family. The *craic* at the dinner table was cheerful and for once I was happy to just sit back and enjoy the banter. Big John spoke with concern and wonder in his voice to Gran.

'What's this I hear about yer Pat being sick again?'

'Ach aye, it's true. Her blood's bad, just like our Síle.'

'What's wrong with Síle?'

'Her blood's high.'

'I thought that was Margaret?'

'No, her blood's low.'

'Jay-sus, if yer family was dogs they'd have all been put down by now.'

And so on and so on. Meanwhile Dan was shooting at me across the table with his fork, pretending it was a gun, and Conor was gurning about wanting a bap instead. I sat still and said nothing. I hadn't found Jean's killer, I had plainly failed in that regard, but I wanted to enjoy this before I had to leave for Australia.

After dinner Sharon came home from work and Kevin, John's brother, rang to tell us that someone had just been kneecapped in the New Lodge. While John was still talking to Kevin on the phone I went upstairs to the attic to record the day's events in my diary. It only took a few minutes before wee Dan, all dressed up in his camouflage Action Man outfit, poked his four year old head up to have a look what was going on. 'Are ye doing yer homework, Simon?' I asked him if he wanted to come up and play while I wrote in my diary. 'Aye, OK.' He lay beside me on the bed for a while until he got bored and started marching around the attic. I looked over at him and couldn't help but smile.

'*A Dhonncha, is buachaill dána thú.*'

The Irish was lost on him.

'I said that you are a bold boy, Dan.'

He smirked and shook his tiny fist at me.

After a while I stopped writing and Dan asked if I could put my underarm deodorant on him, 'Put the smell of an African on me again'. I dutifully daubed his tiny underarms and then he was back over to the ladder on his way downstairs. I was left alone to the cold contemplation of the attic.

25

Sunday Dinner and a Wee Riot

'IRA terror leaders here are now sending their shock troops to war—their own children. Bomb-throwing eight-year olds are in the front line. They steal out at dusk to play games with death, trained to hate and kill. And the children at war chant obscenities to nursery rhyme tunes as the bullets fly.'

The Sun, 8 February 1971

'Wrong place, wrong time... wrong country.'
Front page of *The Mirror* (N. Ireland), 19 January 1998

My head felt like someone had detonated a fragmentation grenade just behind my left eye. I was hearing the constant thud, thud, thudding of British Army helicopters inside my skull although none were visible in the dark morning sky above my bed in the attic. After I'd finished writing in my journal the night before, Sharon had come home from work and suggested that she, Big John and I go down to the Gravediggers Arms for a drink. The Gravediggers Arms, at the junction of the Glen and Falls roads, is so named because it is directly across from Milltown cemetery and in days of yore it was a common haunt of the gravediggers in the employ of cemetery's administrators. A nice spot for a wee drink over the lunch hour or when the dying business was slow. We ourselves only went down for a single quiet cleansing ale that night but the pub was packed and as that 'inebriate of some repute' Brendan Behan was known to say, 'getting in was a bit easier than getting out'. The ale flowed freely. I remember giving a few pound coins to a man who came around collecting money for republican prisoners and I remember being accused of being a Canadian by a man in the toilets, but other than that the night was a bit of a blur. And now, the following morning, my mind was a blur. And yet, somehow, I made it downstairs and limped wretchedly in to the kitchen. Gran was standing at a hissing stove.

'Sit ye down Simon, you've got an awful sickly look about ye. I've a wee Ulster fry on for ye right now. I was just after sending Conor t' go wake ye.'

The scent of baked beans, hot chips, fried egg, bacon rashers, potato bread, toast and everything else wafted over towards me. And good to her word as always, a few moments later Gran placed a plate overflowing with heart-attack food before me. I could practically feel my arteries hardening as I ate and the hangover in my belly was quickly drowned in a sea of delicious grease. Bloated and content I was, if not an entirely new man, then at least a man newly fortified with baked beans, rashers and ambition. So, it was back upstairs with me and into the bathroom to scrape the hair off my face and then slip in to the shower to get busy with the soap and water. It was while I was applying the pear-scented shampoo to my depleted quoife that Big John yelled from outside the door.

'You be long in there Simon? We're all away over t' the New Lodge t' visit me Ma and Da. D'ye want t' take the trip over, like?'

■ ■ ■ ■

As Big John pulled the car into the curb in the narrow street outside his Ma's house a mini-riot was about to start at the corner of the street. About a dozen boys between the ages of nine and fourteen were gathering on wasteground beside a gable wall. They were collecting stones and empty bottles and arguing over tactics as Big John, Sharon, Conor, Wee Dan and I got out of the car about thirty metres away. I could hear a small boy of about eight insisting that he had just seen two Brit armoured jeeps entering at the top of the estate, 'Are you sure?!', the others were saying, and we could hear them arguing over which street they were likely to drive down and where the best place to ambush them was. 'Just getting ready for a wee Sunday afternoon riot', said Big John, nodding in the direction of the boys, as he opened the front door of his mother's house and he, Sharon and the kids nonchalantly walked in. Then, at that exact moment I heard and saw two British Army jeeps turn in to the long narrow street at the end furthest away from the gathering boys and saw them scatter and take up positions in the nearby entries and alleyways. I was fascinated by this and indicated to John and Sharon that I would join them inside in a few moments; in the meantime I might watch the car and make sure it didn't get accidentally hit by any stones. 'Fair enough', says John, and with that I took up a prime spectator's position on the front step as about two hundred metres up the road the ambling armour-plated jeeps of the British Army crept closer towards me and the awaiting ambush.

When the jeeps got about fifty metres from me one of the two soldiers poking out of the top pointed his rifle and trained the barrel on me as the jeep drew slowly closer. And then, just as the jeeps were about even with the front doorstep of John's Ma's house the first empty Coke bottle exploded against the far side of the armour plating, shattering glass and spraying it in to the air. There was then a loud bang and the second jeep in the convoy rocked a little as a large rock slammed in to the side. I heard the young British soldier on top, who was still pointing his rifle at me, call out 'woo-hoo, 'ere we go!' He seemed to smile a little as he flipped down the safety visor on his Army helmet. And then it was on, as they say, for one and all. A dozen young boys converged from the entries and alleyways hurling stones and bottles at the last jeep in the convoy as the first jeep made it to the bottom of the street, turned right and accelerated away. As the second jeep slowly lumbered around the same corner a few moments later about half a dozen of the braver and older boys chased it, throwing stones and bottles at the British soldier who was training his rifle at them as they ran choking into the jeep's exhaust fumes. I could hear the dull thud of stones on armour plating as the jeep carried on down the road.

With the jeeps gone the boys quickly re-convened in the centre of the wasteground with the usual, 'did you see the one I threw that hit the windscreen?', kind of bravado that is universal to young boys in dangerous situations everywhere. 'Which way did they turn?', the older boys were asking and there was much discourse as to which street the jeeps were likely to drive down next and the best place to ambush them again. Stones were re-gathered and they then set off jogging to get themselves in place. I watched them disappear down the street.

The Sunday afternoon riot having moved off to another location, I went inside to John's Ma's house. As soon as I stepped inside the door I was met by Eamonn, John's fourteen year old brother, who had heard the thudding stones and come to see what the *craic* was. I explained that it was just a wee riot but that they had moved along now. Eamonn craned his neck out the door to see if he could catch the last of the action.

'I hate the Brits, so I do. I threw a rock at a jeep the other night and they come after me and I run and they just kept coming and chasing me down all the entries and I had t' climb into a taxi and say, "Please help me, the Brits are after me", so I did. Yer man just told me t' lay on the floor until they passed by and then I came on home.'

'Is that right Eamonn? You best watch yourself or one of those fellas will shoot you with a plastic one day.'

I realised straight away that he didn't need some wide-eyed interloper like myself to tell him this. Between 1970 and 1981 the RUC and British Army fired a total of 98,503 plastic and rubber bullets in Northern Ireland. Despite the warm and fuzzy image the idea of a plastic bullet conjures in the minds of arm-chair commentators in far off shores, they are harder than car tyres and people in the north of Ireland know that they are a deadly. Between April 1972 and April 1982, fourteen people were killed in Northern Ireland by rubber or plastic bullets. Six of them were children. They included eleven year old Stephen McConomy who was shot in the back of the head with a plastic bullet fired by the British Army and died three days later on 19 April 1982. In the Army's (much disputed) version of events, Stephen McConomy was a rioter who had been stoning British soldiers. As such, the eleven year old boy was just another regrettable statistic in the war to pacify Northern Ireland.[1]

Anyway, like I said, none of this was news to young Eamonn and he just shrugged his shoulders at me and went upstairs to play Nintendo with Conor and Dan. I walked into the lounge room where I was greeted by Big

John's Ma and where she, John and Sharon were talking about the knee-capping in the New Lodge the night before. Apparently the word on the street was that 'yer man was a bad boy doing something he shouldn't have outta been doing'. As we sat sipping tea and chatting Mrs McVicker's sister, Bridie, telephoned. It was after she got off the phone that Mrs McVicker mentioned her sister had 'taken a bad turn' lately. Apparently, after her son Gerard O'Hara had been shot in front of her in September 1992, Bridie 'took a breakdown', and 'the poor woman was just wrecked'. Somehow, she eventually snapped out of it. She stopped taking the pills 'for her wrecked nerves' that the doctors had given her and there was a marked improvement until only the previous week when she had seen the face of UFF leader Johnny Adair posing for the television cameras inside Long Kesh jail. Adair was allegedly responsible for the attack on Bridie's New Lodge home and after chatting to reporters Adair had posed for a photograph beneath a banner declaring 'Kill 'em all, let God sort 'em out!'

While we were discussing poor Bridie's troubles someone mentioned the poor young man, 'Just back for a holiday after working in America,' who had been killed by the LVF in the early hours of that very morning as I was lying in bed sleeping off my hangover. This was news to me and I was appalled to learn that such a horrible and senseless death could happen as I spent half the day in decadent slothfulness and knew nothing about it.

■ ■ ■ ■

Fergal McCusker was the fourth Catholic/nationalist to be killed in order to avenge the memory of King Rat. He was shot dead in the small County Derry town of Maghera. Tragically, Fergal had just returned to Northern Ireland from Boston in the United States where he had gone, like so many before him, in search of a job and a better life. Twenty-eight year old Fergal had grown up in Maghera, the third of nine children, and had experienced long periods of unemployment. He had only been back in Maghera two weeks and was leaving a local pub late on Saturday night when loyalists waiting nearby saw the GAA jersey he was wearing and identified him as a Catholic. He was dragged off the street at about 1:15am and shot twice in the head behind Fairhill Youth Club on the grounds of the local Catholic church. According to eyewitness reports, two of the men who killed him had their faces painted orange.

When the LVF 'South Londonderry Brigade' later phoned a Belfast newsroom to claim responsibility for the murder they claimed McCusker was responsible for IRA gun-running between the USA and Ireland. Not even the tabloids—including *The Mirror* which featured a tasteless photo of a wall flecked with McCusker's blood on its front page—wanted to touch that one. The LVF also claimed that McCusker had been involved in the IRA operation which Liam Averill had originally been sent to prison for. Some papers couldn't help but mention that the Youth Club where McCusker's bloodied body had been found was near the Averill family home. Fergal's heartbroken father described the allegations about his son as a 'rotten slur' and it was pointed out that Fergal was the fifth GAA supporter to be killed by the LVF in a year—he was killed simply because he was a Gaelic sports enthusiast.

In the aftermath of Fergal McCusker's death pressure intensified on Sinn Féin to commit itself to the British government 'Heads of Agreement' document in order to hopefully end the killing spree and move the peace process forward. Sinn Féin however, was having none of it. Martin McGuinness, the Shinners chief negotiator at the Stormont peace talks, told British television that over the previous few weeks 'four Catholics have been killed by loyalist death squads, up to a dozen have been wounded'. As such, 'These propositions, the Heads of Agreement, were presented at the talks table from the barrel of unionist and loyalist guns'. In short, the solution was not to force republicans into further concessions, but to face down the not-an-inch faction within Unionism whom the likes of the LVF looked to for political direction. These sentiments were summed up by Gerry Adams, writing in the *Irish News*, where he argued that a 'peace process cannot be built on a minimalist approach to change', and that 'we cannot afford to repeat the failures of the past'. It was all too late for Fergal McCusker. According to *The Mirror* it was a simple case of 'wrong place, wrong time… wrong country'.[2]

■ ■ ■ ■

Sunday appeared to be visiting day in the world of Big John and Sharon, and although the light had already drained from the day, we left the New Lodge and continued on our way to the home of Róisín and Sean O'Reilly,[3] Big John's sister and brother-in-law, for a wee visit. On the way over in the car we passed three British Army jeeps and three RUC jeeps trawling up and down the Cliftonville Road. We also passed the Clifton Tavern, where Eddie Treanor had been shot dead on New Year's Eve. Eventually arriving at the O'Reilly house in another North Belfast Catholic/nationalist enclave, we were ushered in. Again we were fed sweets and triangular sandwiches with the crusts cut off as we sat sipping tea. Big John asked his sister to tell me about the time 'the Brits renovated your kitchen' and the storytelling began.

They arrived uninvited, storming through the front and back doors of the house with their combat uniforms and rifles and promptly informing Róisín that she was not allowed to leave her own house until they were finished. They were in for a search, a thorough one, and she better settle in for a while. They were nothing if not dedicated and enthusiastic in the execution of their duties. Carpets were ripped up, wallpaper was torn back, furniture was probed, cupboards were turned inside out. British soldiers with foreign accents tramped all over Róisín's house sticking their hands all over her most private and personal possessions. Finally an industrial kanga-hammer was brought in to the kitchen and Army engineers set to work on the floor. Róisín was then informed that they had solid intelligence and that they would find the hidden IRA guns they were looking for, whether she told them where they were or not. Her protestations of innocence were ignored. A few minutes later they did indeed find something—an old dog-eared pornographic magazine secreted under the floorboards in the kitchen by a previous inhabitant. And it was while Róisín was sitting captive in her own home going red from embarrassment at the thought of soldiers finding pornography under her kitchen floor that the Army discovered that there was a very good reason why they could not find the IRA guns that they were so sure were hidden in her home—they had the wrong house. They had got the address wrong. So, they simply packed up all their gear and left. Róisín didn't mention whether they took the confiscated girlie mag with them or not.

Interestingly, Róisín's husband Sean and his family come from the Jamaica Street area of Ardoyne and lived there from about 1935 until the 1970s. His parents lived at one point in 100 Jamaica Street which is actually the same house that my Uncle Manuel was standing in when Paddy McAdorey was shot in the front garden. Now this was a complicated business, but if I understood it all correctly, Sean's uncle was David Braniff, the father of my Uncle Manuel's childhood friend Patrick. The Braniffs themselves have suffered terribly during the Troubles. Beside having Paddy McAdorey shot dead in their front garden in August 1971, in September 1981 their own son, Anthony, was mistakenly shot by the IRA as an informer. And finally, in March 1989, when he was sixty-three years of age, old David Braniff himself was shot dead by the UVF.

David Braniff, father to a dozen children, had been kneeling and saying the rosary at the moment when the gunmen burst into his house and killed him. Mrs Braniff had thrown herself over his dead body and later sobbed to a local politician, 'Why didn't they take me with him?' David Braniff was killed because he had converted from Protestantism to Catholicism in order to marry his Catholic-raised wife. Sean went round to his uncle's house immediately after David had been shot dead and remembers that the body was still lying cold on the kitchen floor. He noticed a hole in one of his uncle's socks that needed darning and commented that 'It's funny the things you remember'. In the newspapers a few days later, Bishop Daly would beg the loyalist paramilitaries to end their 'mad dance of death'.[4]

With yet another little link back to Jamaica Street I became convinced that there was simply no denying that half the population of Belfast seem to be somehow related to each other. Just think of the whole Ardoyne, McAdorey-Fairley-Braniff-O'Reilly connection. And then the O'Reilly's connection to the McVickers in New Lodge. The McVickers to the Campbells in Andersonstown and the Campbells to the Fairleys back in Ardoyne. All the stories of Belfast's horrible Troubles are interwoven and it seems sometimes as though the last thirty years of conflict have succeeded in eventually touching everyone with evil. All that remains are the tightly wound little circles of suffering.

It was while I was contemplating all of this that Róisín suggested we all go out for Sunday dinner together and so we all—five adults, four kids—loaded ourselves up in to the car and made our way down to a restaurant on the Antrim Road. With the kids at one table sucking down Coca-Cola and ice cubes and the adults at the other discussing this, that and the other I was allowed to retreat in to my thoughts. Sitting beside me were four ordinary northern Irish Catholics who had all suffered tremendously because of the Troubles but who never really discussed or shared it. Sharon lost her mother to the IRA. Big John and Róisín had their father locked up in prison for most of their young lives, and lost their cousin Gerard to the UFF. Sean lost his uncle to the UVF and his cousin to the IRA. What amazed me was that they seemed to have not discussed many of these things openly with each other before. Their stories seemed to be as much a revelation to each other as to myself.

Sean's brother saw his best friend blown up and killed in front of him. Big John and Róisín's mother got shot in the leg by a plastic bullet fired during a riot after one of the 1981 hunger strikers had died. Róisín, the oldest of the McVicker children, 'didn't want to know about the Troubles when I was young' and remembers prancing up and down the street in oversize high heels on the day her father was taken away to Long Kesh. Another time the British Army informed the McVicker family that there was a large bomb out the back of their house. And then there was Sean's passing remark regarding the trouble the Braniff's had had getting Paddy McAdorey's blood stains out. And so on and so on. Eventually I commented that people back home in Australia would scarcely be able to believe that the stories I was hearing were coming from people who were not scarred, traumatised and institutionalised. Sean had an answer for me.

'You know the suffering people have been through but I guess ye normally just never touch on it really, except like this, or in terms of telling funny stories and stuff. For the *craic*, ye know? Like, I knew Sharon's mammy got killed but I've never said a word about it or asked a thing before tonight because ye know people just don't want t' discuss those things. The hurt. Ye know, it's twenty odd years but people's still hurting and can't heal. Never will. That's why ye usually don't speak about it except t' make fun of it.'

Sharon just nodded and then Sean asked me if I thought the Truth and Reconciliation Commission in South Africa had done any good. We talked and sipped our pints and then finally Sean, a little drunk now, grabbed me by the arm and announced to the rest of the table:

'You can take the boy's family out of the Ardoyne but you can't take Ardoyne out of Australia in the boy!... Wait, I messed that up!'

And we all burst into laughter. 'You know what I mean ye slagging bastards', said Sean and then the general merriment, feasting and imbibing continued apace. I relayed how my father, upon emigrating to Australia, walked in to a shop one day and went to the counter and asked the young sales-assistant, 'Can I have a poke please?' He, of course, had no idea at the time that the Belfast slang for an ice cream was Australian slang for sexual intercourse and was genuinely puzzled by the reddened face of the coy girl behind the counter.

A few hours later a now partially inebriated Big John inquired how my book was going? I made a few comments and then everyone chimed in with literary advice—'an' make sure ye get the accent right'. There were even some suggestions about possible titles until Big John interjected with a big 'No, no, I know what ye have got t' call it'. I noticed that at the kid's table wee Dan was stabbing his cousin with his fork. 'What?' said Sharon and a dramatic hush fell over the lacquered wooden table. I could hear the distant chinking of ice cubes in cool glasses as John sat back in his chair and unburdened himself of his genius.

'Two countries and a poke.'

26

Body Count

'You can shove your dove.'

UFF commander Johnny 'Mad Dog' Adair, 1994.

'The talks, for all their imperfections and uncertainties, represent the only way out of the present nightmare.'

Irish News, 20 January 1998

The next day, 19 January, I was back sitting in the Linen Hall Library doing some research. Yvonne had the radio on softly when the news came on that the INLA had just killed another leading loyalist in Belfast. The RUC were saying that he was a local UDA leader but it was all very confusing. The only clear fact was that the vehicle used in the killing was found burnt out shortly afterwards in Twinbrook. I immediately wondered if any of the various offshoots of my family out there had seen anything. Sitting in the Linen Hall Library amongst thirty years worth of books, newspapers, documents, leaflets and propaganda relating to 'the Troubles' and listening to the news of the latest killing, the future did not look so bright. Another man dead, bringing the total to six (counting King Rat) since I had been back in Belfast. The body count was creeping ever upwards and to top things off the radio also reported that Sinn Féin had now officially rejected the British Government's 'Heads of Agreement' paper. Discussing things with Yvonne as she sipped on her tea, we agreed that the conflict appeared far from over. Yvonne also worried me with a passing comment about the murder that had occurred the day before.

'Ye know Simon, when yer poor wee man got shot by the LVF and killed yesterday and he was only after getting home from America, I thought of you.'

The thought had crossed my own mind as well.

'I thought, imagine if that fella Simon was over here from Australia investigating his aunt's killing and he got shot himself. Maybe one day, years from now, we'd have another Australian relative up the Linen Hall t' investigate yer own death.'

Only in Belfast could a comment like that seem as normal and congenial as it was intended. I smiled and went back to my research. A few hours later I thought I might have actually achieved something with the day so I packed up to make my way home. Sitting in a black taxi driving up the Falls Road we passed a newsagents with a *Belfast Telegraph* advertising poster outside with the headline, 'Adams in crisis talks at No.10'. Driving up the Falls we passed all those familiar streets again, streets I knew from relatives' stories and from history books before I ever set foot in Belfast myself—Leeson Street, Rockville Street, Beechmount ('RPG') Avenue and so on. As we passed Dunville Park, established at a time when the majority of houses in West Belfast were without proper amenities, I thought about the fact that the park had been donated to the people of West Belfast by a family of whiskey merchants who ensured that toilets and running water were kept on site so that 'the working class may learn the art of cleanliness'.[1] The park remains a monument to the insulting philanthropy of turn-of-the-century bourgeois do-gooders.

And most of all, as I travelled along the Falls I thought about everything that had transpired, for better and worse, over the last thirty years. All that 'trouble'. All those dead. Street after street of families making the best of bad times. Enjoying the *craic,* having a pint at the local, and waking the dead in the front room of tiny little matchbox houses with sweets for guests on little trays. To anyone with any sense of history at all, the whole of nationalist West Belfast is a map of human endurance. And on the other side of the 'peace walls' and concrete 'interfaces', was another community revelling in its separateness yet living with its own share of sadness, mourning, poverty and perseverance. I had on occasion breached the peace line and been driven, somewhat nervously, down the Shankill or around Tigers Bay myself. I saw no discernible difference between the poverty and hardship of people living there and that of people down the Falls. All the red, white and blue painted curb-stones and tattered Union Jacks attached to lamp posts could not hide the fact that despite the professed loyalty of these people to their Queen, Mrs Elizabeth Windsor did not appear to care if they continued to be reared in poverty or die violent deaths at the hands of people they considered to be disloyal Fenians.

It was all getting to me. Time was running out for my little investigation and the answers were still few and far between. Perhaps I was just obsessed with death at that moment—which would not have been surprising given that I had spent the last three weeks investigating Jean's killing—but passing those streets branching off the Falls Road my heart grew heavy with the thought of all the suffering that had been inflicted on the people of Belfast. My thoughts travelled up the narrow streets that run off the Falls and down the entries and alleyways where young boys kick tattered soccer balls against gable walls as skinny teenage girls stand around smoking. On these streets plagued by poverty and unemployment local people can still show you the spot where three, or thirteen or thirty years ago so-and-so was shot dead by this group, or that group, or was killed in the crossfire. The blood stains may have faded, but in Belfast they are never truly washed away. And on cold nights when the fog pushes up against the window panes of the pubs along the Falls and people return home to their beds, everything is silently remembered.

As the black taxi passed the IRSP's Advice Centre on the Falls Road I noticed that it was looking decidedly locked up and abandoned today. Laying low, I supposed, after the day's events when some of their political fellow travellers in the INLA put a man in an early grave. Their 'We will not negotiate the Union' placard stood defiantly gazing out over the Falls Road. Beside it was a small tricolour with a red star in the middle. The black taxi rattled on past and we eventually turned on to the Glen Road and drove up past the Glenowen Inn where Jean had spent the last few hours of her life on that dark night in June 1972.

Only a few nights previously Sharon, Big John and I had been walking home from the Gravediggers Arms and stumbled past the Glenowen as the place was emptying out. I looked at my watch and noticed that it was just before midnight, almost the exact time that, twenty six years previously, Jean and Sean McCann probably walked down those same stairs hand in hand and strolled to the car that would deliver Jean to the tragic death that was awaiting her just up the road. On a cold January night a quarter century later none of us said a thing as we walked past the bar in the midnight frost. I did however notice Sharon glance at the establishment as we walked. Her look was casual but I couldn't help but wonder if the place still held an immediate potency for her. Was it just another part of the urban landscape of Andersonstown for her now, its terrible significance diminished by the years, or did she still think of her doomed mother sitting in that bar every time she passed it? I knew I did, but I did not have the heart, nor the guts, to ask Sharon what she felt.

While we had been sitting in the *Gravediggers Arms* earlier that night I had, however, mentioned to Sharon that I had gone down to Milltown Cemetery and spoken to her mother at her grave. Sharon seemed pleased enough, or as pleased as you can be when your idiot cousin from Australia tells you he had a chat with your dead mother. I sat there in the pub that night wishing so much that I could find something, say something, or write the words that could change everything, or at least make Jean's death more comprehensible. But Jean was shot dead because she was in the wrong place at the wrong time. It was as simple and as complicated as that. Sharon knew that already, and I was worried that my researching Jean's death had achieved nothing but the reopening of old wounds. Later, sitting slightly drunk in the kitchen at Tardree Park, in the house that Jean was raised in, everything I had written in my research and personal journals suddenly seemed so brittle, insufficient, contrived and self-defeating. I sat alone eating cold left-over pancakes smothered in butter (a Belfast treat) next to the very room that Jean's coffin had been laid out in for her wake.

Jean was born at 18 Jamaica Street, Ardoyne, my great-granny McGeough's house, but Tardree Park was always her home. She grew up on the same streets that Sharon and now Sharon's own sons are growing up on. When I finally went to bed in the attic that night I tried to imagine Jean in the house at Tardree Park. Tried to think of her sleeping in one of the rooms beneath me. I could almost picture her brushing her teeth in the sink, or sitting watching the telly downstairs. I imagined her fighting with her sisters and playing with her young daughter. But I simply couldn't imagine what it must have been like for the rest of the family that night when the knock came at the door. I couldn't imagine it at all. Even after twenty-six years I had seen the pain in Gran's eyes when I asked her about it and that terrible look still haunts me.

■■■■

When I got out of the snug warmth of the crowded black taxi at the top of the estate near The Pop, I was shattered by cold. It put years on me. Bad years. It was not yet five o'clock in the afternoon and the dark sky above was already in a deep sulk. Behind me snow was visible on Black Mountain and the pavement beneath my feet was cold and hard. I walked down to Tardree Park and promptly changed out of my scholar's outfit and back in to my tracksuit pants before I took it upon myself to make a fresh pot of hot tea. I was sitting on the couch sipping at the side of the mug when the talking hair-do on the telly announced that it was 5:11pm and they were now crossing live to 10 Downing Street where a Sinn Féin delegation was just leaving the Prime Minister's residence after their meeting with Tony Blair. Gerry Adams, Martin McGuinness and the others then sauntered out of 10 Downing Street as if on cue and strode towards the assembled cameras. (When I spoke to my Mum on the phone in Australia the next day she commented that she thought Gerry was wearing a lovely coat.) Lucilita Bhreathnach then stepped up to the microphones to rattle off a few words in Irish and direct the question and answer session. The wind was positively howling down Downing Street and was putting tears on Ms Bhreathnach's cheeks as she handled the media.

The long and the short of it all appeared to be that the Sinn Féin delegation had impressed upon Blair that people out in West Belfast and in what is sometimes described as 'the broader republican family' in Ireland were none too impressed with the 'Heads of Agreement' package. It was basically unsellable in the republican ghettoes of the north and it wasn't much to base a peace process on. I wondered how seriously young Tony took their suggestion that he and his apparatchiks go back to the drawing board.

A short time later there was a knock at the door and Uncle Gerry and Aunt Margaret III dropped around to visit Gran. They sat and chatted with Gran, Big John and I in the lounge room until Aunt Margaret III took umbrage at fifty year old Gerry swearing in front of his mother so much.

'Stop ye cursing ye dirty beast. That's yer mammy sitting righ' there beside ye, ye know? If I got 10p off ye every time ye said the f-word I'd be rich, so I would.'

'Aye,' replied Uncle Gerry, 'an' I'd be fucking skint.'

A good laugh and then they were on their way back out into the coal black night. As I waved them goodbye from the door I could spy the faint white afterglow of snow sitting on Black Mountain in the background. Yet another beautiful but brittle Belfast moment.

Back inside I watched telly and read a wee story to Conor and Dan. Then, just after the boys were away upstairs to bed, the news came through at about 9pm that yet another Catholic civilian had been shot by loyalist gunmen just a few miles away on Belfast's contested Ormeau Road. No one knew if he would live. I slumped back in the couch in dismay. An hour or so later another news flash revealed that the man in question had died.

■ ■ ■ ■

His name was Larry Brennan, a fifty-two year old Catholic, shot four times at 7:23pm as he sat in his taxi on the Ormeau Road. It was still only a matter of hours since the INLA had gunned down Jim Guiney in South Belfast—the killing that had been announced on the radio while I was at the Linen Hall Library. The following day's edition of the *Irish News* (20 January) carried the headline 'Victim follows victim in grim spiral of hate'. The INLA had released a statement claiming responsibility for the killing of Guiney on Monday 19 January and avowing that they would 'not countenance the hypocrisy of loyalist paramilitaries who talk peace during the day and murder Catholics by night'.

Guiney, aged thirty-eight and a father of four, had been shot dead inside his own shop—'Jim's Carpet Showroom'—in Dunmurry on the outskirts of South Belfast. He was an alleged UDA commander in South Belfast and was well known to some of the leading lights in the Ulster Democratic Party (UDP), including its leader Gary McMichael. Shortly after 11am two INLA men had simply walked in to the shop, identified Guiney, and opened fire. The alleged UDA South Belfast commander died on the floor of Jim's Carpet Showroom. An INLA getaway car was found blazing in Twinbrook six minutes later. And just over eight hours afterwards Larry Brennan was shot dead 'in retaliation'.

When Jim Guiney was buried a few days later he was given a loyalist send off. An honour guard of sixteen men accompanied the coffin, some of whom were wearing Orange sashes, and more than 1,000 people turned up to pay their respects. A UDA flag and a Glasgow Rangers jersey were draped over the coffin. Leading loyalist politicians came to pay tribute to the deceased. Glowing obituary notices were also published in the *Belfast Telegraph*. Several mentioned that Guiney had been 'murdered by the enemies of Ulster' and insisted 'Till we meet again. Beat the drum slowly'. There were notices from the Lisburn Ulster Defence Volunteers L.O.L, from the South Belfast Progressive Unionist Party ('Tomorrow is promised to no-one'), the Lisnagarvey Drumming Club, from 'Skey, Scooby and all his friends from South Belfast in the Maze', by the

Bridgeton Loyalist Flute Band, 'West Belfast Loyalist prisoners in the Maze', the West and North Belfast branches of the UDP, Ulster First Flute Band, Ulidia Defence Alliance (Seymour Hill), Tigers Bay UDP, Loyalist Prisoners Association, and the Ulster Defence Flute Band of Lisburn, to mention but a few. There were also personal messages from his poor bereaved family and from Bobby Phillpott, a UDA/UFF commander serving fifteen years in Long Kesh for attempted murder of a Catholic couple in their home near Lisburn in 1992.[2]

Larry Brennan's funeral however, had no such trappings of glory unfulfilled. Brennan's sister Eilish claimed that to his loyalist killers Larry was just 'another score on the wall'. And what was interesting about all of this was that while the newspapers emphasised that Jim Guiney was a well respected member of the UDA, Brennan was almost always characterised as 'apolitical'. It was also mentioned that he was engaged to be married to a Protestant woman.[3] The following edition of the republican weekly *An Phoblacht* made an interesting argument in this regard:

> As in all recent sectarian killings, the family are expected to establish the dead person's status through the media. Like the victim of rape, Catholic victims of sectarian attacks must prove their 'innocence'. It is left to the family to dispel the victim's 'culpability'… But most importantly, to be innocent a Catholic must be apolitical. A Catholic with a political agenda is treated by the media as an accomplice in their own murder. Sectarian killings are 'provoked', they are 'acts of revenge' and if the victim is a republican, in any sense of the word, it becomes 'inevitable'.[4]

Nevertheless, Larry Brennan's mother was quoted as saying that:

> This is the second member of our family we've lost. I lost a nephew in 1972, his father died of a broken heart. I'm sure I will too.

Brennan's fiancée was similarly shattered. Reading her story in the newspapers, I was reminded of Jean. Like Jean, Dorothy Creaney was the survivor of a bad marriage. And like Jean, she had eventually found love with someone else: 'I was just getting over twenty-five years of being married and never thought that I would find happiness again.' Larry Brennan, her Catholic fiancee, had previously been warned not to drop her home to the Protestant estate on which she lived. They carried on regardless and she had kissed Larry goodbye before he went to work. She never saw him alive again.

It was now obvious to everyone that the UDA/UFF were carrying out attacks which were being claimed by the LVF. Indeed, in the words of one commentator, the LVF's only contribution to the loyalist killings in Belfast in January 1998 was to provide the UFF with the official LVF codeword to be used when phoning up newstations and claiming responsibility. Still, when the late news came on at ten o'clock that night it was enough to make you want to weep. You could practically see a black cloud hanging over the news-reader's head. The LVF had shot dead Fergal McCusker on Saturday night, the INLA had killed leading loyalist Jim Guiney Monday morning, Gerry Adams had been in at 10 Downing Street and now the loyalists had shot dead another Catholic, Larry Brennan, on Monday night. It was an important and terrible day in Ulster politics. That brought the total body count to seven. Seven. Seven coffins, seven funerals, seven families bereft forever.

Big John and I sat in the kitchen having an ice cold can of Harp each (chilled naturally on the back porch) and discussing the political situation. I commented that the killing on the Ormeau Road must have had, like the murder of Eddie Treanor in North Belfast on New Year's Eve, some sort of UDA/UFF sanction and/or involvement. Big John had just started work on a new building site directly opposite a loyalist estate where intimidating paramilitary murals were clearly visible. He mentioned that he and some of his fellow Catholic co-workers, whom he was driving to work each morning, might have to alter their route, as well as their start and knock-off times, for a while. John cut straight to the point, as always.

'See, the funny thing is if yer ever going t' get whacked by the Orangies, it's almost certainly going t' be either while arriving at work, while leaving work, or while ye are actually at work. Seems t' me that the safest thing t' do around this place sometimes is just t' avoid paid employment entirely.'

He nodded, earnestly agreeing with himself as the cold brown bubbles settled in my anxious tummy.

'Work, it's fucking bad for yer health, so it is.'

27

Orange Blood

'I do declare that I am not, nor ever was, a Roman-Catholic or Papist; that I was not, or ever will be, a member of the society called: "United Irishmen", nor any other society or body of men, who are enemies to his Majesty, or the glorious constitution of these realms; and that I never took the oath to that or any other treasonable society.'

Orange Oath and Rules, 1834

'If guns are made for shooting,
Then skulls are made to crack.
You've never seen a better Taig
Than with a bullet in his back.'

Loyalist song, circa 1970s

The black crow stared at me. I was worried it might have my eyes out if I gave it half a chance. So we just watched each other from a distance, me admiring its thick oily black feathers, until it got bored and went back to breaking the thin layer of ice with its beak and drinking from the cool puddle of water underneath. I was on my way to the Kennedy Centre on the Andersonstown Road to do a spot of shopping, believing that a crisp morning walk would probably do me no ill. At the bottom of Tardree Park I turned into a real park and walked down the gravel path past the abandoned icy swings and the puddle where the black crow was breaking the ice and sipping cool water. Further down the track I passed a famous mural and I noted that 'Ireland's Soldiers of Freedom' featured on the wall with their balaclavas and AK47s were in need of a new paint job. In particular, the IRA sniper down the bottom was looking positively flaky and in need of a touch-up. I kept walking until I finally reached the Andersonstown Road and realised I was close, once again, to Sean McCann's flat. The temptation to climb back up the stairs was almost overwhelming, but I resisted. It was hard to stomach that the only man with all the answers was the only one not talking. Still, who was I to tell a broken man how to live out the rest of his life?

From there I crossed the road and walked down past Casement Park, near where those two British Army corporals had been stripped, beaten and shot in 1988 after driving their car into the funeral of an IRA man. Finally, with the two degree cold needling in to me I reached the Kennedy Centre and promptly purchased my younger brother the hurley he so desired. With my shopping done for the morning, I walked back home. I did not see the crow on my way.

Cousin Caitlín called me at about lunch time and asked if I fancied coming over for a wee visit to see the Fairleys in the afternoon. I agreed and at about two o'clock Caitlín's Mícheál picked me up at Tardree Park and I was away over to Jamaica Street in Ardoyne. On the way Mícheál took the scenic drive the long way around Black Mountain and we passed down through Ligoniel where Paddy McAdorey and his two comrades allegedly killed those three young Scots soldiers in 1971. I kept my eyes peeled for the names of streets I remembered from reading the newspaper reports up at the Linen Hall Library. On a cold afternoon like that, driving in a warm car with the snow lying on the side of the mountain and the air sharp with winter, it was hard to picture Ligoniel as the scene of such a nasty deceitful death.

Entering the outskirts of Ardoyne from the Crumlin Road, we were stopped near Hesketh Road by two men laying gas pipes. Hesketh Road, at the interface between loyalist Shankill and nationalist Ardoyne, was the perfect place for an ambush. Even Mícheál looked a little nervous as we attempted to find a way around the mechanical digger. Mícheál joked that if anyone approached the car wearing a balaclava and looking like a loyalist then I was to scream out 'G'day mate!' in the loudest possible Australian accent. Eventually one of the men working on the gas pipes found a way of directing us on to the footpath and around the digger and we were on our way once again. As I looked out the back window at the two gas pipe layers Mícheál commented that it was an unsafe place for Catholics to be working.

From Hesketh Road Mícheál took me on a little detour through Deerpark and to several streets near a 'Peace Wall' where you could still see the remains of a dozen Catholic houses burnt out in July 1997 during the last 'Drumcree disturbances' (as BBC reporters like to call the violence associated with the Orange Order's annual siege of the Garvaghy Road). No one was on the streets. The houses, still in neat little rows like Coronation Street, were blackened shells on the inside with white paint, still remarkably pristine, on the outside. There was also black spraypaint on the external walls of some of the abandoned Catholic homes facing on to the street—'UFF', 'UDA', 'Taigs out!' The white paint of the walls looked so frighteningly stark against the charred fingers of soot marking out where flames had licked back the paintwork from burning windows. Never before had the cruel legacy of Ulster's divided history seemed so glaringly apparent to me.

My spirits considerably dampened, we eventually drove through Deerpark (where Elva and her children had been driven out by loyalists) and then on to Alliance Avenue with its Union Jacks hanging off the lampposts and where Sean O'Reilly's uncle, David Braniff, had been shot dead in his home while saying his rosary. You didn't have to be the helmsman on the HMS Brightspark to understand why Catholics/nationalists in North Belfast felt under siege. In this part of Northern Ireland, 'the war' has been extraordinarily real and deadly to all its participants, republican, loyalist or security forces. With the LVF on the warpath and three men dead over the last two days, the atmosphere in North Belfast was tense in the extreme. I got sick of looking out for suspicious cars following us and was pleased as punch when we eventually turned in to Jamaica Street and arrived at Caitlín's house.

Inside, Caitlín and Aunt Gloria were sitting on the couch while Mícheál and Caitlín's kids, Louise and Mícheál Óg (or junior) were watching telly. I sat down and Aunt Gloria immediately commented on the awfulness of the current state of the Troubles.

'I'm up each morning at the minute for t' watch the news and see if anyone's after getting shot and just praying it's not someone ye know. The Troubles is real bad at the minute Simon, so they are. You've got to be awful careful, so ye do.'

We all took tea and somehow we got to talking about sectarianism and Aunt Gloria was immediately away. Given that she was born and raised a Protestant and was now living in a staunchly republican area, she felt she was qualified to discourse on such matters.

'Simon, I've got Orange blood in me, did ye know that?'

First she told us about how she and my Uncle Tony had met and remarked that 'mixed marriages' (ie: Catholics and Protestants) were far more common in those pre-Troubles, pre-1969 days. On occasion Tony, whose stepfather Robert McVeigh (as opposed to his father, my grandfather Old Q'ey) had actually fought in the 1916 Rising, would even go down to the Shankill to watch the Orange parade on the 12th of July. These days he might be killed. As a 'turncoat' or a 'Lundy', a Protestant woman who married an Irish Catholic, Aunt Gloria's own life would also be at risk from loyalist paramilitaries. In Ulster renouncing your religious affiliation is paramount to renouncing your nationality. In Northern Ireland, to be Catholic is (in 99% of cases) to be Irish and to be Protestant is to be British. To be an atheist is not an option—you are either a Catholic atheist or a Protestant atheist. It is all a question of ethnicity and politics. A united Ireland or the United Kingdom?

Eventually Aunt Gloria ran out of breath and we changed the subject. I mentioned that I had seen a wee Sunday afternoon riot in the New Lodge the other day.

'Aye,' said Mícheál, 'the kids round here in North Belfast are all still mad for rioting. No harm t' 'em, I used t' love it myself when I was a kid, like. Sometimes we even used t' riot against each other just for practice.'

This got us laughing but soon enough the topic of the latest round of killings raised its ugly head again. Aunt Gloria recalled the time my Uncle

Tony had worked down at the Docks in the 1970s driving a forklift amongst a mainly Protestant workforce. One day loyalist paramilitaries armed with iron bars and wearing balaclavas came to where Tony was working, 'That's it, you're finished here, don't come back the morra'. And that was it, you didn't need to be told twice.

Mícheál also had a few more things to say about the Troubles.

'When you were a kid the Troubles were great *craic*—rioting, burning cars and throwing rocks at the Brits. I remember one of my pals said the day Bobby Sands died was the best day of his life. My mammy kept me at home but my pal got out and was running about on the streets throwing petrol bombs at the Brits—riots going crazy, 'Ra having a crack 'n all—he says it was brilliant. He got a hiding after he got home from his Ma, but at the time it was magic. The Troubles were like that. It was fun and then someone was after getting shot by the loyalists or the Brits and you saw how it wrecked the family and you realised, fuck, this is serious business. But when you were young like, it was just mad.'

I then asked what it had been like in Ardoyne during the 1997 'Drumcree disturbances'. On the TV in Australia I had seen images of Catholics being burnt out of their homes in mixed areas adjoining Ardoyne. The lead up to the contested march from Drumcree down the Garvaghy Road in Portadown and the twelfth of July parades—which celebrate the victory of William of Orange at the Battle of the Boyne in 1690—usually dredge up all the accumulated tensions of 300 years of Ulster history. The recent sieges at Drumcree in '95, '96 and '97 had ended in riots and violence across Northern Ireland.

'The twelfth', said Caitlín, 'every year, it's just crazy 'round here. I mean we've got the Orangies just over the way and they're burning out people and you can just smell the smoke and feel the tension in the air.'

She spoke of the ongoing fear of being undefended—the fear that after the torching of Bombay Street in 1969 had caused the Provisional IRA, as their supporters said at the time, to rise from the ashes. The fear that had caused men like Paddy McAdorey to take up arms. Each year before the twelfth people in Ardoyne stock up on candles and hoard bread as rumours circulate that loyalists will try to shut their electricity down as they had during the 1974 Ulster loyalist workers strike against power-sharing with nationalists/Catholics. Said Caitlín, 'I've now got enough candles up my way to land a fucking jet down on Jamaica Street with'.

In 1997 during the Siege of Drumcree Part III the cable men had made a mistake and the electricity did go out in whole parts of Ardoyne for a few hours. People in Jamaica Street were beside themselves, fearing a repeat of 1974. Aunt Gloria phoned the electric company.

'I says, my electric's off and if I find out it's because of them Orange bastards, you and them are paying for any food in my fridge what spoils.'

A big meeting of Ardoyne residents at the Shamrock Club discussed the house burnings in nearby districts and the siege on the Garvaghy Road. Cars with loudhailers had driven around the district calling 'all concerned citizens' to the meeting. People began planning the physical defence of the area. Local republican veteran Martin Meehan was there and another republican allegedly said to the assembled crowd, in a thinly veiled message from the IRA, 'We'll defend you, but you've got to defend us'. In the middle of the meeting someone from the crowd yelled out to Meehan, 'Martin, how bad is it really?', to which he apparently replied that he hadn't seen it that bad since 1969.

However, the feared total Orange onslaught never materialised and after accommodating Catholic refugees burnt out of nearby estates, Ardoyne survived yet another marching season. And the electric came back on in Aunt Gloria's fridge.

Eventually we somehow got on to family matters and I inquired if Aunt Gloria (Uncle Tony being absent) had any idea why our family name appeared as 'Farley', rather than 'Fairley' in the old Belfast street directories from when Old Q'ey first brought the name to Jamaica Street. Aunt Gloria's explanation, which was as good as any other, was that when Old Q'ey told his name to the street directory people some Protestant editor probably thought the name was wrong and changed it to Farley, which sounded more Catholic. At about this point Caitlín came back from the kitchen after measuring her wee girl up for her first communion dress and Max the Cat (who really is a cat, just in case you thought he was someone with a very bad nickname) flopped down on the carpet. After rolling over on to his back for a spell, Max the Cat then got back up on to his little padded paws and went and sat next to the electric fire. This caused Aunt Gloria to get all excited and she quickly put down the cup of tea she was sipping and pointed at Max.

'Here, Simon, g'wan and look there, it's gonna snow tonight for sure 'cause that cat's got its back t' the fire. That's what the oul wans would tell ye, so they would. And it'd usually be true.'

Ignoring Aunt Gloria's meteorological predictions, Mícheál then took a trip to the kitchen and got Mícheál Óg to come out and recite the Lord's Prayer in Irish for me while he himself went in search of biscuits. With Mícheál Óg finished and Caitlín, Aunt Gloria and I applauding, Mícheál came back in with an assortment of bikkies on a plate and took them over to Aunt Gloria for first choice. Aunt Gloria took one and as Mícheál came over to me next to offer a biscuit for my tea he whispered, 'Did ye notice she chose the orange one first, so she did', and he winked. Aunt Gloria overheard and smiled.

'I told ye, I can't help it, I've orange in me blood.'

After finishing the cup of tea with Aunt Gloria, Caitlín and Mícheál, it was time to head back to Andersonstown so I bid 'fare ye well' to one and all amongst the Fairleys and company in Ardoyne and promised to visit them again next time I was over from Australia. Mícheál drove me back out to Tardree Park and on the way we went down Jamaica Road in Ardoyne (as opposed to Jamaica Street) where kids had made a rudimentary swing by tying a piece of rope and a wooden board to a lamp post. The venture was obviously successful as it was immediately apparent that the frequency of swinging young Ardoynians had caused the pole to tilt to ten o'clock—like a certain famous Italian tower. As we passed in the car I could see two young girls with long white socks and dirty knees swinging away with reckless abandon.

Leaving Ardoyne, the sky was already bruising darkly and Mícheál detoured past another small estate where the evidence of July's loyalist marching season was still apparent. Another row of Catholic homes torched and the windows boarded up. Facing this row of charred and empty homes were the red, white and blue kerbstones of the neighbouring Protestant loyalist estate. The occupants of one of the abandoned Catholic homes facing the estate had defiantly daubed—in a reference to the Drumcree march—'No walk, no way'.

From there we drove to The Bone and then into Cliftonville. Along the 'peace line' about a dozen houses stood burnt out and boarded up. Many of the homes at another nearby 'interface', as social planners refer to the junctions between Catholic and Protestant areas, had been completely bulldozed in order to create a neutral buffer zone. It was official 'no man's land' except for one lone house—28 Roe Street—surrounded by wasteground and rubble near a peace wall with razorwire atop it. Locals refer to the building as the 'Little House on the Prairie' and for many years a lone family occupied it, refusing to accept that they were living in a sectarian buffer area. On this particular winter's night, with the warm yellow lights of the house still throwing an inviting glow over the desolate pitch of broken glass, bricks and rubble, Northern Ireland's divisions could scarcely have been more starkly posed.

Next we drove on to the lower Shankill, past some loyalist murals and along yet another peaceline separating the loyalist Shankill from nationalist Clonard. As the night fell heavily all around us Mícheál mentioned that there were predictions of snow. I asked Mícheál if he thought someone else would get shot tonight. 'Who knows?,' he said as we accelerated away from the Shankill and out towards Andersonstown, 'Maybe, but hopefully it might be a bit cold for people to go out killing at the minute.'

28

Drawing Breath

'To the living, we owe respect; to the dead, we owe the truth.'

Voltaire

On 26 June 1972, eighteen days after Jean was killed, the IRA called a ceasefire. The temporary cessation of hostilities was precipitated by the terrifyingly high body count during the first half of 1972 and the fact that the IRA genuinely did appear to have the British Army on the back foot. So confident were the Provisionals of an impending military victory that when Sinn Féin's Maire Drumm stood up at Bodenstown on 11 June, three days after Jean's death, and declared 1972 to be the year of victory and destiny, it did not, for once, simply sound like empty words. American historian J. Bowyer-Bell gives something of the flavour of that Bodenstown rally.

> Often the Republican Sunday in June was a reunion of the failed and bitter… This year, 1972, there were thousands upon thousands… They were on a winner. The whole Derry [IRA] staff were there, many of the commanders, most of four generations, and much of the visible movement. They truly sensed the tide was moving out.[1]

Or as Martin Meehan, a former Ardoyne IRA officer, told journalist Peter Taylor over twenty years later:

> We actually believed we could drive the British into the sea. It was raw determination, a gut feeling that if we kept up the pressure, we could do it… We really thought that victory was just around the corner and that with one more push we could do it. All the signs were there that we were on the road and we had moved mountains.[2]

The Provos therefore believed they were coming from a position of strength when they offered the British a tentative olive branch. On 13 June, five days after Jean's death, they held a press conference and announced that they would be willing to call a ceasefire if the British Secretary of State for Northern Ireland, William Whitelaw, was willing to negotiate with them. While the suggestion was initially scoffed at, the British were quite interested to probe the Provos and find out what was on offer. Already in 1972 Britain had endured international political backlash after Bloody Sunday in January (when fourteen unarmed Catholic protesters had been shot dead), had dissolved the partitionist Stormont Parliament in March (and thus reverted Northern Ireland to direct rule from Westminster, suffering the wrath of loyalists) and had sat terrified as the death toll mounted. In all, approximately 150 people, including Jean, had been killed in the first six months of the year alone. A great many of these were British soldiers and the government was open to fresh initiatives. And as if to indicate his willingness to cross into bold new territory, Whitelaw had conceded 'special category' (political prisoner) status to all IRA inmates in Her Majesty's Ulster jails—a gesture designed, in part, to facilitate an IRA-British Army truce.[3]

In response, and following some background negotiations, the IRA announced a bilateral truce to take affect as of midnight on Monday 26 June. However, to make sure the British were under no false illusions that the IRA was coming begging to the peace table, the Provos continued their military campaign literally up to the last five minutes before the ceasefire. Twelve British soldiers and a RUC man were killed between 11-26 June, the last British solider being shot dead just before the midnight deadline in the Short Strand area of East Belfast. His name was Malcolm Banks and he was twenty-nine years of age. He could have been, and should have been, the last British solider ever to die in Ireland.

■ ■ ■ ■

On the morning of 27 June 1972, exactly eighteen days after young Sharon had woken up to be told that her mother was dead, Belfast woke up to relative peace for the first time in almost three years. A ceasefire was in place. The specifics weren't known to the public at the time, but British government representatives and an IRA official had even established a 'hotline' by which they could contact each other when problems arose. The IRA promised not to engage the British Army in combat and the British promised to stay away from sensitive republican areas. Raids, house searches and arrests would be curtailed. The agreement also gave rise to some interesting sights around Belfast. According to Gerry Adams, republicans began openly patrolling Ballymurphy in West Belfast in a Land Rover with IRA painted on the side.[4]

The truce made it through its first week and then, in a remarkable turn of events, on the morning of Friday 7 July a five-man delegation representing the IRA, including Gerry Adams who was specially released from Long Kesh for the purpose, was flown in an RAF helicopter to Britain for a secret meeting with William Whitelaw. Apparently before the republican representatives left Gerry Adams put on an old jumper with a hole in it in order to deliberately emphasise his proletarian pedigree. In his own words, 'I couldn't have dressed up anyway, but... I thought that was appropriate.' IRA Chief of Staff Séan MacStoifáin carried a revolver in a shoulder holster and once in England, Séamus Twomey requested their secret escort stop so he could take a toilet break and do a little sight-seeing before they met with representatives of HRH's government. From the Provos point of view history suddenly seemed to be waking up, offering the possibility of a fresh negotiated alternative to the Troubles of the last years. 'Victory '72' indeed.[5]

That afternoon, in a house of a British junior minister in the posh London suburb of Chelsea, William Whitelaw, the Queen's most senior representative in Northern Ireland, met the IRA leadership face to face. It was the first such meeting since Michael Collins had gone to England to negotiate the Anglo-Irish peace treaty on behalf of *Dáil Éireann* in 1921. The Provo delegates—who claimed political descent from Collins' IRA but considered him a traitor for consenting to partition—were only too aware of the historical legacy of the 1920s negotiations.

The meeting started well enough, with Whitelaw launching into a speech about how the history of Ireland and England had been plagued by mistrust but that here at last was a British politician (meaning himself) upon whom the IRA could rely to stand by his word. Séan MacStoifáin, the IRA Chief of Staff, welcomed the Secretary of State's introductory comments and replied that he hoped that the meeting would now 'lead to the settlement of this dispute between our two peoples'. MacStoifáin then read out a statement which was little more than an IRA list of demands, principal among which was a demand for the British to make a declaration of intent to withdraw from Northern Ireland. Frank Steele, the MI6 agent who escorted the IRA delegation to London, later commented that MacStoifáin 'behaved like Montgomery at Luneberg Heath telling the German Generals what they should and shouldn't do if they wanted peace.' The British must have then realised, if there was still any doubt, that the Provos were not about to be bought off by soft words, fine wines or the vague hint of future British concessions.

In short, there was never anything much on the table in Chelsea that day from either faction which was going to draw in the other side and end the conflict. Given that neither the British government nor the IRA considered itself to have been defeated in war, there were no terms of surrender to discuss and very little political middle ground upon which to meet. And so the meeting ended.

Whitelaw would later dismissively describe the secret exchange of views as a 'non-event' during which the IRA leaders had 'made impossible demands which I told them the British government would never concede'. This retrospective bravado was possibly enhanced by Whitelaw's safe distance from the events and people he was then describing. According to eminent Irish historian, Tim Pat Coogan, based on interviews with members of the IRA delegation, at the time Whitelaw appeared 'nervous and sweating' while meeting these so-called 'terrorists' of such fearsome reputation. After all, they commanded an organisation that had killed nearly 100 of his soldiers over the last two years. Even Gerry Adams later described Whitelaw at the meeting as being 'florid and flustered; his hand was quite sweaty.'[6]

Nevertheless, the IRA delegation was driven to the airport in a British government limousine and flown back to Ulster. According to Bowyer-Bell:

> On the flight Steele suggested that the British casualties were not causing London problems: 'We lose more men through road accidents in Germany in any one year than the losses you fellows are inflicting on us.' MacStoifáin noted that he doubted if the British Army had lost twenty soldiers to cars in the last three weeks and felt it amazing that Steele was so poorly briefed. What was amazing was that none of the Irish grasped how the English worked, how minor and irritating the Irish Troubles were, seen from London—an embarrassment, a tricky dilemma, but hardly the stuff of grand crisis.[7]

I was particularly disturbed, reading Bowyer-Bell's book, by Frank Steele's callous calculations. I doubted if the heartbroken mothers of the twenty young British soldiers who had been killed by the IRA in the lead up to the ceasefire shared his point of view. How little regard these British gentlemen seemed to have for the young working class lads who died in defence of the Crown across the Irish Sea.

The Provo delegation that stepped into that Chelsea home in July 1972 went to find out when and how the British would be leaving Northern Ireland. Realising that no such deal was on offer, and sincerely believing (with due cause) that it was their armalites and bombs which had got Irish republicans to the negotiating table in the first place, the Provos returned to Belfast prepared, if needs be, for a new round of war. Or as the young Martin McGuinness, who at the age of twenty-two had represented the Derry IRA, would later explain:

> The only interest that we had in going to meet Whitelaw wasn't to talk about side issues, this element or that element... The attitude of republicans to the ceasefire was that it was going to be short-term. At the meeting we were going to identify very quickly whether or not we were being played along. We had a single-minded approach to it. If the British weren't going to come up with a declaration of intent to withdraw, then the truce was over.[8]

Similarly, upon finding the Provo delegation not in the mood for compromise and considering their demands for a timetable for British withdrawal to be both unrealistic and unreasonable, the British government huffed and puffed. Above all else, Whitelaw seems to have concluded after the 7 July meeting that there was no way the British government would be able to cut a deal with the Provos. The old British disengagement process, honed to perfection in numerous other colonial contexts, would not wash with these angry men from Belfast's and Derry's backstreets. They were not going to be easily moderated, accommodated and absorbed into some new dispensation which altered the appearance of power in Northern Ireland, but left British influence intact. And that was all the British, in 1972, were really interested in. When they didn't find it on the table in Chelsea, they hunkered down for war.

At the time, both leaderships decided to err on the side of caution, hoping that the meeting at Chelsea was perhaps an awkward prelude to real negotiations. They maintained their ceasefires. Following the 26 June truce, and fearing a secret deal between the IRA and the British government, loyalist paramilitaries had intensified their random attacks on Catholics. In response republicans had unofficially retaliated—but the formal truce between the British Army and the IRA held. Nevertheless, tensions on the ground were mounting. They came to a head on 9 July, just two days after the historic secret meeting in Chelsea.

That Sunday a confrontation broke out between the British Army and a crowd of several thousand Catholic residents as locals attempted to move displaced Catholics into houses abandoned by Protestants on the Lenadoon estate in West Belfast. The Northern Ireland Housing Executive had authorised the move but the decision had been overruled by a senior British Army commander in Belfast under pressure from the UDA, who threatened to burn down the houses if Catholics moved in. Army vehicles were used to forcibly prevent moving vans arriving. Eventually the angry crowd started stoning the British Army and a large riot broke out. The Army responded by firing rubber bullets and tear gas. At about 5pm Séamus Twomey, the senior IRA commander in Belfast who had attended the secret London talks two days previously, approached the British commanding officer and informed him in no uncertain terms that he believed the British had breached the truce. And then the shooting started. The British Army would later claim that in the ensuing gun battle the local IRA fired over three hundred rounds at them.

As the crisis in Lenadoon escalated frantic IRA officials apparently tried to contact the British government by phone via the contacts that had been established during the all too brief ceasefire. Unlike the previous week when they had been accorded the status of limousines, no one appeared to want to talk to them, despite the obvious seriousness of the situation. When they finally got Frank Steele on the other end of a phone line the response to the news that the ceasefire was about to break was apparently that it was 'a pity' but that 'Perhaps we'll see you sometime'. That was it, the ceasefire was over. That night an IRA statement blamed the British Army for ending the bilateral truce and announced that 'all IRA units have been instructed to resume offensive action'. Half a dozen bomb attacks in Northern Ireland followed over the next few hours as well as several shooting incidents. Séan MacStiofáin told the *Irish Press* that the IRA would be prosecuting its new offensive with 'the utmost ferocity'. The war was back on.[9]

■ ■ ■ ■

The IRA released its statement announcing the end of the bilateral truce at 9pm. Less than an hour later an event occurred in republican Ballymurphy which—like Derry's 'Bloody Sunday' earlier in January—drew almost an entire generation of local youth towards the IRA. At about 9:50pm two shots were fired at two civilian cars on Westrock Drive by a British Army sniper positioned nearby in Corry's timber yard. When one of the cars stopped and its occupants got out, the British Army sniper opened up again, shooting nineteen year old Martin Dudley through the back of the head and leaving him near dead and permanently disabled, lying in a pool of his own blood in the street. The same sniper kept Dudley's companions from the car pinned down under heavy fire for the next hour and a half, also preventing an ambulance from attending to the seriously wounded young man. When two local teenagers went to Dudley's assistance in an attempt to pull him to safety, a second British Army sniper in the timber yard opened fire, killing one of them and seriously wounding the other. A few minutes later, with people now fleeing the area or frantically taking cover, a thirteen year old girl, Margaret Gargan, was shot dead a few streets away by a third British sniper firing from the timber yard.[10]

At this point panic set in amongst the locals—the British snipers seemed to be shooting at anything and anyone in Ballymurphy who came into their sights. And as if to prove the point, at approximately 9:57pm, seven minutes after they had first shot Martin Dudley in the head, one of the British snipers shot dead Father Fitzpatrick, a Catholic priest, as well as Paddy Butler and David McCafferty as they attempted to attend to the wounded. Father Fitzpatrick had been waving a white handkerchief and McCafferty was only fifteen years old.

If the gun battle between the IRA and the British Army on the Lenadoon estate earlier in the day had been something of a set piece battle, this was a case of wilful murder. Indeed, if the intention of the British Army was to 'flush out' and hopefully kill local IRA members by indiscriminately firing into Ballymurphy and forcing the Provos to openly defend the area, they failed.

The problem was, as local IRA members later admitted, that most of the Ballymurphy Provos were still making their way back home from the massive gun battle earlier in Lenadoon. The area was virtually undefended and it was some time before the IRA was able to return fire on the sniper's positions in the timber yard. By then the British Army had already killed five innocent people.

In damage limitation mode, a British Army spokesman immediately told the press that 'There has been a heavy exchange of fire between the IRA and troops. Some of the dead and wounded were undoubtedly caught in the crossfire.' The *Belfast Telegraph* of the following day, Monday 10 July 1972, carried the Army press officer's line. In a breath-taking display of Orwellian newspeak, black became white and white became black. On the front page the *Telegraph* led with 'We have hit five terrorist gunmen, say troops', followed by the main headline: 'IRA launch big attack on Army post in Belfast.'

The blackening of the names of innocents in the newspapers did not go down well in Ballymurphy where the bodies of the dead were laid out in the front rooms of small working class houses so that neighbours could pay their last respects. Around Westrock Drive the bullet pocks could still be seen in the gable walls. The blood stains remained on the footpaths and in the back streets. Describing a thirteen year old girl standing in a community centre, a Catholic priest waving a white hankie, and young boys trying to drag their wounded friends to safety, as 'terrorists' did not beguile these people. The local IRA, which finally succeeded in dislodging the British snipers from their positions, stood unchallenged as the armed defenders of the district. The British Army meanwhile returned to the raids, house searches and random arrests that had virtually disappeared during the brief bilateral truce. The war continued.

The 'Springhill massacre', as it is referred to today by locals, started less than an hour after the IRA had issued its official statement declaring the bilateral truce to be over. Ballymurphy local, Gerry Adams, fresh from the secret talks with Whitelaw in his holey proletarian pullover, saw the Springhill massacre as a deliberate signal from the British Army: 'Their preference for war could not have been made much clearer.'[11] A quarter century later Ballymurphy locals can still show you the spot where Martin Dudley was shot in the head or where the wee Gargan girl was killed. A little garden of remembrance has been built by locals to commemorate the dead. At the opening of the memorial in May of 1999 Martin Dudley laid a wreath at the remembrance wall and spoke of events twenty years previously:

> It was a quiet summer evening here and everyone was going about their business—the next thing I was shot through the back of the head. Everyone who tried to help me was then shot at—the priest who thought I was dead and went over to anoint me was killed. I was lying on my back in a sort of a trance, with the bullets chipping round my head. Anyone who tried to help was just getting massacred. The remembrance brings it back, but you have to talk about it to let people know exactly what went on.[12]

At the same opening ceremony a spokesperson for a local activist group representing victims of state violence, Relatives for Justice, commented that:

> There has never been an inquiry into these killings, the truth has never been told. It was the forgotten massacre. It was Belfast's Bloody Sunday.

The Springhill massacre remains for these people a running sore—symptomatic of 'this dispute between our two peoples', as Séan MacStoifáin had told William Whitelaw in London. A dispute that steps should have and could have been taken towards resolving in the summer of 1972. A dispute which still requires fundamental resolution and wounds which still require healing.

■ ■ ■ ■

Although the month of July 1972 had started with a bilateral truce and a ceasefire between the IRA and the British Army, it ended as one of the bloodiest months in the entire history of the Troubles. After Lenadoon and the Springhill massacre the IRA went on the offensive. Three soldiers were killed by the IRA on 13 July 1972, three days after the ceasefire ended. On 18 July an IRA sniper shot dead eighteen year old James Jones in Ballymurphy, the 100th British soldier to die in Northern Ireland. There were shootings and bombings almost every day and at least nine people were killed in the infamous 'Black Friday' bombings of 21 July when the IRA detonated no less than twenty-two bombs in Belfast in a single afternoon. Despite warnings, the sheer number of bombs left police unable to cope with the necessary evacuation of civilians. Television pictures showed horrific scenes of police shovelling the dismembered and charred remains of some of the victims into plastic bags. A number of the explosions were car bombs—a simple but effective weapon invented by the IRA in 1972: the Provos' historic contribution to the arsenal of modern urban guerilla war.

For the statisticians July 1972 provided a grim index of death. Even if one only looks at the period from 13 July, the day on which the IRA seriously swung back into action, to the end of the month, approximately sixty-five people were killed. The dead included fifteen British soldiers, three other members of the security forces, six Provisional IRA members, eighteen Protestant civilians (mainly innocent bystanders caught in bomb attacks) and over twenty Catholic civilians (mainly killed at random by loyalists). Seven people died on the narrow streets of Ardoyne alone. Fifty people died the following month, forty were killed in September, until by the end of the year nearly 500 people had gone to early graves. When the security forces collated their end-of-year figures it was revealed that there had been 10,628 shooting incidents in 1972 and that 1,853 bombs had been planted. The darkest and bloodiest year of the Troubles by any measure.[13]

If the bilateral truce and the secret meeting in Chelsea on 7 July 1972 had represented a moment during which both the IRA and the British Government drew breath and tentatively stepped back from war, the period after the breakdown of the ceasefire on 9 July represented a full-scale intensification of the conflict. On the last day of the month the British launched Operation Motorman, designed to end the 'no go' zones in republican areas. More than twenty thousand British troops backed up with helicopters, bulldozers and light tanks, moved in to demolish barricades and 'restore order'. Nine days later, republicans commemorated the first anniversary of internment with riots and petrol bombs. Belfast and Derry burst into flames once again. The second half of 1972 also marked the emergence of the 'Shankill Butchers'—a small collection of loyalists who trawled the streets for unsuspecting Catholics to hack to death. Overall, the die was cast in a conflict that would rage on for another twenty-two years before a fragile opportunity like the one offered in June of 1972 would emerge again.[14]

Jean's young daughter, who was still in mourning at the time of the 1972 bi-lateral truce, would be a mother herself by the time of the IRA ceasefire in August 1994. And thousands more people would be dead.

29

Cuimhne/
Memory

'The nearer we come to the light, the more vicious comes the attacks from darkness.'

Fr O'Connell at funeral of Fergal McCusker

'It's nothing to do with you, it's just the stupid country we live in.'
Brother of wounded victim, *Irish Times*, 23 January 1998

I was safely sitting in front of the telly with Big John, Conor, wee Dan and Gran when Sharon arrived home from work. She'd been down in Dublin (or Dubbo as I called it, in honour of the great town of the New South Wales deep west) for the day and had just got back on the train. As she sat down on the couch beside Conor and Dan the news started. The Orange Order was on again about the siege of Drumcree. Sharon, in an uncharacteristic outburst, was incensed by the Orange Order's demand to be allowed to parade down the middle of the Catholic Garvaghy Road in Portadown in honour of William of Orange's defeat of James II at the Battle of the Boyne in 1690.

'I hate them triumphalist marches, so I do. What are they going on about anyway? It was just a stupid wee row in a river!'

This caused an eruption of merriment on my behalf and John, who had taken to calling me 'Gerry' on account of my last name, was similarly impressed.

'Do ye like that one Gerry? She's some fucking historian our Sharon, so she is.'

Sharon then mentioned that when she was on the train back from Dublin she had seen graffiti saying '26+6=1' and had to explain its thirty-two county united Ireland message to the Protestant co-worker she was travelling with. Her co-worker eventually nodded in understanding and mentioned that on some trains she had seen a similar, loyalist equation of political mathematics—'6 into 26 won't go!'

Later Big John and I watched the Liverpool versus Newcastle match and I spared a thought for my mate Buzz Perkins back in Sydney who would undoubtedly be watching it live at some ungodly hour. John and I knocked the tops off a few cans of lager and Colm from across the road must have got a whiff, as he came over for a drink or two. We watched and drank. And watched some more.

The next day I caught a black taxi down the Falls and into the city to meet Sharon for lunch at a wee Italian cafe. We talked over tea and pasta and then Sharon had to go back to work. I got myself into another black taxi and went back out West. Staring out the windows I noticed a roughly spray-painted message on a brick wall just off the Lower Falls that I had somehow never noticed before—'Either ballot or gun, our day shall come.' Inside the taxi everyone was talking about the loyalist killings and trying to guess when and where they would strike again. An Oul Wan in the corner with a blue rinse and scarf around her head just kept muttering, 'It's terrible, isn't it? Just terrible.' Everyone agreed. It was.

I got out at the top of the Glen Road and walked down to Tardree Park where I was enthusiastically greeted by Conor, Dan and wee Rebecca. Amanda called from Australia soon afterwards and with only two days to go before I returned to Sydney she promised she would make some space in the bed for me when I got back. I then went upstairs to lie on my bed for a while and write in my journal.

At about 5:15pm a man was shot five times in an alley off the Donegall Road while sitting in his car. His name was Ben Hughes, he was Catholic, fifty-five years old and married. He had just finished work at P&E Motor Factors, where he had been employed for thirty years despite being 'in a minority' within the workforce. The loyalist who shot him had been waiting for him outside. He was wearing 'dark clothes, had a scarf over his face' and was 'hunched over'. The killer walked straight up to the driver's side of the car that Ben Hughes had just got into and pointed the gun, held with both hands, at him. The grim faced newsreader on the six o'clock news reported that Mr Hughes had been pronounced dead on arrival at Royal Victoria Hospital. It was later reported that a teenager had yelled at one of the journalists covering the killing, 'Do you know what I think— it's one less Taig on the streets!'[1]

All in all I felt fantastically depressed. Therefore, when Big John suggested that myself and himself go down to the Felon's Club for a 'swall-ee', if for no other reason than that the house was full of people and Sharon needed some time to herself, I leapt at the opportunity. John seemed to feel that if we let the LVF and/or the UFF get between ourselves and a little liquid refreshment, then they had won. Still, even John was a bit worried about going for a pint at the Felon's—a club set up and run by ex-republican prisoners. To this Sharon chastened him with a curt, 'What do ye think this is, friggin' Beirut? Away and take Simon out for a drink.' And with that we were into our winter coats and out the door. In the back of my head I wondered if somewhere in downtown Beirut right at that moment some Palestinian refugee was going out for a night on the town and chastising the naysayers at the door by remarking, 'What do you think this is, Belfast? Let's go!' It was possible.

Anyway, after a pint in the Felons, where the signs are in Irish and

English, we took a walk down the road to a pub nicknamed Jurassic Park (on account of the average age of the drinkers there) for another jar of the black stuff. As we were buzzed in through the security grill we discovered that in the hall off the main bar they were holding line dancing lessons. We had a pint and then went next door to the off-license for a few takeaways. We packed and paid and walked up to Tardree Park. Back in the house I had a few more and then, a bit full, I crawled up the ladder to the loft and to bed. I lay under the skylight with the cold air stabbing in through the little holes in the roof shingles and I thought about the poor man shot dead on the Donegall Road. At that stage I didn't even know his name. We had also heard that another taxi driver in North Belfast had had a lucky escape after loyalists had opened fire on him when he turned up to a hoax call. He had been hit once in the head by a bullet but managed to drive off and lived to tell the story.

The night sky above me was as black as death itself. Everything was falling apart; the peace process seemed to be in tatters and I was leaving Belfast for Australia in a little more than a day. I felt treacherous in going. That was the whole point wasn't it? I could always walk away, I could always get on a plane and go. I could turn the other cheek if I wanted to and just pretend the Troubles didn't exist. They couldn't touch me in Sydney. I would be gone and everyone else, everyone in Belfast who I cared about, would be left behind to deal with the LVF, UFF, and the ghost of King Rat. For the first time in my life I felt like an ambulance chaser.

■ ■ ■ ■

I woke up with a slight hangover after a night without dreams. As I pulled myself from my slumber and sat on the side of the bed with my fuzzy head in my hands, I recall thinking that I better go down and have some cornflakes and find out how many people ended up dying last night. The last news I had heard was that at least three had been shot, the man on the Donegall Road was already dead, and I was hoping the other two had lived: the taxi driver wounded by loyalists in North Belfast and the other man wounded by loyalists in a 'punishment shooting'.

As I tried to stand up my hangover got a grip on me and I felt compelled to retreat from sit to supine position on the bed. A weakness came over me. As I lay there dehydrated and tired, I thought back to that morning only three and a half weeks previously when I had woken up on my first day back in Belfast and had listened to music on my walkman as I gazed at the colliding dawn clouds above me through the skylight. I think I had written in my diary of the rumbling British Army helicopters that disturbed my slumber that morning as being like dull metal birds. It was with such a thought in mind, and with the hangover still embracing me like a familiar enemy, that I thought I might remain lying down on the bed for a while before facing the cornflakes on my last day in Belfast.

The morning papers were gloomier than ever. Four men had been killed in as many days and there seemed to be no end in sight. One paper revealed that the ambulance that carried a dying Ben Hughes to Belfast City Hospital had actually passed his wife, who worked at the hospital and was waiting outside for Ben to come pick her up. She got home to find out her husband was dead. Meanwhile the SDLP, Sinn Féin and several other parties were calling on the UDA/UFF to come clean and admit responsibility for the killings. And the IRA had rejected the Heads of Agreement document as a basis for a peace settlement. It was one crisis after another. An editorialist wrote that 'Even those who have experienced the ups and downs of the various peace processes, over the years, have difficulty making any sense of what is happening… These are truly black days.'[2]

That afternoon Sarah-Jane, wee Rebecca and I went up to pick up Conor and Dan from school at St Theresa's. The lollipop man waved us across the road and I walked with the boy's wee hands wrapped in mine. At that moment, with dozens of screaming children running to mums and dads and the lollipop man standing there with his sign trying to make sure none of us got run down on the Glen Road, all I could think of was that I wanted Conor and Dan to be able to grow up without the bloody conflict that killed their grandmother.

Back home at Tardree Park I helped Conor with his homework and then Amanda phoned from Australia to tell me that the uni had written to let me know that I had been conferred my doctorate and would graduate in May. And so that night, my last in Belfast, Gran, Sharon, Big John and I went out for a 'last supper' and to celebrate my success with the Ph.D. However, before we left we found out that another Catholic had been shot by loyalists. Chris McMahon, aged twenty-nine, had been shot twice as he was closing up the bakery where he worked at about 6pm. As his brother comforted him the wounded man had asked 'Why me?', to which his brother apparently replied, 'It's nothing to do with you, it's just the stupid country we live in'. Thankfully, Chris McMahon survived.[4]

That evening in the car, with a soupy rain drenching the world outside, we ran into several British Army patrols as we were driving out of Tardree Park. Up and down the North Link there were no less than three armoured jeeps plus two separate foot patrols armed to the teeth and crouching beside garden hedges in the drenching rain. John put on the car radio as we drove out of the estate and we listened some more to the news about the shooting. As our car slipped on through the cold black rain and past the soldiers, Gran, who was sitting beside me on the backseat, shook her head in disbelief, 'Ach, you're better off away from all this Simon'.

We drove up near Cave Hill where in 1795 Theobald Wolfe Tone and Henry Joy McCracken had looked out upon Belfast and sworn an oath to free Ireland from the scourge of English colonial rule. Dinner was taken at Belfast Castle, a special treat from Sharon and John for which they refused to let me pay, and afterwards I stood outside in the slow misty rain taking it all in. I was reminded yet again, as if I needed reminding, that I would really miss Sharon and John when I got on a plane for Australia in the morning. And then, strangely, it was while we were in the car on the way back to Andersonstown, after four weeks of silence on the subject, that Gran suddenly and unexpectedly started talking about Jean. Sharon immediately swivelled around in her seat in the front so she could better hear her grandmother talking about her mother. What we got wasn't much, but it was more than Gran had said about Jean in the entire time I had been there. Sharon and I both sat hanging on every word.

According to Gran, Sharon looks like Jean, except in the eyes 'which are all her Da's'. She walks like Jean too and gets her sense of organisation and endearing bossiness from her. Jean had a nickname at Bass Brewery, where she worked right up until she was killed, which was based on her tendency to organise people and delegate tasks. Gran was also aware that Jean had collected money for IRA prisoners amongst the Bass workers while she worked there, which was ironic on account of how she died. Sharon and Jean are very alike in personality and after a pause Gran nodded her head and turned back to the window again, 'you can see her mother in her, right enough'.

That was it. A half dozen sentences. It was the most I ever heard Gran say about Jean. It was the closest she ever came to talking about what her beloved daughter was like as a person. I was grateful to have heard. Sharon, however, wasn't finished. She started again on how she wasn't even allowed to have a bike when she was a child because Gran was so afraid of her hurting herself. Gran cut her off mid-sentence.

'I lost our Jean. I wasn't going t' lose you too.'

And with that the car fell silent as we drove on into the dark rain. As we passed West Belfast travelling along the Westlink, Milltown cemetery loomed up on our right. I thought of Jean and wondered if anyone else in the car did too. For once, thankfully, I asked no questions.

30

Slán Abhaile

'Whole communities feel fearful and close to rejection in this land, our land, the land we call home. Sometimes we have wondered were we welcome in the North of Ireland.'

Father Denis McKinley at funeral of James McColgan

'Hearts are beating for you from which time and space cannot separate you. Prove worthy of their interest in you, and for the rest—Courage, and trust in God. Adieu.'

Fenian newsletter produced on
a convict ship bound for Australia, 1867[1]

It was Friday 23 January. The time was 7:51am precisely and I was sitting alone in an empty departure lounge with a hurley (a gift for my brother), my backpack, and a box of *bon voyage* sweets given to me by Peggy, Hector's mother. The Belfast weather had been consistent to the last—raining, cold and miserable. My own senses were dulled. I had been up since about 6am and had had a quick shower before John and Sharon drove me out to the airport. As we pulled slowly out of Tardree Park the sun had not yet even bothered to make the pretence of a rising and Big John had the headlights on to cut through the heavy black mist. I waved goodbye to The Pop as we turned left onto the Glen Road and then we were away up past Bass brewery, the Traveller's camp and the spot where Jean was killed. We turned right, off the Glen Road, and headed out through Hannahstown and then up Black Mountain and towards the airport. That cold January morning, with the sky still dark and unforgiving, the mountain was covered with the milkiest fog I can ever remember seeing in my life.

The conversation in the car on the way to Belfast International was light enough although John did mention, for some reason, that his memories of the early Troubles in the 1970s were coloured by two pop songs: 'Bridge over troubled waters' and 'Tie a yellow ribbon 'round the old oak tree'. The latter was played, in particular, whenever an internee was released from Long Kesh camp—an occasion of considerable rejoicing in the district. Sharon recalled that the song had in fact been played at

Hector's homecoming when he got out of prison in 1986. We then talked about this, that and the other until the red runway lights of Belfast International loomed out from the black fields alongside us and we arrived at the airport. I got out of the car. As we exchanged hugs and handshakes I thought, ironically, of a Maori farewell song from New Zealand that I learnt in Irish translation at *Conradh na Gaeilge* classes in Sydney.

> Anois tá an uair
> Nuair a chaithfimid slán a rá.
> Go luath beidh tú ag imeacht
> Fada I bhfad uainn.
> Tamall a bheith tú as láthair
> Bí tú ag cuimhneamh orainn.
> Nuair a thiochfaidh tú ar ais
> beimid ag fanacht leat.[2]

So, until next time, *slán go foill col cuig. Ná déan dearmad orm.*[3]

■ ■ ■ ■

On the plane out of Belfast I read that morning's papers. The RUC Chief Constable, Ronnie Flanagan, was now claiming that forensic and investigative evidence pointed to direct UFF involvement in the murders of Eddie Treanor on New Year's Eve, Larry Brennan on the Ormeau Road on Monday, and of Ben Hughes on the Donegall Road on Wednesday. Although the Ulster Democratic Party, the political wing of the UDA/UFF, had been stridently claiming that their men were still on ceasefire, they were now forced to admit that something had gone horribly wrong and that the rumours may have been true all along. David Adams from the UDP said that he had 'no intentions of calling the Chief Constable a liar' and that he would now 'go back to the UFF and ask for explanations, and ask exactly what is going on'. If nothing else, it was clear the UDP were about to be expelled from the peace talks. Later that day, Friday 23 January, the UFF released a statement admitting to some of the recent killings and arguing that 'The current phase of republican aggression by the INLA made a measured military response unavoidable. That response is now concluded.' It went on to claim that the UFF was committed to the UDP's peace strategy and that the republican movement 'must now rein in its dogs of war'. The statement must have been of little comfort to the families of the six Catholics killed since Billy Wright was assassinated inside Long Kesh on 27 December.[4]

I arrived in England. London was London, albeit only briefly and in transit, and then I arrived in Rome gaining an hour somewhere along the way. After finding my luggage I headed outside to wait for the courtesy bus to take me to my hotel. There, I immediately collapsed on the big bouncy bed feeling tired, hungry and disoriented. I kept thinking of Belfast, my inability to unravel all the secrets of Jean's death, and the current trials and tribulations of the peace process. I somehow managed to find some Irish news on the cable news service and discovered that yet another man had been shot in Belfast. He had been working on gas pipes on Hesketh Road, just off the Crumlin Road in North Belfast; his name was Liam Conway. He was thirty-nine years old and had been shot twice in the head and chest at close range at about 4:45pm. So much for the UFF's renewed ceasefire. It was then that it struck me—Hesketh Road! He was one of the men Mícheál and I had passed on our way into Ardoyne the other day. We had been blocked in by a mechanical digger and I had had a minor panic attack, fearing a loyalist trap. Now one of the two men who waved us through and directed us around the digger was dead. When Liam Conway was buried a few days later, his blind brother Brian 'clasped the coffin awkwardly' and helped carry his dead brother through the narrow streets of North Belfast. The following day floral tributes left at the scene of Liam's murder in Hesketh Road were set on fire by local loyalists.[5]

Meanwhile back in Rome I knew that in the morning I would be boarding a plane for a twenty hour flight home. I resolved to go to sleep early. I undressed and lay on my back for a while staring at the white ceiling and feeling vaguely uncomfortable. And then I realised what was bothering me: no Army helicopters buzzing above. For the first time in a month I was in almost complete silence. It was also the first time in a month that I had really been alone. No library, or interviewing, or playing with the boys or talking with Gran or Big John or Sharon, or anyone else who happened to drop by. The sounds of Rome were dulled by the heavy hotel doors and I was all by myself on a crisp double bed. Just me, Rome and four air-conditioned walls. Strangely, my thoughts turned to a very famous poem by Belfast poet Maurice Craig, and I recited a few lines to myself before I drowsed off.

> O the bricks they will bleed and the rain it will weep,
> And the damp Lagan fog lull the city to sleep;
> It's to hell with the future and live on the past:
> May the Lord in his mercy be kind to Belfast.

And then I slept and dreamt of *an domhan nua*.

■ ■ ■ ■

I was met at Sydney airport after twenty hours of flying, with a stopover in Bangkok, by my brother Marty. Earlier, while still on the plane flying over somewhere I managed to get hold of a copy of the *International Herald Tribune*, a newspaper compiled from the *New York Times* and *Washington Post* and distributed solely on international aircraft. I read more about the UFF press statement from the day before in which they admitted to some of the King Rat 'retaliation' killings. I also learned that even after the shooting on Hesketh Road some loyalists had shot yet another Catholic taxi driver. Thirty-three year old John McColgan was shot five times in the back of the head at point blank range. His murder brought the final death toll, including King Rat, to ten.

John McColgan had been killed after picking up a fare on the Andersonstown Road near the Whitefort Inn—the pub where Big John, the others and I had been drinking on New Year's Eve—at about 9pm on Saturday night. His loyalist killers, who had ventured behind enemy lines and into Andersonstown in order to hail a cab in the street, had shot him from the back seat of the taxi and then dumped his body on the road near Hannahstown Hill. Sharon, Big John and I had driven along the same stretch of road on our way to Belfast airport early on Friday morning. After dumping John McColgan's corpse onto the cold dark lonely road they had driven his taxi to the Giant's Ring in South Belfast, and set fire to it.

John McColgan was the sixth person to die in Northern Ireland in a week. The following day Lorraine McColgan, the dead man's distraught wife, spoke to the *Irish News*:

> He kissed me goodbye and said: 'I love you', like he always did, and then he was gone… I said to him on Friday, before he went out to work: 'John, just watch yourself love', and he said: 'Sure the UFF have made a statement, that their ceasefire has been reinstated and I'll be alright', but I never slept all Friday night until he came home. And again when he went out last night, I said to him, 'John, watch yourself love'. He was always looking over his shoulder, but he felt he was safe now… It is senseless what they are doing. It is getting us nowhere. I don't think they realise what these people are doing to families like mine… I want no retaliation for my husband's death. I don't want anybody else to go through this.[6]

When John McColgan was buried a few days later his widow Lorraine was so overcome with grief that she collapsed and had to be carried to a car in order to attend his funeral. One of her sons, eleven year old Sean, walked behind his father's coffin all the way to the church. He later asked a television crew that was attempting to interview him, 'Why did they kill my daddy? I loved him. He was big and he brought me everywhere.' His nine year old sister Mairead wrote a letter to her dead father—'I will help mummy in the house. I will not fight with Sean. We will never forget you.' His three children each carried a red rose to his grave.[7]

■ ■ ■ ■

Back in Australia I had the wonder of return to deal with. I was missing Belfast of course, but I also felt a joyous celebration at being back in Australia with Amanda and being far away from the bullets and blood and funerals of Ulster. As my plane circled Sydney before landing the Italian couple next to me pointed out the window and in broken English had asked, 'Your city, no?' I had nodded yes, 'My city, si', and I did feel a deep sense of contentment rise up within me. I was coming home to *an domhan nua*—the new world.

I never really thought I'd get to the bottom of Jean's death. I knew the very nature of the bitter conflict in Northern Ireland meant that I would never get a final definitive sense of truth. All I could hope for were fragments of truth. A faint trace of it. I didn't get the answers to my questions, but some questions are important in and of themselves. If nothing else, I hope that I have succeeded in recapturing something of Jean for Gran, Sharon, John, Conor, wee Dan and the latest addition to the family—baby Liam Patrick.[8] I hope I have provided some fresh perspective on the senseless tragedy of Jean's death for everyone who ever knew and loved her. For all of her family and friends. And I hope that through examining the intrigue surrounding her death I have been able to provide some insight into the tangled fabric that has made the conflict in the north of Ireland so resistant to resolution. That bitter season of bloodletting known colloquially as 'the Troubles' has lasted for my entire lifetime. Thirty years. I was born at the start of it in 1968 and I would like to live to see the end of it.

So here I am, writing this in August 1999, re-dispersed or 'scattered' to the antipodes and loving it. Confident in my hyphenated existence, I'm enjoying being caught between two cultures and countries—Ireland and Australia. Investigating Jean's death I uncovered a sense of blood and of connections that run deep across oceans of time. I have a sense of place and distant belonging. I have a sense of my people and of my family. And, of course, I have a new sense of self. *Mhúin Síne an méid sin dom, agus is fearrde mé é. Is fada marbh í. Fágaimis sin mar atá sé.*[9]

31

Epilogue: The Trembling Hand of History

I found peace
in the graveyard
between the carved stones
of our terrible history.

'The iron grip of history may loosen… But then again it may not. For this is Northern Ireland. Where we are not only war weary. But peace wary. We have been there so many times before with New Dawns, Fresh Hope, Complete Cessations and Peace in Our Time. Foreign correspondents and visiting politicians who come here hoping to wrap up our Troubles once and forever, must wonder at such caution.'

Belfast Telegraph, 11 April 1998

en people were killed during the three and a half weeks I was in Belfast. About a dozen more were shot and wounded. Soon after I arrived back in Sydney and in response to the UFF's statement admitting responsibility for several of the recent killings, the UDP were forced out of the peace talks for several weeks. Then in March Sinn Féin were themselves expelled from the talks for several weeks after RUC Chief Constable Ronnie Flanagan decided that the IRA was responsible for a shooting in Belfast.

The entire peace process was put on hold once again.

March was also dominated by news of the murder of two lifelong friends, Damian Trainor (25) and Philip Allen (34) in the small village of Poyntzpass. The LVF had simply burst into a local pub and shot the friends—one Catholic, the other Protestant—dead. Around the same time the LVF also released a policy document to the press. Its position on the peace talks was unequivocal, especially with regard to those from the Protestant community whom the LVF felt were selling out Ulster.

> The LVF recognises that key Protestant leaders in the church,
> politics, industry and commerce, and, last but not least,
> paramilitary world, have succumbed to this blackmail and are
> presently colluding in a peace/surrender process designed to break

the union and establish the dynamic for Irish unity, within an all-Ireland Roman Catholic, Gaelic, Celtic state.

With tension and despair mounting the chairman of the peace talks, US Senator George Mitchell, set a deadline of 9 April for a political settlement. This led to an intensified round of negotiations, increased international interest in the peace talks, and on 23 March I did an interview on an Adelaide radio station about the Irish peace process in my capacity as a lecturer at UNSW and a supposed expert in Irish history. My mum, who heard the broadcast when it was re-played on national radio, called me up positively exuberant: 'It was fantastic. You sounded just like yourself, but clever!'

With Mitchell's deadline looming there were three more killings at the start of April—one carried out by the INLA and two by loyalists. Twenty-four hours of virtual non-stop negotiations on 9 April failed to reach final agreement but somehow at about 5:30pm on Good Friday 10 April 1998 the participants in the peace talks at Stormont announced that a deal had been done. The proposed deal, immediately coined the Good Friday Agreement, proposed North-South cross-border bodies, a Northern Ireland power-sharing assembly, and a British/Irish council. Its most controversial elements were the release of all political prisoners and the acceptance of a postponement of decommissioning of illegal weapons. First, however, the Good Friday Agreement would have to go to referendum north and south of the border.

The referendum was held on 22 May in both Northern Ireland and the Irish republic. Public advertisements calling on people to vote 'YES' carried the subtext of 'Make your own history'. In all 71.12% of people in the north and 94.4% in the south voted 'YES'. Soon afterwards elections were held for the new northern power-sharing assembly and when the results were published it was revealed that David Trimble's UUP had won 28 seats; John Hume's SDLP 24; Ian Paisley's DUP 20 and Sinn Féin came fourth with 18. The loyalist PUP, political wing of the UVF, picked up two seats while the UFF/UDA's political wing, the UDP, did not win any.

A few months later on Thursday 2 July I was at the computer, sitting in my study, drinking my morning cup of tea and reading the Belfast newspapers on the internet. There were worrying developments at Drumcree where the Orange Order's annual siege of the Garvaghy Road was back on. British troop levels were up to 18,000, all police leave had been cancelled and riots were breaking out nightly on loyalist estates all across the north. By the eleventh of July, the night before the most significant day in the loyalist political calender, the loyalist crowd in the Drumcree churchyard had grown thousands strong. LVF men could be seen throwing pipe bombs, petrol bombs and flares at the lines of British soldiers amassed before them and preventing their passage down the Garvaghy Road. Those loyalists opposed to the peace process and the Good Friday Agreement seemed to be growing stronger by the minute when tragedy struck once again. On the night of 11 July three young brothers born to a Catholic mother—Richard (10), Mark (9) and Jason Quinn (8)—were burnt to death when loyalists petrol-bombed their house on a loyalist estate in Ballymoney. The horrific sectarian murder made the front page of most major newspapers throughout the world the following morning. The affect on Drumcree was palpable. Overnight the numbers of loyalist hardliners dwindled from thousands to about 200. Even within the Orange Order leaders like Reverend William Bingham declared that 'no road is worth a life' and that the Orangemen should leave Drumcree.

Then on 10 August 1998, the twenty-second anniversary of the death of Danny Lennon and the Maguire children on Finaghy Road North, it was announced that the LVF had called a permanent ceasefire. Despite their relatively recent arrival on the scene, the LVF had established themselves as one of the most vicious paramilitary groups of the entire Troubles. Now the LVF was apparently calling it quits, although it was suggested that their ceasefire was perhaps a ruse to get their prisoners out of jail within the terms of the Good Friday Agreement and that some of their members immediately set up a new group, the Red Hand Defenders.

Just as things seemed to be improving, on a Saturday afternoon, 15 August, a 500lb car bomb belonging to dissident republicans of the so-called 'Real IRA'—who were opposed to Sinn Féin's involvement in the Good Friday Agreement— exploded in Omagh killing twenty-nine innocent civilians. This heinous bombing undoubtedly represented one of the all-time low points in the Troubles. The dead were both Catholics and Protestants, including three generations of one family. In the aftermath of Omagh political and repressive pressure mounted on those republican groups not on ceasefire. Two of them, the INLA and 'Real IRA', eventually relented, suspending their armed campaigns.

In September the first political prisoners—both loyalist and republican—were released under the terms of the Good Friday Agreement and the power-sharing assembly had its first sitting. Gerry Adams turned fifty on 6 October and did a rare personal (as opposed to political) interview with a republican journalist. He was asked if there wasn't something else he'd rather be doing with his time, other than leading Irish republicanism out of three decades of conflict and war. His reply provided an interesting estimation of 1998:

> If you take this year, for example. It began with a killing spree by loyalists, then the Stormont talks, the Good Friday agreement, the referendum, the Assembly elections, then Drumcree. It's been traumatic for everyone… If I think back, this year was probably as difficult as during internment in 1972…

At the end of October—after being named a joint recipient of the 1998 Nobel Peace Prize only a week or so previously—First Minister designate of the new Northern Ireland Assembly, David Trimble, breached the Good Friday Agreement. The 31 October deadline for setting up an Assembly executive approached and then passed by as Trimble refused to allow Sinn

Féin to take the executive seats they were entitled to under the Good Friday Agreement. Trimble succeeded in doing this by resurrecting IRA decommissioning as a pre-condition. It was not his intention, but hardline anti-agreement loyalists took their cue. Just after midnight on Halloween, Saturday 31 October 1998, a new paramilitary group calling itself the Red Hand Defenders shot dead an innocent man by the name of Brian Service near the junction of Alliance Avenue and Deerpark Road in North Belfast. Brian Service was dutifully recorded as the 3,630th fatality of Northern Ireland's Troubles.[2]

In the aftermath of the murder of Brian Service politicians of all ilk rushed to denounce the Red Hand Defenders. The *Belfast Telegraph* derided the group as 'a coalition of rouge loyalists', as a 'cancer in our midst', and emphasised that Brian Service's family had begged for no retaliation. Even former loyalist paramilitaries like David Ervine, leader of the Progressive Unionist Party, struggled for words with which to adequately denounce the Red Hand Defenders—'right-wing fundamentalist going-nowhere buffoons'.[3]

Perhaps the most biting comment however was made by Gerry Adams. Referring to David Trimble's condemnation of the killing and his pledge that he would not allow it to collapse the peace agreement, Adams retorted that 'There is no point in Mr Trimble making statements about not allowing the process to be derailed on a Sunday and then delaying the process on Monday'. Such sentiments were perhaps unconsciously echoed by the Catholic Bishop who attended Brian Service's funeral a few days later and who argued that the real evil in society that needed to be 'decommissioned' was the sectarian hate that had consumed Brian's life. Nevertheless, Trimble continued to insist, in breach of the Good Friday Agreement, on IRA decommissioning prior to Sinn Féin taking its seats in the executive. To complicate matters, in December the LVF handed over a few rusty weapons for monitored destruction. As sparks flew under the glare of television lights in the Belfast headquarters of the official decommissioning body, one couldn't help but wonder what Billy Wright would make of all of this. As the first anniversary of his death approached, the ghost of King Rat still loomed large.

A lot can happen in just one year. On 24 December 1998 the *Belfast Telegraph* commented that 'In terms of historic events, 1998 will go down as a year that went close to matching 1798'. The year's historical significance included 'the horrific killings of January, which could have aborted the whole peace process'. In another editorial published on 11 January 1998, the first anniversary of the murder of Terry Enright, the *Irish News* mentioned that 'At this stage last year, a horrendous sectarian murder campaign was at its height and a political breakthrough seemed as far away as ever'. Meanwhile the southern *Irish Times*, as part of its official 'Ireland Review '98', commented that the year was 'Marked by extraordinary highs and lows' and that '1998 may well go down as the most momentous year in the history of this island since 1921'. Deaglán de

Breadún reported that 'Around this time last year there was deep gloom at the heart of the peace process'. In Mr de Breadún's opinion '1998 marked the beginning of the end of the war'.

Meanwhile Terry Enright's widow, Deirdre, his two daughters, Ciara and Aoife, and his friends published forty-six memorial notices in the *Irish News* on the first anniversary of his death.

> ENRIGHT Terry, First Anniversary occurs January 11. I can't believe a year has gone by Terry without seeing your big happy smile… I will never forget that night because part of me died with you. Your last words to me were, I will see you in the morning kid… we were going to grow old and grey together. Well that's what we thought, but we will in my heart and that's where you will remain forever… every time I look at our two beautiful daughters I know I have the best part of you… Love and miss you forever, your wife Deirdre XXX.
>
> ENRIGHT Terry, First Anniversary occurs January 11. Beautiful memories of our daddy Terry who died a year ago today. Daddy we love you so much it hurts, sometimes we miss your silly jokes, your big happy smile. We miss watching for the bus and you coming in for your dinner and wrestling with us and mummy giving off, saying you would have us mad, and we all just laughed…
>
> Christmas was no fun and so lonely without you. Now instead of having you here with us, we know we have a special guardian angel up in Heaven who will look after us always. Your two beautiful daughters Ciara and Aoife. Ta gra mor againn duit Daidi XXX.[4]

Remembering Terry's tearful funeral, I recalled the warm tears slowly carving their way down his wife's cheeks as she walked behind his coffin and the cold lonely flowers of his two daughters. I remembered the trail of sorrow from the church through the Turf Lodge. And I thought of Sharon and Jean.

■ ■ ■ ■

Back in Australia I had my own minor troubles to contend with. I was on a NSW organising committee of people from Australian Aid for Ireland (AAI—an Irish republican solidarity group) who were supposed to organise Gerry Adams' impending visit to our sunburnt shores. Gerry Adams had previously been denied a visa to visit Australia and the Liberal government's reversal on this matter didn't especially please the traditionally conservative section of the media. Piers Akerman, a right-wing hack at the *Daily Telegraph*, dredged the depths of traditional anti-Irish stereotyping in a piece published on 14 January 1999 and publicised on the front page with the heading 'Why we should shun Gerry Adams'. Describing him as 'IRA political boss Gerry Adams', Akerman attacked any Irish-Australians who would want to listen to the Sinn Féin president, suggesting that:

...most of those who pay to hear this creature [Adams] will throw back a few jars and sing a few verses of Danny Boy or Kevin Barry... Let's hope his sympathisers temper their adoration with a dose of reality along with the obligatory Jamesons and Guinness.

On Saturday 16 January the *Daily Telegraph* published an article I wrote in response to Piers Akerman's ill-informed diatribe. I put Jean's death at the forefront.

The IRA killed my Aunt. Her name was Jean Smyth and she was shot dead on 8 June 1972 while out driving in West Belfast.
The IRA thought her car belonged to British Army intelligence and opened fire on it, killing our Jean with a single bullet to the head. Aunt Jean was the 366th person to die in the dirty little war in Northern Ireland. She was twenty-four years of age...
Given all of the above, it may appear remarkable to some people to discover that I am completely in favour of Gerry Adams' visit to Australia next month...

I discussed the marginalisation of Irish republicans and its deadly results, and ended by returning to the issue of Jean.

The real point, as Gerry Adams himself has often stated, is that no one has a monopoly on suffering in Northern Ireland. 'The Troubles' have harmed and hurt everyone they have touched...
Every Australian who is able to, should go see Gerry Adams while he is in Australia and listen to what he has to say.
I know I will be there. And I'll be thinking of Aunt Jean, knowing that it is only people like Gerry Adams who can make the terrible conflict that killed her a thing of the past.

On the Wednesday after the article appeared I got my first strange letter in the mail. It came in a plain brown envelope with a rather nice Australian 45 cent stamp of a colourful weedy seadragon on the front. Addressing me as 'Dear Sir', my correspondent implored me to rally in defence of freedom of speech and to support the campaign to allow Nazi-apologist and Holocaust-revisionist David Irving into Australia. 'After all', wrote my new friend, 'he has not knee-capped, wounded, or murdered anyone. All he wants to do is present facts and information he has located in various archives.' It was signed, 'Faithfully yours'. Still, overall I thought it was quite a polite letter for a neo-Nazi until Amanda, who is privy to such matters of etiquette, informed me that writing a letter in red ink meant you wished sickness and death upon the recipient. I immediately resolved not to read anything written in red ink ever again, even if it was addressed to me as 'Dear Sir' and even if it arrived bearing a stamp of a weedy seadragon.

A few days later the serious hate mail arrived. One piece will suffice. I opened the plain white envelope to find a copy of my article ripped in half, accompanied with a one page typed diatribe. The fact that the *Telegraph*'s editor had entitled my article on Gerry Adams' visit 'Opening the doors to tolerance and peace' particularly rankled my correspondent. In what followed, the terrible politics was only matched by the paucity of the syntax.

> I doubt if this vile, snide, sleekit killer-posing as a choir-boy and some man of wisdom would appreciate these two hackneyed words [peace and tolerance]… The Adams's venture into Australia is a fund-raising campaign for armaments, along the way the usual anti-British, spiel, whines of Cromwell, the potato famine, the protestants in Ulster and the dream of a united Ireland, where a foreign Pope can crucify the poor bastards not knee-bending to Rome.

I was then informed that my personal support for Gerry Adams would supply 'another bomb or gun to back-shoot some unfortunate British soldier in Northern Ireland' and that I was just as bad as 'Adams, McGuinness and all the other scumbag bastards who blew up Mountbatten and his grandson'. The letter culminated with something of an implied threat. Whilst myself and all the other 'Fenian bastards are whining over your guinness, singing Danny Boy' and listening to the 'claptrap spewing forth from the forked gob of terrorist Adams', I should always remember that 'you are as culpable when you contribute to his campaign'.

When Gerry Adams did finally arrive in Australia I was busier than ever. On Friday night we had organised a fundraising dinner at the Australian Jockey Club in Sydney. After dinner and before the speeches, I walked with Gerry to the men's toilet. He entered the bathroom behind me and before I knew it people were asking him questions as we all stood in a row peeing. 'On'ya Gerry!', 'Are ya giving the Unionists heaps in the Assembly, Gerry?', 'What d'ya think of Australia, Gerry?' and so on. Not a moment's peace. Standing there urinating, I was genuinely worried that any second now one of the men beside him was actually going to lean over and attempt to shake Gerry's hand as he was still directing business with the other. It was an altogether ridiculous situation. Gerry took it all in good humour but I got a glimpse of what his life must have been like for these last few media-frenzied years.

Saturday day was the Wallace Wurth memorial lecture at the University of New South Wales which was televised to an audience of over 100,000 people that night. Up to a few minutes before Gerry went on stage I was still worried about exactly what the response would be from the audience when he walked in. Standing in the guest room with Gerry, the rest of the Sinn Féin delegation, Michael Morgan (the president of AAI who had done all the hard work getting Gerry into the country), Richard O'Brien (the Irish Ambassador) and the Vice Chancellor of the University of NSW, John Niland, I nervously worried over last minute technical hitches. As it happened, Gerry received a standing ovation from the 800 people in the lecture hall and went on to give one of the best speeches of his entire stay in Australia.

A press conference, a private reception and a small chat with selected dignitaries later, my role in Gerry's first visit to Australia was almost over. Those of us who organised the NSW leg had only the AAI function at the Harold Park Racetrack that night left. Standing behind a bookstall as Gerry walked in I calculated how many hours sleep I had had in the last week. Fifteen? Eleven? I couldn't remember anymore. It was, I believed, the least I could do to help the peace process in Ireland. And of course, Jean was never far from my mind in this regard. So when Gerry Adams stole my pen later that night I decided not to hold it against him. If all that the road to a peace settlement in the north of Ireland requires of me is the sacrifice of sleep and the occasional forfeiture of a writing implement then I am indeed one of the blessed.

When an exhausted Gerry Adams left Australia a few days later he commented on the rigorous publicity and speaking tour that we had arranged for him—'At least they had the decency to shoot Michael Collins, they're trying to work me to death.' And with Gerry gone I was able to relax for the first time in two months and think about everything that had transpired. In particular, the threats to me from displaced loyalists made me think back to the previous year and the time I had spent in Belfast during that season of death and despair.

Looking back on my time in Belfast in December 1997 and January 1998, I can see the desperation of those weeks much more clearly now. The entire peace process was almost brought crashing down by the assassination of King Rat on 27 December and the resulting loyalist killing spree. Ten people lost their lives as I sat in an Andersonstown attic researching the death of a relative killed twenty-six years previously. Yet, despite the bullets that cost those ten lives and wounded so many others, the peace process limped on. It was one of those moments where an entire society seemed poised on the brink of something heinous and slowly drew back from it in fear. The ordinary people of Northern Ireland pressed their respective political leaders for an alternative to a future soaked in blood. In doing so they made the Good Friday Agreement possible. Maybe my Gaelic teacher had been right all along, *bíonn gach tosú lag*.[5]

Sin é.

Notes

CHAPTER 2   **(PAGES 7-17)**

1 The Times, *Ireland of To-Day*, London, 1913, pp. 61-62.
2 See, for instance, figures published in *Irish News*, 27 January 1927.
3 See, for example, Mitchel McLaughlin in *Irish News*, 2 February 1998.
4 Devenney was beaten at his home on 19 April, but died of his injuries on 16 July.
5 For figures see, for instance, P. Bew & G. Gillespie, *Northern Ireland: A chronology of the Troubles, 1968–1993*, Dublin, 1993, p. 18; D. Sharrock & M. Devenport, *Man of War, Man of Peace: The Unauthorised Biography of Gerry Adams*, London, 1997, p. 62.
6 G. Adams, *Free Ireland: Towards a Lasting Peace*, Dingle, 1995, pp. 9, 54. For numbers of IRA men in 1961-62, see also Sharrock & Devenport, *Man of War, Man of Peace*, p. 37.
7 D. McKittrick *et al*, *Lost Lives*, London, 1999. See statistical index. See also, M. Sutton, *An Index of Deaths from the Conflict in Ireland, 1969-1993*, Belfast, 1994. All statistics in this chapter come principally from these two sources. In particular, *Lost Lives* provides a brief summary of the circumstances of every death arising from the Troubles and was used by the current author to double-check stories regarding various fatalities.
8 S. Bruce, *The Red Hand: Protestant Paramilitaries in Northern Ireland*, New York, 1992, pp. 46-49. Also, D. Boulton, *The UVF 1966–73: An Anatomy of Loyalist Rebellion*, Dublin, 1973, pp. 144-145.
9 Quoted in M. Dillon & D. Lehane, *Political Murder in Northern Ireland*, Ringwood, 1973, pp. 56-57.
10 Wright quotes from interview published in M. Dillon, *God and the Gun: The Church and Irish Terrorism*, London, 1997, pp. 77-98.
11 *Irish Times*, 21 October 1998. Interestingly, despite his tea-totler image, during his autopsy it was discovered that Wright had illegal drugs in his bloodstream. See, *Irish News*, 23 October 1998.
12 For more on the activities of King Rat, see for example, S. McPhilemy, *The Committee: Political Assassination in Northern Ireland*, Colorado, 1998.
13 *Irish Times*, 28 April 1997. Also, *INLA Communiqué Concerning the Execution of Billy Wright AKA 'King Rat'*, 27 December 1997.
14 Those tried along with Crip McWilliams for Wright's murder were John 'Sonny' Kennaway (35) and John Glennon (32). All were from Belfast. They were sentenced to life imprisonment for murder, plus an additional twenty years for possessing illegal firearms. For more details, see *Irish News*, 20 October 1998; *Belfast Telegraph*, 20 October 1998; *Irish News*, 21 October 1998; *Irish Times*, 21 October 1998. For coverage specifically on the death of Billy Wright, see for instance, *Sunday Life*, 28 December 1998; *The Mirror* (N. Ireland edition) 29 December 1997; *Irish News*, 22 February 1999.
15 *Belfast Telegraph*, 21 October 1998. For more on the INLA and IPLO, see J. Holland & H. McDonald, *INLA: Deadly Divisions*, Dublin, 1994.
16 *Irish News*, 23 October 1998.

CHAPTER 3   **(PAGES 18-31)**

1 On Belfast during World War II, see for instance, B. Barton, 'The Belfast Blitz, April-May 1941', *History Ireland*, Autumn 1997, pp. 52-57; M. Farrell, *Northern Ireland: The Orange State*, London, 1976, pp. 159-160; T. Gray, *The Lost Years: The Emergency in Ireland, 1939-1945*, London, 1998, pp. 117-123.
2 Not his real name.
3 *Irish Times*, 29 Dec 1997. Also, *Belfast Telegraph*, 29 Dec 1997.
4 *Belfast Telegraph*, 29 Dec 1997.
5 Not her real name.
6 *Irish Times*, 30 Dec 1997; *Irish News*, 30 Dec 1997.
7 *Irish Times*, 31 Dec 1997. See also, *Irish News*, 31 Dec 1997; *The Mirror* (N. Ireland edition), 31 Dec 1997.

CHAPTER 4   **(PAGES 32-43)**

1 Quote from *Irish Times*, 21 January 1998. For coverage of Treanor's murder, see also, *Irish News*, 2 January 1998.
2 On McClinton see M. Dillon, *God and the Gun: The Church and Irish Terrorism*, London, 1997, p. 23, 37-40, 106.
3 Information on the inquiry into the death of Eddie Treanor from *Irish News*, 28 November 1998.
4 For more on McGurk's Bar, see S. Bruce, *The Red Hand: Protestant Paramilitaries in Northern Ireland*, New York, 1992, pp. 51-53. In 1976 Robert Campbell, a UVF man from the Shankill, confessed to planting the McGurk's Bar bomb. He was given fifteen life sentences in September 1978. On 4 December 1998 a single wreath was laid at the former site of McGurk's bar, now an underpass on the westlink motorway, by friends and relatives of those killed.

CHAPTER 5   **(PAGES 44-59)**

1 *Irish News*, 3 January 1998.
2 T. Pakenham, *The Year of Liberty: The History of the Great Irish Rebellion of 1798*, New York, 1993, p. 231. See also J.B. Woodburn, *The Ulster Scot: His History and Religion*, London, 1914, pp. 297-299. *An Phoblacht*, 11 June 1998.

3 *The Mirror (N. Ireland edition)*, 29 December 1997.
4 E. Fairweather, R. McDonough, M. McFadyean, *Only Our Rivers Run Free: Northern Ireland—The Woman's War*, London, 1984, p. 107.
5 Name changed on request.
6 Name and number changed.
7 The Ranger's goalkeeper, Andy Goram, later claimed that the armband was in honour of his aunt who had died three months previously. This was denied by his family. See *Belfast Telegraph*, 8 February 1999.
8 The best account of 'Operation Tollan' is in the republican prisoner's magazine *The Captive Voice (An Glór Gafa)*, Vol. 8, No. 3, Summer 1997.
9 Irish Street survey details published in *Irish News*, 19 December 1998.
10 For more see 'The Rise of John McKeague', in D. Boulton, *The UVF, 1966-73: An Anatomy of Loyalist Rebellion*, Dublin, 1973, pp. 108-129.
11 Details on the RHC can be found in J. Cusack & H. McDonald, *UVF*, Dublin, 1997; S. Bruce, *The Red Hand: Protestant Paramilitaries in Northern Ireland*, Melbourne, 1992.

CHAPTER 6   (**PAGES 60-72**)
1 Name changed.
2 Figures provided in this paragraph are based principally on M. Sutton, *An Index of Deaths from the Conflict in Ireland, 1969–1993*, Belfast, 1994. They differ slightly from the updated, expansive and more detailed study, D. McKittrick *et al*, *Lost Lives*, London, 1999. I've tried to take account of both sources.
3 *Sydney Morning Herald*, 10 June 1972; *New York Times*, 9 June 1972.
4 The death toll for 1972 is often recorded as 472 but this is due, in part, to the fact that a number of sectarian killings which were originally not reported as such at the time. *Lost Lives* provides probably the most up to date and detailed summary, providing the figure of 492. See, *Lost Lives*, p. 138.
5 P. Bishop & E. Mallie, *The Provisional IRA*, London, 1997, p. 192.
6 P. Taylor, *Provos: The IRA and Sinn Féin*, London, 1997, pp. 109-110.
7 Taylor, *Provos*, p. 139.
8 J. Bowyer-Bell, *The Irish Troubles: A Generation of Violence, 1967–1992*, Dublin, 1994, pp. 332-333. For more information on the MRF etc, see Mark Urban, *Big Boy's Rules: The SAS and the Secret Struggle Against the IRA*, London, 1992, pp. 35-39 and M. Dillon, *The Dirty War*, London, 1990, pp 27-59. Details in this section are based largely on these accounts. See also, G. Adams, *Before the Dawn: An Autobiography*, London, 1996, pp. 212-213.
9 F. Kitson, *Low Intensity Operations*, London,

1971, pp. 13, 24, 69.
10 Kitson, *Low Intensity Operations*, p. 49.
11 The MRF is variously stated as standing for Mobile Reconnaissance Force, Military Reaction Force or Mobile Reaction Force.
12 The two 'Freds' were apparently Seamus Wright and Kevin McKee. In an April 1999 public statement the IRA admitted court-martialling, executing and secretly burying Wright and McKee in 1972. The IRA statement claimed Wright and McKee were both MRF members. There have been recent attempts by the IRA to recover their bodies for proper burial. See, Dillon, *The Dirty War*, pp. 32-44, 48-51; *An Phoblacht*, 1 April 1999; *Irish Times*, 31 May 1999.
13 Adams, *Before the Dawn*, p. 213.
14 T.P. Coogan, *The Troubles: Ireland's Ordeal 1966-1996 and the Search for Peace*, Sydney, 1996, p. 286. Dillon, *The Dirty War*, pp. 45-48, 51-53.
15 Dillon, *The Dirty War*, p. 47. Another account of the trial appears in M. Dillon & D. Lehane, *Political Murder in Northern Ireland*, Middlesex, 1973, pp. 304-309.
16 Martin Dillon is, to my knowledge, the only writer to cover Jean's death in a book. In *The Dirty War* he dedicates 22 lines to her death and links it to British military intelligence operations in Belfast, although blaming the actual killing on the IRA. An IRA man allegedly told him that Jean's death was 'an unfortunate hit'. However, I have not quoted Dillon's coverage of Jean's death as he gets some facts completely wrong. Among other things, he gives the month of her death as October 1973, after the Four Square Laundry shoot-out in Twinbrook. Dillon, *Dirty War*, p. 59.

CHAPTER 7   (**PAGES 73-78**)
1 *Belfast Telegraph*, 3 January 1998. Also, *Belfast Telegraph*, 5 January 1998.
2 Name changed.

CHAPTER 8   (**PAGES 79-88**)
1 RUC figures from *Irish Times*, 23 May 1998.
2 Freeland and Meehan quoted in *Irish News*, 3 January 1999.
3 See, 'North Belfast's years of turmoil', *Irish News*, 15 June 1998; 'North Belfast constituency profile', *RM-Distribution*, 10 June 1998.

CHAPTER 9   (**PAGES 89-103**)
1 Names changed.
2 E.R.R. Green, 'The Beginnings of Industrial Revolution' in J.C. Beckett & T.W. Moody (eds), *Ulster Since 1800*, London, 1995, Vol. 1, p. 37. For more on Belfast's development see for instance, J. Bardon, 'Belfast at its Zenith', *History Ireland*, Winter 1993, pp. 48-51.
3 M. Farrell, *Northern Ireland: The Orange State*, London, 1976, pp. 14-18, 91.

4 Unemployment and emigration figures from Farrell, *The Orange State*, pp. 91-93.

5 Quoted in E. Fairweather, R. McDonough, M. McFadyean, *Only the Rivers Run Free: Northern Ireland, the Woman's War*, London, 1984, p. 192. 'Papish rioters' from Shankill Defence Association quoted in *Irish News*, 4 August 1969.

6 *Irish News*, 16 August 1969.

7 Quoted in M. Arthur, *Northern Ireland Soldiers Talking*, London, 1987, p. 161.

8 Quoted in Fairweather, McDonough, McFadyean, *Only the Rivers Run Free*, p. 189.

9 K. Torr & J. Brosnan, *The Ardoyne Report: A Forsaken People*, Belfast, 1982, p. 6.

10 For Rose McAllister's account of internment day in Ardoyne and McAdorey's death, see Fairweather, McDonough, McFadyean, *Only the Rivers Run Free*, pp. 197-203.

11 There was a reciprocal move during this wave of violence. Many Ardoyne Protestants in the area around Farringdon Gardens, moved north-west to the loyalist estates of Ballysillan and Glencain while Catholics moved from mixed or Protestant areas in to Ardoyne.

12 M. Sutton, *An Index of Deaths from the Conflict in Ireland*, 1969-1993, Belfast, 1994.

13 For more details on this episode, see P. Bishop and E. Mallie, *The Provisional IRA*, London, 1997, pp. 177-178. Also, M. Dillon, *The Dirty War*, London, 1990, pp. 234-236.

14 Inquest details from *Belfast Telegraph*, 12 August 1971.

15 J. Bowyer Bell, *The Irish Troubles: A Generation of Violence, 1967–1992*, Dublin, 1994, pp. 198-199.

16 Bishop & Mallie, *The Provisional IRA*, pp. 177-178. On the Scots soldiers killings, see also M. Dillon & D. Lehane, *Political Murder in Northern Ireland*, Penguin, Middlesex, 1973, pp. 254-255. The latter source alleges the other two Provos rumoured to be responsible for the deaths of the Scots soldiers were Martin Meehan and Anthony 'Dutch' Doherty.

17 Dillon, *The Dirty War*, pp. 44-45. Dillon implies, as this quote reveals, that he has established this fact with contacts within the republican movement. Wilson was killed on 25 June 1973 at a quarry outside Ligoniel where his loyalist killers also stabbed his female Protestant friend 19 times. One of the men convicted of the double murder was John White, now a leading spokesman for the UDP.

18 On Tartan gangs see, for instance, P. Taylor, *Loyalists*, London, 1999, pp. 81-82.

19 See the entry for Malcolm Hutton and McAdorey in McKittrick *et al*, *Lost Lives*, London, 1999, p. 79

CHAPTER 10   (**PAGES 104-107**)
1 Name changed.

CHAPTER 11   (**PAGES 108-119**)
1 *Irish News*, 31 January 1996; *Irish Times*, 1 October 1997.

2 G. Adams, *Cage Eleven*, Dingle, 1990, pp. 83-84.

3 On the 200th anniversary of Henry Joy McCracken's hanging, the *Irish News* and *Belfast Telegraph* reproduced articles on his execution originally published two centuries earlier. See, *Irish News*, 18 July 1998; *Belfast Telegraph*, 18 July 1998.

4 A.T.Q. Stewart, *The Ulster Crisis*, London, 1979. See also, T. Bowman, 'The Irish at the Somme', *History Ireland*, Winter 1996, pp. 48-52.

5 One of the UFF members that attacked Greysteel and was sentenced to life in prison, Jeffrey Deeney, later transferred to the LVF wing in Long Kesh. For more on the Greysteel attack, see E. Mallie & D. McKittrick, *The Fight For Peace: The Inside Story of the Irish Peace Process*, London, 1996, pp. 204-205.

CHAPTER 12   (**PAGES 120-126**)
1 *Irish News*, 9 January 1998; *Irish News*, 10 January 1998.

CHAPTER 13   (**PAGES 127-135**)
1 For more on these various reports etc, see T.P. Coogan, *The Troubles: Ireland's Ordeal 1966-1995 and the Search for Peace*, 1995, pp. 271-273.

CHAPTER 14   (**PAGES 136-146**)
1 Fógra Fáilte, *An Illustrated Guide to the Counties of Ireland*, Dublin, 1953, p. 198.

2 R. Kee, *Ireland: A History*, London, 1995, pp. 44-45.

3 Cromwell quoted in M.F. Cusack, *An Illustrated History of Ireland from AD 400 to 1800*, Middlesex, 1995 (originally published 1868), pp. 502-503. For a full account of Cromwell's 'adventures' in Ireland, see A. Fraser, *Cromwell: Our Chief of Men*, Suffolk, 1976, ch. 13.

4 The full poem appears in B. Behan, *Brendan Behan's Island*, London, 1962, p. 32.

5 For information on the death of Terry Enright, see *Irish Times*, 12 January 1998; *Irish News*, 12 January 1998; *Irish News*, 28 November 1998; *An Phoblacht*, 3 December 1998.

6 Paramilitary loyalism is very fragmented. The two largest groups, the UDA/UFF and the UVF, have been traditional rivals and since the 1970s their feuds have often ended in bloodshed. The UDA/UFF's political wing is the UDP. The UVF's political wing is the PUP. From the UDA/UFF's perspective therefore, embarrassing the PUP's David Ervine would have been a good thing.

CHAPTER 16   **(PAGES 150-162)**
1   Many of the biographical details presented here come from *Belfast Graves*, Dublin, 1985, pp. 145-146.
2   *Belfast Newsletter*, 9 August 1976. Drumm was later arrested and detained for making this speech. Other details from *Belfast Telegraph*, 10 August 1976.
3   A British soldier, Charles Coleman, had also been killed near the junction of Rossnareen Avenue and Tullymore Gardens the day before Jean was killed.
4   Also known as John Green or Sean Glass.
5   D. O'Donnell, *The Peace People of Northern Ireland*, Camberwell—Australia, 1977, p. 2. According to information on the Peace People's website, a march in support of the Peace People was held in Australia and Mairead Corrigan spent 'six weeks on an exhausting tour of Australia and New Zealand in early 1977'. www.peacepeople.com.
6   G. Adams, *Cage Eleven*, Dingle, 1990, pp. 134-137.
7   L. Curtis, *Ireland: The Propaganda War*, London, 1984, p. 201.
8   M. Dewar, *The British Army in Northern Ireland*, London, 1996, pp. 116-117. I have used this quote because it encapsulates the Army's 'line' at the time of the killings. Dewar's book was originally published in 1985. Despite the fact that this version has been challenged by evidence in the public domain it appears unchanged in the 1996 edition.
9   See for instance, E. Fairweather, R. McDonough, M. McFadyean, *Only the Rivers Run Free: Northern Ireland, the Women's War*, London, 1984, p. 27. Also, *Belfast Newsletter*, 14 August 1976; *Belfast Graves*, p. 146.
10 R. Francis, 'Broadcasting to a Community in Conflict—The experience in Northern Ireland', in B. Rolston & D. Miller (eds), *War and Words: The Northern Ireland Media Reader*, Belfast, 1996, p. 64.
11 L. Curtis, *Ireland: The Propaganda War*, London, 1984, p. 202. For a full account of the 'Peace People', see J. Bowyer Bell, *The Irish Troubles: A Generation of Violence, 1967-1992*, Dublin, 1994, pp. 482-490, 520-523.
12 Fairweather, McDonough, McFadyean, *Only the Rivers Run Free*, p. 27.
13 But not completely. They are also repeated in C. Keena, *A Biography of Gerry Adams*, Dublin, 1990, p. 66.
14 G. Adams, *The Politics of Irish Freedom*, Dingle, 1986, p. 70.
15 Details and quotes from Curtis, *Propaganda War*, pp. 99-100.
16 G. Adams, *Free Ireland: Towards A Lasting Peace*, Dingle, 1995, p. 58.
17 *Belfast Graves*, p. 146.
18 Figures from M. Sutton, *Index of Deaths from the Conflict in Ireland, 1968-1993*, Belfast, 1994, pp. 195-206.

CHAPTER 17   **(PAGES 163-169)**
1   Some of the names of relatives have been changed.

CHAPTER 18   **(PAGES 170-174)**
1   'Hector' requested that his prison nickname be used for the purposes of this book.

CHAPTER 19   **(PAGES 175-182)**
1   S. Adams, 'In Search of an Irish Mandela?: South Africa's Negotiated Transition and the Northern Ireland Peace Process in Comparative Context', *Discussion Document*, November 1997.
2   *Belfast Telegraph*, 11 January 1990; *Irish News*, 11 January 1990; *Belfast Telegraph*, 15 April 1991; *Irish News*, 16 April 1991.
3   Because of prisoner releases under the Good Friday Agreement, Long Kesh prison is due to close by 2001.
4   For more on Terry Enright's funeral, see *Irish Times*, 15 January 1998.

CHAPTER 20   **(PAGES 183-191)**
1   Quoted in C. de Baróid, *Ballymurphy and the Irish War*, London, 1990, p. 116.
2   See, J. Cusack & H. McDonald, *UVF*, Dublin, 1997, pp. 99-100.
3   For more on Joe McDonnell and the 1981 Hunger Strikes, see D. Beresford, *Ten Men Dead*, London, 1987, pp. 281-310.

CHAPTER 21   **(PAGES 192-202)**
1   P. Taylor, *Provos: The IRA and Sinn Féin*, London, 1997, pp. 108-109.
2   G. Adams, *Cage Eleven*, Dingle, 1990, pp. 14-15.
3   Quotes and information on the death of Gerard O'Hara from *Belfast Telegraph*, 28 September 1992; *Belfast Telegraph*, 29 September 1992; *Irish News*, 28 September 1992; *Irish News*, 29 September 1992; *Belfast Newsletter*, 28 September 1992.

CHAPTER 22   **(PAGES 203-215)**
1   *Irish News*, 31 January 1996; *Irish News*, 2 February 1996; *Irish News*, 3 February 1996.
2   In 1993 republicans killed a total of 38 people while loyalists killed 48. M. Sutton, *An Index of Deaths from the Conflict in Ireland, 1969-1993*, Belfast, 1994. Prior to the Shankill bombing, republicans had already attempted to assassinate Adair six times. In September 1995 Adair was finally sentenced to sixteen years in prison after RUC officers made recordings of him admitting his role in 'directing' UFF activities.
3   October 1976 was the bloodiest month of the entire Troubles with 28 people dying. Sutton, *An Index of Deaths*. For other details

on the Shankill bombing and Begley, see for instance, B. Rowan, *Behind the Lines: The Story of the IRA and Loyalist Ceasefires*, Belfast, 1995, pp. 53-55; E. Mallie & D. McKittrick, *The Fight For Peace: The Inside Story of the Irish Peace Process*, London, 1996, pp. 194-212.

4 Copeland quoted in *Irish News*, 19 Jan 1998. Eddie's father John had been shot dead by the British Army in disputed circumstances in October 1971. He was not a member of the IRA.

5 Potter quoted in *Irish News*, 20 Jan 1998.

6 Quoted in *An Phoblacht*, 28 Jan 1999. Copeland was later given £27,500 compensation by the courts. See, *An Phoblacht*, 27 May 1999.

7 On the media, see, for instance, D. Miller & G. McLaughlin, 'Reporting the Peace in Ireland', in B. Rolston & D. Miller (eds), *War and Words: The Northern Ireland Media Reader*, Belfast, 1996, p. 424; Mallie & McKittrick, *The Fight For Peace*, pp. 213-217.

8 *Belfast Graves* Vol 2, Belfast, 1994, p. 52.

9 See for instance Peter Taylor's interviews with Hugh Annesley and Albert Reynolds in P. Taylor, *Provos: The IRA and Sinn Féin*, London, 1997, pp. 338-339.

10 Quoted in D. Sharrock & M. Devenport, *Man of War, Man of Peace: The Unauthorised Biography of Gerry Adams*, London, 1997, p. 310.

11 *Belfast Telegraph*, 1 January 1998.

12 Quote from *Irish News*, 4 March 1998. For more on the controversy over the documentary see R. Bolton, 'Death on the Rock', in Rolston & Miller (eds), *War and Words: The Northern Ireland Media Reader*, Belfast, 1996.

13 Murphy was released from prison in November 1998 under the terms of the Good Friday Agreement. See, *Irish News*, 25 November 1998. Stone was released in July 2000.

CHAPTER 23   (PAGES 216-227)

1 Quoted in G. Adams, *Before the Dawn*, London, 1996, p. 242.

2 E. Fairweather, R. McDonough, M. McFadyean, *Only The Rivers Run Free: Northern Ireland—the Woman's War*, London, 1984, p. 53.

3 For a revealing interview with Clarke, see P. Taylor, *Provos: The IRA and Sinn Féin*, London, 1997, pp. 103-105, 299-301.

4 Quoted in B. Campbell, L. McKeown, F. O'Hagan (eds), *Nor Meekly Serve My Time: The H-Block Struggle 1976-1981*, Dublin, 1994, p. 80.

5 G. Adams, *An Irish Voice: The Quest for Peace*, Dingle, 1997, p. 142.

6 Thatcher quoted in T.P. Coogan, *The Troubles: Ireland's Ordeal 1966-1996 and the Search for Peace*, London, 1996, p. 281.

CHAPTER 24   (PAGES 228-235)

1 On Averill's escape, see *Irish Times*, 11 December 1997; *Irish Times*, 12 December 1997.

2 Averill from *An Phoblacht*, 8 January 1998.

CHAPTER 25   (PAGES 236-243)

1 See, L. Curtis, *They Shoot Children: The Use of Rubber and Plastic Bullets in the North of Ireland*, London, 1982; L. Curtis, *Ireland: The Propaganda War*, London, 1984, pp 80-82, 252-253.

2 *Irish News*, 19 January 1998; *Irish News*, 20 January 1998; *Belfast Telegraph*, 19 January 1998.

3 Names changed.

4 *Irish News*, 23 March 1989; *Irish News*, 21 March 1989; *Irish News*, 20 March 1989.

CHAPTER 26   (PAGES 244-250)

1 Quoted in G. Adams, *Falls Memories*, London, 1993, p. 23.

2 Phillpott was one of the UDA/UFF leaders who had recently met with Mo Mowlam inside the prison. He was released from jail in October 1998 under the provisions in the Good Friday Agreement. For Guiney's notices, see *Belfast Telegraph*, 21 January 1998.

3 One newspaper claimed Brennan's fiance had been told by loyalists that she would be killed if she attended his funeral. *Irish Times*, 24 January 1998.

4 *An Phoblacht*, 22 January 1998. For other details on the killing of Guiney and Brennan, see *Irish Times*, 20 January 1998; *Irish News*, 20 January 1998; *Irish News*, 21 January 1998; *Irish News*, 23 January 1998; *Irish Times*, 23 January 1998.

CHAPTER 28   (PAGES 257-265)

1 J. Bowyer-Bell, *The Irish Troubles: A Generation of Violence, 1967-1992*, Dublin, 1994, p. 328.

2 P. Taylor, *Provos: The IRA and Sinn Féin*, London, 1997, p. 135. Taylor's full account of the 1972 ceasefire is on pp. 128-147.

3 When this concession was taken away in 1976 it led to a crisis that would eventually provoke the 1981 hunger strike.

4 G. Adams, *Before the Dawn: An Autobiography*, London, 1996, p. 202.

5 Adams, *Before the Dawn*, p. 202.

6 Whitelaw quoted in P. Bew & G. Gillespie, *A Chronology of the Troubles, 1968-1993*, Dublin, 1993, p. 54. Remarkably, it was later claimed that the BBC actually recorded the secret meeting. See, *Irish News*, 7 Jan 1999. Steele quoted in Taylor, *Provos*, p. 142. Adams, *Before the Dawn*, p. 204. Also, T.P. Coogan, *The Troubles: Ireland's Ordeal 1966-1996 and the Search for Peace*, London, 1995, p. 175. Coogan provides a very good overview of the secret talks in London on pp. 174-177.

7 Bowyer-Bell, *The Irish Troubles*, p. 334. For Bowyer-Bell's full account of the 1972 ceasefire, see pp. 329-337. Adams confirms Steele's comments in *Before the Dawn*, pp. 205-206.

8 McGuinness quoted in M.L.R Smith, *Fighting for Ireland?: The Military Strategy of the Irish Republican Movement*, London, 1995, p. 108.

9 Quoted in Bowyer-Bell, *The Irish Troubles*, p. 337.

10 On the 'Springhill massacre', perhaps the best account is in a locally produced booklet, *The Springhill Massacre*, Belfast, 1992(?). See also, *Irish News*, 5 May 1999.

11 Adams, *Before the Dawn*, p. 207.

12 *Irish News*, 5 May 1999.

13 There are some minor variations regarding figures/casualties within the main sources. Figures provided here are based on information provided in Bew & Gillespie, *A Chronology*, p. 57; M. Sutton, *An Index of Deaths Resulting from the Conflict in Ireland, 1969–1993*, Belfast, 1994; D. McKittrick *et al*, *Lost Lives*, London, 1999. Sutton gives the total death toll for 1972 as 472. McKittrick *et al*, using updated information, give the figure as 496.

14 There was in fact another IRA-British Army truce in early 1975. However, despite its longevity, it lacked the initial sense of possibility generated, on both sides, during the 1972 ceasefire. Merlyn Rees, the British Secretary of State, would later reveal, with disarmingly honesty (or bravado?), British intentions towards the IRA during the 1975 ceasefire: 'We set out to con them and we succeeded'. Not surprisingly, eventually the ceasefire collapsed and within the republican movement the more-militant 'northern faction' based around Gerry Adams and Martin McGuinness were able to displace the Dublin leadership whom they blamed for the 1975 ceasefire. Rees quoted in Coogan, *The Troubles*, p. 260.

Chapter 29   (Pages 266-270)

1 'Memory'.

2 Quote from *Irish News*, 22 January 1998. At the time of writing no one has been charged with Mr Hughes' murder. According to the RUC the gun used in the killing had been used in previous loyalist attacks. Details from Coroner's inquest as reported in *Belfast Telegraph*, 11 February 1999.

3 *Belfast Telegraph*, 22 January 1998.

4 *Irish Times*, 23 January 1998; *Irish News*, 23 January 1998. McMahon was sometimes alternatively quoted as saying 'It's nothing to do with you. It's because of this stupid country where we live.'

Chapter 30   (Pages 271-275)

1 Quoted in T. Keneally, *The Great Shame: A Story of the Irish in the Old World and the New*, Sydney, 1998, p.487.

2 'Now is the hour, when we have to say goodbye. Soon you will be leaving, far away from us. You will be away for a while, remember us. When you come back, we will be waiting.'

3 'Farewell until later cousin. Do not forget me.'

4 *Irish Times*, 23 January 1998; *Irish Times*, 24 January 1998; *Irish News*, 23 January 1998.

5 The UFF later admitted killing Liam Conway. On his death, see *Irish Times*, 24 January 1998; *Irish News*, 24 January 1998; *Irish News*, 27 January 1998; *Irish Times*, 26 January 1998.

6 *Irish News*, 26 January 1998.

7 *Irish Times*, 26 January 1998; *Irish News*, 28 January 1998; *Irish Times*, 28 January 1998. At the inquest over a year later it was revealed that the handgun used to kill McColgan had also been used in the murder of Sean Brown in Bellaghy during May 1997. Brown's murder was claimed by the LVF. No one claimed responsibility for the murder of John McColgan. See, *Irish News*, 27 March 1999.

8 Sharon and John's new baby was conceived when we were all in Dublin during January 1998. That's why John never ended up sharing the bed with me that night; he got his dirty weekend away after all!

9 'Jean taught me that and I am a better person for learning it. She has been dead a long time. Say no more about it.'

Chapter 31   (Pages 276-283)

1 D. McKittrick *et al*, *Lost Lives*, London, 1999, p. 1463.

2 *Belfast Telegraph*, 2 November 1998. Other details on the death of Brian Service and the Red Hand Defenders from: *Belfast Telegraph*, 2 November 1998; *Irish News*, 4 November 1998.

3 *Irish News*, 12 January 1999.

4 'Every beginning is weak.'

CROSSING
PRESS